The News of Empire

The News of Empire

Telegraphy, Journalism, and the Politics of Reporting in Colonial India, c. 1830–1900

Amelia Bonea

OXFORD
UNIVERSITY PRESS

Oxford University Press is a department of the University of Oxford. It furthers the University's objective of excellence in research, scholarship, and education by publishing worldwide. Oxford is a registered trademark of Oxford University Press in the UK and in certain other countries.

Published in India by
Oxford University Press
YMCA Library Building, 1 Jai Singh Road, New Delhi 110 001, India

First Edition published in 2016

ISBN-13: 978-0-19-946712-9
ISBN-10: 0-19-946712-9

Typeset in Minion Pro 10.5/12.5
by Tranistics Data Technologies, Kolkata 700 091
Printed in India at Rakmo Press, New Delhi 110 020

Pentru mami, tati şi măicuţa

CONTENTS

List of Illustrations, Map, and Tables ix

List of Abbreviations xi

Acknowledgements xiii

Note on Spelling and Transliteration xvii

Introduction 1

1. Technologies of News Transmission 42
2. Sites of Practice and Discourses of Telegraphy 95
3. Journalists and Journalism in Nineteenth-Century India 148
4. Making News and Views: Colonial Policy and the Role of Reuters 204
5. Reporting Foreign and Domestic News 266

Conclusion 321

Glossary 332

Select Bibliography 334

Index 361

About the Author 377

ILLUSTRATIONS, MAP, AND TABLES

Illustrations

2.1 Delhi Telegraph Memorial, 2010 133

3.1 Telegraphic news on its journey from London to Bombay, *The Leisure Hour*, 1901 172

5.1 News composing room, *Times of India*, November 1898 273
5.2 Bulletins of overland news, *Hindoo Patriot*, 11 July 1860 284
5.3 Foreign and domestic telegrams at the end of the century, *Madras Times*, 5 July 1897 308

Map

Map showing the main trunk telegraph lines of communication of the world, 1887 (at the beginning of the volume)

Tables

3.1 Traffic of news-free messages, 1867–1900 177
3.2 Traffic of press telegrams, 1873–1900 180
3.3 Abstract of press messages sent by Reuters and other associations and individuals, 1873–9 182

4.1 Telegrams sent by Roper Lethbridge to the press, April–October 1877 228
4.2 The press commissioner's establishment 231

5.1 Telegrams reporting the Poona murders, 24 June–5 July 1897 309

LIST OF ABBREVIATIONS

BPMA	British Postal Museum and Archive
CR	*Calcutta Review*
DNCJ	*Dictionary of Nineteenth-Century Journalism in Great Britain and Ireland*
GPO	General Post Office
NAI	National Archives of India
NNR	*Native Newspaper Reports*
IOR	Oriental and India Office Records, British Library
P&O	Peninsular and Oriental Steam Navigation Company
RA	Reuters Archives

ACKNOWLEDGEMENTS

This book was written, sometimes quite literally, on the move—moving between continents, countries, institutions of education, and languages. The frustrations of academic nomadism will be familiar to many of my colleagues, but so will the joy of making new friends, learning new languages, and being exposed to the writing and research conventions of different academic environments. I like to think that this work, just like my life, has been enriched by each of the institutional and cultural contexts in which I have lived and studied during the last two decades. It has certainly benefited tremendously from the help of many wonderful people I have encountered along the way. My gratitude, like my life, is geographically distributed.

In Romania, I would like to thank my first mentor, Dora Stanca, who discovered and nurtured my interest in history. During a period of post-communist soul-searching, the most important thing she taught me is that history should never be univocal.

In Japan, paradoxically the place where I began to study the modern history of South Asia, I am particularly indebted to my former supervisor, Riho Isaka (Isaka-sensei), for introducing me to this field of research and for remaining my mentor and friend. Toshie Awaya, Takashi Miyamoto, Tsukasa Mizushima, Nariaki Nakazato, Nobuhiro Ohta, Michihiro Ogawa, and the late Haruka Yanagisawa have welcomed the eccentric *ryūgakusei* (international student) in their midst, offering intellectual support and friendship over the years. Clive Collins has been an exceptional teacher and friend, whose lectures stimulated our interest in the English language and also taught us how to be in the world. Without the generous financial support of the Japanese government, which funded my undergraduate and graduate education through their Monbukagakushō (MEXT) Scholarship scheme, neither this book nor my current career would have been possible.

In Australia, I thank Matt Tomlinson for infusing my work with anthropological insight and for showing me some of the nuts and bolts of academic research.

In Germany, where I completed the doctoral dissertation on which this book is based, my biggest debt is to my supervisor Roland Wenzlhuemer, for his professionalism, friendship, and guidance in all things telegraphic. The project benefited from the financial support of the German Research Foundation, through the Cluster of Excellence 'Asia and Europe in a Global Context' at the University of Heidelberg. I wish to thank the administrative staff of the Cluster as well as Anna Andreeva, Antje Flüchter, Martin Gieselmann, Hans Harder, and Madeleine Herren-Oesch for support at various stages of this project. Michael Mann has shared my interest in telegraphy and journalism in South Asia and I thank him for his encouragement and critical feedback. While studying for my PhD in Heidelberg, I was also fortunate to be surrounded by a group of friends whose penchant for conversation was rivalled only by their cooking skills. I am grateful to Ahmet Bekil, Paul Fletcher, Prabhat Kumar, Eleonor Marcussen, Sridevi Padmanabhan, and Swarali Paranjape for making my postgraduate years such an unforgettable experience. To Nitin Sinha, I am also indebted for conversations about the history of communications in South Asia and generous advice on many other details that go into the making of a book.

In India, I thank Dhruv Raina for always asking questions I was not able to answer, for reading drafts, and for his willingness to share his vast knowledge of the history and historiography of science. The staff at the Nehru Memorial Museum and Library and the National Archives of India (both in New Delhi), in particular the archivists Jaya Ravindran and G. A. Biradar, were helpful in locating and accessing archival material. My knowledge of telegraphy has also benefited from discussions with Deep Kanta Lahiri Choudhury. Niladri Chatterjee, Vinod Pavarala, and Charu Singh have been partners in animated conversations about various aspects of South Asian history. To Biswamoy Pati and the staff and research fellows at Nalanda University I am indebted for inviting me to present my work at their respective seminar series in Delhi. I thank the editorial team at Oxford University Press, India, for their professionalism as well as the two anonymous reviewers for their useful comments on an earlier draft of this book. In Delhi, Shalini and Arun Shamnath have been my family away from home.

In the United Kingdom, the staff at the British Library's Asian and African Studies Reading Room and the Postal Museum and Archive (both in London) have been particularly helpful and accommodating. At Thomson Reuters, a special word of thanks is due to John Entwisle for generously allowing me to use the Reuters Archives. During the final stages of writing, I also benefited from conversations with Anindita Ghosh, Chandrika Kaul, Francesca Orsini, Manu Sehgal, Samiksha Sehrawat, Amrita Shodhan, David Trotter, Teja Varma Pusapati, Cressida Jervis Read, and Sally Shuttleworth. The European Research Council (Grant Agreement Number 340121) covered some of the costs associated with the publication of this book.

Elsewhere around the world I acknowledge the help of Mark Ravinder Frost, for an illuminating debate on postal communication in the British Empire; Robin Jeffrey, for his congenial support and countless discussions about journalism in India; and Sanjay Joshi, for generously sharing a conference paper on the *Native Newspaper Reports*. Isabel Hofmeyr has been an inspiring model for research on the history of print media and I thank her for taking the time to read and comment on Chapter 5 of this book.

Parts of Chapter 4 have been published as '"All the News That's Fit to Print?" Reuter's Telegraphic News Service in Colonial India', in *Global Communication Electric: Business, News and Politics in the World of Telegraphy*, edited by M. Michaela Hampf and Simone Mueller-Pohl (Frankfurt and New York: Campus Verlag, 2013). Similarly, the section on the reporting of the Austro-Prussian War in Chapter 5 was published as 'The Medium and Its Message: Reporting the Austro-Prussian War in the *Times of India*', *Historical Social Research*, 35 (2010): 167–87. I thank both publishers for their kind permission to reuse this material, which appears here in a revised form.

My last words of gratitude are reserved for my family. Özlem, Temi, Pelumi, Raluca, Kate, and Yordanka have shared with me almost every step of the journey which began in Japan a decade-and-a-half ago.

They are now part of my extended family and I count myself fortunate for having them in my life. My cousin Adela provided shelter, food, and much-needed moral support during my research trips to London. Above all, I am grateful to my parents, Viorica and Lucian; to my maternal grandmother, Armina; to Dominik for his constant support and for painstakingly reading the whole manuscript; and to Johannes, Renate, and Michael for making me feel at home in Bavaria. My mother was always supportive of my scholarly endeavours: I seem to have 'inherited' my penchant for debate and eye for detail from her. My father, who is an electrician, made it his mission to initiate me into the mysteries of electricity from an early age, presciently predicting that 'you will need it one day'. But it was my grandmother who taught me to love people and their stories. Her creative ways of dealing with the contrivances of 'modern' life always remind me that academic learning is only one of the many paths to knowledge. I might be a grown-up now, but I still dream of being like her.

NOTE ON SPELLING AND TRANSLITERATION

This book does not employ any conventional system of transliteration for words in Indian languages, but uses the anglicized forms which appeared most frequently in the nineteenth-century documents examined. Thus, Pune is written as Poona, Mumbai as Bombay, *ḍāk* as *dak*, *Bhārat Jīvan* as *Bharat Jiwan*, and so on. In quotations, the original spelling is retained. To facilitate understanding, especially for readers less familiar with the history of South Asia, I also indicate in brackets the contemporary name of a locality after its first mention in the text.

For the transliteration of Japanese words, I follow *Kenkyūsha's New Japanese–English Dictionary* (4th edn, 2003), which uses a modified version of the Hepburn system of romanization. In my experience, this system of transliteration usually makes it easier for English-language speakers to interpret the original pronunciation.

Introduction

On 20 December 1865, a few months after Britain was successfully connected to India by means of electric telegraph cables that crossed the Ottoman and Persian territories, the *Times of India* published an editorial criticizing the colonial state's deficient administration of its telegraph network. According to this report, communication was unreliable and prone to frequent interruptions. The telegraph was also used primarily to 'serve ... political and official purposes', at the expense of the 'mercantile public' and the newspaper press. The 'selfishness' of the Indian administration, the editor continued, was illustrated by a recent episode that involved the governor of Bombay, Sir Henry Bartle Frere:

> The case of Sir Bartle Frere's telegram, sent from Sattara the other day, announcing the close of the Bhootan war, is one still more to the point. Dated on the 14th November it arrived in London on the 15th; but the former date, on being compared with the commercial telegrams also received on the 15th, was not believed to be correct by the London merchants. Their telegrams bore date the 4th, so it was generally concluded that the additional figure had been granted by the signallers in pursuance of their daily attempts at mystifying the public. But the date was correct; Sir Bartle Frere's telegram could flash to London, from more than a hundred miles beyond Bombay, in twenty-four hours, while those of our merchants require ten days before their *disjecta membra* [fragments, lit. scattered limbs] arrive in London to puzzle the wits of acute City clerks.[1]

The episode is intriguing, offering as it does an alternative perspective on a technology which has been more often remembered, in Shakespeare's popular verse, for 'put[ting] a girdle round about the earth' and making the world smaller in the process.[2] During a time when the latest telegraphic news from London published by the *Times of India* was, on average, between five and ten days old, the allegation that official intelligence travelled the distance between colony and metropole within a day is curious enough to warrant attention. As the *Times of India* suggested—rather predictably for a period marked by animated debate about the state of telegraphic and postal communication with India and the role of private enterprise therein—the key to solving the crisis of communication was to resort to 'outside assistance'. Indeed, London 'projectors' were reportedly ready to take over the working of the Indian and Indo-European telegraphs. All that was needed was the sanction of colonial authorities![3]

This editorial gives us a taste of the complex politics that surrounded the construction and use of the telegraph network in the nineteenth century. In fact, one could argue that the electric telegraph, by many contemporary accounts a 'useful' technology which enabled communication across vast physical distances, also helped to divide people over myriad issues connected with its construction and use. Examples included the layout and ownership of lines, the cost of communication, and the formulation and implementation of imperial regulations that circumscribed access to technology and generated hierarchies of communication. The episode is thus a fitting entry point into this study about journalism, technologies of communication, and the politics of news reporting in nineteenth-century India, all the more so since it also anticipates some of its protagonists: colonial administrators, editors, correspondents, and other people connected with the production and circulation of newspapers, merchants, engineers, telegraph companies, news agencies, and readers.

The book uses the example of the electric telegraph and its incorporation into news reporting as a springboard for pondering how technology and English-language journalism intersected in colonial India. As is well known, the newspaper press has been an indispensable historical resource for scholars of colonial South Asia and has inspired substantial scholarship over the years.[4] This study draws on such precursors—some of which will be discussed in the following pages—but aims to make a contribution to the field by addressing two interrelated questions: What were the mechanisms of news reporting in nineteenth-century South Asia and the factors, historical actors, and events that shaped the content and form of news? What role did telegraphy and, by extension, other technologies of communication play in the development of journalism during this period? Put differently, the aim of the study is to re-examine the history of the press in colonial South Asia through the lenses of technologies of communication like the telegraph and to show how the changing technological landscape of the nineteenth century enabled the articulation of certain practices and visions of journalism in a colonial landscape that was set on controlling and even repressing the circulation of intelligence.

News assumed a variety of guises in nineteenth-century India, but this study focuses on printed, occasionally manuscript intelligence publicized through the pages of the English-language press. The primary audience of such newspapers was a relatively small group of Anglo-Indian merchants, soldiers, administrators, and other civilians resident in the subcontinent as well as a growing group of English-educated Indians, representing colonial South Asia's emerging middle class.[5] Significantly, the expanding network of postal and telegraphic communication also enabled the public at 'Home' (that is, in Britain) to gain access to Indian news on an increasingly timely and regular basis. Such items of intelligence also reached, in English or in translation, a broader international audience in continental Europe, Asia, North America, and Australia. Although the present study does not engage in detail with this global process of news exchange, it does occasionally draw on newspapers published outside the confines of South Asia, especially in Southeast Asia, Japan, and the United States, in an attempt to map the geographical ramifications of this interconnected world of journalism.

Despite its relatively narrow focus, the book does not endorse a rigid distinction between printed or written news on the one hand and spoken news on the other. In fact, it argues that in the field of news reporting, as in other fields of literary production—journalism being itself considered a type of literary endeavour during much of the period examined—the boundaries between the oral and the written were porous.[6] The two categories of news continuously interacted with each other, with spoken news entering the domain of the printed word via rumours and correspondents' letters, and printed news returning to the sphere of the oral as it was discussed and communicated from one person to the other.

News played a crucial role in every domain of social life in colonial India, as illuminated, among others, by C. A. Bayly's study of intelligence gathering and social communication.[7] From the perspective of the British colonizers, it was an indispensable ingredient in the conduct of military campaigns, administration, and trade. Indeed, access to intelligence was central to the making and preservation of empire. Despite a relatively strong current of opinion that has insisted on examining the history of the press in South Asia primarily through the lenses of conceptual binaries such as 'colonial' or 'nationalist', news reporting remains one dimension of journalism that clearly demonstrates how much more complicated the press world of nineteenth-century India was. A cursory glance over the pages of newspapers provides useful hints about their ideological and informational diversity and shows that they were interconnected projects that drew on each other for information and opinion. The intelligence they published reflected various levels of spatial aggregation: local, regional, national, imperial, or global. It was also topically diverse, featuring political and financial information, reports about the weather, famines, floods, earthquakes, fires, epidemic outbreaks, and crime, but also about education, literature, science, technology, sporting events, and other 'amusements'.

People read the newspaper press for a variety of reasons in the nineteenth century. For some groups, such as merchants and traders, keeping up with the 'latest news' was central to the successful conduct of their business. For others, news was a source of education and inspiration and the newspaper itself a vehicle through which to engage and participate in public debates, to call for socio-political reform, to denounce offenders, to express support for the imperial cause, or to mobilize caste, class, regional, and national sentiment. Finally, news was also a source of amusement, entertainment, and gossip as well as a source of reassurance or distress for those anxiously awaiting the safe arrival of a steamer or the results in the matriculation examination. By exploring simultaneously the various facets of news production and circulation, this book shows that news and interest in news in nineteenth-century India were a function of specific socio-economic and political circumstances which mitigated certain visions of journalism and reporting, not only the result of a 'natural' curiosity for the unknown and the sensational. In short, my aim is to identify and discuss some of the political, technological, economic, and ideological factors that shaped the content and form of newspapers in colonial South Asia.

As the editorial published in the *Times of India* suggested at the beginning of this chapter, the relationship between technology and the exchange of intelligence in the nineteenth century was not always easy to grasp. Seen from the vantage point of many of its contemporaries—and indeed, many of its later historians and theorists—the telegraph often appeared as a 'revolutionary' technological device which helped to 'shrink' the world by enabling the transmission of information at speeds hitherto unattainable.[8] Such accounts are a valuable record of the unprecedented acceleration of communication in the course of the nineteenth century. They also provide important insights into contemporary perceptions of telegraphy and the ways in which it was connected with projects of modernity and empire-building. The challenge for the historian of technology, as I see it, is this: how do we write a history of the telegraph that strikes the right balance between technological enthusiasm and technological scepticism, between 'grand narratives' of communication and the myriad 'little' stories or microhistories that went into the making of this history, between the practices and discourses of telegraphy, and between the role of the state and non-state actors? In this book I do not claim to provide an answer to all these questions, but I do hope to take a step in this direction. My attempt is to write a history of the telegraph in colonial India that weaves together a number of interrelated threads of inquiry, some of which have been pursued before, others less so. This includes discussion of technologies of news transmission in nineteenth-century India, processes of knowledge production and popularization in the field of telegraphy, electromagnetism, insulation, and so on, the role of telegraphy in imaginations of modernity and empire as well as the role of the state and news agencies in shaping the circulation of intelligence and advocating particular 'visions' of journalism, the development of news reporting in colonial India, and the incorporation of telegraphy into journalism.[9]

Revolutionary though it might have been in its ability to transmit messages rapidly, the electric telegraph was neither a technology 'invented' overnight nor a 'neutral' technology at that. On the contrary, its use was deeply imbricated in the socio-economic and political realities of its time and was subject both to the vagaries of the natural environment and to insufficient knowledge. Furthermore, the technological 'revolution' triggered by telegraphy was gradual and piecemeal rather than sudden and dramatic: it took time for lines to be constructed, for knowledge to be acquired, for colonial regulations to be discussed, drafted, and implemented, for the cost of communication to decrease, and for people to familiarize themselves with the new technology. Indeed, lack of knowledge, technical failures, moments of 'panic', personal rivalries, or internal bureaucratic malfunctions were just as much part and parcel of the history of telegraphy in colonial South Asia as were grand narratives of scientific discovery and progress, such as the idea that telegraphy would help to reform both individuals and nations. In a similar vein, the news published in the pages of the nineteenth-century press was not an uncontested category, but a field where different visions of journalism vied with each other and where power relations were constantly played out.

The book examines the practices and discourses which surrounded telegraphy and journalism in colonial South Asia, and aims to situate local debates and developments within a broader imperial and international framework of relevant discussions and developments. It is an exercise in establishing connections and comparisons, which is particularly important in the context of the present study, since journalism was (and remains) an enterprise predicated upon the circulation of intelligence and opinion. In addition, the history of telegraphy in the nineteenth century cannot be divorced from the movement of capital and scientific expertise that crossed national and imperial borders. This is not to say that all news and scientific knowledge circulated, or that they all circulated to the same extent. Rather, it is to emphasize that newspapers were printed forms which thrived on the exchange of intelligence and opinion; their financial survival usually depended on the patronage of advertisers, readers, and the government. As Sheila Jasanoff has remarked in a different context, journalists in colonial South Asia were 'actors [who] … themselves compare[d], shaping their personal visions in accordance with imagined elsewheres and elsewhens, and those comparisons in turn got woven into social meaning-making'.[10]

The book focuses primarily on the electric telegraph, first opened for public use in India on 1 February 1855. It also makes reference to other technologies of transport and communication such as steamers and railways, which were equally instrumental in the circulation of intelligence in the British Empire and the Indian subcontinent. It weaves together two distinct strands of Indian historiography, the history of journalism and the history of technology, and is the first systematic account of the development of English-language news reporting in nineteenth-century India and the role of technologies of communication therein. In the remaining part of this introduction, I discuss some of the ways in which technology and journalism have intersected in scholarly literature during the last century and a half and consider how communication perspectives can offer new insights into the history of the press in colonial South Asia. My aim is to highlight relevant themes which allow us to place the historiography of journalism and means of communication in India within a broader international context. This is an attempt to bring different media and communication histories 'in dialogue with each other' and to overcome what Manu Goswami has called, in her discussion of railways in colonial South Asia, the 'internalist focus' of some of the previous literature.[11] The chapter ends with a description of the book's methods and an outline of its structure.

Sources for the History of Journalism: International Perspectives

In their survey of scholarly literature on journalism history, Kevin Barnhurst and John Nerone identify two principal sources that have generated interest in this field of investigation. One is a long-standing preoccupation with the development of communication media, which some scholars trace as far back as antiquity, a claim they illustrate by reference to Plato's critique of rhetoric and writing in *Phaedrus* (c. 370 BCE). The other source of interest is occupational and was inextricably connected with the gradual professionalization of journalism, a process with roots in the nineteenth century that was accelerated significantly over the course of the twentieth century.[12]

In Britain and the United States, the nineteenth century was marked by an explosion of print, due, among other factors, to the abolition of taxes on knowledge, new technological innovations, and increased literacy. This was also a time when historical writing about the newspaper press proliferated. Perhaps unsurprisingly, histories of printing and publishing were among the earliest genres of 'journalism history'.[13] These accounts were especially popular during the first decades of the nineteenth century. They frequently highlighted the interrelated development of printing technology and the press. In fact, as Charles A. Macintosh was to observe in mid-century, a book about the press was incomplete without also addressing 'the progress of typefounding and stereotyping, together with the manufacture of printing-ink'.[14]

Later genres of journalism history, encompassing a growing corpus of (auto)biographies of journalists and general press histories—early precursors of a substantial body of 'national' histories of the press—also highlighted the role of technologies of transport and communication in the development of this field of activity. As industrialization and mechanization proceeded apace, railways, steamers, and telegraphs came to play an indispensable role in the practice of journalism, facilitating the transmission of intelligence and the distribution of newspapers to their subscribers. As observers pointed out, steamers delivered correspondents' reports from various parts of Britain to London and enabled newspapers to travel back to their readers. Late railway despatches brought in news from the colonies, while telegraphs allowed information to travel back and forth between Britain and the rest of the world.[15]

In the twentieth century, the gradual crystallization of a professional ethos, promoted by the establishment of schools of journalism and professional associations, provided an additional layer of interest in the study of press history.[16] During the same period—and particularly in the North American context—the study of press history and journalism more generally began to be shaped by theoretical and methodological insights developed by scholars connected with the emerging field of Communication Studies (later, Media and Communication Studies). For the purposes of this book, James Carey's work on communication and the telegraph, to which I shall return later, is particularly relevant. His popular essay, 'The Problems of Journalism History', inspired scholars to conceptualize the 1960s–1970s as a period which marked a break with what Carey had called, following Herbert Butterfield, the 'Whig model' of journalism history.[17] Histories of journalism written in the nineteenth and twentieth centuries thus came under scrutiny for their preference for the biography genre, with its emphasis on strong individuals and organizational models like news agencies, and linear narratives of progress and gradual expansion of press freedom.[18]

Indeed, since the 1970s, journalism history has been among the fields which have benefitted from the shift of emphasis from political, military, and diplomatic history to a new type of social history that focused on the study of subaltern groups like labourers, women, and ethnic minorities. These new developments have also been accompanied by occasional calls for a more consistent engagement with the history of communication and the work of media theorists like Harold Innis and Marshall McLuhan. Whether or not these approaches represented a radical departure from past scholarship has been a matter of some debate. Making an argument for historical continuity, Tom O'Malley points out that specialist and more popular scholarship produced in the decades prior to the 1960s also addressed many of the concerns which have informed contemporary media histories. One such example can be found in Robert Albion's 1930s work on canals, railways, and telegraphs, which O'Malley credits with introducing the concept of 'communication revolution' and 'signal[ling] the much broader importance of communications within historical developments'.[19]

Histories of Journalism in South Asia: Sources and Genres

The sources of interest outlined in the previous section, communicational and professional, have also been relevant to the history of journalism in the Indian subcontinent. In his *A History of the Press in India*, published in 1962 under the auspices of the Audit Bureau of Circulations, Swaminath Natarajan acknowledged that '[t]he history of journalism is closely linked to the development of the printing press and the growth of communication'.[20] Professional interest in the study of press history in South Asia has remained conspicuous since the first half of the twentieth century, when Pat Lovett's Adhar Chandra Mukherjee Lectures at the University of Calcutta were published posthumously under the title *Journalism in India* (1929). This booklet was followed shortly by similar publications emanating from the pen of experienced journalists, such as E. P. Menon's *Journalism as a Profession* (1930) and S. P. Thiaga Rajan's *Introduction to Journalism* (1938).[21]

In the first half of the twentieth century, the lack of publications in the field of journalism began to attract the attention of a number of Indian commentators, many of whom were themselves engaged in the practice of journalism. The period was marked by a growing professional consciousness and a widespread feeling of inadequacy about the state of journalism education in the subcontinent. At a time when the country was moving slowly towards independence and when journalism itself was undergoing significant transformations both locally and globally, the gaze of the Indian press turned not only upon the colonial state's repressive policies and actions, but also inwards, to question the suitability of extant models of journalism. As Thiaga Rajan and, fifteen years later, the American journalism educator Roland E. Wolseley expressed, there was growing concern among Indian journalists that journalism literature and education were lagging behind other countries, most notably the United States.[22] The models embodied by journals 'at Home', which had been emulated, adapted, and contested by journalists in the subcontinent since the late eighteenth century, were coming under scrutiny not only as a result of increased nationalist agitation, but also as a result of professionalization, growing interest among 'young, educated' Indians in journalism as a 'new avenue of employment', the proliferation of other models of journalism like 'yellow journalism', changes in printing and office technologies, and the diversification of media technologies in the form of wireless telegraphy and radio.[23]

This crisis of identity continued in the postcolonial period, when the initial confidence in the benefits of American journalism, as illustrated by Wolseley's own visit to India in 1952, appears to have dissipated. In the 1960s, the famous Nehruvian journalist M. Chalapathi Rau surveyed press systems in the Soviet Union, China, the United States, and Britain, and voiced concern that instead of creating its own system of journalism, independent India was merely imitating others. The void created by the demise of the 'nationalist' and 'Fleet Street' traditions of the colonial era, he warned, was now in danger of being filled by 'Americanization', which was 'fast becoming a substitute for Anglicisation'.[24] The problem was how to transform newspapers, this ubiquitous 'item of everyday modernity', into a truly indigenous medium, which both addressed and reflected the reality of local society.[25] It is a topic to which I shall return in the other chapters of the book, to argue, for example, that this association between colonial modernity and European ideas and practices of journalism has not only encouraged superficial distinctions between colonial and pre-colonial forms of news reporting, but has also led to the conceptual relegation of local forms of news communication, such as handwritten Mughal news-sheets (*akhbarat*), to the 'prehistory' of journalism. As Margrit Pernau and Yunus Jaffery have pointed out in their recent study of the akhbarat of 1810, 1825, and 1830—the former two prepared for the British Resident at Delhi and the latter for King Akbar Shah II—there were 'astonishing lines of continuity between the *akhbarat* and the new print media [newspapers]; continuities firstly in the use of *akhbarat* as sources of information, but also in what was considered to be "news" and in the ways it was presented'.[26] In other words, the boundaries between pre-colonial and colonial forms of news reporting were not always as clear-cut as we have been accustomed to assume.

Like in other cultural contexts, the beginnings of press history in India have been intimately associated with the history of printing and publishing. Surveys of printing presses and literary production were a common modality for the colonial government to gauge and control the production of printed matter in the nineteenth century, albeit in an imperfect and 'limited' manner, as A. R. Venkatachalapathy has demonstrated in his work on printing in south India.[27] In Bengal, the first efforts in this direction can be traced to the work of the Baptist missionaries of Serampore (Srirampur), especially to the activity of Rev. James Long, whose catalogues and 'returns' of Bengali printing presses and publications included sections on the history of Bengali newspapers and periodicals.[28] The importance of printing to Christian missionary projects in India and across the British Empire more generally has been extensively studied, with scholars highlighting the often ambiguous relationship between missionary enterprise and colonial rule.[29] Indeed, Long's own catalogues appear to be the outcome of personal interest and missionary zeal, combined with the influence of a colonial government that was becoming increasingly interested in the compilation of statistics which could be used to monitor the field of print production in Bengal.

The association between the history of the press and the history of printing and publishing continued throughout the twentieth century. For example, Sushil Kumar De's *History of Bengali Literature in the Nineteenth Century, 1800–1825* (1919) contained a chapter on the early Bengali journalism of the Serampore Mission. Perhaps the best illustration of this approach in the twentieth century is B. S. Kesavan's impressive three-volume history of printing and publishing in India which includes, among other topics, comprehensive sections on Tamil journals and magazines, James Augustus Hicky's publication of the 'first' newspaper in India, and the development of Hindi periodicals and of journalism in Karnataka, Andhra Pradesh, and Kerala.[30]

Broadly speaking, histories of the press in India can be divided into three genres: (auto)biographies, general histories, and topical histories. The former enjoyed a certain degree of popularity in the nineteenth and twentieth centuries. For the colonial period, some of the notable publications in the English language were, in chronological order, William Knighton's account of his editorship of the *Ceylon Herald*, *Tropical Sketches; Or, Reminiscences of an Indian Journalist* (1855), J. H. Stocqueler's *Memoirs of a Journalist* (1873), Ram Gopal Sanyal's *The Life of the Hon'ble Rai Kristo Das Pal Bahadur, C. I. E.* (1886), F. H. B. Skrine's *An Indian Journalist: Being the Life, Letters and Correspondence of Dr. Sambhu C. Mookerjee* (1895), and R. P. Karkaria's *India: Forty Years of Progress and Reform: Being A Sketch of the Life and Times of Behramji M. Malabari* (1896). Many nineteenth-century public figures were actively involved in journalism, either as editors, proprietors, occasional contributors, or as correspondents. As a result, memoirs published during this period often contain references to their journalistic activities. A case in point is that of Surendranath Banerjea's autobiographical work, *A Nation in the Making* (1925), which includes an account of his activity as an editor of the *Bengalee*. The biography genre has enjoyed only a minor presence in the landscape of journalism history in the post-independence period, although in recent years scholars like Edwin Hirschmann and Nariaki Nakazato have published excellent studies of Robert Knight and Harish Chandra Mukherjee respectively. The former journalist, also discussed in Chapter 4, was the founder of two of India's most enduring newspapers, the *Times of India* and the Calcutta *Statesman*, while the latter edited the *Hindoo Patriot*.[31] Samples of reporting from this newspaper will be discussed in Chapter 5.

By comparison, the genre of general histories of the press has been prolific, especially in the post-independence period. In the nineteenth century, the precursors of such publications may be found in the essays on press history occasionally published in the periodical press, which were popular in India as well as in Britain. The *Calcutta Review* was one important platform for the publication of such condensed histories of the press. The articles featured focused almost exclusively on the Indian or 'native' newspapers. They suggest a growing preoccupation with this section of Indian journalism in the second half of the nineteenth century, which usually took the form of attempts to diagnose its 'character', monitor its opinions, and evaluate its performance as an instrument of education and improvement.[32] This attitude was reflected, for example, in Rev. Long's 1850 piece on 'Early Bengali Literature and Newspapers', which emphasized the utilitarian value of the vernacular press 'as a grand means for working on the *masses* in this country'.[33]

In the last decades of the nineteenth century, preoccupation with the history of the press extended to other parts of the subcontinent, especially to western India, where the publications of nationalist leaders like Bal Gangadhar Tilak repeatedly came to the attention of colonial authorities.[34] In 1877, William Digby, journalist and writer with experience in Ceylon (*Ceylon Observer*) and south India (*Madras Times*), published a comprehensive article on 'The Native Newspapers of India and Ceylon', in which he surveyed the vernacular press in the Bengal, Bombay, and Madras Presidencies, the North-West Provinces, the Punjab, and Ceylon.[35] Two decades later, R. P. Karkaria, otherwise known for his biography of the Parsi author and journalist Behramji Malabari, contributed articles on the history of two pioneering Gujarati newspapers, *Rast Goftar* and *Bombay Samachar*, while the sixtieth anniversary of the *Times of India* in 1898 prompted the publication of an article documenting the history of this newspaper.[36]

Almost invariably, the publication of such material was used as an opportunity to advance opinions about the role of the Indian press in the subcontinent, in particular to discuss the relationship between the colonial government and the press and the thorny issue of press censorship. Reflecting on the future of the vernacular press, Digby wrote—rather ironically if we consider that his essay was published shortly before the passing of the Vernacular Press Act of 1878 which was designed to curtail the freedom of expression of the Indian-language press—that 'it may fairly be taken for granted that no official censorship of the press, corresponding to what is the rule in France, will be necessary, or will be established, in India'.[37] Similarly, Karkaria was keen to emphasize the benefits of political liberalism not only for the development of the vernacular press, but also for British rule in the subcontinent. In a political climate which discouraged and attempted to suppress overt criticism of the colonial government's attitude towards the press, such publications often became a medium through which to argue for—or indeed, against—press freedom. As Chapter 4 will also discuss, arguments in favour of press freedom were often premised on the more or less implicit understanding that this freedom would not be abused: while 'rational', 'objective' criticism of the British rulers was accepted, 'seditious' material was not.

With regard to general histories of the press, their number remained limited in the first half of the twentieth century, when Margarita Barns published her pioneering book, *The Indian Press: A History of the Growth of Public Opinion in India* (1940). This set the tone for a host of similar publications and remains, to this day, one of the main works of general reference for historians of journalism in India.[38] The genre continued to grow in the second half of the period, with many new publications appearing in the 1960s, in the wake of the First Indian Press Commission. More recently, such texts have also been published in connection with the establishment of departments of mass communications and journalism at Indian universities and usually function as introductions to the history of journalism in India.[39]

Another prolific category of press histories is that of topical studies. Such texts have been particularly popular in the post-independence period. By and large, they belong to the genre of political historiography and have addressed topics which resonate with the particular historical circumstances of the Indian subcontinent. Debates about press freedom and colonial censorship represented a staple of journalistic content in the nineteenth century, not only as part of general accounts about the history of journalism, as we have seen above, but also as regular news reports published in the Indian and British press under familiar titles like 'Government and Journalism in India', 'Curbing the Native Press in India', and so forth. But the first studies of press laws, sedition, and press freedom date from the early decades of the twentieth century.[40] The topic remained relevant in independent India, especially in the 1970s and 1980s, when the experience of the Emergency rekindled interest in the role of the press in society and its relationship to the institutions of the state.[41] In the post-independence period, the impulse to study journalism history has also been inextricably connected with the desire to rescue the history of the vernacular press from the derision in which it was held during the colonial period. Many of the histories published in the aftermath of independence reflected this agenda, aiming, for example, to understand the role of vernacular newspapers as instruments of social and political mobilization. The topic remains relevant, especially in the last three decades, when economic liberalization, increasing literacy, and technological innovations have created a favourable climate for the proliferation of the press in Indian languages.[42]

In short, of all genres of print available in colonial India, the newspaper and periodical press has so far attracted the greatest amount of scholarly attention. As Ulrike Stark has pointed out, this is especially so if we compare the newspaper with its 'twin manifestation', the printed book.[43] But this situation has not been devoid of contradictions. Despite its popularity as a target of scholarly investigation, the history of the press in colonial South Asia has also remained relatively immune from the broader concerns and theoretical debates which have reinvigorated the field of book history over the last decade.[44] By and large, the thematic repertoire of press histories has followed predictable trajectories of investigation, and work remains to be done on many aspects connected with the material, visual, institutional, and technical dimensions of newspaper production and circulation. In what follows we will look more closely at one such field, that of technologies of communication, and consider how their study has intersected with the history of journalism both in South Asia and abroad.

Theories of Communication, Telegraphy, and Journalism

In the American context, interest in communication(s) as a field of inquiry and an academic discipline has generated fruitful overlaps between the history of technology and the history of journalism. Indeed, technology has been instrumental in shaping American perceptions of itself and the world; for many students of journalism history in the United States, technology proved to be, in the famous words of Claude Lévi-Strauss, something that was 'good to think with'.[45] The telegraph proved 'useful' for the study of press history, as a body of works that examine its connections to journalism in the United States, Britain, Australia, and Russia demonstrates.[46] Recent years, in particular, have also witnessed the development of new theoretical approaches and frameworks of interpretation. While earlier studies of journalism were characterized by a narrower geographical and ideological nation-state perspective, more recent work, infused with the concerns of global history for recovering patterns of interaction and integration, is committed to investigating the role of the telegraph as an instrument of globalization, and its relation with the newspaper press in a broader transnational context. This research is part of a substantial body of scholarship which aims to understand how various technologies and media of communication have facilitated the circulation of ideas and information since the nineteenth century, leading to new levels of integration in fields of activity as diverse as commerce, journalism, diplomacy, science, and literature.[47]

As a major technology that changed the face of communications in the nineteenth century, the electric telegraph has always received a certain degree of attention from historians of technology, starting from nineteenth-century accounts of its 'history and progress' to early twentieth-century studies of the 'telegraph industry' or of the related technologies of the telephone and the wireless.[48] For the purposes of this book, I would like to draw attention to a little-acknowledged, albeit defining moment in the historiography of telegraphy, namely the publication in the early 1980s of James Carey's essay, 'Technology and Ideology: The Case of the Telegraph'. A well-known media and communications theorist, Carey emphasized the importance of telegraphy as a technology which 'determined, even to this day, the major lines of development of American communications', and identified several key sites where the social impact of telegraphy could be studied. Journalism was one of them.[49]

Carey's statement about the historical relevance of telegraphy must be seen in the context of his lifelong preoccupation with understanding the mechanisms, technologies, and ideologies of communication which enabled American society to perpetuate itself collectively as a nation.[50] Drawing on various strands of communication research, but also profoundly influenced by the work of anthropologist Clifford Geertz, Carey is often credited with introducing 'the "interpretive turn" to communication studies long before it became the fashion in the humanities and sociology'.[51] His call for a cultural history of journalism went beyond the traditional view of newspapers as a means of transmitting information and knowledge. For Carey, communication was a 'ritual' which brought people together not only for the purpose of exchanging information, but also for the purpose of reproducing social relations and structures.[52] News, as Carey described it, was 'drama':

> It [news] does not describe the world but portrays an arena of dramatic forces and action; it exists solely in historical time; and it invites our participation on the basis of our assuming, often vicariously, social roles within it.[53]

Drawing on Harold Innis's insights about the spatial and temporal bias of communication media, Carey conceptualized the telegraph not as a mere technological tool, but as the product of a particular set of cultural and historical circumstances which enabled new ways of thinking about communication by separating it from transportation. The telegraph thus made possible a 'transmission view of communication' which provided an alternative to older religious worldviews.[54] The 'consequences' of the telegraph, according to Carey, were registered in many domains of social life: in the conduct of business and administration, both at a national and imperial level, in the coordination of trains and time, in language and literature, and, more generally, in the structures of knowledge as well as the 'spatial and temporal boundaries of human interaction'.[55] In the field of journalism, the telegraph promoted the rise of 'objective' news by forcing journalists to report 'bare facts' instead of detailed accounts of events, a process which eventually resulted in the replacement of correspondents with stringers. The use of telegraphy also eliminated 'the local, the regional, and the colloquial' from the language of news, leading to the creation of a vocabulary of reporting which was accessible to a national public, and purging journalism of older styles of reporting that drew on satire, the hoax, and the tall story. The establishment of news wire services which relied on telegraphy to sell news also precipitated the commodification of news.[56]

Carey proved prescient in anticipating some of the future directions of scholarly investigation. From diplomacy, administration, labour relations, tramp fishing, trade, and cartography to journalism and literature, there are few domains of social life that have not received some amount of attention from scholars interested in the history of the electric telegraph.[57] In what follows I will highlight the ways in which the study of telegraphy has intersected with the study of journalism history in the aftermath of Carey's work, emphasizing some of the main points of contention and debate.

Broadly speaking, arguments about the relation between technological innovation and the development of journalism have followed two scenarios. For some authors, the electric telegraph was an important agent of social change. Richard Kielbowicz and Allan Bell, for instance, have argued that the telegraph promoted a non-chronological format of news writing and facilitated the development of the inverted pyramid, a style of reporting which places the most important information at the beginning of the news story.[58] Other scholars, however, chose to place less emphasis on technology itself and focused instead on the socio-economic and political context which surrounded its use.[59] The work of sociologist Michael Schudson on the rise of objectivity in American journalism has been particularly prominent in this respect. Already, at the end of the 1970s, Schudson argued that the nineteenth century demand for 'objective' news resulted not from the use of telegraphy, but from developments in the business and political culture of the time, which, in turn, fuelled the American press's search for improved means of transport and communication. The birth of news as we know it was, in other words, connected to the 'democratization of politics, the expansion of a market economy, and the growing authority of an entrepreneurial, urban middle class'.[60]

Subsequent scholars built on these arguments to question the extent to which the telegraph had altered perceptions of time and space. According to Menahem Blondheim, preoccupation with speed in journalism preceded the advent of telegraphy; long-held notions of time and space were already undergoing a process of change in American society as a result of the 'transportation revolution' which took place at the end of the eighteenth and the beginning of the nineteenth century. Against Innis and Marshall McLuhan, Blondheim argued that the telegraph allowed news agencies like the Associated Press to exercise a 'monopolistic control of knowledge' and fuelled conflicts and crisis just as much as it promoted a sense of 'brotherhood' and the creation of a 'global village'.[61] Similarly, arguments about the role of the telegraph in the development of the inverted pyramid have also come under scrutiny. Based on the analysis of news published in the *New York Herald* and the *New York Times*, Horst Pöttker has suggested that the emergence of this style of reporting had little to do with the use of telegraphy and was instead connected with 'the professional effort to strengthen the communicative quality of the news' during the last decades of the nineteenth century.[62]

It might be tempting to discard these two perspectives on the nexus between telegraphy and journalism as binary opposites, but their relationship is often more difficult to grasp. Though not necessarily subscribing to a crude technological determinism, the first group of studies can be described as a form of 'impact talk', which tends to promote a mechanistic view of the world and to explain technology as the main agent of social change, separating it from the social milieu in which it was created and used. Such approaches can also be located within the broader tradition of 'effect research' in communication studies and social sciences, which usually employs a 'stimulus–response' model and subscribes to a relatively narrow view of communication.[63] By contrast, the second group of studies, with which this book identifies, uses a model of communication that incorporates and moves more confidently between various resources, institutional frameworks, and categories of actors involved in the communication process—the state, publishers, printers, newspaper readers, entrepreneurs, scientists, and news agencies.[64]

Turning to the example of India, we notice an interesting and little-acknowledged parallel between much of the previous work on journalism history, which has often followed the tradition of 'effect research'—visible, for example, in studies of the 'growth' of public opinion and of the press as a catalyst of national, regional, or caste sentiment discussed in the previous section—and the trajectory followed by communication research, where this particular approach has been for a long time the preferred paradigm of investigation.[65] As Biswajit Das has convincingly argued, although communication 'has always remained topical and vibrant in Indian society', communication research as such has failed to morph into a full-fledged discipline like other social sciences.[66] Ironically, it has also attracted little attention from historians of journalism, although the last two decades have witnessed attempts to recognize and conceptualize communication as an essential category of investigation for historians of colonial South Asia, a point to which I shall return shortly.

Part of the issue is that many scholars and media practitioners in India have for a long time drawn on and subscribed to a vision of communication which is largely informed by the ideologies of Enlightenment and universalism. As Bernard Bel et al. point out in their excellent study of media and mediation, communication research in India has been inextricably connected to the nation-building imperatives of the postcolonial Indian state and the UNESCO-endorsed vision of communication as an instrument of development and social change.[67] Particularly since the 1960s, this has led to the establishment of institutions of research which by and large worked within two models of investigation: studies of the structure and content of the press, and studies of public opinion. Not surprisingly, perhaps, these models have also been particularly influential in historical studies of the press in India.

Since the 1990s, the rise of neoliberalism, accompanied by the explosion of print and audio-visual media, especially in vernacular languages, and the failure of the developmentalist model have posed new challenges to these modes of investigation. The last decades, in particular, have witnessed the topical diversification of research, visible, for example, in attempts to examine the history of the colonial press from less-explored angles such as medical journalism and advertising.[68] Another important body of scholarship, infused with the concerns of global historians for investigating connections and interactions beyond the traditional framework of the nation-state, has also set out to examine the role of the press and news agencies as agents of globalization and to recast the history of the press and journalism as 'media history'. Chandrika Kaul's work, especially her pioneering account of the reporting of the Raj in the British press, has been particularly influential in this regard.[69] Research in this vein demonstrates that practices of journalism in colonial India were much more complex than analyses based on a simplistic dichotomy of 'nationalist' and 'Fleet Street' traditions have suggested.[70]

These recent developments, through their emphasis on the role of global telecommunications in forging press and imperial networks, provide an opportunity to examine anew the history of the press in nineteenth-century India.[71] This is all the more important since technology has not featured prominently in previous histories of the press in colonial South Asia. Although some studies acknowledge the role of steam navigation and telegraphy in shortening the communication time between Britain and India, they are less preoccupied with understanding how newspapers made use of these technologies.[72] Indeed, reflecting European and American trends, the most conspicuous field where technology and journalism have intersected so far is in the genre of institutional histories of news agencies such as Reuters and the Press Trust of India. Examples include Graham Storey and Donald Read's official histories of Reuters as well as S. Sapru and G. N. S. Raghavan's studies of news distribution practices in the subcontinent, which highlight Reuter's monopolistic position in the system of news exchange.[73]

Raghavan's study is one of the few that attempt to trace systematically the development of news reporting in the subcontinent and to consider the ways in which technologies of communication have shaped journalism. Focusing on the first half of the twentieth century—which in itself mirrors a scholarly preference for the study of press history during the late nineteenth and early twentieth century, a period that coincided with the rise of Indian nationalism—his book also examines at some length the connection between news values and a newspaper's vision of its role in society. In a familiar inversion of colonial rhetoric, Raghavan appropriates technology for national purposes, emphasizing the role of telegraphy in nation-building. Thus, he points out, 'An unintended consequence [of telegraphy] was the strengthening of national consciousness through speedy and widespread communication between national leaders and the people, and through improved mutual awareness among people living in different parts of India.'[74]

While it is relatively easy to demonstrate that the telegraph facilitated communication between nationalist leaders and between leaders and the rest of the population, the connection between the use of telegraphy and the rise of a 'national consciousness' is more tenuous to prove. After all, many British colonizers also believed, in the nineteenth century, that improved means of communication would translate into a consensus of opinion.[75] Rather than succumbing to the temptation to invest technology with the power to shape collective thinking and behaviour, it might be more useful to examine how and for what purposes it is used by various categories of social actors.

While drawing on Raghavan's insights into the development of news reporting, this study nevertheless departs from his in its temporal emphasis on a 'longer' nineteenth century. My aim is to trace the development of news reporting since the late eighteenth century, with occasional references to earlier periods as well, in order to understand how new technologies of communication were located within a broader system of communication in the Indian subcontinent. Unlike Raghavan, I am also more critical about the ability of technology to bridge the gaps between individual aspirations and collective formations.[76] This is not to deny the role of telegraphy and technology more generally in projects of nation-building (or empire-building, for that matter). But it is to argue that we need to probe deeper into the relation between the practices and discourse of telegraphy in nineteenth-century India—in other words, to acknowledge that technology-in-practice and technology-in-discourse are not necessarily overlapping domains—into how technology worked, how audiences shaped and responded to the process and content of news reporting, and so on. More than three decades ago, Benedict Anderson taught us that the nation is 'imagined'.[77] My concern, in relation to telegraphy and journalism, is to understand what the relationship between imagination and practice was, but also who 'imagined', why, and how various imaginations competed with each other.

Communication, the State, and the Role of Non-state Actors

This introduction would be incomplete without reference to another body of works that has provided inspiration for the current study. These can be subsumed broadly, for lack of a better term, under the rubric of histories of transport and communication in colonial South Asia. One of the first scholars to engage systematically with the notion of communication and its relation to processes of knowledge-making and colonial state formation in South Asia was C. A. Bayly, in his now classic work *Empire and Information*. Bayly's agenda in writing this book was to move away from the study of institutions to a 'sociology of knowledge', a shift which, as we have already seen, had parallels in other areas of investigation such as media and communication studies. Drawing on the work of renowned sociologist Manuel Castells, Bayly coined the term 'information order', a heuristic device that he used to investigate the relationship between state and non-state actors ('autonomous networks of social communicators') in the making of colonial India.[78] His work drew attention to the ways in which the emerging system of communication of the colonial state intersected (or not) with indigenous networks of communication and knowledge exchange, leading to slippages he famously labelled 'information panics'. Bayly's scepticism in the ability of the colonial state to grasp the complexities of Indian society has proved enduring. In its emphasis on the role of communication in shaping political organization, his book can also be located within a broader tradition of research which goes back to the work of the Canadian political economist Harold Innis.

In the present study I draw on some of Bayly's insights—for example, his observation about the increasing centralization of the information order during the nineteenth century, which has also been documented in a different context by Chandrika Kaul—but I aim to provide an account of processes of communication in colonial India that is concerned both with the nature and functioning of institutions and with processes of knowledge-making. Such a perspective is particularly relevant in the field of journalism and news reporting, where state and non-state actors constantly interacted with each other and where newspapers did not only report events and opinions, but also played a crucial role in the creation of knowledge about India, Britain, and other parts of the world. Here,

I follow John B. Thompson in conceptualizing communication as a 'form of action' which mobilizes multiple layers of participants (both state and non-state actors) and is shaped by the degree of power—political, economic, symbolic, or coercive—an individual possesses as part of a social group or institution.[79] In this context, the book uses news reporting in nineteenth-century India as a springboard for pondering how technology functions as a resource which can generate various forms of power. Drawing on the perspectives of a wide range of actors—journalists, colonial administrators, news agencies, members of the self-styled 'mercantile community'—all of whom had a stake in processes of news reporting in the nineteenth century, the study also highlights the symbiotic relationship between these various forms of power.

The role of telegraphy in acting as an instrument of and conduit for imperialism has been discussed in a handful of studies, most notably in Daniel Headrick's work on technologies as 'tools' of empire, David Arnold's account of science, technology, and medicine in colonial India, and D. K. Lahiri Choudhury's more recent history of the Indian telegraph.[80] Building on Bayly's notion of 'information panics', Lahiri Choudhury also emphasizes the precarious nature of British control over India and conceptualizes the 1850s as a turning point in the history of colonial South Asia, when a 'New Imperialism [was] driven by technologies such as telegraphy'.[81] The emphasis on the technical limitations of telegraphy and its consequences for the role of the telegraph in suppressing the Indian Mutiny is relevant for the purposes of this book, as is the discussion of the changing contexts of scientific activity, which demonstrates how knowledge about telegraphy became increasingly professionalized and metropolitan in outlook.[82] While I accept Lahiri Choudhury's proposition that the 1850s–1860s marked a break with the past, particularly on account of the ways in which the telegraph infrastructure was built and the telegraph staff was recruited, I also argue that in relation to the specific field of journalism, that turning point must be located in the later part of the century, namely the period around the 1870s–1880s. The picture that emerges from corroborated archival evidence and newspaper files suggests the existence of informational hierarchies and the fact that the use of telegraphy in journalism was gradual and piecemeal. It was only in the last decades of the period that telegraphy 'came of age' with regard to domestic and international reporting. The colonial state was slow to endorse the use of this technology for purposes other than political, military, and commercial. The cost of transmission remained high in the nineteenth century, shaped as it was by the geopolitical and financial interests of various state players and telegraph companies. It was only in the last three decades of the nineteenth century that the colonial government introduced measures which allowed newspapers to send press telegrams at concessionary rates. The press took advantage of this situation by sending more and increasingly longer telegrams, especially domestic news.

During the last decade and a half, the topic of communication has also become vibrant in studies of 'public works' in colonial India. In this connection, Ravi Ahuja's exploration of the public nature of 'public works', with its focus on multiple technologies of communication, is particularly relevant.[83] Indeed, as Dwayne Winseck and Robert Pike have also shown in their study of global telegraphic communication, colonial regulation of telegraphy, coupled with the increasing influence of global market forces, worked in tandem to privilege certain categories of users at the expense of other less financially and politically viable competitors, thus circumscribing significantly the 'public' utility of telegraphy in the nineteenth century.[84]

Nitin Sinha's recent study of communication in eastern India also advocates a comprehensive view of communication that does not single out already privileged technologies—that is, the railways—but examines them in conjunction with other technologies of transport and communication like roads and waterways.[85] The present work subscribes to this line of investigation, particularly in its attempt to demonstrate how a newer technology like the telegraph was used alongside older technologies such as steamers, carts, and even carrier pigeons to report news in nineteenth-century India. Sinha's emphasis on the symbiotic relationship between technology and processes of knowledge-making, as reflected in his insightful remark that '[w]ays of seeing … interacted with the ways of travelling', is also important in the context of the present study.[86] As far as the technologies discussed in this book are concerned, this statement can be qualified with the observation that 'seeing' in nineteenth-century India was a two-way process. The telegraph mediated ways of knowing not only for the colonial state, but also, as the next chapters will show, for the Indian population. This did not prevent it from also functioning as a technology that 'occlude[d] vision and limit[ed] transparency', as Sheila Jasanoff has pointed out in a different context.[87] Overall, many of the actors discussed in this study showed a remarkable ability to adapt to the changing circumstances of their environment and to use a wide range of means and modes of communication, be they old or new, to transmit news.

In conclusion, the present book draws inspiration from many valuable precursors, but remains sceptical of grand narratives of technology-driven social change and 'media revolutions', aiming instead to show how developments in news reporting in nineteenth-century India were shaped by a host of political, technical, and socio-economic factors which circumscribed the production and circulation of telegraphic intelligence. Unlike other historical studies of journalism and news reporting, I take a longer view of the nineteenth century that does not prioritize the last decades of the period, but aims to understand how news reporting in India made use of and developed alongside various technologies of communication from the beginning of the century. Although the telegraph has often been described as a technology which dematerialized communication, I aim to recover and bring to the fore, whenever possible, the importance of its 'material substratum', as demonstrated by surviving telegrams, cables, newspapers, colonial records, and so forth. By conceptualizing newspapers as a site of practice that illustrates how telegraphy was used in the field of journalism, I hope that we can begin to bridge the gap between the discourses and practices of telegraphy in colonial India and to recuperate some of the practices of news reporting of this period.

Methods

This book reconstructs the use of telegraphy and other technologies of communication in the field of journalism from three complementary angles: (*a*) by tracing the geographical routes along which news circulated and considering how technology enabled this process of circulation; (*b*) by embedding the use of technology in the specific socio-economic and historical circumstances of the period examined and identifying the social networks which shaped the exchange of news; and (*c*) by examining specific instances of reporting in order to understand how the format and content of news journalism developed in nineteenth-century India. The advantage of this approach is that it allows us to examine news reporting as a dynamic process which drew on multiple media of communication such as runners, pigeons, telegraphs, railways, and steamers. Each of them responded to a particular need in the system of communication, helping to overcome or circumvent existing natural, technical, political, and economic obstacles faced in collecting and disseminating news.

As is the case with most studies concerned with the history of news and newspapers, the primary material which could be used as a springboard for analysis and discussion was overwhelming. In 1885 alone, for example, 421 English-language and vernacular newspapers were published in British India and the princely states, of which 116 were published in the Bombay Presidency, 77 in Bengal, and 39 in Madras.[88] Considering the vast number of potential newspaper sources, a selection had to be made based on criteria outlined below.

The bulk of the newspapers examined consisted of publications in the English language, although there are occasional references to the Hindi-language weekly *Bharat Jiwan* published in Benares. The sample covers the period from the late eighteenth century to the end of the nineteenth century, with a focus on the interval from the 1830s to the 1900s. The emphasis on the nineteenth century is deliberate: as discussed above, previous histories of the press have tended to focus on developments spanning the late nineteenth and twentieth centuries, a period in which the history of journalism in South Asia was profoundly shaped by the rise of Indian nationalism. By contrast, in this book I am also concerned with the earlier phase of journalism history, aiming to highlight its foundational role in the future development of the press in South Asia. In addition, I also use specific events in the history of telegraphy in South Asia as points of reference around which to organize the narrative of the book. These are the opening of the Indian telegraphs for public use on 1 February 1855, the breakthrough in communications between Britain and India represented by the opening of telegraph lines via the Ottoman Empire and Persia in 1865, and the opening of the Red Sea route in 1870. The analysis ends in 1900 short of the introduction of wireless telegraphy. On 10 February 1905, after a few years of experiments, the Telegraph Department reported that a successful and functional wireless connection had been established between Diamond Island and Port Blair, thus marking the beginning of a new era in the history of telegraphy in India.[89]

Some newspapers allowed for a more detailed examination than others; this usually depended on their lifespan and current availability. There is, unfortunately, a bias towards major newspapers that enjoyed a longer lifespan and were usually published in the main administrative and commercial centres of Calcutta, Bombay, and Madras. While such publications offered the opportunity of analysing news reporting over a longer period of time and enabled the identification of specific trends and variations, it must be remembered that they occupied a privileged position in the nineteenth-century circuit of news exchange. Nevertheless, I have strived to counterbalance this bias by reading across a wider range of publications which appeared in the Indian subcontinent in the nineteenth century, such as the *Delhi Gazette* and the *Lahore Chronicle*, reportedly the first journals in India to make use of the telegraph for the transmission of news; the *Hills*, a weekly published in Mussoorie in the early 1860s; or the *Kandahar News*, a manuscript newspaper published in the eponymous locality at the end of the 1870s.

The years surveyed were those available at the British Library in London and the Nehru Memorial Museum and Library in New Delhi. Only two of the newspapers selected, the *Bombay Gazette* and the *Englishman*, were published throughout the entire period covered by this study. Others, such as the *Times of India* and the *Madras Times*, were founded in the early 1860s and have survived, as is the case with the former, for a long period of time. By contrast, the *Lahore Chronicle* was a relatively short-lived paper, while, for the *Delhi Gazette*, microfilm copies are only available for three decades of its existence, despite its longer lifespan.

The study combines the long-term analysis of several newspapers with the in-depth examination of two case studies. The long-term analysis focuses on the *Englishman* of Calcutta and the *Bombay Gazette*. In the case of the former, the issues examined cover the period 1840–1900; for the latter, the sample covers a slightly longer period, 1830–1900. The aim of the analysis was to gain an understanding of the overall development of news reporting during this time and to evaluate the role of telegraphy therein. Since reading the whole run of the selected newspapers would have been impossible, a sample was examined based on a method proposed by S. R. Brooker-Gross which was adapted to the specific requirements of the present study.[90] In the first instance, two complete issues of each newspaper—the first Wednesday and the third Thursday in July—were analysed at intervals of ten years. The issues were scanned for quantitative and qualitative information, namely the number of columns occupied by news, the source of news, the order in which news was published, the content of news (political, commercial, general interest, and so on), the form of news (headlines, bylines, fonts, white space), as well as any other type of relevant information about telegraphy and the newspaper press (for example, opinions expressed in editorials). Second, the conclusions drawn from the examination of this sample were tested by reading other issues of that particular newspaper, in order to assess their relevance and validity, and also by comparing it to other publications from the period in order to identify possible similarities and differences.

In addition, two specific events were examined in detail: the Austro-Prussian War of 1866 as an example of foreign reporting, and the murder in Poona (Pune) in 1897 of W. C. Rand and Lieutenant Ayerst, two European officers associated with the enforcement of plague relief measures, as an example of domestic reporting. The former event was examined comparatively across the *Times of India*, the *Englishman*, the *Madras Times*, and the *Lahore Chronicle*, while for the latter the sample was based on issues of the *Bombay Gazette*, the *Englishman*, and the *Madras Times*. Occasional reference was also made to translations from vernacular newspapers published in the *Native Newspaper Reports* compiled by the colonial government. Apart from illustrating the reporting of foreign events in India, the Austro-Prussian War was also considered relevant because it coincided with the completion of overland telegraphic communication between Britain and India, and because in histories of journalism war reporting has often been linked to developments in the field of communication technologies. Similarly, the 'disturbances' or 'outrages' in Poona, as they were commonly referred to in the Anglo-Indian press, received a considerable amount of coverage both in India and abroad and illustrate well the transformations in domestic news reporting visible by the end of the nineteenth century. The incident also had significant ramifications for the vernacular press, leading to allegations of sedition and to Tilak's eventual conviction to eighteenth months' rigorous imprisonment.

Structure of the Book

The book continues with Chapter 1, which sets the background to the ensuing discussion by mapping the channels of communication that connected Britain and India, integrating them into a network of news. In order to understand the complex geography of communication in nineteenth-century South Asia, the chapter traces the establishment of the main routes that facilitated the circulation of news between Britain and India before and after the introduction of electric telegraphy. It focuses, in particular, on the 'discovery' of the overland route to India via the Suez in the 1830s, the opening of the Indian telegraph system for public use on 1 February 1855, the completion of the telegraphic lines which linked Britain to India via Russia and Turkey in 1865, and finally the opening of the first submarine cable between the two countries via the Red Sea in June 1870. The aim here is to recover some of the complex interplay of state policy, private enterprise, and individual agency by focusing not only on the physical layout of the lines, but also on the ways in which technologies of communication were used. Furthermore, the discussion shows how older forms of communication coexisted with newer ones, and how the availability and use of a certain technology was shaped by a combination of factors of a political, economic, technological, and ecological nature.

Chapter 2 focuses on the sites of practice and discourses of telegraphy. It uses a variety of historical material in the form of the popular and specialist press, memoirs, (auto)biographies, folk songs, and literary texts to capture the wide range of experiences with and responses to telegraphy, electricity, and other related 'modern' technologies in colonial India. The chapter begins by identifying some of the contexts of use of telegraphy—from administration, to money transfer, to the communication of urgent personal news and even blessings—and then considers how knowledge about telegraphy and electricity was disseminated via the newspaper press and scientific publications in vernacular languages. The aim of the chapter is to recover a wider range of experiences of telegraphy than those previously examined in scholarly literature, while not losing sight of the ways in which this technology functioned as a powerful instrument and symbol of imperial rule. The medical applications of electricity made telegraphy particularly amenable to representations as an instrument of modernity by which to cure India's 'diseased' social and political body. In this respect, the telegraph was not only a conqueror of physical distance, but also a creator of difference between the colonizers and the colonized.

In Chapter 3, attention shifts to journalism as I discuss the various stages of news production and dissemination in nineteenth-century India and consider how telegraphy was incorporated into the field of news reporting. The chapter explores some of the most common strands of opinion that informed discussions about the role of telegraphy in journalism, in particular the nature and extent of change in processes of news-making and circulation as well as their relation to perceptions of time and space. It then reconstructs the production and dissemination of news in the nineteenth century, with a focus on the various stages of this process: the collection and transmission of information by the available means of communication, the publication of news in the newspaper press, its eventual return into the public domain via subscription and distribution practices, and its 'consumption' through reading practices. Here, again, the attempt is to balance colonial records of how telegraphy was regulated and colonial statistics about its use—for example, data about the number and cost of press telegrams in the second half of the nineteenth century—with accounts of how the technology worked in practice, many of which originated with people who had first-hand experience of this technology.

Chapter 4 examines the ways in which colonial policy shaped news reporting and the role of Reuters in facilitating the exchange of news between Britain and India. It discusses early colonial attempts to monitor and centralize the distribution of official intelligence to the press through the establishment of Editor's Rooms, government gazettes, and the institution of the press commissioner. It shows how the Indian government attempted to reconcile the aim of minimizing the financial costs incurred in the process of distributing official news with that of monitoring and controlling the publication of official intelligence in the newspaper press. At the same time, the chapter highlights the gradual expansion of Reuters in the Indian subcontinent, its success in taking over other ventures for news distribution such as the *Times of India* Telegraphic Agency, and its role in promoting a vision of news as a commodity that needed to be protected through copyright. This notion of news was at odds with another, promoted by many representatives of the press and, occasionally, by colonial officials, that insisted on regarding official intelligence as a 'public good' which should be distributed to the press by the government.

Finally, in Chapter 5, attention turns to the newspapers themselves, in an attempt to understand how news-reporting practices developed in the nineteenth century and how telegraphy was incorporated into English-language journalism in colonial South Asia. The first section approaches news reporting from a long-term perspective, by examining its evolution, over a period of seven decades, as reflected in two major Anglo-Indian newspapers, the *Bombay Gazette* and the *Englishman*. The discussion also includes references to a wider sample of English-language newspapers published in the subcontinent during this period. The next section focuses on the reporting of two specific events: one international, the Austro-Prussian War of 1866, and one domestic, the murder of two European officers in Poona in 1897. The analysis captures not only the hierarchies and paradoxes of telegraphic communication, but also the ways in which it facilitated the exposure of readers to highly similar—if not identical—types of informational content.

The conclusion summarizes the findings of the book and suggests future lines of inquiry which could build on and complement the present study. In all but name, this chapter is not a closure, but a call to explore anew the multifarious life of newspapers as printed media and purveyors of news and views in colonial India.

Notes

1. *Times of India*, 20 December 1865.
2. For nineteenth-century examples of this widespread trope, see Anon., 'The Romance of the Electric Telegraph', *New Monthly Magazine and Humorist*, 89 (1850): 296–307; J. A. Wyllie, 'The Telegrapher's Song', in Anon., *Lightning Flashes and Electric Dashes: A Volume of Choice Telegraphic Literature, Humor, Fun, Wit & Wisdom* (New York: W. J. Johnston, 1877), p. 75.
3. *Times of India*, 20 December 1865.
4. For an earlier outline of a research agenda that centres on South Asian newspapers, see Edwin Hirschmann, 'Using South Asian Newspapers for Historical Research', *Journal of Asian Studies* 31, no. 1 (1971): 143–50.
5. In this book I follow nineteenth-century conventions and use the expression 'Anglo-Indian' to refer to British residents in India, not to people of mixed European and Indian descent (Eurasians), which is how the term has been used from 1911 onward. 'Anglo-Indian newspapers' thus refers to newspapers published by Anglo-Indians, usually in the English language, while 'Indian newspapers' refers to newspapers published by Indians both in English and Indian languages. However, we must remember that the latter expression was also used by Anglo-Indian journalists to distinguish themselves from the journalism practised at 'Home' (that is, in Britain), especially during the first half of the nineteenth century. James Silk Buckingham, for example, referred to the 'Indian community' that subscribed to his *Calcutta Journal*, by

which he understood 'English people in India'. I will indicate when this is the case. See Douglas Dewar, *Bygone Days in India* (London: John Lane the Bodley Head, 1922), p. 65. During the period covered in this book, newspapers published by Indians were usually described generically as the 'native press' (currently obsolete) or, when published in one of the Indian languages, as the 'vernacular press' (which this study uses) and the 'language press'. See Kirti Narain, *Press, Politics and Society: Uttar Pradesh, 1885–1914* (New Delhi: Manohar and The Book Review Literary Trust, 1998), pp. 17–18, for a discussion of the latter notions in the context of north India. Finally, the term 'English-language newspapers' as used in this book refers to newspapers published both by Indians and Anglo-Indians.

6. For an example of how oral and print cultures intersected in colonial India, see Francesca Orsini, *Print and Pleasure: Popular Literature and Entertaining Fictions in Colonial North India* (Ranikhet: Permanent Black, 2009), especially her discussion of Urdu and Hindi songs in print (pp. 49–105).
7. C. A. Bayly, *Empire and Information: Intelligence Gathering and Social Communication in India, 1780–1870* (Cambridge: Cambridge University Press, 1996).
8. For more contemporary references to the 'revolutionary' effects of telegraphy, see K. Shridharani, *Story of the Indian Telegraphs: A Century of Progress* (New Delhi: Government of India Press, 1953), p. 61; and Mel Gorman, 'Sir William O'Shaughnessy, Lord Dalhousie and the Establishment of the Telegraph System in India', *Technology and Culture* 12, no. 4 (1971): 581–601, 597.
9. I borrow the term 'vision' from Mark Hampton, *Visions of the Press in Britain, 1850–1950* (Urbana and Chicago: University of Illinois Press, 2004).
10. Sheila Jasanoff, 'Future Imperfect: Science, Technology, and the Imaginations of Modernity', in *Dreamscapes of Modernity: Sociotechnical Imaginaries and the Fabrication of Power*, edited by Sheila Jasanoff and Sang-Hyun Kim (Chicago: University of Chicago Press, 2015) p. 25.
11. Manu Goswami, *Producing India: From Colonial Economy to National Space* (Chicago: University of Chicago Press, 2004), p. 32; Kevin G. Barnhurst and John Nerone, 'Journalism History', in *The Handbook of Journalism Studies*, edited by Karin Wahl-Jorgensen and Thomas Hanitzsch (New York and London: Routledge, 2009), p. 23.
12. Barnhurst and Nerone, 'Journalism History', p. 17.
13. One example is Isaiah Thomas's two-volume *History of Printing in America*, first published in 1810. Thomas was a radical printer and journalist who published the long-lived *Massachusetts Spy* from 1770

until 1801. A later example from Britain is Henry R. Plomer's *A Short History of English Printing, 1476–1898* (London: Kegan Paul, Trench, Truebner & Co., 1900). See Peter Simonson, Janice Peck, Robert T. Craig, and John P. Jackson, Jr., 'The History of Communication History', in *The Handbook of Communication History*, edited by Peter Simonson, Janice Peck, Robert T. Craig, and John P. Jackson, Jr. (New York: Routledge, 2013), p. 19.

14. Charles A. Macintosh, *Popular Outlines of the Press, Ancient and Modern* (London: Wertheim, Macintosh, and Hunt, 1859), p. 178.
15. See, for example, Charles Pebody, *English Journalism and the Men Who Have Made It* (London: Cassell, Petter, Galpin & Co., 1882), p. 162.
16. Although the beginning of journalism education proper is usually associated with Joseph Pulitzer's decision to establish the first School of Journalism at Columbia University in 1912, the first attempts to teach journalism in the United States date from the 1860s. Across the Atlantic, in 1895 the University of Heidelberg offered its first course on the 'History of the Press and Journalism in Germany'. See Beate Josephi, 'Journalism Education', in *The Handbook of Journalism Studies*, edited by Karin Wahl-Jorgensen and Thomas Hanitzsch (New York and London: Routledge, 2009), p. 44; Simonson et al., 'The History of Communication History', p. 20.
17. James Carey, 'The Problem of Journalism History', in *James Carey: A Critical Reader*, edited by Eve Stryker Munson and Catherine A. Warren (Minneapolis and London: University of Minnesota Press, 1997), p. 88.
18. Carey, 'The Problem of Journalism History'; Barnhurst and Nerone, 'Journalism History', pp. 19–20.
19. Tom O'Malley, 'History, Historians and the Writing of Print and Newspaper History in the UK, c. 1945–1962', *Media History* 18, nos 3–4 (2012): 289–310, 295.
20. S. Natarajan, *A History of the Press in India* (Bombay: Asia Publishing House, 1962), p. 3.
21. Pat Lovett, *Journalism in India* (Calcutta: Banna Publishing Company, [1929]); E. P. Menon, *Journalism as a Profession* (Tellicherry: Vidya Vilasam Press, 1930); S. P. Thiaga Rajan, *Introduction to Journalism* (Madras: Educational Publishing Company, 1938).
22. Wolseley's decision to edit *Journalism in Modern India* (Bombay and Calcutta: Asia Publishing House, 1953) was the outcome of discussions with Indian students in the United States and journalists in India, in the course of which it emerged that 'books on India's journalism are scarce'. In his 'Foreword' to Thiaga Rajan's book, the editor of the *Bombay Chronicle*, Syed Abdullah Brelvi, also remarked that 'unfortunately there are very few books published which may be said to do adequate justice

to this great and fascinating subject [journalism]'. See S. P. Thiaga Rajan, *Introduction to Journalism* (Madras: Educational Publishing Co, 1938), p. iii.

23. Menon, *Journalism as a Profession*, p. 1.
24. M. Chalapathi Rau, *The Press in India* (Bombay: Allied Publishers, 1968), pp. 30–1.
25. Tapti Roy, 'Disciplining the Printed Text: Colonial and Nationalist Surveillance of Bengali Literature', in *Texts of Power: Emerging Disciplines in Colonial Bengal*, edited by Partha Chatterjee (Minneapolis: University of Minnesota Press, 1995), p. 30.
26. Margrit Pernau and Yunus Jaffery (eds), *Information and the Public Sphere: Persian Newsletters from Mughal Delhi* (New Delhi: Oxford University Press, 2009), pp. 1–2, italics original.
27. See especially his discussion of a 'limited Raj' in the field of print surveillance. A. R. Venkatachalapathy, *The Province of the Book: Scholars, Scribes, and Scribblers in Colonial Tamilnadu* (New Delhi: Permanent Black, 2012), pp. 169–207.
28. Roy, 'Disciplining the Printed Text', p. 32. See also J. Long, *A Descriptive Catalogue of Bengali Works, Containing a Classified List of Fourteen Hundred Bengali Books and Pamphlets, etc.* (Calcutta: Sanders, Cones, and Co., 1855); James Long, 'Returns Relating to Native Printing Presses and Publications in Bengal; and A Return of the Names and Writings of 515 Persons Connected with Bengali Literature, Either as Authors or Translators of Printed Works. Chiefly during the Last Fifty Years; And a Catalogue of Bengali Newspapers and Periodicals Which Have Issued from the Press from the Year 1818 to 1855', in *Selections from the Records of the Bengal Government*, no. 22 (Calcutta: 'Calcutta Gazette' Office, 1855).
29. For example, R. E. Frykenberg (ed.), *Christians and Missionaries in India: Cross-cultural Communication since 1500* (Grand Rapids, Michigan: Wm. B. Eerdmans, 2003); Anna Johnston, *Missionary Writing and Empire, 1800–1860* (Cambridge: Cambridge University Press, 2003).
30. B. S. Kesavan, *History of Printing and Publishing in India: A Story of Cultural Re-awakening*, 3 vols (New Delhi: National Book Trust India, 1997). A similar, albeit less comprehensive, example is P. A. Mohanrajan's study of early printing and publishing in India which surveys the history of Tamil-language newspapers and journalism. P. A. Mohanrajan, *Glimpses of Early Printing and Publishing in India: Their Contribution towards Democratisation of Knowledge* (Madras: Mohanavalli, 1990).
31. E. Hirschmann, *Robert Knight: Reforming Editor in Victorian India* (New Delhi: Oxford University Press, 2008); Nariaki Nakazato, 'Harish Chandra Mukherjee: Profile of a "Patriotic" Journalist in an Age of Social Transition', *South Asia: Journal of South Asian Studies* 31, no. 2 (2008): 241–70.

32. For a discussion of the development of print censorship in colonial India, see Sanjay Joshi, 'Historicizing the Archive: Making of the Native Newspaper Reports in Colonial India', paper presented at the Western Conference of the Association for Asian Studies, Provo, Utah, 27 September 2002; Priya Joshi, *In Another Country: Colonialism, Culture, and the English Novel in India* (New York: Columbia University Press, 2002), pp. 48–9.
33. J. Long, 'Early Bengali Literature and Newspapers', *Calcutta Review* (henceforth *CR*) 13 (1850): 124–61, see 124, 144, emphasis original.
34. See also N. K. Wagle (ed.), *Writers, Editors and Reformers: Social and Political Transformations of Maharashtra, 1830–1930* (New Delhi: Manohar, 1999).
35. W. M. Digby, 'The Native Newspapers of India and Ceylon', *CR* 65 (1877): 356–94.
36. R. P. Karkaria, 'The Oldest Paper in India: The *Bombay Samachar*', *CR* 106 (1898): 218–36; R. P. Karkaria, 'The Revival of the Native Press of Western India: The *Rast Goftar*', *CR* 107 (1898): 226–43; Anon., 'Sixty Years of the *Times of India*', *CR* 108 (1899): 86–104; R. P. Karkaria, *India, Forty Years of Progress and Reform: Being A Sketch of the Life and Times of Behramji M. Malabari* (London: Henry Frowde, 1896).
37. Digby, 'The Native Newspapers of India and Ceylon', 387.
38. Margarita Barns, *The Indian Press: A History of the Growth of Public Opinion in India* (London: George Allen & Unwin, 1940).
39. J. Natarajan, *History of Indian Journalism* (New Delhi: Publications Division, 1954), but also H. P. Ghose, *The Newspaper in India* (Calcutta: University of Calcutta, 1952); N. Krishnamurthi, *Indian Journalism: Origin, Growth and Development of Indian Journalism from Asoka to Nehru* (Mysore: University of Mysore, 1966); S. P. Sen (ed.), *The Indian Press* (Calcutta: Calcutta Press, 1967); M. Moitra, *A History of Indian Journalism* (Calcutta: National Book Agency, 1969); G. N. S. Raghavan, *The Press in India: A New History* (New Delhi: Gyan Publishing House, 1994); Muniruddin, *History of Journalism* (New Delhi: Anmol, 2005); Sunit Ghosh, *Modern History of Indian Press* (New Delhi: Cosmo, 1998); G. S. Bhargava, *The Press in India: An Overview* (New Delhi: National Book Trust, 2007), and so on. For a study that focuses on the history of Hindi journalism, see R. Bhatnagar's important *The Rise and Growth of Hindi Journalism* (Varanasi: Vishwavidyalaya Prakashan, 2003).
40. 'Government & Journalism in India', *Daily News*, 3 January 1879; 'Curbing the Native Press in India', *Belfast News-letter*, 15 March 1878; G. K. Roy, *Law Relating to Press and Sedition* (Simla: Station Press, 1915); K. B. Menon, *The Press Laws of India* (Bombay: Tutorial Press, 1937).
41. Durga Das Basu, *Law of the Press in India* (New Delhi: Prentice-Hall of India, 1980); Sushila Agarwal, *Press, Public Opinion and Government in India* (Jaipur: Asha Publishing House, 1970). See also Milton Israel's

important study on propaganda: Milton Israel, *Communications and Power: Propaganda and the Press in the Indian Nationalist Struggle, 1920–1945* (Cambridge: Cambridge University Press, 1994).

42. M. T. Boyce, *British Policy and the Evolution of the Vernacular Press in India, 1835–1878* (Delhi: Chanakya Publications, 1988); P. S. Khare, *The Growth of Press and Public Opinion in India, 1857 to 1918* (Allahabad: Piyush Prakashan, 1964); Prem Narain, *Press and Politics in India, 1885–1905* (Delhi: Munshiram Manoharlal, 1970); Narain, *Press, Politics and Society*; S. K. Singh, *Press, Politics and Public Opinion in Bihar, 1912–1947* (New Delhi: Manak Publications, 2010); and many others. For an excellent analysis of the development of the Indian press in post-Emergency India, especially with regard to the vernacular language press, see Robin Jeffrey, *India's Newspaper Revolution: Capitalism, Politics and the Indian-Language Press, 1977–99* (London: C. Hurst & Co., 2000).
43. Ulrike Stark, *An Empire of Books: The Naval Kishore Press and the Diffusion of the Printed Word in Colonial India* (New Delhi: Permanent Black, 2009), p. 6.
44. See for example the works of Orsini, *Print and Pleasure*; Stark, *An Empire of Books*; Anindita Ghosh, *Power in Print: Popular Publishing and the Politics of Language and Culture in a Colonial Society, 1778–1905* (New Delhi: Oxford University Press, 2006).
45. David E. Nye, *American Technological Sublime* (Cambridge, MA: MIT Press, 1994). See also Sumita S. Chakravarty, 'Cultural Studies Legacies: Visiting James Carey's Border Country', *Cultural Studies—Critical Methodologies* 9, no. 3 (2009): 412–24, especially p. 413; John Pauly, 'Introduction: On the Origins of Media Studies (and Media Scholars)', in *James Carey: A Critical Reader*, edited by Eve Stryker Munson and Catherine A. Warren (Minneapolis and London: University of Minnesota Press, 1997), p. 9.
46. For studies of telegraphy and journalism in the United States, see R. A. Schwarzlose, 'Early Telegraphic News Dispatches: Forerunner of the AP', *Journalism Quarterly* 51, no. 4 (1974): 595–601; R. B. Kielbowicz, 'News Gathering by Mail in the Age of the Telegraph: Adapting to a New Technology', *Technology and Culture* 28, no. 1 (1987): 26–41; Menahem Blondheim, *News over the Wires: The Telegraph and the Flow of Public Information in America, 1844–1897* (Cambridge, MA: Harvard University Press, 1994). For Britain, see Roger N. Barton's recent study, 'The Birth of Telegraphic News in Britain, 1847–68', *Media History* 16, no. 4 (2010): 379–406, which points out that '[t]he birth of telegraphic news in Britain has so far received wholly inadequate attention' (399). For Australia, see Peter Putnis's work: 'Overseas News in the Australian Press in 1870 and the Colonial Experience of the Franco-Prussian War', *History Australia* 4, no. 1 (2007): 6.1–6.19; and 'Reuters in Australia:

The Supply and Exchange of News, 1859–1877', *Media History* 10, no. 2 (2004): 67–88. For Tsarist Russia see Louise McReynolds, 'Autocratic Journalism: The Case of the St. Petersburg Telegraph Agency', *Slavic Review* 49, no. 1 (1990): 48–57. For a study of the influence of telegraphy on other media such as the radio, see J. S. Smethers and Lee Jolliffe, 'The Partnership of Telegraphy and Radio in "Re-creating" Events for Broadcast', *Journal of Radio Studies* 1, no. 1 (1992): 83–96.

47. For example, Terhi Rantanen, *When News Was New* (Chichester, West Sussex: Wiley-Blackwell, 2009); M. Michaela Hampf and Simone Mueller-Pohl (eds), *Global Communication Electric: Business, News and Politics in the World of Telegraphy* (Frankfurt: Campus Verlag, 2013); Peter Putnis, Chandrika Kaul, and Juergen Wilke (eds), *International Communication and Global News Networks: Historical Perspectives* (New York: Hampton Press, 2011); Dwayne R. Winseck and Robert M. Pike, *Communication and Empire: Media, Markets, and Globalization, 1860–1930* (Durham and London: Duke University Press, 2007); Roland Wenzlhuemer, *Connecting the Nineteenth-Century World: The Telegraph and Globalization* (Cambridge: Cambridge University Press, 2012); Roland Wenzlhuemer (ed.), 'Global Communication: Telecommunication and Global Flows of Information in the Late 19th and Early 20th Century', *Historical Social Research* (special issue) 35, no. 1 (2010).
48. Some examples include: E. Highton, *The Electric Telegraph: Its History and Progress* (London, 1852); A. F. Harlow, *Old Wires and New Waves: The History of the Telegraph, Telephone and Wireless* (New York and London: D. Appleton-Century Company, 1936); R. L. Thompson, *Wiring a Continent: The History of the Telegraph Industry in the United States, 1832–1866* (Princeton: Princeton University Press, 1947).
49. James Carey, 'Technology and Ideology', in *Communication as Culture: Essays on Media and Society*, rev. edn (New York and London: Routledge, 2009), p. 156.
50. Chakravarty, 'Cultural Studies Legacies', p. 419.
51. Eve Stryker Munson and C. A. Warren, 'Introduction', in *James Carey: A Critical Reader*, edited by Eve Stryker Munson and Catherine A. Warren (Minneapolis and London: University of Minnesota Press, 1997), p. x.
52. Carey, *Communication as Culture*, p. 12.
53. Carey, *Communication as Culture*, p. 17.
54. Carey, *Communication as Culture*, p. 157.
55. Carey, *Communication as Culture*, pp. 156–7.
56. Carey, *Communication as Culture*, pp. 162–4.
57. For general histories of telegraphy, see K. G. Beauchamp, *History of Telegraphy: Its Technology and Application*, History of Technology

Series, no. 26 (London: Institution of Engineering and Technology, 2001); J. L. Kieve, *Electric Telegraph: A Social and Economic History* (Newton Abbot: David and Charles, 1973); C. R. Perry, 'The Rise and Fall of Government Telegraphy in Britain', *Business and Economic History* 26, no. 2 (1997): 416–25; Bruce J. Hunt, 'The Ohm Is Where the Art Is: British Telegraph Engineers and the Development of Electrical Standards', *Osiris* 9 (1994): 48–63; Soli Shahvar, 'Iron Poles, Wooden Poles: The Electric Telegraph and the Ottoman-Iranian Boundary Conflict, 1863–1865', *British Journal of Middle Eastern Studies* 34, no. 1 (2007): 23–42; Margot Fuchs, 'The Indo-European Telegraph System 1868–1931: Politics and Technical Change', *Berichte zur Wissenschaftsgeschichte* 13, no. 3 (1990): 157–66. On telegraphy and electrical science, see Iwan Rhys Morus, 'The Electric Ariel: Telegraphy and Commercial Culture in Early Victorian England', *Victorian Studies* 39, no. 3 (1996): 339–78; Richard Noakes, 'Industrial Research at the Eastern Telegraph Company, 1872–1929', *British Journal for the History of Science* 47, no. 1 (2013): 119–46. For labour in relation to telegraphy, see G. J. Downey, *Telegraph Messenger Boys: Labor, Communication, and Technology, 1850–1950* (London and New York: Routledge, 2002). For telegraphy and diplomacy, see D. P. Nickles, *Under the Wire: How the Telegraph Changed Diplomacy* (Cambridge, MA: Harvard University Press, 2003); A. Knuesel, 'British Diplomacy and the Telegraph in Nineteenth-Century China', *Diplomacy and Statecraft* 18, no. 3 (2007): 517–37. On telegraphy, trade, and tramp shipping, see B. Lew and B. Cater, 'The Telegraph, Co-ordination of Tramp Shipping, and Growth in World Trade, 1870–1910', *European Review of Economic History* 10, no. 2 (2006): 147–73. For telegraphy in literature, see Richard Menke, *Telegraphic Realism: Victorian Fiction and Other Information Systems* (Stanford: Stanford University Press, 2008); Susan Shelangoskie, 'Anthony Trollope and the Social Discourse of Telegraphy after Nationalisation', *Journal of Victorian Culture* 14, no. 1 (2009): 72–93; J. H. McCormack, 'Domesticating Delphi: Emily Dickinson and the Electro-Magnetic Telegraph', *American Quarterly* 55, no. 4 (2003): 569–601; P. Gilmore, 'The Telegraph in Black and White', *English Literary History* 69, no. 3 (2002): 805–33.

58. Kielbowicz, 'News Gathering by Mail', 33, 35–6; Allan Bell, 'Text, Time and Technology in News English', in *Redesigning English*, edited by S. Goodman, D. Graddol, and T. Lillis (New York: Routledge, 2007), p. 79. See also Stephen J. A. Ward, *Invention of Journalism Ethics: The Path to Objectivity and Beyond* (Montreal: McGill-Queen's University Press, 2004), pp. 187–8; and Paul Wouters, Katie Vann, Andrea Scharnhorst et al., 'Messy Shapes of Knowledge: STS Explores Informatization, New Media and Academic Work', in *The Handbook of Science and Technology Studies*,

edited by Edward J. Hackett, Olga Amsterdamska, Michael Lynch, and Judy Wajcman (Cambridge, MA: MIT Press, 2008), pp. 319–20.

59. Wouters, Vann, Scharnhorst et al., 'Messy Shapes of Knowledge', p. 321.
60. M. Schudson, *Discovering the News: A Social History of American Newspapers* (New York: Basic Books, 1978), see especially pp. 12–60.
61. Blondheim, *News over the Wires*, pp. 1–7, 12; Menahem Blondheim, '"Slender Bridges" of Misunderstanding: The Social Legacy of Transatlantic Cable Communications', in *Atlantic Communications: The Media in American and German History from the Seventeenth to the Twentieth Century*, edited by N. Finzsch and U. Lehmkuhl (Oxford and New York: Berg, 2004), pp. 155–62.
62. Horst Pöttker, 'News and Its Communicative Quality: The Inverted Pyramid—When and Why Did It Appear?', *Journalism Studies* 4, no. 4 (2003): 501–11.
63. Biswajit Das, 'The Quest for Theory: Mapping Communication Studies in India', in *Media and Mediation*, vol. 1, edited by Bernard Bel, Jan Brouwer, Biswajit Das, Vibodh Parthasarathi, and Guy Poitevin (New Delhi: Sage Publications, 2005), p. 40.
64. Nevertheless, we must remember that within the tradition of 'impact talk' itself, there have been various levels of engagement with the environment in which communication takes place. Conversely, even for those subscribing to the theoretical tenets of contextualism, the convenience of 'impact talk' as a rhetorical device has often proved difficult to overcome. As Henry Örnebring points out, part of the reason why the language of 'impacts' and technological determinism has been successful in studies of journalism is because it provides recognizable points of reference for many journalists for whom technology has been an essential part of their work routines. According to him, such approaches not only offer a 'philosophical perspective' on the relation between technology and journalism, but are also a 'practical discursive processing of embodied experience'. Henrik Örnebring, 'Technology and Journalism-as-Labour: Historical Perspectives', *Journalism* 11, no. 1 (2010): 57–74, see 57.
65. Das, 'The Quest for Theory', p. 38.
66. Das, 'The Quest for Theory', p. 35.
67. Bel, Brouwer, Das et al. (eds), *Media and Mediation*, pp. 25–8.
68. A. Chaudhuri, *Indian Advertising, 1780 to 1950 A.D.* (New Delhi: Tata McGraw-Hill, 2007); Madhuri Sharma, 'Creating a Consumer: Exploring Medical Advertisements in Colonial India', in *The Social History of Health and Medicine in Colonial India*, edited by Biswamoy Pati and Mark Harrison (London: Routledge, 2009); Douglas E. Haynes, 'Selling Masculinity: Advertisements for Sex Tonics and the Making of

Modern Conjugality in Western India, 1900–1945', *South Asia: Journal of South Asian Studies* 35, no. 4 (2012): 787–831.

69. Chandrika Kaul, *Reporting the Raj: The British Press and India, c. 1880–1922* (Manchester: Manchester University Press, 2003).
70. In the 1980s, G. N. Barrier also highlighted the shortcomings of such a model of analysis in his discussion of newspapers in Punjab. Taking the example of the *Lahore Tribune*, a paper which has been frequently portrayed by historians as a 'powerful voice of nationalism in Punjab', he showed that the fact that it was run by Bengali editors and patronized by a small group of Hindu professionals drastically limited the *Tribune*'s potential for political mobilization. The paper assumed a clear pro-Hindu stance despite the editors' efforts to avoid involvement in factional and communal politics. See N. G. Barrier, 'Punjab Politics and the Press, 1880–1910', in *Aspects of India: Essays in Honor of Cameron Dimock, Jr.*, edited by M. Case and N. G. Barrier (New Delhi: Manohar and American Institute of Indian Studies, 1986), p. 130.
71. Kaul, *Reporting the Raj*. See also Simon J. Potter (ed.), *Imperial Communication: Australia, Britain, and the British Empire c. 1830–50* (London: Menzies Centre for Australian Studies and University of London, 2005); Putnis et al., *International Communication and Global News Networks*. On press networks as a category of investigation, see Bryna Goodman, 'Semi-Colonialism, Transnational Networks, and News Flows in Early Republican Shanghai', *China Review* 4, no. 1 (2004): 55–88; Peter O'Connor, *The English-Language Press Networks of East Asia, 1918–1945* (Folkestone, Kent: Global Oriental, 2010).
72. Julie F. Codell, 'The Nineteenth-Century News from India', *Victorian Periodicals Review* 37, no. 2 (2004): 106–23.
73. Graham Storey, *Reuters' Century, 1851–1951* (London: Max Parrish, 1951), pp. 62–8; Donald Read, *The Power of News: The History of Reuters* (Oxford: Oxford University Press, 1999), especially pp. 49–68; Uma Das Gupta, 'The Indian Press, 1870–1880: A Small World of Journalism', *Modern Asian Studies* 11, no. 2 (1977): 213–35; S. Sapru, *The News Merchants: How They Sell News to the Third World* (New Delhi: Dialogue Publications, 1986); G. N. S. Raghavan, *PTI Story: Origin and Growth of the Indian Press and the News Agency* (Bombay: Press Trust of India, 1987).
74. Raghavan, *PTI Story*, p. 51.
75. Michael Mann's preliminary study on this topic is relevant here. See Michael Mann, 'Telegraphy and the Emergence of an All-India Public Sphere', in *Global Communication Electric: Business, News and Politics in the World of Telegraphy*, edited by M. Michaela Hampf and Simone Mueller-Pohl (Frankfurt: Campus Verlag, 2013).
76. Or, to use Jasanoff's inspired formulation, to examine the role of technology in 'connecting the individual's subjective self-understanding to a shared social or moral order'. Jasanoff, 'Future Imperfect', p. 5.

77. Benedict Anderson, *Imagined Communities: Reflections on the Origin and Spread of Nationalism* (12th edition, London and New York: Verso, 2003).
78. Bayly, *Empire and Information*, pp. 2, 366.
79. John B. Thompson, *The Media and Modernity: A Social Theory of the Media* (Cambridge: Polity Press, 1995), pp. 12–13.
80. D. R. Headrick, *The Tools of Empire: Technology and European Imperialism in the Nineteenth Century* (Oxford: Oxford University Press, 1981). For the case of telegraphy in India, see D. K. Lahiri Choudhury, *Telegraphic Imperialism: Crisis and Panic in the Indian Empire, c. 1830* (Basingstoke: Palgrave Macmillan, 2010); D. K. Lahiri Choudhury, 'Sinews of Panic and the Nerves of Empire: The Imagined State's Entanglement with Information Panic, India c. 1880–1912', *Modern Asian Studies* 38, no. 4 (2004): 965–1002. For science, British imperialism, and modernity, see Deepak Kumar, *Science and the Raj, 1857–1905* (New Delhi: Oxford University Press, 1995); Dhruv Raina, *Images and Contexts: The Historiography of Science and Modernity in India* (New Delhi: Oxford University Press, 2003).
81. Lahiri Choudhury, *Telegraphic Imperialism*, p. 5.
82. Lahiri Choudhury, *Telegraphic Imperialism*, pp. 11–28. In this connection, see also Kumar, *Science and the Raj*.
83. Ravi Ahuja, *Pathways of Empire: Circulation, 'Public Works' and Social Space in Colonial Orissa, c. 1780–1914* (Hyderabad: Orient BlackSwan, 2009). See also Goswami, *Producing India*; Ian J. Kerr, *Building the Railways of the Raj, 1850–1900* (New Delhi: Oxford University Press, 1997); I. D. Derbyshire, 'Economic Change and the Railways in North India, 1860–1914', *Modern Asian Studies* 21, no. 3 (1987): 521–45; Lahiri Choudhury, *Telegraphic Imperialism*; Nitin Sinha, *Communication and Colonialism in Eastern India: Bihar, 1760s–1880s* (London: Anthem Press, 2014).
84. Winseck and Pike, *Communication and Empire*.
85. Sinha, *Communication and Colonialism in Eastern India*, pp. xxii–xxiii.
86. Sinha, *Communication and Colonialism in Eastern India*, p. xxv.
87. Jasanoff, 'Future Imperfect', p. 13.
88. Narain, *Press and Politics in India*, p. 53.
89. *Administration Report of the Indian Telegraph Department for 1904–5*, V/24/4288, p. 13, Oriental and India Office Records, British Library (henceforth IOR).
90. S. R. Brooker-Gross, 'The Changing Concept of Place in the News', in *Geography, the Media and Popular Culture*, edited by J. Burgess and J. R. Gold (New York: St Martin's Press, 1985), p. 65.

1 Technologies of News Transmission

> The post office doesn't issue receipts for letters posted. Both letters were stamped. It's out of the question that my two letters are stranded at the post office here. If the Shaikhupur postmen didn't deliver them, is that my fault? I grant you I wrote only your name and 'Shaikhupur' as the address. I didn't write the muhalla, and perhaps that's why the letters didn't reach you.
>
> Your letter has just this moment come, and I am writing these lines lying down. Now I'll send Inayatullah to your [Delhi] house and get him to find out and bring me the details of your Shaikhupur address.
>
> Well, sir, Inayatullah is back with a note. I'm addressing the envelope accordingly, but I shan't have time to catch the post, so I'll send it off tomorrow morning.
>
> —Ghalib to Hakim Ghulam Najaf Khan (1865)

During the nineteenth century, English-language newspapers in India relied on a variety of means and routes of communication to obtain their foreign and domestic news. The mode of transmission of intelligence was reflected in the very format of news: telegrams were shorter and more compact than correspondents' letters, although, as Chapter 5 will discuss, telegrams themselves became increasingly longer as the century advanced. In addition, highlighting the mode of communication of various items of intelligence, either through special font and spacing techniques or through explicit mentions in editorials and other newspaper matter, was an important practice of news reporting during much of the period examined. Foreign intelligence was usually published under headlines which indicated the mode of conveyance, thus 'Overland Mails', 'News by the Mail', or 'Mail News' when transmitted by post, and 'By Indo-European Telegraph', 'Latest Intelligence', and 'Latest Telegrams' when transmitted by the electric telegraph. Apart from facilitating reading by providing readers with a sense of chronology, the emphasis on the modes of communication of intelligence also helped newspapers to build symbolic and economic capital, testifying to their ability to tap into existing networks of technology and patronage. Details indicating the source of news, the mode of transmission, and the time of dispatch also facilitated a certain degree of control over the circulation of intelligence by allowing the Telegraph Department and the colonial state to track down errors in transmission and to prevent potential 'abuses'.

Journalism in nineteenth-century India drew on a variety of technologies and media of communication, both old and new, in order to obtain its news. The manner in which new modes of transmitting information coexisted with older ones is instructive of how the social incorporation of a new technology is contingent upon a variety of economic, political, and environmental factors. In this chapter I reconstruct the 'arteries', as they were sometimes referred to, along which news, in the form of letters, official reports, or telegrams, travelled within and towards India in the nineteenth century. The discussion sets the stage for the more detailed examination of practices of news reporting in the following chapters, by enabling us to visualize the trajectories along which intelligence moved, more or less regularly, between Britain and India and within the Indian subcontinent. Although the analysis focuses on the postal and telegraphic routes of communication developed on the basis of two major technologies, the steamer and the electric telegraph, I aim to provide a more comprehensive account of the communications system in nineteenth-century India and to show how more recent innovations—including railways—existed in a symbiotic relationship with older modes of communication by means of runners, horses, and boats.

Early Modes of Distance Communication

Practices of news-writing and circulation in the Mughal period have been documented by a number of scholars who show, in the words of C. A. Bayly, that pre-colonial India was an 'information-rich society' in which news travelled along a variety of formal and informal channels of communication.[1] This literature also demonstrates that while the newspaper in its modern guise might have been a European import to India, the idea of the newspaper itself was by no means a European invention. As Iqbal Husain has pointed out, in South Asia the precursor of the newspaper took the form of manuscript newsletters prepared at the Mughal court, but also by regional powers such as the Marathas, and, privately, by people involved in trade and commerce.[2] Although the circulation of these newsletters was more restricted than that of the modern newspaper—Mughal akhbarat were intended for imperial officials, landholders, merchants, and, occasionally, officers and soldiers—their principal role was to disseminate information in a relatively regular manner. Depending on their particular type, the newsletters contained official news, advice, predictions, rumours, and so on, and moved between various parts of India with the help of runners and horses, as part of a formal relay system which spanned the subcontinent and coexisted with non-fixed private and commercial postal networks.[3]

In the nineteenth century, far from becoming obsolete, runners and horses were integrated into the emerging postal system organized by the British rulers.[4] Until 1837, when the Post Office Act XVII was passed, each of the three presidencies of Bombay, Bengal, and Madras had its own postal arrangements.[5] Private *dak*s (postal services) operated by Indians and Europeans did not disappear after this date, but the East India Company was keen to suppress unlicensed postal systems, especially when they competed with its own.[6] For example, in 1850, when a commission was set up to inquire into the state of postal communication in the subcontinent—eventually leading to the postal reforms introduced by Act XVII of 1854—many of those who testified were asked to comment on the existence of 'private dawks'. On 28 May 1850, Nilratan Haldar, *dewan* (financial administrator) of the Board of Customs, Salt and Opium, reported that 'the Nawab Nazim of Moorshedabad has a dawk from Calcutta to Moorshedabad, which, I believe, goes daily, and is called the Nizamut dawk. The shroffs of the Burrabazar have also a dawk of their own to Mirzapoor and the Upper Provinces.'[7] Pestonji Dhunjibhoy, an opium trader who worked for Dossabhoy Framjee, Cama & Co., also mentioned the existence of three 'native dawks' in Rajputana, but claimed he had no knowledge of similar arrangements in any of the territories of the East India Company. Yet, at this point in time, the practice of employing special messengers or organizing private daks for the conveyance of both commercial and personal communications remained relatively widespread. As Haldar explained, private daks often travelled faster than the government post and local businessmen and potentates preferred to send their private communications 'by their own servants'.[8]

The distances covered by runners varied from one period to the other, according to the length of the stages into which postal routes were divided. During the time of Emperor Aurangzeb (1658–1707), the route from Ajmer to Ahmedabad, stretching over a distance of approximately 300 miles, was divided into 27 stages and manned by 62 *harkaras* (runners).[9] In the mid-nineteenth century, the distance between dak stations in the Bengal Presidency varied between 8 and 10 miles.[10] Runners were usually paid Rs 4 per month and were expected to cover an average of 5 miles per hour. They received an additional 8 annas per 1/2 mile of increased speed, but were also penalized with deductions when they fell short of 4 miles per hour, except when the delay had been caused by the bad condition of the road.[11] The speed of the runner could also be a function of the degree of importance attached to the intelligence he conveyed. As Colonel Armine S. H. Mountain wrote from Poonamallee (Poovirundhavalli) in 1829, 'When the dâk-bearer carries an express, he wears a bell about his neck; if it is of great importance he has two bells; but if three, it is a signal of haste and then he is bound to run for his life.'[12]

The conveyance of mails was transformed in the second half of the nineteenth century, with the development of roads and the incorporation of new technologies like the railways, but the introduction of new means of communication was gradual and by no means uniform throughout the Indian subcontinent. This meant that mail delivery was often dependent upon a combination of newer and older modes of communication, which during the 1850s and 1860s included runners, mail carts, boats, railways, and horse-drawn vehicles like accelerators.[13] As Geoffrey Clarke pointed out, runners continued to do much of the work of conveyance until and even after the introduction of railways in 1852 and the establishment of the Public Works Department in 1854, when road-building began to be undertaken on a larger and more organized scale, making possible the use of wheeled carriages.[14] G. Paton, director general of the Post Office in India, reported that in 1860–1 the total extent of mail roads was 43,570 miles, of which 36,784 miles were covered by runners and boats, 5,740 miles on horseback and by mail carts, and 1,046 miles by railway.[15] As the network of railways continued to expand in the following decades, longer runner lines became increasingly affected. By the beginning of the next century, the postmaster general declared, 'In many parts of the country the railway has supplanted the mail runner, and with the completion, during the year under report [1900–1] of the East Coast Railway into Calcutta, the last links of the longest runners' line in India have been closed.' The line in question connected Calcutta to Madras; 863 runners were 'thrown out of employ' upon its closure.[16]

The importance of the runner in the communication circuit of the nineteenth century is also demonstrated by his representations in the popular press of the time. A visual documentary of Udaipur and Rajputana produced by the English painter William B. Wollen for the *Illustrated London News* of 12 October 1889 included, along with the 'Water Palace' of Udaipur, Maharana Fateh Singh's portrait, and scenes of dak travelling, an illustration of two harkaras carrying mail through the desert. Like other representations of runners—such as the 'Dawk Walas of Bengal', published in the same periodical three decades earlier—this illustration conveyed the impression of dynamism and movement. It also underscored the symbolic incorporation of the runner, exponent par excellence of a pre-colonial order of communication, into a newer, 'modern' system of postal communications.[17] The old and the new thus coalesced in the romanticized figure of the runner, whose more extraordinary exploits, which included being exposed to 'mail dacoities', tiger attacks, and cobra bites, provided fascinating source material for the newspaper and periodical press.[18] The dangers, as Chitra Joshi has shown, were all too real. The runners themselves frequently invoked the hazardous nature of their occupation in their attempts to negotiate better terms of employment.[19] The harkara, carrying the familiar bamboo stick and mail bag with jingling bells on his shoulder, remained an important figure in the communication landscape even in the twentieth century, despite the introduction of more 'modern' means of communication.[20]

Arguably the fastest method of transmitting information before the invention of the telegraph was by means of pigeons. If runners covered an average of 5–6 miles per hour and the first mail horses from Bombay to Indore travelled at a speed of approximately 7 miles per hour, taking 52 hours and 25 minutes to reach, pigeons bred in Calcutta were reportedly able to fly as many as 20 miles in the same amount of time at the beginning of the nineteenth century.[21] Messenger pigeons could be useful in the absence of new technologies or, indeed, as an alternative to them, especially in situations when there was a breakdown in the usual channels of communication or when there were concerns about security, as was the case with the tapping of telegraphic messages.[22] Although I found no evidence of their actual use in connection with the exchange of military and commercial intelligence in nineteenth-century India—apart from a number of stray proposals, which are discussed below—there is evidence that they were used for these purposes in other parts of the world and the British Empire.

The practice of employing pigeons as messengers, especially in times of war, had ancient roots. In the nineteenth century, pigeon posts became particularly popular in the aftermath of the Franco-Prussian War of 1870–1, when countries like Britain, Germany, France, Russia, Austria, Italy, Spain, and Portugal began to set them up as an 'auxiliary means of communication' in the event of a breakdown in the usual channels of intelligence transmission.[23] It is unclear whether a similar system existed in India, but proposals were occasionally floated, especially from individuals who were commercially invested in pigeon-keeping. Lt Col A. H. Osman, an authority in the field and a pioneer in pigeon-racing in Britain, wrote in 1900 that 'several lofts have been established at Secunderabad and Deccan by "Tommy Atkins", and it is hoped that now the valuable services have been so strikingly proved by the [Siege of] Ladysmith pigeons, no time will be lost in establishing military lofts throughout India'.[24]

In the nineteenth century, with the expansion of the newspaper press and the emergence of news agencies like Havas, Wolff, and Reuters, carrier pigeons were also used to transmit stock quotations between various European capitals. Businesses and newspapers often operated their own pigeon lofts. Julius Reuter, founder of the eponymous news agency, famously established a pigeon post from Aachen to Brussels in the 1850s to cover a gap in the emerging telegraph network and to facilitate the rapid transmission of stock intelligence between Brussels and Paris.[25] Years later, the Dutch-born editor of the American magazine *Manufacturer and Builder*,

Dr Peter Henri van der Weyde, recollected witnessing the training routine of pigeons during occasional trips to Paris and Amsterdam. The practice was to transport the birds by railway for increasingly longer distances of 40, 80, and 90 miles and to set them free to find their way back. Young, inexperienced birds often perished during these hazardous journeys. To prevent this, Weyde recommended the use of a Chinese device consisting of small bamboo whistles, whose 'very loud and shrill sound' would ward off potential predators when attached to the backs of the birds.[26]

Messenger pigeons were commonly bred in Bengal in the early nineteenth century. The idea of using them to convey commercial and other types of intelligence was certainly not absent from the public imagination.[27] In the early 1820s, when the topic of communication by means of semaphores began to engage the attention of the public in Calcutta, a correspondent for the *Calcutta Journal of Politics and General Literature* suggested that pigeons should be used to send messages between the town and the shipping establishment at Saugor (Sagar) Island.[28] The proposal to use 'winged Hurkarus' was quickly dismissed by another writer on account of the costs involved, but the anecdote illustrates a recurrent trend in the history of communications in colonial India, namely that the impulse for faster and more efficient modes of communication was strongly rooted in the desire to obtain commercial, and not only military and political intelligence.[29] Indeed, access to timely and accurate information was just as vital for the conduct of commerce and trade as it was for military campaigns and the discharge of administrative duties. The trend had parallels in earlier periods, when merchants (*mahajans*) and other prosperous communities organized their own systems of mail distribution. For the eighteenth century, G. H. Khare and G. T. Kulkarni document the case of a Delhi-based agency which sold news to the Maratha government. Known as Khemkaran Mansaram, this firm of bankers also functioned as a news agency from the 1730s–1740s until the last decade of the century and sold news in the northern part of India, where most of its operations were based.[30]

Like runners, carrier pigeons continued to operate in the subcontinent long after the introduction of more rapid means of transport and communication. The Orissa state police was famous for its pigeon service, which it used as late as the 1980s to communicate with stations in remote areas.[31] Far from suggesting an overlap between pre-colonial and colonial networks of communication—after all, as

D. K. Lahiri Choudhury has shown for the electric telegraph, the new routes of communication designed by the British in the nineteenth century did not always follow established indigenous routes due to the divergent military and economic interests of the East India Company—this excursus into the modes of communication which pre-dated, but also coexisted with, the 'big' technologies of the nineteenth century, namely the steamer, the railway, and the telegraph, shows that the old and the new were not mutually exclusive.[32]

This situation resulted from a combination of factors. Ecological features, especially a difficult geographical terrain, made some regions less accessible to other modes of communication than runners. The construction of the telegraph was to encounter similar problems: for example, the line between Srinagar and Gilgit, which reached altitudes of 12,000 feet, was only completed in 1894 and was in constant danger of being carried away by avalanches.[33] In addition, the utilitarian logic of the East India Company made the establishment of new routes and modes of communication subservient to its military and trading imperatives. The degree of economic, political, or military importance of a locality influenced its position in the emerging communication network. Bani Madhub De, an assistant in the Board of Customs, Salt and Opium, was among a group of petitioners from the district of Burdwan who protested against the extant postal arrangements, pointing out that they were particularly unfavourable to localities like his native village of Koormoon (Kuhrmun). The location of the village, some 8 miles north-east of Burdwan and a similar distance from the Grand Trunk Road, made it not only expensive but also inconvenient to send letters to family members. As De testified on 1 July 1850, he wrote home 'very seldom, because the letters are detained at the Burdwan Post-office, and are generally seven or eight days in reaching their destination; on this account we send our letters by hired cossids [courier, runner]'.[34]

Cost, particularly before the introduction, in 1854, of a uniform rate of postage irrespective of distance, was a vital factor in the choice of a particular mode of communication. When testifying before the postal commissioners, many Indian merchants pointed out that they were in the habit of enclosing all letters in one packet, rather than paying individual postage for them. The problem was even more acute for the poorer sections of the population of Calcutta, who could not afford to communicate regularly with their distant relatives. Babu Ram Anand, who employed between thirty and thirty-five servants from various villages in the Upper Provinces, estimated in 1850 that approximately a third of the population of Calcutta consisted of migrants from that region who had left their families behind. His practice was to ask the servants from a certain village to write their letters 'on small bits of thin paper, so that the whole may not weigh more than a quarter of a tolah'. Each month, he paid the postage fee for approximately thirty to forty bundles of letters sent in this manner.[35]

The problem of cost remained important after the introduction of the telegraph, when the post became the cheaper, albeit slower, alternative for communication. Even Reuters, which made a name for itself by selling telegraphic news, used the cheaper postal system to send its less important intelligence from India to Britain. As Henry M. Collins, Reuter's agent at Bombay, wrote to the secretary to the Government of India on 7 September 1867, '[S]ummaries are now forwarded by every Bombay mail for transmission to London via Suez, or the various Mediterranean ports, and in cases of special interest by direct overland telegraph.'[36]

Discussing the American context, Richard Kielbowicz has pointed out that the post and the telegraph responded to different 'niches' or needs in the communication system: if the former allowed the transmission of detailed communications, the latter was particularly useful for concise, brief messages.[37] But it was not merely a matter of technical characteristics. Cost was also an important consideration. As one contributor to the *Manufacturer and Builder* wrote in 1871, in the case of mails, the expenses increased but little with the increase in the quantity of mail. By contrast, in the case of telegraphic communication,

> every message takes its time and its separate manipulation; and if a wire is worked to its full capacity, the doubling of the number of messages requires a new wire, new operators, batteries, etc. In fact, the running expenses are in a direct ratio to the amount of business. Moreover, for long distances, repeaters or relays are necessary; hence expenses increase to some extent in the ratio of the distance also.[38]

This opinion also had advocates in India. In his 1866 account of telegraphy in the subcontinent, Charles Adley remarked that a train could carry a thousand letters at the same time and for the same cost, but telegrams had to be sent individually and their price increased with distance.[39]

Postal Communication between Britain and India

Rapid, reliable, and regular communication between Britain and India was central to the British imperial project, playing an important role not only in the conduct of administration, but also in the circulation of troops, goods, and passengers. It was an ideal to which colonial administrators, merchants, entrepreneurs, journalists, and other members of the public aspired, although aspiration rarely translated into consensus about the course of action to be followed. In fact, communication remained a topic of heated debate during much of the nineteenth century. Discussions revolved around a number of issues, from the geographical layout of the routes, the cost of communication, and the technical characteristics of the technologies employed, to the role of the state in controlling communication, the distribution of responsibility between the 'Imperial Government' and the Government of India, or the quality of service and the companies entrusted with the delivery of mails. In this section I will highlight some of the debates and turning points in the development of postal communication between Britain and India, aiming to show how they influenced the circulation of news and newspapers in the nineteenth century.

Before the advent of steam, mails regularly took between four and six months to complete the 9,000-mile voyage to India via the Cape of Good Hope. By the end of the eighteenth century, as imperial expansion continued apace, the need for an organized system of postal communication became increasingly apparent. The ensuing battle over communication pitched the British Post Office against the East India Company: despite the former's occasional attempts to regulate and assume control of overseas postal communication, at the beginning of the nineteenth century the Company continued to enjoy a monopolistic position in the conveyance of Indian mails. The Ship Letter Act of 1814, an act of Parliament which led to the establishment of a monthly post office packet to Calcutta, Madras, and occasionally Bombay, was at best a compromise, since most postal matter continued to be dispatched to India in vessels owned by the East India Company.[40]

The same period also witnessed important developments in shipping technology. Successful experiments with steam power began to change the face of ocean navigation. By the late 1820s, efforts to connect Britain with India by means of steamers were already under way. In 1825, the *Enterprise* became the first steamer to complete the journey to India via the Cape of Good Hope. Five years later, the East India Company's armed steamer *Hugh Lindsay*, built in Bombay by master builder Naoroji Jamsetji, sailed successfully from Bombay to Suez in a month, demonstrating the practicability of this route of communication during most of the year, with the exception of the period coinciding with the south-west monsoon (June to September).[41] Based on this experiment, a select committee appointed to enquire into the state of steam navigation to the subcontinent concluded on 14 July 1834 that a 'regular and expeditious communication with India, by means of steam vessels, is an object of great importance both to Great Britain and India'.[42]

These developments went hand in hand with attempts to establish a shorter overland route of communication with India via Egypt. Thomas Waghorn, a lieutenant in the Bengal Marine, became particularly invested in this project. His exploits eventually earned him the reputation of 'pioneer of the overland route'.[43] Waghorn's initial plan of using steamers on a route to India via the Cape of Good Hope was frustrated by lack of financial support from the mercantile communities in London, Liverpool, and Manchester. Acting upon the advice of John Loch, chairman of the East India Company, he eventually decided to turn his attention to the different route via the Red Sea. As he testified in front of the select committee in 1834, steam navigation between Britain and India was a topic to which he dedicated his 'undivided attention both night and day'.[44] Later evidence suggests that this might not have been an overstatement. Recollecting his meeting with the adventurous projector many years later, the Anglo-Indian journalist J. H. Stocqueler described him, in his characteristically sneering 'journalese', as suffering from a form of steam mania. The episode took place sometime in or around October 1828, when Waghorn departed from India after failing to enlist the financial support of the Bombay community, but nevertheless raising subscriptions to the value of approximately Rs 50,000 in Calcutta and Madras:

> I was heartily glad to get rid of Waghorn, for his mania on the subject of steam navigation was irrepressible. He talked of nothing else. He dreamt of nothing else. He bored every one, and nearly drove his host frantic. At breakfast, tiffin, and dinner it was steam, steam, steam—*rien que cela*. Previous to his departure [for England] I invited a few friends to meet him at dinner, and wish him God-speed, but I privately begged of them not to say too much about steam, for it would certainly set off our

> friend at a tangent. But at the very outset he broke loose. I introduced him to Major Hawkins of the Engineers—'Hawkins, the adventurer Mr. Waghorn; Waghorn, my *esteemed* friend Major Hawkins'. '*Steamed*, did you say?' screamed the pioneer of the overland route—and from that moment we were in for it. The steam of a jug of hot-water, the smoking dishes, the vapour emitted by the *hookah*-smokers, were all painfully suggestive.[45]

Stocqueler's account might have been exaggerated, but it was hardly surprising in an age marked by commercial and scientific fervour, when fortunes were easily made and lost in a bewildering range of schemes and projections that involved almost everything from mining to shipping, steam companies, and railroads, to timber, silk, sugar, or soda. In this context, 'manias' emerged as a common diagnosis for a host of social problems which included speculation, fraud, and bankruptcy.[46]

Over the following years, Waghorn undertook several journeys to the subcontinent, in the course of which he experimented with various modes of transportation in an attempt to demonstrate the practicability of the Red Sea route. His first journey began in 1829. He set off from London on 28 October hoping to meet the *Enterprise* at Suez on 8 December and to exchange his despatches from Lord Ellenborough, president of the Court of Directors, for political correspondence from the Indian government. His travels, publicized in the press of the time, took him from Trieste to Alexandria, Cairo, and Suez. Having failed to meet the expected steamer at the latter destination, he then proceeded to Cosseir (Koseir) and Judda (Jeddah), eventually reaching Bombay on 20 March 1830.[47]

Notwithstanding financial, political, and technical obstacles—the East India Company continued to refuse to endorse his projects—Waghorn eventually succeeded in establishing a relatively regular overland mail service to India. In 1836, he used English steamers, caravans, and Indian Navy steamers to transport newspapers along a route that passed Marseilles, Malta, Alexandria, Cairo, and Suez. The postal fee was 6 pence per item, and newspapers had to be 'open at the ends, without any mark or writing except the address on the envelope, and not more than 7 days old'.[48] The most difficult part of this route, before the completion of the railway link in 1858, was the overland journey from Alexandria to Suez, where mails, passengers, and freight had to be transported across the desert.[49] According to one observer, caravans of approximately 3,000 camels were needed to carry the cargo of a single steamer, while mail and passengers were transported in carriages, on horseback, and on donkeys.[50]

By 1840, Waghorn's service via Egypt was facing serious competition from the newly established Peninsular and Oriental Steam Navigation Company (henceforth P&O). Formed three years earlier, the new shipping venture would also prove to be a serious competitor for the East India Company, despite its attempts to retain its former privileges.[51] The first P&O steamer, the *Hindostan*, set off from Southampton for Calcutta on 24 September 1842, on a voyage via the Cape of Good Hope which lasted approximately three months. Two years later, a mail contract for the Suez–Calcutta line was secured. This became effective on 1 January 1845 and allowed steamers to ply along a route that passed from the Suez to Aden and onwards to Galle, Madras, and Calcutta.[52] On 1 January 1853, these arrangements were replaced with a new postal contract for the conveyance of the India and China mails, which led to the establishment of fortnightly mails between England, Calcutta, and Hong Kong via Southampton and Marseilles.[53] The point of exchange of mail packets travelling onwards to East Asia was Galle: the steamer headed to Calcutta passed the mails to a vessel in waiting, which continued its journey to Penang, Singapore, and Hong Kong.[54]

The mails via Southampton left Britain on the 4th and the 20th of each month, while those via Marseilles were scheduled for the 9th and the 25th.[55] The price of a newspaper not exceeding 4 ounces was 1 penny via Southampton and 3 pence via Marseilles.[56] Since the former route was cheaper, 'all heavy official communications and … all the soldiers' letters' as well as 'an immense number of newspapers' were sent to India via Southampton.[57] In addition to the Calcutta mails, there was also the option of sending postal matter to Bombay via bimonthly mails which left London on the 2nd and the 17th of each month.[58] The line from Bombay to Aden, operated by the East India Company since 1834, was only acquired by the P&O on 7 July 1854, under pressure from the British government, and began to operate on 1 January 1855.[59]

As Mark R. Frost has pointed out, apart from facilitating the circulation of people and freight, these nineteenth-century sea routes were essential in mediating the flow of printed matter in the form of books, newspapers, and pamphlets, weaving maritime Asia into a web of information and knowledge.[60] Despite its monopolistic position, the P&O was by no means the only company that facilitated this traffic of people, goods, and ideas. In 1869, for example, the route to Calcutta was also serviced by the French Messageries Impériales (via Marseilles), Austrian Lloyd's (via Trieste), and the Societa Anonima Italiana di Navigazione Adriatico Orientale (via Venice).[61] A few years later, as the calendar of mail steamer departures shows, the British India Steam Navigation Company—founded in 1856 in Calcutta by William Mackinnon and Robert Mackenzie as the Calcutta and Burmah Steam Navigation Company—operated steamers to Karachi, the Persian Gulf, Calcutta, and a number of intermediate ports on the west and east coasts of India, as well as Ceylon.[62] From the perspective of the newspaper press, this plurality of choices proved particularly beneficial. The Bombay–Suez line, which was also operated by the Bombay and Bengal Steamship Company, enabled newspapers to receive foreign news on a more frequent basis and to overcome the information gaps between the arrivals of P&O mails. During the Austro-Prussian War of 1866, for example, the *Times of India* published news received by the P&O's 'regular mail' service, but also intelligence delivered by steamers of the Bombay and Bengal Steamship Company 'in anticipation of the regular mail'.[63]

Contemporary accounts from travellers to India also testify to the extent and scale of these exchanges with and within South Asia. Upon his arrival in India in 1839, Albert Fenton, a cadet of infantry with the Bengal establishment, remarked that the Hooghly teemed with activity, with 'ships of all sizes and nations' plying up and down the river.[64] A similar observation came from William Russell, special correspondent of *The Times* in India, who identified American, British, French, and Indian vessels—several of them 'of large tonnage'—upon his arrival at the river on 28 January 1858.[65]

Ensuring that mails reached their final destination in a timely manner was one of the main preoccupations of colonial officials, merchants, and journalists in the nineteenth century, a topic to which I shall return in Chapter 4. The concern with speed preoccupied the official mind to such an extent that in 1855, the postmaster at Aden wrote to the political resident in that place to complain about the 'great hindrance to the public service caused by the unnecessary detention of H. M.'s Mails on board the P&O S[team] N[avigation] Company's steamers'.[66] The 'public' whose interest the postmaster aimed to protect was the restricted circle of British administrators stationed in Aden. His initial reaction of charging the local delivery peons with negligence in delivering the mails from the *bunder* (or *bandar*, Persian for 'port') to the post office is a perfect example of that widespread colonial practice which Charles Adley was to describe a decade later, in his severe indictment of the Indian Telegraph Department, as a case of the 'bad workman always complain[ing] of his tool'.[67] Fortunately for the peons, in this particular case the postmaster decided to examine the matter personally and came to the conclusion that the culprit was the officer in charge of the mails, who refused to 'make greater haste' and only parted with the mails an hour and a half after the arrival of the vessel. As the postmaster alleged, the officer disregarded the rule according to which 'the commander of every vessel who does not land the mails "as speedily as possible"' was liable to pay a fine of Rs 1,000.[68]

Efforts to ensure the speedy delivery of mails usually began aboard steamers, before the vessels reached their ports of destination. The system was first implemented on homeward-bound steamers plying from Alexandria to Southampton and Marseilles, where sorting clerks were employed in 1859. Attempts to establish a similar service for India-bound mails were initially discarded on account of high costs and the argument that 'English clerks could not sort letters correctly for stations in India, where there were many places with the same name'.[69] But in 1868, sorters began to operate on steamers which travelled east of Suez. The system proved successful and expedited the delivery of mails to other post offices in India by at least six hours, which was the amount of time usually required to sort mails in the Bombay port.[70]

Complaints about the difficulty of delivering letters and telegrams in India were not unusual, especially in the 1850s and 1860s. One of the most common charges was that mistakes occurred because the delivery peons were unable to read English. Local names and addresses were also deemed too difficult to decipher on account of their similarity, vagueness, or misspelling. Language was, indeed, a problem, as Deputy Postmaster General J. R. B. Bennett told the Commission of Inquiry into Postal Communication in India in 1850. Since peons did not usually speak or read English, 'The only way they have of distinguishing letters is to catch the name of the addressee from the delivery clerk, and write an abbreviation of it in Bengalee on the back of the letter'.[71] It was for this reason—and the fact that they were penalized for mistakes and misdeliveries—that most peons preferred to work in the 'native town' rather than in Chowringhee or 'anywhere where there are only mercantile houses, or the residence of English gentlemen'.[72]

But the delivery peons also showed a remarkable ability to adapt to their circumstances. Khadim Hosein, originally from Burar in the district of Burdwan, had been employed as a delivery peon on a monthly salary of Rs 8 for four years at the time he appeared before the Postal Commission. He admitted to not being able to read English, Persian, or Hindi addresses, but he read Bengali and, as he pointed out, 'Some of the peons by constant habit are able to make out English addresses.'[73] Another peon, Muniruddin from Peeta in Zillah Hooghly, had worked for the General Post Office (GPO) for an impressive twenty-eight or twenty-nine years at the time of the inquiry. He also earned a monthly salary of Rs 8, in addition to Rs 20–5 per annum which he received as a 'customary present at the time of Hindoo festivals from the residents of my beat'.[74] His testimony makes for fascinating reading, providing insights into how geography and language shaped the work of delivery peons:

> The limits of our delivery extend in the north direction to Banstollah-street, but there are two Mahajunee houses in Patoorea Ghatta-street, near the riverside, where we have to deliver Nagree letters. The boundary of the delivery extends on the east side to the Chitpore-road, and some way up to Colootollah-street, so as to include Amratollah-lane, Soorty Bagun, Cheenaparah and Tiretta Bazar. On the south and west the delivery is bounded by the end of Sukeas-lane, Old China Bazar-street, and the river. We deliver all Nagree, Persian, Teloogoo, Mahratta and English letters within these limits. The peons of the fourth and six divisions deliver only Bengalee letters.[75]

This testimony suggests a much more complex scenario than the predominant colonial narrative of local incompetence usually depicts. The picture is further complicated by information about the inadequate number of peons employed with the GPO in Calcutta and their unsatisfactory working arrangements. According to the reports of the Postal Commission, the furniture in the dispatching room was 'broken' and 'dilapidated' and the pigeonholes in which letters were placed after being sorted and registered were too small for the purpose. This meant that letters had to be arranged in heaps on the table and on top of the pigeonholes and could be easily misplaced.[76] Perhaps ironically, the peons appeared to be particularly familiar with the names and addresses of European residents in Calcutta. One reason for this was the smaller size of the population; the other was fear of penalties and punishment. As John Thomas, head of the Letter Mail Receipt Department, pointed out, once the overland mail was open, the procedure was for all the delivery peons to sit on the ground and collect the post for their respective divisions:

> The delivery clerks know where the residents live, and as they throw each letter to its proper division, they call out the name of the addressee. The peons generally know the residence of every person who receives letters by the overland mail, but in every case of doubt the peons inquire the direction from the delivery clerk, and make a note of it on the back of the letter.[77]

In fact, as Maulvi Ahmed and Babu Ram Anand alleged, a letter, when addressed to a 'native', was much more likely to find its way to its destination if the address was written in English rather than in Persian or other vernacular languages.[78]

Once the overland mail reached India, postal matter entered the last segment of its journey towards its final destinations in the subcontinent. Vans were sent to Garden Reach upon the arrival of the steamer from Europe and mail bags were brought to the GPO to be opened, with the boxes arriving via Marseilles enjoying precedence on account of the prepaid postage. In 1850, postal matter travelled from Calcutta towards the interior along six routes: the Western Road towards Benares and the North-West Provinces; the Berhampur Road, which serviced places like Monghyr, Darjeeling, and Cooch Behar; the Dacca Route, towards Dacca, Chittagong, and Arracan; the Kedgeree Road, towards Diamond Harbour and Kedgeree, which was used for packets that left Calcutta by ship; the Madras Road, towards Jellasore, Balasore, Cuttack, and Ganjam; the Bombay Road, towards Midnapore and Nagpur; and, finally, the Bancoorah Old Road towards Hazaribagh and Chota Nagpur.[79] On the Western Road, the mails were carried in a mail cart from the GPO in Calcutta to Benares, and thence by runners. Similarly, on the Bombay line, a combination of runners, horses, and camels were employed. Runners took the mail to Midnapore, Kumerara, and Sambalpur. Horses then carried it from Sambalpur to Raipur, on the basis of a contract with a Mr Babington, postmaster of Sambalpur. Finally, from Raipur to Nagpur the mail was transported either by horses or by camels, 'according to the convenience of the contractor, Jumnath Dass'. The rest of the routes were manned entirely by runners.[80]

In the Indian subcontinent, local newspapers could be sent either individually or by *banghy* (parcel) post. By mid-century, the traffic had become substantial. In 1852, for example, it was estimated that the number of newspapers dispatched inland through all the post offices of India had reached a monthly average of 106,756 (for comparison, by 1898–9 the number had increased to 32,122,502).[81] Postage was relatively high, particularly during the first half of the nineteenth century, when it was calculated according to distance. Act XVII of 1854 prescribed a uniform rate irrespective of distance, but retained the distinction between imported and local newspapers first introduced in 1837, despite complaints that this preferential treatment was unfair and 'overloaded the mails', adding to the costs incurred by the post office. The commissioners appointed to inquire into the state of postal communication found it difficult to endorse the earlier regulations that had made postal fees for imported newspapers cheaper than for local ones:

> The overland summaries, printed exclusively for Indian circulation, may be compressed, without inconvenience, to the maximum weight of 3.5 tolas allowed for Indian newspapers and summaries; and it would be no hardship on those who are in the habit of taking in the weightier English weekly and daily newspapers, either to pay for the luxury of receiving them by letter post, or to submit to the delay of receiving them by banghy.[82]

Notwithstanding such opposition, the postage fee for an imported newspaper not exceeding 6 tolas was fixed at 2 annas in 1854; for a paper weighing between 6 and 12 tolas, the cost doubled. By contrast, for local newspapers, the fee was 2 annas for papers not exceeding 3.5 tolas and 4 annas for papers weighing between 3.5 and 6 tolas.[83]

The distinction was eventually removed through an order of the governor general on 9 March 1860, when the postage rate on every newspaper not exceeding 6 tolas was fixed at 1 anna.[84] However, official sanction of the measure came only with the passing of Act XIV of 1866, a situation which generated further debate between the representatives of the newspaper press and the Government of India. The authorities insisted that the preferential treatment was the result of the British Post Office's insistence on a uniform rate of postage for India. Other motives included the desire to encourage communication between colony and metropole, and the fact that in the 1850s the average weight of a newspaper in India was usually under

3 tolas (the *Englishman*, for example, weighed 2.75 tolas).[85] For their part, newspaper proprietors argued that the rule had hampered the development of the press in India. As Messrs Townsend and Smith, owners of the *Friend of India*, pointed out,

> Your Excellency in Council cannot be aware, that while for one penny at least forty-four pages of a weekly paper like the *Saturday Review*, on thick paper, can be sent all over the United Kingdom, and that for two pence the same paper is sent by Southampton to India, and all over India, for one anna, or three half pence, thirty pages only of the *Friend of India* (and that on very thin paper) can be sent in India. The result is that your petitioners have been forced to use very thin paper for their post edition, and to restrict the size of their journal most inconveniently, rather than force their subscribers to pay double postage.[86]

As far as delivery times were concerned, in the 1850s runners required approximately eleven days to cover the distance from Calcutta to Bombay.[87] With the exception of a short gap between 1853 and 1857, from 1840 until 1870 an express mail operated each way between Calcutta and Bombay, carrying postal matter for an additional fee beyond that charged for the ordinary post. Similar arrangements also existed for various periods of time between Bombay and Madras (1830s to 1853), Bombay and Delhi, and Bombay and Lahore (1848–52). The express was particularly beneficial for newspapers in Calcutta and Madras as it allowed them to receive up to two newspapers at the ordinary inland postal rates, with additional titles being charged an extra Rs 5.[88]

Newspapers closely monitored the arrival of expresses and regular daks, publicizing them in their pages. The issue of 3 April 1841 of the *Bombay Times and Journal of Commerce* announced, for example, that both the Calcutta express and regular dak had been received 'up to 22d inclusive'. In addition, the Madras regular dak had been received up to the 25th and the express up to the 26th, the Agra regular dak up to the 24th and the express up to the 23rd, while 'an express from Madras of the 27th was received too late for the steamer'.

The readers themselves proved no less anxious about the performance of the post. Writing to the same newspaper, a correspondent from Agra known only as 'MacAdam' praised the postal arrangements in the Bombay Presidency, which had enabled him to 'read your extra of the 10th instant from Bombay by the same day's dawk I received that of the Calcutta Star of the 20th March'. The achievement was all the more exceptional, it seems, since 'the transit from Bombay to Agra is not in such first rate order as that of the Calcutta road to our own presidency'. MacAdam's agenda in writing to the newspaper was to enlist the editor's support for the establishment of an improved and direct route of communication between Madras and Agra, which would 'ensure a more speedy delivery of our overland letters and newspapers from Madras direct instead of by the circuitous route of Calcutta or Bombay'. His musings about the best available route illustrate not only the importance of the Grand Trunk Road, but also the ways in which the press could shape the face of postal communication:

> Then the query that comes next is—which is the best line for the road to be? I don't at present know whether this road joins the Grand Trunk road—or that of Jhansee and Gwalior. Under present circumstances I would prefer the Madras line; joining the Grand Trunk road somewhere at or about Cawnpore—for the speed of the post on this line is very excellent—thanks to the *Delhi Gazette* and the Post Master General.[89]

The express system came to an end in 1870 due to the use of railways, which allowed the transmission of mails in bulk—unlike the 'dribs and drabs' spread over a period of almost a week from Calcutta to Bombay—but also due to the use of the telegraph which made possible the transmission of important information at considerably faster speeds.[90] Apart from significantly impacting the distribution of mails in the Indian subcontinent, the expansion of railways also prompted a re-evaluation of the relationship between Calcutta, Madras, and Bombay in the system of postal communication. The postal arrangements in use during the first six decades of the nineteenth century suggest that Bombay occupied only a secondary position as a port of entry of mails into India, with Calcutta and Madras enjoying a more prominent status. As the members of the Select Committee on East India Communications observed in 1866, this situation was motivated by the 'political and commercial importance of those cities' and the fact that the arrangement was convenient for the redistribution of mails to other parts of India.[91]

By the 1860s, however, it had become increasingly obvious that the system was unsatisfactory and that dispatching the mails only to Bombay and distributing them by rail to the rest of India would considerably improve the transit time of mails.[92] In 1865, Director General of the Post Office of India H. B. Riddell compared the delivery times of mails from Calcutta via Galle and Bombay and concluded that the former route had become redundant, since mails reached London approximately one week later than via Bombay. It was only at Madras that the mail still reached 12–18 hours ahead of the Bombay packets. In addition, there were numerous complaints that the mails via Galle did not reach the North-West Provinces, the Punjab, Sindh, Bombay, and even an important part of the Madras Presidency.[93]

The completion of railway communication between Bombay and Calcutta, as well as between Bombay and Madras, was the decisive development which shifted the balance in favour of Bombay becoming, as one observer put it, '*the* port of India'.[94] In 1866, when the British government set up the committee to investigate the state of postal and telegraphic communication with India, it was decided that the fortnightly mails to Bombay and Calcutta should be replaced by a weekly service to Bombay.[95] A year later, the P&O's mail contract for the Bombay–Suez line was renewed, an agreement which transformed Bombay into 'the port of arrival and departure of all English mails', effectively boosting its importance as a centre of news and benefiting the newspapers published in this town.[96]

Railways also helped to change the face of communication on the European segment of the overland mail. In Britain, they had been used occasionally for the conveyance of mails since 1830, although the regular service of the Post Office was inaugurated in 1838, upon the passage of the Railways Conveyance of Mails Act. As Jehangir Naoroji and Hirjibhoy Merwanji recorded in their account of residence in Britain, in 1839 the mail train from London to Birmingham took five hours to complete its journey, a performance which also included twenty-five minutes of 'stoppages'.[97] A decade later, overland mails via Marseilles could travel by train for part of their journey through France—between Abbeville and Paris—while the network continued to be expanded towards the Italian ports of Genoa and Trieste.

In October 1869, the mail to India gained an additional 'supplementary' route via Ostend, Brussels, Cologne, Brindisi, and Alexandria.[98] Initially used only occasionally, since services via Southampton and Marseilles were cheaper, this new route proved particularly useful during the Franco-Prussian War (1870–1), when railway communication was stopped in France. After the completion of the Mont Cenis Tunnel in 1871, which linked France with Italy by rail, the conveyance of mails via Brindisi became regular, with England paying approximately 500,000 francs annually for the transport of almost 200 tons of newspapers and 40 tons of letters.[99] This remained the principal mail route to India until World War I.[100]

Similarly, the opening of the Suez Canal in 1869 led to a considerable reduction in the cost of transport from Alexandria to the Suez, a situation which severely affected the P&O and forced it to reorganize its traffic to India. The British Post Office was initially opposed to the conveyance of mails via the Canal, emphasizing the advantages offered by the use of the Egyptian Railways. However, the P&O gradually diminished its financial investment in the conveyance of mails by land, a fact which led to the closure of the overland route from Alexandria to the Suez in 1888.[101]

Thus, in the course of a century, the travelling time of mails between Britain and India had diminished considerably. If, in 1840, the voyage between Britain and Bombay via Alexandria took an average of six or seven weeks, by the end of the century the average time of transit for mails from London to Bombay was 14 days, 3 hours, and 40 minutes.[102] The rates of postage also decreased in the course of this period. In 1871, the governor general in council granted a reduction in inland rates, which allowed newspapers not exceeding 10 tolas to be sent for half an anna, while those below 20 tolas were charged 1 anna.[103] In 1897, the rate was 0.25 anna for newspapers below 3 tolas and 0.5 anna for those between 3 and 10 tolas. Exchange copies of newspapers which were sent to other proprietors or editors were exempt from postage, while newspapers sent in bundles to agents for sale to persons other than regular subscribers were charged half the postage fee.[104]

With regard to imperial postage, on 27 December 1870, a delegation of bankers, merchants, newspaper proprietors, brokers, and other people engaged in trade in India, China, and Australia, submitted a memorial to the postmaster general of Britain, the Marquis of Hartington, asking for a reduction in the rates charged for newspapers via Brindisi. Ironically, the switch to this route, while deemed safer and faster, had proved disadvantageous for newspapers published in India, leading to an increase in postage rates from 3 to 4 pence per 4 ounces of weight. The request was refused on the grounds that when the Indian mails were dispatched via Marseilles, only a French transit rate was required, while in the case of transport via Brindisi, the passing of the mail through several European countries generated a higher transit fee.[105] The last two decades of the century thus witnessed increased agitation, by men such as the Conservative member of Parliament John Henniker Heaton, for the introduction of penny postage in the British Empire. On 25 December 1898, in the wake of the Imperial Postal Conference held in London, a postage fee of 1 penny per 0.5 ounce was introduced for letters exchanged between Britain and most of its colonies, including India. But it was only in 1913 that the Empire Press Union, an organization established in London in 1909 for the purpose of representing the interests of English-language newspapers published throughout the empire, managed to secure a postage rate of 0.5 pence per copy for newspapers.[106]

Mechanical Telegraphs in Colonial India

If the previous sections have focused on postal communication, in the remaining part of this chapter I turn my attention to the telegraph, the other important technology which newspapers used in the nineteenth century for the communication of news. Historical accounts of telegraphy in the Indian subcontinent usually begin in the 1830s with William Brooke O'Shaughnessy's pioneering experiments in electric telegraphy. These culminated, more than a decade later, in Lord Dalhousie's decision to construct the first network of telegraphs in the Indian subcontinent. But electric telegraphy was not the only type of telegraphy used in colonial South Asia. From the end of the eighteenth century, a number of proposals for the introduction and use of mechanical telegraphs, in the form of shutters and semaphores, were submitted. Some of them will be discussed below.[107]

Unlike their electric counterparts, visual telegraphs have so far occupied only a marginal place in histories of communication in the Indian subcontinent. Gunakar Muley's essay on semaphore telegraphy is one of the few studies dedicated exclusively to this subject. Despite its title, much of the discussion focuses on the history of semaphores in Europe, not in the Indian subcontinent.[108] While the subject deserves its own book, my interest in the topic is necessarily tangential and motivated by the role 'semaphoric telegrams' played in early processes of news reporting. In the 1840s, more than a decade before 'electric telegrams' became a more or less regular feature of news reporting, semaphoric news was already being published in the pages of Calcutta newspapers like the *Englishman* and the *Calcutta Courier*.[109] Apart from supplying newspapers with shipping intelligence and familiarizing readers with the format of telegraphic news, mechanical telegraphs also anticipated the electric telegraph in other ways, for example in the field of administration, through the organization of a 'Telegraph Department', the appointment of a 'Superintendent of Telegraphic Communication' in the 1830s, and the administrative amalgamation of postal and telegraph services.

Like in Europe, interest in visual telegraphy in and for the Indian subcontinent was motivated primarily by considerations of a military and naval nature, although commercial interests also became increasingly prominent during the first decade of the nineteenth century. Some of the earliest proposals for the introduction of semaphores date back to the eighteenth century. One suggestion originated with Thomas Barnard (1746–1830), a British engineer responsible for surveying the *Jaghire* (*jagir*) lands in the Chengalpattu District of present-day Tamil Nadu during 1767–74. In 1767, Barnard proposed the construction of a line of 'visual telegraphs' in India on the grounds that it would 'give warning of invasion of the Carnatic by Haidar Ali's horsemen'.[110] Two decades later, in 1788, a similar proposal was submitted to the governor of Madras, Archibald Campbell, for the purpose of 'alarming the country in case of invasion'.[111]

Over the following decades, telegraphy became increasingly popular in Europe, especially after the Chappe brothers established their semaphore system in France, which was successfully used for the transmission of military and political news. Following suit, in 1795 the British Admiralty decided to construct a line of shutter telegraphs from London to Deal, Portsmouth, based on a model proposed by Lord George Murray. This instrument was less efficient than the Chappe telegraph: communication was done with the help of six boards, as opposed to moveable arms in the case of the Chappe device, which had the advantage of being lighter and more easily visible from a distance.[112] Shortly thereafter, the Napoleonic Wars (1803–15) provided an additional layer of interest in visual telegraphy, encouraging the submission of various proposals for the improvement of extant instruments and codes of signalling.

In the case of India, military and naval officers vied with each other for the support of the government and the Court of Directors, each confident that their system was 'most valuable' and 'superior' to its predecessors.[113] The projectors advocated visual telegraphs as particularly useful in facilitating communication between military stations and posts, along the coast, and between headquarters and detachments. Needless to say, official reception of these schemes depended not only on the technical qualities of the instruments and their ability to communicate messages in as convenient, efficient, and accurate a manner as possible, but also on the projectors' ability to tap into the existing networks of political and financial patronage.[114]

Among those who advocated telegraphy as 'the principal new object that attracted attention' was Lieutenant Colonel John Macdonald, a long-time resident in the Indian subcontinent.[115] In 1797, upon his return from India, Macdonald set about improving the extant shutter telegraph in use in England at the time. He devised a system of boarded telegraphs for land communication, which was based on the 'lettering' of words and used a numerical code that assigned numbers to individual words. Following contemporary practice, Macdonald actively advertised his innovations in the periodical press of the time, particularly in the *Gentleman's Magazine* and the *Asiatic Journal*. In addition, he also aimed to obtain public recognition through the publication of his *Treatise on Telegraphic Communication, Naval, Military and Political* (1808) and *Telegraphic Dictionary* (1818).

Macdonald's correspondence with the Admiralty emphasized the potential military applications of his innovation at a time of British imperial expansion in South Asia. Sir John Barrow, second secretary to the Admiralty, praised the telegraph for its potential to facilitate communication 'between the interior frontier line of India and the several Presidencies'.[116] But the Court of Directors proved unwilling to endorse Macdonald's project, deciding instead to purchase fifty copies of his *Treatise* and to dispatch them to India together with a model of his instrument so 'that they may come under the observation of men whose employment or studies have led them to the consideration of subjects of that nature'.[117] Perhaps more remarkable than the technology itself were Macdonald's accurate prediction about the future geographical trajectory of telegraphic communication in the Indian subcontinent and his implicit recognition of the naval and commercial significance of telegraphy. As he wrote on 5 August 1815, 'The first Line of Telegraphic Communication to be established in India will, probably, run between Calcutta, the Capital, and Diamond Harbour.'[118]

Plans for the establishment of telegraphic communication were not confined to Bengal, but extended to other parts of India as well. In 1813, William Boyce, a land surveyor with experience on the coast of Ireland, submitted a proposal to the Government of Bombay for the establishment of a network of telegraphs which was to span the Indian subcontinent. As Boyce put it, the instrument he had devised was 'infinitely superior' to those of Claude Chappe and Lord George Murray because of its ability to transmit news faster: 'When an overland dispatch arrived or any news of importance by sea, it could be communicated to the Supreme Government in half an hour, and an answer received back in the next half an hour'.[119] The two routes he proposed were: Bombay–Poona–Hyderabad–Cuttack–Calcutta, with a total of 75 stations, and Bombay–Mangalore–Seringapatam–Bangalore–Madras, with a total of 133 stations. The proposal was rejected by Colin Mackenzie, future surveyor general of India, on the grounds that the plan was impracticable without an appropriate survey of the terrain, the wooden towers were liable to destruction by white ants and invisible in jungle areas, they were exposed to attacks from Pindaris (here, marauders), and could not be easily supplied with water and provisions.[120]

In July 1817, much to the dismay of the Court of Directors, who did not approve of such 'experiments of great expense', the government decided to set up a committee to investigate the possibility of establishing a line of telegraphs from Calcutta to Nagpur.[121] Led by Colin Mackenzie, the committee appointed George Everest and Lieutenant Ferguson to survey the line from Calcutta to Chunar, a task which was completed in May 1818 and resulted in the establishment of an experimental line of telegraphs. Everest's account suggests that he did not find the terrain particularly suitable to the construction of visual telegraphs. For example, the tract between Calcutta and Burdwan was described as 'flat and swampy … [and] peculiarly ill calculated for telegraphic communication, from there being scarcely any rising grounds, either natural or artificial, so that the edifice must be raised from the ground'. With the survey coming to an end in October 1818, the signal stations were also closed down shortly thereafter.[122]

The project was revived in 1820, as the government was keen to maintain a line of telegraphs along the New Military Road and eventually decided to appoint a superintendent in charge of the forty-five stations between Calcutta and Chunar.[123] A correspondent for the *Calcutta Journal* reported that the two-storey high Martello towers erected at intervals of 10 miles were each attended by a *tindal* (petty officer) whose task was 'to take observations, repeat signals, make entries, and send reports to the inspectors', and by five *lascar*s (here, soldiers) who 'work[ed] the machinery'.[124] Initially, this consisted of four movable spheres erected on a mast which were later replaced by shutters of wooden boards. As the instruments were improved and the signallers became more experienced, whole words and sentences, instead of letters, could be transmitted based on a code known only to the inspectors. The time of transmission also became shorter: from two-and-a-half hours for a distance of approximately 350 miles from the River Sone to Calcutta to only fifty minutes from Chunar to Calcutta. By November 1827, the line was used daily for the transmission of messages, despite the fact that clouds of dust and the absence of a second telescope made work difficult at times.[125] The expenses generated by this 'costly and ill-advised experiment', which were estimated to have reached almost six lakh rupees since its commencement a decade earlier, made the Court of Directors increasingly impatient. Acting on the suggestion of Charles Metcalfe (then member of the Supreme Council), the governor general in council eventually sanctioned the closure of the line on 1 September 1828.[126]

In the meantime, proposals for the establishment of telegraphic communication in other parts of India continued to be submitted. In fact, one newspaper report mentions 10 October 1835, 5.37 p.m., as the time when the first telegram was transmitted in Mysore. The message consisted of ninety-six words and was sent by Lingaraja Urs on behalf of the maharaja to the British commissioner.[127] In Bombay, on the other hand, where the postal lines from Calcutta, Hyderabad, and Madras converged, Governor John Malcolm also proposed to link Poona to the city by semaphores in 1830. Weary of further expenses on behalf of telegraphic communication, the governor general rejected this plan on account of the considerable costs incurred by the establishment of the telegraph system in Bengal. Notwithstanding the lack of official support, Malcolm pointed out the advantages of such a system, emphasizing the ideal position of Bombay as a point of entry of information into India:

> The Court of Directors ... will see ... the many important advantages, as well as saving of expenditure, that might have resulted from the adoption of this measure, of conveying rapid intelligence in a country so favourably situated for it as Bombay, and for communication with vessels in the harbour.[128]

Although the plan did not materialize, the government was not prepared to renounce the idea of telegraphic communication, at least not in Bengal. Amid protests from the Court of Directors, it went ahead and sanctioned the construction of semaphores along a second axis of communication which stretched southwards from Fort William to the shipping establishment at Saugor Island. The terrain had been surveyed in 1802, albeit without much practical consequence.[129] Two decades later, correspondents of the *Calcutta Journal* decried the absence of an efficient mode of transmitting shipping intelligence from Saugor to Calcutta, pointing out that this had a negative impact on trade. Eager to find a remedy, members of the mercantile community expressed their willingness to sponsor the construction of semaphores and even suggested alternative modes of communication by means of pigeons and flagstaffs.[130] Indeed, in 1830, the 'Mercantile Establishments and Insurance Offices of Calcutta' offered to pay a monthly subscription fee of Rs 900 to support the construction of the line on the condition that they should be provided with telegraphic intelligence from Kedgeree and Saugor. Their other request was that 'the line from Diamond Harbour upwards should follow that of the river'.[131]

For the purposes of this axis of communication, semaphores were considered preferable to shutters, as they were 'lighter, more manageable, offering less surface to violent winds, and possessing besides the power of being turned to any quarter'.[132] The semaphore towers between Kedgeree, with its important post office, and the Calcutta Exchange, were eventually completed in May 1830 and opened for public use on 21 June 1831.[133] Stations were located at Kedgeree Light House, Coverdale's Tree, Mud Point, Moyapore, Fort William, Middle, and Diamond Point.[134] The total cost of construction was estimated at Rs 29,299, and the Semaphore Telegraph Establishment was placed under the superintendence of Captain Harington.[135] The line was used for the transmission of shipping intelligence until the opening of the first line of electric telegraphs in 1851.[136]

The construction of shutters and semaphores clearly followed the strategic military interests of the Company Raj. Telegraphs were built along military roads, such as the one linking Calcutta to Benares, in order to facilitate the movement of troops and the transmission of information about the state of the road. The pairing of important routes of communication and telegraphs was hardly surprising: in fact, the same principle would also inform the construction of the network of electric telegraphs. As one anonymous traveller remarked in 1860, 'All along the Trunk Road the electric telegraph wires are placed, and messages can be communicated from one important station to another with the same facility as in England.'[137] At the same time, however, the advantages of semaphore telegraphy, like the advantages of electric telegraphy, did not escape the attention of other members of the public. Since commerce and trade depended on the rapid communication of information, members of the mercantile public often expressed their willingness to endorse and fund such projects, on occasion even trying to influence the layout of the lines.

Wiring India

The electric telegraph was different from its mechanical counterpart in that it used electricity to transmit messages, a process that enabled information to travel faster and farther. Unlike visual telegraphs, which used flags, shutters, movable arms, telescopes, and so on, the electric telegraph required wire (usually made of copper), a battery to produce the electric voltage, an electromagnet to produce the magnetic field which could deflect the pointer, and a key to interrupt or complete the circuit. The telegraph did not appear in a vacuum, but was built on previous scientific discoveries and experimentation. Although European and American imaginations of modernity in the nineteenth century depended primarily on narrow, nation-based narratives of scientific discovery and progress, which emphasized the primacy of Western science and appropriated scientific inventions as national achievements, some commentators like Peter Henri van der Weyde conceded that innovation in the field of science was a multi-sited process which depended on the transnational exchange of knowledge and collaboration:

> One of the first duties in Science is to 'give honor to whom honor is due'; as later brilliant inventions tend to eclipse former more valuable discoveries on which they are based, and as even the names of former great investors and laborers in the field of scientific progress become forgotten, we think it highly useful to give here a kind of chronology of the discoveries on which our knowledge of electricity, and the subsequent series of inventions, which culminated in the modern electric telegraph, are based. It will show the reason why Switzerland, Germany, France, England, America, and even Russia, claim this invention, while the fact is that they all had their share in it, and that no single nation and much less any single individual, can lay any other claim, than having taken advantage of the investigations of others, and perhaps sometimes added some novelty very trifling when compared with the knowledge inherited from predecessors.[138]

But even in such accounts, colonies like India—and Weyde was rather open-minded in his assessments of non-European technology by comparison to many of his contemporaries—when mentioned at all, functioned more as a site for the collection of information and knowledge and the transfer of science and technology rather than a place where 'science' and 'technology' were produced.[139] This was visible in the relatively regular publication in the pages of the *Manufacturer and Builder* of articles on topics of interest such as brick-making, methods of cleaning solid silver, and the architectural characteristics of temple construction in India; paper production in Japan, China, and Korea; carpentry, metal works, oil, and felt-hat making in Japan; and road and bridge construction in China.[140]

In line with his philosophy of 'giving honor to whom honor is due', Weyde was also one of the few who included William O'Shaughnessy's 1839 experiments with underwater telegraphy in Calcutta as part of the historical timeline of electric telegraphy. In that year, O'Shaughnessy, who had arrived in India in 1834 and was by now a professor of chemistry at the Calcutta Medical College, reportedly succeeded in sending signals across the Hooghly River with the help of a copper wire insulated with cotton and tar.[141] Although it took the discovery of the insulating properties of gutta-percha and the passing of another three decades for submarine telegraphy to come of age on the occasion of the successful laying of the transatlantic cable in 1866, O'Shaughnessy's experiments with electric telegraphy gained enough recognition for Lord Dalhousie to entrust him in 1851 with the construction of the early network of telegraphs in the subcontinent.

As John Macdonald had predicted decades earlier, the first line of electric telegraphs built by O'Shaughnessy did indeed run along the Hooghly River, linking Calcutta with Diamond Harbour. It was an experimental line of approximately 82 miles, which was completed on 4 October 1851 and was used primarily to transmit shipping intelligence.[142] Encouraged by this initial success, Dalhousie and the Court of Directors sanctioned the extension of the lines to the rest of India in the following year: by 1856, telegraphs ran from Calcutta to Agra and further on to Peshawar and Bombay, which were then connected to Madras. Communication was also established between Ootacamund and Bangalore, as well as Meeday and Rangoon.[143]

As Lahiri Choudhury has pointed out, there were no duplicate lines at this time and no direct connection between Calcutta and Madras, a fact that undermined the efficiency of the system and was partly responsible for the failure of communication during the Mutiny of 1857.[144] Although O'Shaughnessy was aware of contemporary achievements in the field of telegraphy, the instruments he devised for use in India were unique in their own right, not only because he was keen to use local materials and expertise, but also because he was concerned about infringing already registered patent rights.[145] Among his most notable innovations—which were to come under severe scrutiny from his successors—were the use of bamboo poles and heavy iron rods as conductors instead of copper wire and a telegraphic instrument similar to that of Cooke and Wheatstone's, but which had a separate receiver and transmitter.[146] In 1857, the Morse system of signalling was introduced in India, the instruments being manufactured by the German firm Siemens & Halske.[147]

As Colonel D. G. Robinson, director general of the Indian Telegraph Department, testified before the Select Committee on East India Communications on 15 May 1866, the primary object of the government in sanctioning the construction of telegraphs in India had been to facilitate 'speedy communication between the different military stations'.[148] Indeed, as the next chapter will discuss in more detail, this belief in the importance of the telegraph for imperial administration and rule was reinforced on the occasion of the Indian Sepoy Mutiny of 1857. Nevertheless, a decade after the opening of the lines for public use, it had also become increasingly clear that to view the telegraph solely or primarily as an instrument of imperial administration was no longer tenable, especially if the government was to make up for some of its reported annual financial loss of £40,000 incurred in running the system. Furthermore, there was growing pressure from other sections of the public, in particular the merchant community and some representatives of the press, for improved and cheaper communications. Robinson's words captured well this gradual change of direction when he said that 'the Government and the public, as well as the telegraph administration, consider the telegraph department an institution like the Post Office, *pro bono publico*.'[149]

This was also a time when the contours of scientific activity in colonial India were undergoing significant changes. As Lahiri Choudhury has pointed out, O'Shaughnessy had belonged to a generation of 'gentleman scientists'—although his claim to that title was not necessarily by virtue of his birth—who had used local materials to devise his own system of telegraphic communication. The tide was changing by the 1860s, and O'Shaughnessy's successors at the helm of the Telegraph Department proved largely unsympathetic to both his scientific method and his managerial skills. Telegraphic science and practice became more institutionalized and standardized from the mid-1860s onwards, which also meant that it became more European and metropolitan in outlook.[150] In addition, this period witnessed intense debate, not only in India but also in Britain, about the role of the state in the administration of the telegraph system. Arguably the most severe indictment of O'Shaughnessy came from Charles Adley, civil engineer and superintendent of telegraphs on the East Indian Railway. In his book *The Story of the Telegraph in India* (1866), Adley dismissed O'Shaughnessy's achievements as head of the department and called for the privatization of the Indian telegraphs.[151]

At the time of their opening for public use on 1 February 1855, the total length of telegraph lines in India amounted to some 3,050 miles and the number of telegraph offices was 41. By 1900, there were 55,055 miles of line and a total of 1,939 offices (see map at the beginning of the volume for the overall layout of the network).[152] In addition to these lines, telegraphs were also built along railways and canals. For example, at the end of 1864, there were more than 3,000 miles of telegraph lines in the subcontinent which had been built by railway companies.[153] Signallers working for the railways were predominantly Indian and were paid lower wages than government telegraphists. In terms of geographical layout, the relationship between government telegraphs and railways was symbiotic, with the former usually following the latter. As Robinson put it in 1866,

> We can make no use of a [railway] line until it is open, especially in a hilly country, or where there are rivers; it is easier to travel on any country footpath. One of my best measures was to alter the line from Benares to Allahabad, because the Jumna Bridge was opened; to have done so before would have been inexpedient. We take the best communication that we have, and when that communication ceases to be the best we take the new one; we open a new line and take down the old one, and utilise the materials.[154]

The expansion of the telegraph network facilitated a higher amount of traffic. In 1870–1 a total of 581,234 telegrams were sent on the Indian lines, while by 1898–9 the traffic had increased to 5,448,600. Of these, inland state messages accounted for 659,304 telegrams; foreign state messages for 9,726; inland private, especially press messages, had the biggest share with 4,036,510; while foreign private messages reached 743,060.[155] The turning point was the decade 1871–81, when the increase in the circulation and value of telegrams was almost threefold. Although the Telegraph Department had existed for more than two decades, it was only in 1877–8 that its receipts exceeded substantially its working expenses. According to the annual report for that year, there was an increase in all classes of telegrams, state and private, inland and foreign.

As Chapter 5 will discuss in more detail, there was a correlation between various categories of telegrams and particular events such as famines, military operations, and the fluctuations of trade. But the increase in telegraphic traffic during the 1870s was also due to a great extent to the gradual decrease in the price of inland telegraphic communication. In 1855, when the charge for sixteen words was Re 1 per 400 miles of telegraph line, a message of twenty-four words from Calcutta to Karachi cost Rs 10, while in 1873, when the charge was Re 1 for six words regardless of distance, the same message could be sent for Rs 4. Similarly, the price of a telegram from Calcutta to Bombay was reduced by half, from Rs 8 in 1855 to Rs 4 in 1873. The uniform charge rate was designed to lower the cost of messages transmitted over long distances, and was particularly beneficial to cities like Calcutta, Madras, Bombay, Galle, Rangoon, and Karachi, which accounted for about 40 per cent of the entire telegraph traffic. However, the measure had less impact on the transmission of messages over short distances.[156]

Thus, as in the case of postal communication, cost was an important factor which circumscribed the use of telegraphy as a means of information transmission. It often operated in conjunction with another important consideration: language. Messages needed to be refashioned and condensed in order to save money; they also needed to be written in the officially sanctioned language of telegraphic communication. Originally, communication was only possible in English and messages in other languages were returned. In 1861 the government prohibited signallers from translating vernacular messages into English, arguing that '[s]enders of [vernacular] messages must have their messages written by other agency than that of the signallers or others attached to the Department'.[157] In 1873 it was decided that Indian customers could send telegrams in their own language at the same rates charged for English-language messages, provided that the message was written in the Roman alphabet. But D. G. Robinson, director general of Telegraphs in India, argued that the measures had failed to increase the popularity of the telegraph among Indian users, most of whom still preferred to send their correspondence by post:

> The liberty to telegraph in their own language at the same rates as they can in English is not appreciated, and the natives show sound judgment in so seldom availing themselves of it. Whatever the language be, it must be expressed in the Roman character, and there is more liability to error in making this conversion and in transmitting it when converted, that when the telegraph-master converts the Hindustani message into English for transmission, and the telegraph-master at the terminal translates it back for delivery to the addressee. But neither the very complete address nor the facilities placed at their disposal appear to influence the ordinary Hindu bunniah [*bania*, merchant]. With him a penny saved is a penny gained. He therefore prefers the post at half an anna, and has yet to learn the value of time and how many pounds may be earned by spending rupees on the saving of some of it.
>
> The Marwarees are exceptional; they telegraph freely and they enjoy the excitement of gambling. When the cotton season is over, they will make time bargains by telegraph for opium or any other article of fluctuating value.
>
> I have often heard it argued that a lower tariff would induce the natives to telegraph more freely. It would, but it would not pay. Unlike the post, the carrying power of a telegraph is limited, the distances in India are enormous, the people are poor, and the cost of all material and skilled labor is great.[158]

On 1 January 1882, a new unit of eight words and a new classificatory scheme were introduced for inland state, private, and press messages. Telegrams were now divided into four classes, their price depending on the time of transmission and delivery. Thus, local telegrams were defined as messages tendered during the working hours of a telegraph office and transmitted 'in ordinary course' within a radius of 6 miles of a central government telegraph office. Their cost was 4 annas per eight words. Deferred telegrams were sent at night and delivered to their recipients early on the following morning for the price of 8 annas per eight words. Ordinary telegrams were sent and delivered in the ordinary course and charged Re 1 irrespective of distance, while urgent telegrams enjoyed precedence over ordinary messages and were transmitted and delivered immediately for the price of Rs 2 per eight words.[159] The same prices remained valid at the end of the century.[160] This revision was yet another attempt on the part of the Indian government to encourage private use of the telegraph. Although the new tariffs brought an increase in private messages, it was soon discovered that they did not bring the expected increase in revenue as well, since most people preferred to send their messages as deferred telegrams due to the cheaper rates. For example, in 1882–3 there was a remarkable increase of 14.9 per cent in the number of private messages, but the increase in value only amounted to 5.3 per cent.[161]

Connecting India and Britain by Telegraph

Wiring India was only one aspect of the colonial preoccupation with electric telegraphy. The other, equally important concern for the purposes of military operations, administration, and trade was to establish a telegraphic connection with Britain. As Dwayne Winseck and Robert Pike have discussed, there were altogether four attempts to achieve this goal, in which British capital and subsidies from European governments joined forces with the Indian government through its Indo-European Telegraph Department, the Central Telegraph Administration of the Ottoman Empire, and the Persian Telegraph Department.[162] Three of these trials—which involved ventures like the Mediterranean Electric Telegraph Company, the Mediterranean Extension Telegraph Company, and the Red Sea and India Telegraph Company—ended in failure.[163] For example, in 1859, in the wake of the Indian Mutiny, F. Gisborne and R. S. Newall made an attempt to lay a submarine cable via the Red Sea, but failed on account of insufficient surveys of the seabed and inadequate knowledge about insulation. To make matters worse, the cable was light and weak, and the laying too tight.[164] The experiment proved costly for the British government, which had subsidized the venture by entering into a fifty-year contract with the Red Sea and India Telegraph Company that guaranteed the firm a dividend of 4.5 per cent on its £800,000 capital.[165] This failure deterred the government from subsidizing further telegraph ventures for the next two decades, while also prompting it to turn its attention from submarine cables to landlines.

As a number of scholars have pointed out, the 1850s and 1860s were marked by a 'veritable hunt' for concessions, with telegraph entrepreneurs and the British government vying to secure favourable terms for the construction of the lines through the Ottoman Empire and Persia.[166] Among the most contentious issues to be settled were the trajectory of the routes, the amount of capital to be invested, the authority in charge of the construction and control of lines, the distribution of revenues, and the amount of royalty to be paid to the Ottoman government.[167] Amid intensive negotiations between the British, Ottoman, and Persian governments, the construction of the overland line was undertaken simultaneously from the Middle Eastern and the Indian side. Upon the completion of the Constantinople–Baghdad line in 1861, the Ottoman government began the construction of two alternative routes to Fao, located at the head of the Persian Gulf. One was a 'loopline' which linked Baghdad with Teheran via Khanaqin and was completed in October 1864; the other stretched directly from Baghdad to Fao and was completed in January 1865.[168]

This event marked the beginning of regular telegraphic communication between Britain and India. From the Indian side, the lines were gradually extended from Gwadur (Gwadar) to Bushire (Bushehr) and reached Fao in April 1864, while Gwadur was connected with Karachi in May 1864. In addition to this route, which came to be known as the Turkish route, a Russian line via Tiflis, Teheran, Bushire, and Karachi was also available by 1865, but it was usually avoided on account of the time and quality of transmission.[169] The Turkish route and the Russian route were different on their European leg. On the former, messages travelled from London to Constantinople via Vienna or Turin. From Vienna, they were directed through Serbia and, occasionally, Wallachia; from Turin, they travelled by way of Thessaloniki. On the Russian route, communications passed via the Hague and Berlin, and then onwards to Tiflis.[170]

The construction of an extensive network of telegraph lines further reduced the amount of time it took messages to travel between Britain and India, although goods, military troops, and passengers remained necessarily dependent on the overland routes. The telegraph routes followed roughly the established trajectory of the overland mail, but the difference in the speed of communication was significant, despite the fact that the performance of the lines improved only gradually in the course of the nineteenth century. In the first half of February 1866, for example, the longest time occupied in the transmission of a message to India via the Turkish route was 6 days and the shortest 2.5 hours. On the Russian route, the performance was considerably poorer, with the longest transit time amounting to 20 days and 15 hours and the shortest to 17 days, 8 hours, and 3 minutes.[171] The traffic for 1865 amounted to a total of 11,070 telegrams sent from Britain to India—of which 8,055 were sent via Fao and 3,015 via Bushire—as opposed to 8,403 telegrams sent during the same year from India to Britain, and 1,467 from Europe to India.[172]

As members of the Committee on East India Communications observed in 1866, a message had to pass through the hands of many foreign administrations on its way from London to India by either of the above routes.[173] Predictably, complaints about the operators' lack of adequate knowledge of English, their work ethic, and the inability to protect the lines from destruction and tapping were common. Such rhetoric was often invoked in support of the argument that an 'all-British' route to India was necessary.[174]

In 1870, communication with India gained two additional routes: the first, known as the Indo-European route, was built by Siemens with the support of the British government and was opened for public use on 31 January of that year. The section from London to Teheran was operated by the Indo-European Telegraph Company, while the one from Teheran to Karachi via Bushire was placed under the supervision of the Indo-European Telegraph Department, a section of the Government of India established in 1862.[175] The Indo-European Telegraph Department's system consisted of two parts: the Persian Gulf section from Karachi to Bushire, with an extension to Fao, where it was connected with the line of the Ottoman government. The second was the Persian section, comprising the line from Bushire to Teheran. The administration of the department was amalgamated with the administration of the Indian telegraphs in 1888, but was eventually returned to London on 1 April 1893.[176] In the same time, John Pender's British-Indian Submarine Telegraph Company, later known as the Eastern Telegraph Company, brought London in direct communication with Bombay via a submarine cable laid across the Red Sea.[177] Known as the Eastern Route, this line of communication was inaugurated in June 1870. These two routes became the preferred channels of communication between Britain and India until the outbreak of World War I (see map at the beginning of the volume).

The time of transmission improved considerably in the aftermath of these new developments, amounting to an average of 6 hours and 7 minutes on the Indo-European Line in 1871.[178] On the other hand, the price for international telegrams fluctuated and remained relatively high until the end of the nineteenth century. At the time of the opening of the Turkish route, the price of a twenty-word message travelling between Britain and all important places in India was £5.1 (except to Karachi, where it was approximately £1 cheaper). This tariff was reduced to £2.17 in 1869.[179] Messages were accepted in English, French, and German, but they had to be written in the Roman alphabet.[180] In 1871, due to the low traffic on the Eastern and Indo-European lines, the tariff on these routes was raised to £4.10 per twenty words, while on the Turkish line the rate remained the same as before. This led to a temporary increase in traffic, until the Ottoman authorities were induced to raise their charges as well. At the end of the century, telegraph rates to Europe from any office in India were 3 rupees 4 annas per word via Suez or Teheran and 2 rupees 15 annas via Turkey.[181]

***

The use of electric telegraphy added a new dimension to the circulation of intelligence between Britain and India, complementing the more comprehensive, albeit less timely, method of dispatching correspondents' letters and newspapers via the overland mails. As we have seen in this chapter, prior to and even after the introduction of electric telegraphy into India, the circulation of news—in the subcontinent as well as between Britain and India—drew on an impressive array of technologies and modes of communication, which included runners, mail carts, boats, railways, steamers, semaphores, shutters, bicycles, and even less familiar vehicles like accelerators.

New technologies and modes of communication replaced older ones to a certain extent: for example, the electric telegraph supplanted shutters and semaphores and runner lines succumbed to competition from the railways towards the end of the period discussed. Yet, this statement only partially reflects the complex practices of technology use for the purposes of communication in nineteenth-century India. In particular, it eclipses the processes—not the abrupt break with the past—which led to the accumulation of scientific knowledge, the introduction and use of new media of communication, and the ways in which the old often coexisted with the new and the fact that different technologies responded to different communication needs. Runners could travel where railways could not. Similarly, the telegraph could reach regions that were not always easily accessible by train. But railways and steamers could carry more than one letter at a time and letters were cheaper than telegrams, conveying longer accounts of events or decisions of the colonial administration.

The availability and use of a certain medium of communication thus depended on a combination of factors of a political, socio-economic, ecological, or technical nature. Furthermore, the process of communication was marked by hierarchies which were visible, for example, in the layout of routes, the price, and the language of communication. Needless to say, the telegraph served British colonial power, with routes of communication designed to facilitate the speedy and regular exchange of intelligence with points of military and commercial interest, such as military roads or urban centres of political significance like Calcutta and Bombay. But within this colonial framework of power, prescription, and coercion, various sections of the public in India attempted to negotiate their positions vis-à-vis the communications system, promoting their own visions of telegraphy. In some cases this took the form of calls for the privatization of the Indian telegraphs, as the example of Charles Adley has demonstrated. In others, people tapped messages and perpetrated telegraphic frauds. In yet others, they used the telegraph to contest death sentences or to send money to friends in need, even before the introduction of money-order services in the subcontinent. The social life of technology was varied: the telegraph came to mean different things to different people. It is this plurality of visions and uses that we will attempt to explore in the following chapter.

Notes

1. C. A. Bayly, 'Knowing the Country: Empire and Information in India', *Modern Asian Studies* 27, no. 1 (1993): 3–43, 7. As Bayly points out, the circulation of information in the Indian subcontinent was facilitated not only by military and political imperatives, but also by travelling 'in connection with marriage, pilgrimage, and networks of trade and marketing'.
2. Iqbal Husain, 'Primitive Newspapers: The Eighteenth Century *Akhbarat*', in *Webs of History: Information, Communication and Technology from Early to Post-colonial India*, edited by A. K. Bagchi, Dipankar Sinha, and Barnita Bagchi (New Delhi: Institute of Development Studies Kolkata and Manohar, 2005), p. 140; Bayly, 'Knowing the Country', p. 8; Michael H. Fisher, 'The Office of Akhbār Nawīs: The Transition from Mughal to British Forms', *Modern Asian Studies* 27, no. 1 (1993): 45–82, 50–6.

3. For a detailed discussion of the two types of newsletters prepared at the Mughal court for dispatch to various 'subscribers'—the formulaic type and the interpretive type—see Fisher, 'The Office of Akhbār Nawīs', 48–51, 54; Irfan Habib, 'Postal Communications in Mughal India', *Proceedings of the Indian History Congress, 46th Session* (Amritsar: Guru Nanak Dev University, 1985), pp. 236–52; Michael H. Fisher, 'The East India Company's "Suppression of the Native *Dak*"', *Indian Economic and Social History Review* 31, no. 1 (1994): 311–48.
4. As Chitra Joshi has pointed out, the use of horses was highly localized due to their high cost relative to the limited increase of speed (by comparison with runners), the absence of an efficient road system, as well as opposition from local communities of runners. Chitra Joshi, 'Dak Roads, Dak Runners, and the Reordering of Communication Networks', *International Review of Social History* 57, no. 3 (2012): 169–89, 185–7.
5. M. M. Inamdar, *Bombay G.P.O.* (Mysore: Mysore Philatelics, 1983), pp. 1–5. Calcutta was the first to open a General Post Office (henceforth GPO) in 1774, with Madras following in 1786, and Bombay in 1794. Communication between the three presidencies was not only overland by means of runners, but also by sea. For example, letters from Madras to Bombay were sent by runners to a point near Trivandrum and thence by sea to Bombay.
6. Fisher, 'Suppression of the Native Dak', 342–3.
7. United Kingdom, Parliament, House of Commons, *Report by the Commission Appointed to Inquire into Postal Communication in India* (London, 27 and 28 December 1852), p. 369.
8. *Report by the Commission Appointed to Inquire into Postal Communication in India*, pp. 369, 379, 386, 390. Cf. Nitin Sinha, *Communication and Colonialism in Eastern India: Bihar, 1760s–1880s* (London: Anthem Press, 2014) p. 102.
9. Jean Deloche, *Transport and Communications in India Prior to Steam Locomotion*, vol. 1: *Land Transport* (New Delhi: Oxford University Press, 1993), p. 221.
10. 'Dawk Walas of Bengal', *Illustrated London News* 32 (1858), p. 196.
11. *Report by the Commission Appointed to Inquire into Postal Communication in India*, p. 354. See also Joshi, 'Dak Roads, Dak Runners', pp. 176, 179, for a discussion of the problems encountered by runners in accomplishing the average speed and the role of fines in controlling this speed.
12. Mrs Armine S. H. Mountain (ed.), *Memoirs and Letters of the Late Colonel Armine S. H. Mountain, C.B., Aide-de-Camp to the Queen and Adjutant-General of Her Majesty's Forces in India* (London: Longman, Brown, Green, Longmans & Roberts, 1858), p. 102.
13. An accelerator was a horse-drawn vehicle similar to an omnibus. An illustration and description of an earlier model can be found in 'The Accelerator', *Mirror of Literature, Amusement, and Instruction* 33 (1839),

p. 193. It is unclear whether this model was in actual use in Britain. The London GPO used accelerators to transport letter carriers to their beats: 'The postmen are packed in these carriages after the same principle adopted in placing the Mail bags in the sack; the man who has the greatest distance to go, gets first into the carriage, while he who has to quit it the earliest, gets in the last.' There were two accelerators in Calcutta in the 1850s which were used to take the delivery peons from the GPO to Garden Reach and Bhowanipore. See *Report by the Commission Appointed to Inquire into Postal Communication in India*, p. 358; *Report of the Commissioners for Post Office Enquiry, with Appendixes* (Calcutta: Military Orphan Press, 1851), Appendix C, No. 3, p. CLI.

14. Geoffrey Clarke, *The Post Office of India and Its Story* (London: John Lane the Bodley Head, 1921), pp. 29–30.
15. *Statement Exhibiting the Moral and Material Progress and Condition of India during the Year 1860–61, Part I* (London: George Edward Eyre and William Spottiswoode, 1862), p. 25. First introduced in 1830 in the Bombay Presidency to transport mails between Poona and Panvel (in present-day Maharashtra), mail carts were, unlike runners, particularly useful for the transportation of larger quantities of postal matter and in regions where the railways had not yet been constructed. Horse and bullock cart mails—the Indian version of the mail coach—usually operated on the Trunk Road and were also used for the transport of military troops and ammunition, as was the case during the Indian Mutiny. See Inamdar, *Bombay G.P.O.*, p. 8; 'The Mail Cart in India', *Illustrated London News*, 51 (1867), p. 472; Clarke, *The Post Office of India*, pp. 153, 195–6.
16. *Annual Report of the Post Office of India for the Year 1900–1901* (Calcutta: Superintendent of Government Printing, 1901), p. 4.
17. 'Sketches of Oodeypore and Rajputana', *Illustrated London News* 95 (1889), p. 475; 'Dawk Walas of Bengal', p. 196.
18. 'Dawk Walas of Bengal', p. 182. Also, 'Little Coo-Coo, Or the Khitmutgar's Revenge', *Belgravia* 21 (1873), pp. 309–40, at p. 317; 'Dacoity of a Mail Bag', *Times of India*, 13 August 1880 and 9 May 1899; 'Recovery from a Cobra Bite', *Times of India*, 17 July 1885, and so on. In 1898–9, thirty cases of highway mail robberies were reported. See *Statement Exhibiting the Moral and Material Progress and Condition of India during the Year 1898–1899* (London: Eyre and Spottiswoode, 1900), p. 158.
19. Joshi, 'Dak Roads, Dak Runners', p. 170.
20. An article published in the *Indian Post and Telegraph Magazine* in 1920 discussed the length of stages on the letter and parcel mail lines, the appropriate speed of the runner, and estimated that 'an ordinary day's work for a man is equal to 300 foot tons of energy'. See 'The Indian Postal Runner', *Times of India*, 14 September 1920. Runners also continued to operate in certain parts of India which were not easily

accessible by other means of communication, such as in Purulia District in West Bengal. See 'The Letter and the Spirit', *India Today*, 31 March 1994, available at: http://indiatoday.intoday.in/story/vestiges-of-a-bygone-era-harkaras-still-carry-mail-in-indian-villages/1/292961.html (accessed 2 July 2014).

21. Time occupied in the transmission of the first mail by horses from Bombay, Foreign Department, Political Branch, 8 March 1850, File 71, National Archives of India (henceforth NAI); Mountain, *Memoirs and Letters*, p. 102; 'Carrier Pigeons', *Calcutta Journal of Politics and General Literature*, 24 March 1823, p. 316.
22. William G. FitzGerald, 'The Romance of Our News Supply', *Strand Magazine* 10 (1895), pp. 77–8.
23. A. H. Osman, 'Pigeons as Messengers of War', *Strand Magazine* 19 (1900), p. 160.
24. Osman, 'Pigeons as Messengers of War', p. 164. Osman was a lieutenant colonel in the British Army and founder of the *Racing Pigeon* magazine in 1898. The Siege of Ladysmith (1899–1900) was an event during the Second Boer War, when racing pigeons were used to communicate with Durban.
25. Grahan Storey, *Reuters' Century, 1851–1951* (London: Max Parrish, 1951), pp. 10–11.
26. 'Travelling Pigeons', *Manufacturer and Builder* 6 (1874), p. 91. The longest reported distance travelled by a carrier pigeon was that between Madrid and Brussels, amounting to a total of 750 miles.
27. 'Pigeon Dawks', *Calcutta Journal of Politics and General Literature*, 17 June 1822, p. 654. *Kabūtar bāzī* (pigeon-rearing and racing) was a favourite Mughal pastime. Its historical association with Delhi is beautifully captured in Ahmed Ali's *Twilight in Delhi* (London: Hogarth, 1940).
28. 'Pigeons and Telegraphs', *Calcutta Journal of Politics and General Literature*, 1 October 1822, p. 414.
29. 'Carrier Pigeons', p. 316.
30. G. H. Khare, 'News-Letters of the Medieval Period', in *The Indian Press*, edited by S. P. Sen (Calcutta: Calcutta Press, 1967); G. T. Kulkarni, 'M/s Khemkaran Mansaram: The World's First Ever News Selling Agency during the Eighteenth Century Maratha Rule', in *Webs of History*, pp. 146–7.
31. Daniel Lak, 'South Asia Keeping the Police Pigeons Flying', BBC News, 11 February 1999, available at: http://news.bbc.co.uk/2/hi/south_asia/277047.stm (accessed 15 March 2012).
32. Lahiri Choudhury, *Telegraphic Imperialism*, p. 34.
33. *Times of India*, 3 October 1895. It wasn't only the telegraph lines which were exposed to the vagaries of the environment. Smritikumar Sarkar points out that roads in rural Bengal 'swung between existence and

non-existence with the season, surfacing in dry months and lost to fields in the monsoon'. He also discusses the example of the railway line between Calcutta and Kushtea which was opened in November 1862 only to find that the shifting course of the Ganges prevented the construction of a bridge over it. See Smritikumar Sarkar, *Technology and Rural Change in Eastern India, 1830–1980* (Oxford: Oxford University Press, 2014), pp. 25, 42–3.

34. *Report by the Commission Appointed to Inquire into Postal Communication in India*, p. 390.
35. *Report by the Commission Appointed to Inquire into Postal Communication in India*, pp. 386–7. A *tola* was a unit of weight equivalent to 180 Troy grains or approximately 0.4 ounces.
36. H. M. Collins to Secretary to the Government of India, 7 September 1867, Foreign Department, General A, October 1867, Nos 7–10, NAI.
37. Richard B. Kielbowicz, 'News Gathering by Mail in the Age of the Telegraph: Adapting to a New Technology', *Technology and Culture* 28, no. 1 (1987): 26–41, see 26, 28.
38. 'Telegraph Statistics', *Manufacturer and Builder* 3 (1871), p. 27.
39. Charles C. Adley, *The Story of the Telegraph in India* (London: E. & F. N. Spon, 1866), p. 44.
40. John K. Sidebottom, *The Overland Mail: A Postal Historical Study of the Mail Route to India* (London: George Allen & Unwin, 1948), pp. 6–7; Daniel Headrick, 'British Imperial Postal Networks', Paper presented at the International Economic Congress, Helsinki, August 2006, pp. 2–3, available at: http://www.helsinki.fi/iehc2006/papers3/Headrick.pdf (accessed 15 March 2016).
41. Anne Bulley, *The Bombay Country Ships, 1790–1833* (Richmond, Surrey: Curzon Press, 2000), p. 245.
42. United Kingdom, Parliament, House of Commons, *Report from the Select Committee on Steam Navigation to India* (London, 14 July 1834), p. 3.
43. Waghorn might have found posthumous fame, but he died in indigent circumstances, a situation resented by his surviving family. In 1885, two years after the architect of the Suez Canal, Baron de Lesseps, paid homage to Waghorn as the 'first [who] conceived the idea', one of his descendants, T. Comyns Waghorn, complained in the Australian journal *Once a Month* that Waghorn's widowed sisters, now residing in Melbourne, struggled to survive on a cumulative annual pension of £50 paid by the Imperial Civil List and the Indian government, despite the huge 'commercial gains accruing from Waghorn's services'. Perhaps ironically, the sisters were granted an additional £1 per week from the Government of Victoria 'in recognition of Waghorn's labours in establishing the Overland Route and subsequently steam communication from Singapore to Australia'. T. Comyns Waghorn, 'The Pioneer of the

Overland Route to India and Australasia', *Once a Month: An Illustrated Australasian Magazine*, 3 (1885): 204–8, at 208.

44. *Report from the Select Committee on Steam Navigation to India*, p. 210.
45. Sidebottom, *The Overland Mail*, p. 29; J. H. Stocqueler, *The Memoirs of a Journalist* (Bombay: Times of India, 1873), p. 75, italics original.
46. For a discussion of 'railway mania' see James Taylor, 'Business in Pictures: Representations of Railway Enterprise in the Satirical Press in Britain, 1845–1870', *Past & Present* 189, no. 1 (2005): 111–45. For a contemporary report of the problem, see Anon., 'Speculation Mania', *Examiner*, 907 (1825): 383–4.
47. 'Mr. Waghorn's Route to India', *Asiatic Journal and Monthly Register*, 3 (1830), p. 11.
48. *The Gazetteer of Bombay City and Island*, vol. 1 (Bombay: Times Press, 1909), p. 377; Sidebottom, *The Overland Mail*, p. 65.
49. 'Mr. Waghorn's Route to India', p. 13; Sidebottom, *The Overland Mail*, pp. 16–20.
50. *The P&O Pocket Book* (London: Adam and Charles Black, 1908), p. 10; James Barber, *The Overland Guide-Book: A Complete Vade-Mecum for the Overland Traveller* (London: Wm. H. Allen and Co., 1845), p. 34.
51. See Freda Harcourt, *Flagships of Imperialism: The P&O Company and the Politics of Empire from Its Origins to 1867* (Manchester and New York: Manchester University Press, 2006), p. 4; Shin Gotō, 'Indo e no kisen kōtsū no kakuritsu: Igirisu kaiun kigyō P&O no seiritsu ni yosete' [Establishment of steam communication with India: On the formation of the P&O Steam Navigation Company], *Kagawa Daigaku Keizai-Ronsō* 57, no. 3 (1984): 151–73 (in Japanese).
52. R. Kirk, *British Maritime Postal History*, vol. 2: *The P&O Lines to the Far East* (Heathfield, Sussex: Proud-Bailey Company, n.d.), p. 11. One of the ways in which the company compensated for the lack of government subsidies was by becoming involved in the opium trade in India and China. In fact, the route from India to China followed that of the opium clippers, passing from Calcutta to Penang, Singapore, and Hong Kong. See Kirk, *The P&O Lines to the Far East*, p. 163.
53. Weekly Postal Communication between England and Calcutta, c. 1859, British Postal Museum and Archive (hereafter BPMA), POST 29/88A.
54. George Dodd, *Railways, Steamers and Telegraphs* (London and Edinburgh: W. & R. Chambers, 1867), pp. 155–6.
55. Dodd, *Railways, Steamers and Telegraphs*, p. 13; *Allen's Indian Mail and Official Gazette*, 19 August 1858.
56. *Allen's Indian Mail and Official Gazette*, 19 August 1858.
57. United Kingdom, Parliament, House of Commons, *Report from the Select Committee on East India Communications* (London, 20 July 1866), p. 14.

58. *Allen's Indian Mail and Official Gazette*, 19 August 1858; Instructions re the transmission to Calcutta by telegraph of the commercial intelligence that may be received at Madras by each mail, Home Department, Public Branch, 5 March 1858, Nos 58–9, NAI.
59. *Report from the Select Committee on East India Communications*, p. iv; Harcourt, *Flagships of Imperialism*, pp. 5, 7.
60. Mark R. Frost, 'Asia's Maritime Networks and the Colonial Public Sphere, 1840–1920', *New Zealand Journal of Asian Studies* 6, no. 2 (2004): 63–94.
61. *Street's Indian and Colonial Mercantile Directory for 1869* (London: G. Street, 1869), p. 10.
62. *Calendar of Mail Steamer Departures from Bombay* (Calcutta, 1873), p. 1.
63. J. Forbes Munro, *Maritime Enterprise and Empire: Sir William Mackinnon and His Business Network, 1823–93* (Rochester, NY: Boydell Press, 2003), p. 60. Compare, for example, the overland mail published in the *Times of India* of 7 May 1866 with the one published on 10 July 1866.
64. [A. Fenton], *Memoirs of a Cadet* (London: Saunders and Otley, 1839), p. 4.
65. William Howard Russell, *My Diary in India, in the Year 1858–9* (London: Routledge, Warne & Routledge, 1860), p. 94.
66. Regarding the detention of mails on board the P&O's steamers, 10 April 1855, R/20/A/130, File 199, IOR.
67. Adley, *The Story of the Telegraph in India*, p. 53.
68. Regarding the detention of mails on board the P&O's steamers, 10 April 1855.
69. Clarke, *The Post Office of India*, p. 127.
70. Clarke, *The Post Office of India*, pp. 127–8.
71. *Report by the Commission Appointed to Inquire into Postal Communication in India*, p. 358.
72. *Report by the Commission Appointed to Inquire into Postal Communication in India*, p. 361.
73. *Report by the Commission Appointed to Inquire into Postal Communication in India*, p. 405–6.
74. *Report by the Commission Appointed to Inquire into Postal Communication in India*, p. 407. The practice of offering gifts to the peons came under official scrutiny at the time of the inquiry. Predictably, the officials were keen to discourage the receipt of money other than the postage fee and to make the peons responsible for cases of misdelivery or mistakes. But, as Nilratan Haldar testified on 28 May 1850, the interaction between the peons and the recipients of post was part of a social give and take: 'A man who can afford one or two annas for a letter, does not care about paying one or two pice more as a gift to the peon.' As Haldar pointed out, his own extensive correspondence in Bengali and English arrived regularly, but 'once a year, at the Doorga Poojah, I make the peon a present, generally eight annas. I make a similar present to the peon who delivers letters

at the Board's office.' *Report by the Commission Appointed to Inquire into Postal Communication in India*, p. 369.

75. *Report by the Commission Appointed to Inquire into Postal Communication in India*, p. 407.
76. *Report by the Commission Appointed to Inquire into Postal Communication in India*, pp. 358, 380.
77. *Report by the Commission Appointed to Inquire into Postal Communication in India*, p. 363.
78. *Report by the Commission Appointed to Inquire into Postal Communication in India*, pp. 385, 387. Mistakes and misdeliveries also baffled postal clerks in Britain. It was for this very reason that the GPO at St Martin's-le-Grand employed 'blind men' whose job was to solve the puzzle of 'unintelligible' directions either by correcting bad spelling or by trying to figure out the directions 'from the sounds of the letters'. As Rev. W. Quekett, who visited the GPO at Lord Canning's order, told his audience during a lecture in Warrington in 1854, one of the letters he examined 'read Mary Bruts, Stanes, Oxton, by putting spaces between the words, and supplying the capitals; but being in one line, and no divisions, it puzzled the ordinary sorters'. W. Quekett, 'The History and Progress of a Post-Letter from a Rag to India', in *Warrington Church Institute Lectures* (Warrington: Guardian Office, 1854), pp. 10–11.
79. *Report by the Commission Appointed to Inquire into Postal Communication in India*, pp. 353–4.
80. *Report by the Commission Appointed to Inquire into Postal Communication in India*, pp. 354–5.
81. *Report by the Commission Appointed to Inquire into Postal Communication in India*, p. 46; *Statement Exhibiting the Moral and Material Progress and Condition of India during the Year 1898–1899*, p. 154.
82. *Report by the Commission Appointed to Inquire into Postal Communication in India*, p. 46.
83. *The New Postage Act (XVII of 1854-Rules, etc.)* (1855), pp. 4–5.
84. *Allen's Indian Mail*, 20 April 1860, p. 295; *Abstract of the Proceedings of the Council of the Governor-General of India, Assembled for the Purpose of Making Laws and Regulations, 1865*, vol. 4 (Calcutta: Military Orphan Press, 1866), pp. 244–6. I am grateful to Mark Ravinder Frost for an illuminating discussion about postal rates for newspapers and for pointing me to these records. Email communication, 16 July 2012.
85. *Abstract of the Proceedings of the Council of the Governor-General of India*, pp. 245–6.
86. *Abstract of the Proceedings of the Council of the Governor-General of India*, p. 245.
87. Headrick, 'British Imperial Postal Networks', p. 4. At the beginning of the nineteenth century, opium merchants also operated their own lines

for the conveyance of mails between Calcutta and Bombay. A similar situation was encountered in the early days of electric telegraphy, when newspapers in India received private telegrams from various merchants who were willing to pay the high cost of delivery for timely intelligence from Europe. See Clarke, *The Post Office of India*, p. 30.

88. Max Smith and Robert Johnson, *Express Mail, After Packets and Late Fees in India before 1870* (Stuart Rossiter Trust, 2007), p. 51.
89. *Bombay Times and Journal of Commerce*, 30 April 1845.
90. Smith and Johnson, *Express Mail*, pp. 43–4.
91. *Report from the Select Committee on East India Communications*, p. v.
92. In 1858, *Allen's Indian Mail* was already advising its readers that mails reached India faster via Bombay. *Allen's Indian Mail and Official Gazette*, 19 August 1858.
93. For example, the mail which left Calcutta on 8 December 1865 reached London via Galle on 12 January 1866, while the one via Bombay reached London on 5 January 1866. *Report from the Select Committee on East India Communications*, pp. vi, 19, 611–12.
94. H. W. Tyler, 'Routes of Communication with India', *Journal of the Royal United Service Institution* 10 (1867), p. 278, emphasis original.
95. *Report from the Select Committee on East India Communications*, p. iv.
96. Harcourt, *Flagships of Imperialism*, p. 105; *Gazetteer of Bombay*, pp. 377–8.
97. Jehangir Nowrojee and Hirjibhoy Merwanjee, *Journal of a Residence of Two Years and a Half in Great Britain* (London: Wm. H. Allen & Co., 1841), p. 87.
98. United Kingdom, Parliament, House of Commons Debate, 20 May 1870, vol. 201, cols 1058–9.
99. Headrick, 'British Imperial Postal Networks', p. 4; H. L. Hoskins, *British Routes to India* (London: Frank Cass & Co., 1966), p. 408; 'Overland Mail to India via Brindisi', *Journal of the Society of Arts*, 23 (November 1874–November 1875), p. 14.
100. Correspondence between the Director General of the Post Office of India and the Secretary General of the Post Office London, 7, 22, 24, 29 January and 18 May 1880, BPMA, POST 29/88A; Hoskins, *British Routes to India*, p. 411.
101. *The P&O Pocket Book*, pp. 12–13.
102. Smith and Johnson, *Express Mail*, p. 8; *Statement Exhibiting the Moral and Material Progress and Condition of India during the Year 1898–1899*, p. 160.
103. *Times of India*, 8 June 1871.
104. *Indian Postal Guide, August 1897* (Calcutta: Office of the Superintendent of Government Printing, 1897), pp. 13–14.

105. *Times of India*, 6 March 1871.
106. *Times of India*, 25 October 1913. For a discussion of the Imperial Press Conferences and the Empire Press Union, see Chandrika Kaul, *Reporting the Raj: The British Press and India, c. 1880–1922* (Manchester: Manchester University Press, 2003), pp. 37–40; Simon Potter, *News and the British World: The Emergence of an Imperial Press System* (Oxford: Oxford University Press, 2003), especially pp. 132–59.
107. As the name itself suggests, the shutter telegraph used a combination of shutters to transmit messages, while the semaphore did so by means of a horizontal arm with two moveable planks which could be positioned at different angles. The stations were constructed at a distance from each other and were usually operated by three people: one person read the message with the help of a telescope, another wrote it down and communicated it to a third man who operated the instruments and transmitted the message to the next station.
108. Gunakar Muley, 'The Introduction of Semaphore Telegraphy in Colonial India', in *Webs of History*, pp. 165–72.
109. For an example of such 'semaphoric intelligence', whose lapidary style clearly anticipates telegrams, see the *Half Weekly Calcutta Courier* of 15 June 1839 and the *Englishman and Military Chronicle* of 11 June 1840. The advantages derived by the newspapers of Calcutta from the use of semaphores are also mentioned in K. Shridharani, *Story of the Indian Telegraphs: A Century of Progress* (New Delhi: Government of India Press, 1953), p. 62.
110. M. D. Srinivas, T. G. Paramasivam, and T. Pushkala, *Thirupporur and Vadakkuppattu: Eighteenth Century Locality Accounts* (Chennai: Centre for Policy Studies, 2001), pp. 1–2. The Jaghire lands, as they came to be known, had been granted to the British by the Nawab of Arcot, Mohammed Ali, in October 1763. A jagir was a grant of land which conferred upon the grantee the right to collect revenue. See also R. H. Phillimore (ed.), *Historical Records of the Survey of India*, vol. 1 (Dehra Dun: Surveyor General of India, 1946–58), p. 311.
111. Phillimore, *Historical Records of the Survey of India*, vol. 1, p. 311.
112. 'On Telegraphic Communications', *Penny Magazine*, 9 (1840), p. 61.
113. For example, R. M. Shearman, *Copy of a Plan for a Day and Night Telegraph, and Proposed for General Communication of Intelligence throughout India* (London: T. Jones, 1807[?]); Thomas Lynn, *An Improved System of Telegraphic Communication* (London: Cox and Baylis, 1814). An illustration of the shutter telegraph proposed by Captain Swiney of the Bengal Artillery can also be found in C. W. Pasley, *Description of the Universal Telegraph for Day and Night Signals* (London: T. Egerton, 1823), p. 32.

114. See, for example, the elaborate 'vocabulary' for naval, military, and general communication with the help of flags devised by Thomas Lynn at the beginning of the nineteenth century. This consisted of two-flag signals for auxiliary verbs, personal pronouns, articles, prepositions, and so on, three-flag signals designed to convey approximately 10,000 words and sentences, and single-flag signals for modifying the meaning of words and sentences. Flags had different colours (for example red, white, and blue) and could be positioned at different angles. Lynn, *An Improved System of Telegraphic Communication*, pp. i–iv. For comparison, at the end of the nineteenth century, the Indian field post offices used a telegraphic code which allowed the transmission of long sentences like: 'Letters and newspapers should be enclosed in separate bags marked "Letter Mail" and "Newspapers"' as single words, in this case 'Delimit'. *Telegraphic Phrase-Code for Indian Field Post Offices*, 3rd edn (Lahore: Tribune Press, 1904), p. 479.
115. John Macdonald, *A Treatise Explanatory of a New System of Naval, Military and Political Telegraphic Communication* (London: T. Egerton's Military Library, 1817 [1808]), p. 6.
116. Letter from Mr Barrow to John Macdonald, 1 September 1814, quoted in *Indian Historical Records Commission: Proceedings of Meetings*, vol. 11, Nagpur, December 1928 (Calcutta: Government of India Central Publication Branch, 1929), p. 16.
117. Letter from James Cobb to John Macdonald, 10 May 1817, quoted in *Indian Historical Records Commission*, vol. 11, p. 18; Public letter to Bengal, 3 September 1817, quoted in *Indian Historical Records Commission*, vol. 11, p. 19.
118. Letter from John Macdonald to J. P. Blunt, 5 August 1815, quoted in Macdonald, *Treatise*, pp. 11–12.
119. Lord George Murray developed the first optical telegraph in Britain. Phillimore, *Historical Records of the Survey of India*, vol. 3, pp. 269–70.
120. Phillimore, *Historical Records of the Survey of India*, vol. 3, p. 270. On Pindaris, see S. R. Bakshi and O. P. Ralhan, *Madhya Pradesh through the Ages*, vol. 2: *Pindaris and Marathas* (New Delhi: Sarup and Sons, 2007), especially pp. 171–98.
121. Further papers regarding the Bengal Telegraph Department, Court of Directors to Bengal Government, 14 November 1832, F/4/1492/58679, IOR. On the construction of the New Military Road and its role in facilitating the movement of troops see Sinha, *Communication and Colonialism in Eastern India*, pp. 107–13.
122. Phillimore, *Historical Records of the Survey of India*, vol. 3, p. 271–2.
123. Phillimore, *Historical Records of the Survey of India*, vol. 3, p. 272.
124. 'Selections—Telegraph', *Calcutta Journal of Politics and General Literature*, 19 April 1822, p. 544. A Martello tower was a defensive

building in the shape of a small, round, two-storeyed fortress, used in various parts of the British Empire during the nineteenth century.

125. 'Selections—Telegraph', p. 544. Also Phillimore, *Historical Records of the Survey of India*, vol. 3, p. 272.
126. Phillimore, *Historical Records of the Survey of India*, vol. 3, p. 272; Further papers regarding the Bengal Telegraph Department, Court of Directors to Bengal Government, 14 November 1832, F/4/1492/58679, IOR.
127. K. N. V. Sastri, 'History of Mysore in the XIX Century Illustrated from Contemporary Newspapers', in *Indian Historical Records Commission: Proceedings and Meetings*, vol. 22, Peshawar, October 1945 (Calcutta: Superintendent Government of India, 1945), p. 74.
128. Appendix A, 'Minute by the Honourable the Governor, 30 November 1830', in John Malcolm, *The Government of India* (London: John Murray, 1833), pp. 88–9.
129. 'Pigeons and Telegraphs', p. 414. See also the correspondence on this subject between John Macdonald and J. P. Blunt, in Macdonald, *Treatise*, pp. 11–14.
130. 'Selections—Telegraph', p. 544; 'Telegraphs and Flagstaffs', *Calcutta Journal of Politics and General Literature*, 25 September 1822, p. 331; 'Pigeons and Telegraphs'.
131. Further papers regarding the Bengal Telegraph Department, 27 April 1830 and 27 July 1830, F/4/1492/58679, IOR.
132. Further papers regarding the Bengal Telegraph Department, 27 April 1830, F/4/1492/58679, IOR.
133. W. H. Carey, *The Good Old Days of Honorable John Company: Being Curious Reminiscences Illustrating Manners and Customs of the British in India*, vol. 2 (Calcutta: R. Cambray & Co., 1907), pp. 92–3.
134. Further papers regarding the Bengal Telegraph Department, 22 September 1830, F/4/1492/58679, IOR.
135. Further papers regarding the Bengal Telegraph Department, 24 July 1832 and 18 November 1833, F/4/1492/58679, IOR.
136. Saroj Ghose, 'Commercial Needs and Military Necessities: The Telegraph in India', in *Technology and the Raj: Western Technology and Technical Transfers to India 1700–1947*, edited by Roy MacLeod and Deepak Kumar (New Delhi: Sage Publications, 1995), p. 155. At Fort William, a shutter telegraph had also been in use before being destroyed by strong winds in 1821; nine years later, this was replaced with an improved two-armed semaphore. 'Semaphoric Telegraph', *Calcutta Journal of Politics and General Literature*, 1 March 1821, p. 185.
137. 'Travelling in India', *Leisure Hour* 457 (1860), p. 616.
138. 'Condensed History of the Electric Telegraph', *Manufacturer and Builder* 5 (1873), p. 62.

139. For a discussion and critique of 'diffusion' and 'technology transfer' as heuristic tools for the study of the history of science and technology in colonial South Asia, see David Arnold, *Science, Technology and Medicine in Colonial India* (Cambridge: Cambridge University Press, 2004), especially pp. 92–168; Deepak Kumar, *Science and the Raj: 1857–1905* (Oxford: Oxford University Press, 1995), pp. 1–31.
140. 'Notes on Japanese, Korean, and Chinese Paper', *Manufacturer and Builder*, 2 (1870), pp. 262–3; 'Japanese Carpenters', *Manufacturer and Builder*, 4 (1872), p. 23; 'Indian Method of Cleaning Solid Silver', *Manufacturer and Builder*, 4 (1872), p. 109; 'Japanese Metal Works', *Manufacturer and Builder*, 4 (1872), pp. 181–2; 'A Hindoo Temple', *Manufacturer and Builder*, 4 (1872), p. 212; 'Roads and Bridges among the Chinese', *Manufacturer and Builder*, 4 (1872), p. 244; 'Brick-Making in India', *Manufacturer and Builder*, 4 (1872), p. 278; 'Industries and Invention in Japan', *Manufacturer and Builder*, 5 (1873), pp. 82–3, and so on.
141. 'A Contribution to the History of Submarine Telegraphy', *Manufacturer and Builder* 11 (1879), p. 135; William B. O'Shaughnessy, *The Electric Telegraph in British India: A Manual of Instructions for the Subordinate Officers, Artificers, and Signallers Employed in the Department* (London, 1853), pp. 2–3.
142. *Imperial Gazetteer of India*, vol. 3: *The Indian Empire: Economic* (Oxford: Clarendon Press, 1908), p. 437; Ghose, 'Commercial Needs and Military Necessities', p. 155.
143. Shridharani, *Story of the Indian Telegraphs*, pp. 27–8.
144. Lahiri Choudhury, *Telegraphic Imperialism*, pp. 36–7.
145. D. K. Lahiri Choudhury, '"Beyond the Reach of Monkeys and Men"?: O'Shaughnessy and the Telegraph in India, c. 1836–56', *Indian Economic and Social History Review*, 37 (2000): 331–59, 346.
146. Gorman, 'Sir William O'Shaughnessy', p. 592. The telegraph instruments devised by Charles Wheatstone and W. F. Cooke used magnets to deflect needles fixed on a diamond-shaped grid to indicate the letters of the alphabet. See Beauchamp, *History of Telegraphy*, pp. 36–8.
147. M. Adams (comp.), *Memoir of Surgeon-Major Sir W. O'Shaughnessy Brooke, in Connection with the Early History of the Telegraph in India* (Simla: Government Central Printing Office, 1889), p. 15; Beauchamp, *History of Telegraphy*, p. 96.
148. *Report from the Select Committee on East India Communications*, pp. 158, 161. In fact, as the following chapters also discuss, merchants and representatives of the press never conceived of the telegraph only in these terms.
149. *Report from the Select Committee on East India Communications*, pp. 158, 161.

150. Lahiri Choudhury, *Telegraphic Imperialism*, pp. 51, 75. On 'gentlemanly science', see James A. Secord, *Victorian Sensation: The Extraordinary Publication, Reception, and Secret Authorship of Vestiges of the Natural History of Creation* (Chicago: University of Chicago Press, 2000), pp. 403–36.
151. Adley, *The Story of the Telegraph in India*.
152. Shridharani, *Story of the Indian Telegraphs*, p. 28; *Imperial Gazetteer of India*, vol. 3, p. 445.
153. *Report from the Select Committee on East India Communications*, p. xiii.
154. *Report from the Select Committee on East India Communications*, p. 159.
155. *Imperial Gazetteer of India*, vol. 3, p. 445; *Statement Exhibiting the Moral and Material Progress and Condition of India during the Year 1898–1899*, p. 160.
156. *Administration Report of the Indian Telegraph Department for 1872–3*, V/24/4284, p. 19, IOR.
157. *Administration Report of the Indian Telegraph Department for 1861–2*, V/24/4283, pp. 44–5, IOR. The rule had been revised by 1897, when postmasters were allowed to transcribe vernacular telegrams into the Roman alphabet or to translate them into English free of charge. *Indian Postal Guide, August 1897*, p. 158.
158. *Administration Report of the Indian Telegraph Department for 1873–4*, V/24/4284, pp. 11–12, IOR.
159. *Administration Report of the Indian Telegraph Department for 1881–2*, V/24/4286, p. 4, IOR.
160. *Indian Postal Guide, July 1900* (Calcutta: Superintendent of Government Printing, 1900), pp. 157–8.
161. *Administration Report of the Indian Telegraph Department for 1882–3*, V/24/4286, p. 4, IOR.
162. Dwayne Winseck and Robert M. Pike, *Communication and Empire: Media, Markets, and Globalization, 1860-1930* (Durham, N.C.: Duke University Press, 2007), pp. 25–6.
163. Winseck and Pike, *Communication and Empire*, pp. 25–6.
164. *Report from the Select Committee on East India Communications*, p. 30.
165. Daniel R. Headrick, *The Invisible Weapon: Telecommunications and International Politics, 1851–1945* (Oxford: Oxford University Press, 1991), pp. 19–20.
166. See, for example, Soli Shahvar, 'Concession Hunting in the Age of Reform: British Companies and the Search for Government Guarantees—Telegraph Concessions through Ottoman Territories, 1855–58', *Middle Eastern Studies* 38, no. 4 (2002): 169–93.
167. Maurice G. Simpson, 'The Indo-European Telegraph Department', *Journal of the Royal Society of Arts* 76, no. 3928 (1928): 382–94, at 384–5.

168. Julius Possmann, *Official History of the Persian Gulf Telegraph Cables Compiled under Instructions from the Director General of Telegraphs* (Karachi: Mercantile Press, 1889), p. 1.
169. Possmann, *Official History of the Persian Gulf Telegraph Cables*, p. 1.
170. *Report from the Select Committee on East India Communications*, p. x; Winseck and Pike, *Communication and Empire*, p. 33.
171. *Report from the Select Committee on East India Communications*, p. 625.
172. *Report from the Select Committee on East India Communications*, pp. 625–6.
173. *Report from the Select Committee on East India Communications*, pp. ix–x.
174. See, for example, 'Anglo-Indian Telegraphy', *Daily News*, 24 March 1868, which gave voice to complaints about the system of telegraphic communication with India being 'badly arranged and thoroughly inefficient, and … to a great extent … at the mercy in Asia of a set of incapable and unimproveable [*sic*] Arabs, Turks and barbarians'.
175. Daniel R. Headrick, *The Tentacles of Progress: Technology Transfer in the Age of Imperialism, 1850–1940* (Oxford: Oxford University Press, 1988), p. 100.
176. *Statement Exhibiting the Moral and Material Progress and Condition of India during the Year 1898–1899*, p. 162.
177. Simpson, 'The Indo-European Telegraph Department', 386.
178. Simpson, 'The Indo-European Telegraph Department', 386.
179. James Anderson, 'Statistics of Telegraphy', *Journal of the Statistical Society of London* 35 (1872): 272–326, at 300; *Report from the Select Committee on East India Communications*, p. 26.
180. Government Indo-European Telegraph Department, *The Tariff of Rates for Messages between Any Telegraph Station, etc.* (Bombay: Times of India, 1865), p. 1.
181. *Indian Postal Guide, August 1897*, p. 159.

2 Sites of Practice and Discourses of Telegraphy

> I grab my dictionary feverishly and begin to compose two messages to the police chiefs at Delhi and Calcutta. Upon arrival at Lahore, we rush to the telegraph. The babu telegraphist turns my telegram on all sides. His expression tells me that he does not understand a word of my kitchen English (*anglais de cuisine*). We, for our part, don't comprehend anything he says. The situation is hopeless. The same dialogue with an English employee does not produce a better outcome: [the mess] is complete!
>
> —Jean de Pontevès-Sabran (1887)[1]

Dionysius Lardner, an Irish science writer and professor of natural philosophy at the University College London, echoed a widespread sentiment when he remarked in the mid-nineteenth century that the electric telegraph was fast transforming Puck's promise to encircle the earth 'in forty minutes' from a mere Shakespearean twist of imagination into an everyday reality.[2] The telegraph was a remarkable scientific achievement by the standards of the age. For many of Lardner's contemporaries, it was nothing short of a technological marvel that had transformed the face of communication by enabling the transmission of messages in the 'blink of an eye' through the 'wonderful agency of electricity'. Members of the public welcomed it with a sense of wonder and anticipation, 'wax[ing] lyrical over the ways in which [it] would bring nations closer together, break down boundaries, and foster commerce', as Iwan Morus has aptly observed.[3]

For many contemporary commentators, the telegraph also became an important 'tool of Empire'.[4] The ability to exchange military, administrative, and commercial intelligence in a timely and regular manner was considered useful in 'preserving' Britain's overseas possessions. As a product and symbol of Western scientific 'progress' and modernity, the telegraph also came to be regarded as an instrument of civilization that could help to bridge gaps of race, culture, and class. Much like electricity, which had been harnessed for the treatment of a wide range of physical and mental disorders since the end of the eighteenth century, the telegraph became a tool of reform and improvement. Along with canals and railways, it assumed the metaphorical mantle of a 'great physician' who was expected to 'resuscitat[e] the inhabitants of India of all creeds and nations from the long deep lethargy which has afflicted them'.[5]

Such widespread narratives had to contend with the many contradictions and paradoxes of telegraphic science and practice. The system was vulnerable to 'crises' and 'panics', as Lahiri Choudhury has shown.[6] The Mutiny might have been the archetypal example of this, but it was by no means the only one. Myriad other problems circumscribed the use of telegraphy and challenged triumphalist discourses of scientific prowess and 'progress'. To begin with, the technology was neither perfect nor infallible. The Indian telegraph was exposed to the vagaries of the natural environment: wild elephants knocked down posts and violent storms caused interruptions and breakdowns, as lightning and jungle fires led to the destruction of posts, cables, and caused trees to fall on the line.[7] In 1890–1, for example, 1,947 cases of interruption were reported, amounting to a total of 39,716 hours. These were due to falling trees (364 cases), defects in lines and cables (353 cases), faults in offices (215 cases), 'malice' (152 cases), cyclones and 'exceptional storms' (133 cases), birds and animals (110 cases), and so on.[8]

Far from being perused only by a restricted circle of colonial officials, such statistics circulated widely. The Japanese Telegraph Association, eager to keep the engineering community in that country up to date with the latest developments in telegraphic science around the world, published regular reports about the expansion and performance of the Indian lines in the pages of their *Denshin kyōkai kaishi*

(Bulletin of the Telegraph Association). On one occasion, the Bulletin reported that there had been '1,473 hours of interruption to communication for the current year [1897], as opposed to 1,389 in the previous year'. The causes of interruption clearly fascinated the Japanese observers and were listed in great detail. Thus, thunder and lightning were responsible for disruption in 48 cases, while birds and wild animals caused interruptions in 110 cases. In one instance, rats reportedly ate through the insulation of submarine cables, and, in two other instances, termites had entered the instrument used to prevent lightning. Finally, in Burma, wild elephants had interrupted telegraphic communication on three occasions, leading to 201 hours of stoppages.[9]

Technological innovation was also time-consuming and piecemeal, a fact which had important implications for the size and performance of the network. In 1861, the editor of the *Times of India* estimated that of a total of more than 1,000 messages received over the past eighteen months, only one in four had been correctly transmitted.[10] The volume of traffic increased only gradually in the course of the nineteenth century, as engineers improved extant instruments to enable the transmission of two and eventually four messages in both directions over the same cable (duplex and quadruplex telegraphy).[11] The speed of communication also increased gradually. In 1876–7, it took an average of 1 hour and 13 minutes to transmit a message from Bombay to Calcutta and 46 minutes from Bombay to Madras. By the end of the century (1898–9), the time of transmission had dropped to 22 and 23 minutes respectively, although it continued to fluctuate from one year to the other.[12] Insulation and infrastructure created additional problems. The uninsulated cables submerged in the Red Sea during the first attempt to connect Britain with India in 1859 soon began to corrode and eventually 'crumbled into hundreds of pieces' under the weight of barnacles and corrals. A few years later, it was reported that brick pillars in the Madras Circle occasionally collapsed.[13]

The construction and use of the telegraph network led to alterations of the natural environment and was based on the exploitation of exhaustible resources like gutta-percha. A rubber-like substance derived from the milky latex of *Isonandra* trees in Southeast Asia, gutta-percha had been used as an alternative to *caoutchouc* or India rubber since around mid-century. As a non-conductor of electricity, it became a perfect insulator for submarine cables. It was also commonly employed in the manufacture of a wide range of household, sports, and medical products. But by the end of the century, the scale of exploitation, coupled with the rudimentary and unsustainable methods of extracting the gum, had almost depleted the tropical rainforest in the Malay Peninsula of its trees, leading to one of the most serious ecological disasters of the Victorian era.[14] For many contemporary commentators, the crisis became one of imperial and global communications: as one anxious writer pointed out, the 'world [was] threatened with the loss of the submarine cables' and 'telegraphic intercourse' will soon be 'paralyzed'.[15]

In what follows, I aim to complicate previous accounts of electric telegraphy in colonial South Asia by recovering and engaging with the diversity of practice and discourse that surrounded it. The distinction I draw between these two categories can also be understood as a distinction between telegraphy-in-use and telegraphy-in-discourse. Admittedly, nineteenth-century practices of technology can be difficult to recuperate on account of insufficient historical evidence, especially for non-elite groups, as well as the obvious challenges of distilling practice from an overwhelmingly textual (that is, discursive) record. Yet, as Richard Evans has cogently pointed out, 'Discourse does not construct the past itself; the most that it is possible to argue is that it constructs our attempts to represent it.'[16] Drawing on this observation, I use official records in conjunction with other historical sources in the form of (auto)biographies, memoirs, newspapers, periodicals, folk songs, and literary texts to examine the practices and discourses of telegraphy not only in the 'high' domain of imperial politics and administration, but also in a myriad of other, less familiar situations in which it facilitated or, indeed, precluded communication. Some of the questions that drive this inquiry are: How and why was telegraphy used in nineteenth-century India? How did information and more specialized knowledge about telegraphy circulate? What kind of imaginations of modernity did the telegraph help to mediate? How and why did this technology become such a potent symbol of imperial power and colonial modernity?

In addressing these topics, my contention is that technology gains meaning through its use in specific social contexts and situations.[17] Thus, in order to understand the history of telegraphy in nineteenth-century India, we need to examine simultaneously the ways in which technology was enshrined in various institutions, ideas, and practices. Colonial narratives of technology as an instrument of social and moral improvement usually represented telegraphy as a neutral tool whose incorporation into social activities was conducive to moral and material progress. In doing so, they aimed to mask, downplay, and erase not only the politics that circumscribed the construction and use of the telegraph network, but also the wide variety of practices and discourses associated with this technology in the nineteenth century. Such discourses helped to obscure the fact that experiences of modernity as mediated by telegraphy and, by extension, other contemporary technologies, were fraught with tensions and contradictions both in colonial South Asia and in the imperial metropole itself.

Like other scientific innovations of the age—railways, typewriters, sewing machines, and even steel pens included—the telegraph generated both enthusiasm and uneasiness about the ability of individuals and society to cope with the increasing demands of 'modern' life or, as Partha Chatterjee has aptly put it, with the 'difference posed by the present'.[18] The aim of this chapter is to recover some of this diversity of discourse and practice and to show how the telegraph was used and debated in a variety of contexts, from imperial administration to private affairs. As such, it fuelled utopias of community and improvement, but also generated counter and alternative narratives that raised concerns about its role as an instrument of empire, or about changing patterns of life, work, and human interaction.[19]

Administration by the Telegraph

For many people in nineteenth-century India, experiences of telegraphy were mediated predominantly by the specific circumstances of their employment. The most obvious example is that of the employees of the Indian Telegraph Department. They played a crucial role in the expansion and running of the telegraph network as superintendents, assistant superintendents, inspectors, overseers, signallers, line artificers, *sowars* (line riders), peons, messengers, clerks, accountants, and bookkeepers.[20] In the mid-1860s, approximately 10 per cent of the signallers were Eurasian and Indian, with the more senior positions being monopolized by Europeans. During this period, the department also became interested in recruiting more Indians as line riders and artificers.[21] Other social groups whose work depended on the use of the electric telegraph included colonial administrators, meteorologists, members of the mercantile community, and journalists.

Most of the previous literature on the history of telegraphy in South Asia has focused on the military and administrative applications of this technology, an approach that has rightly underscored the importance of telegraphy for imperial designs and purposes. Yet, if we consult the statistics of the Indian Telegraph Department, we see that state messages represented a relatively small percentage of the total number of telegrams sent annually over the lines: in 1866–7, for example, this number amounted to approximately 10 per cent, with most of the remaining messages being classed as 'private'. Merchants and other people associated with trade and commerce as well the newspaper press were among the most prominent users of telegraphy in the nineteenth century.[22] In addition, as we will shortly see, the telegraph was also used for a variety of other types of communication, by people who were not necessarily associated with administration, trade, or journalism.

In his study of colonial Ceylon, Paul Fletcher has shown that telegrams became an important tool of communication for colonial administrators from around the mid-nineteenth century, complementing a well-established, if complicated and confusing, system of correspondence by means of letters.[23] Telegrams were exchanged at various levels of the imperial administration: between the secretary of state for India and the governor general, between the secretaries to the local governments of Bombay and Madras and the secretary to the Government of India, between the press commissioner and the director of the Indian Telegraph Department as well as other, less prominent officials. They were also used for communication between administrators, army officers, representatives of the mercantile community—such as the secretaries of the Chambers of Commerce in Calcutta and Bombay—and civilians like Reuter's agent at Bombay.

It wasn't only British officials who used the telegraph to conduct their affairs. During his stay in Europe, the maharaja of Baroda Sayajirao Gaekwar reportedly communicated with his administration in India by telegraph. In this manner, he sanctioned agricultural funds for the benefit of cultivators in his state, a decision which he later confirmed by post. The maharaja was keen to emphasize that physical distance did not preclude work: 'I often dispose of more work when I am out of Baroda than when I am in the State, so, as a matter of fact, my absence in this respect is not a matter of inconvenience. Telegraph, post, and means of rapid communication have annihilated distances.'[24]

In theory at least, the rules of telegraphic communication were simple. As the Duke of Argyll, secretary of state for India, intimated on 20 January 1869, 'any intelligence of great importance', such as meteorological information which could signal the approach of a storm or the onset of a famine, was to be transmitted regularly by the telegraph.[25] Other, less important intelligence was communicated by letter via the usual channels of correspondence. Indeed, the number of state messages increased considerably in the aftermath of events in which the colonial administration took a particular interest, such as the 1877–8 famine in southern India, the camp of exercises held in Delhi in 1871–3, the Kooka Revolt of 1871–2, the visit of the Prince of Wales to India, and the outbreaks of cholera in 1875–6.[26] Important political intelligence emanating from senior officials enjoyed precedence, a principle enshrined in the 'clear the line' rule which allowed such messages to be transmitted ahead of other types of telegrams. But the lines were not 'cleared' only for this type of communication. On 24 July 1855, after merchants in Bombay and Calcutta had complained about the unsatisfactory speed at which their commercial despatches travelled, O'Shaughnessy issued a special order for the exchange of such telegrams between the two cities: 'For every Mercantile Message received from England for Calcutta, *the line is to be cleared* by the established signal, all private Messages from the Calcutta side are to wait at each Station, till those now referred are passed on. But the despatches of Government are not to be detained. These take precedence of all others in either direction' (emphasis in original). O'Shaughnessy even threatened to 'immediately remove' from the department any officer who did not comply with his order.[27]

At the same time, however, the very fact that Argyll reprimanded his peers about the absence of adequate communications from India suggests that rules were often eschewed. The speed of communication was shaped not only by the technical characteristics of available technology, but also by the specific agendas of the colonial administrators themselves. The telegraph might have been a technology which enabled the rapid transmission of intelligence, but it was of little use when there was no desire to communicate. Argyll was certainly not the only secretary of state to complain that information about important events in India had reached him first via reports published in the British press rather than through the usual channels of internal communication (in this connection, see also Chapter 4).

The administration of the Indian telegraphs was guided by the logic of frugality. Telegraph officials repeatedly complained that it was 'the political lines and offices chiefly on the frontier that are the drag upon the telegraph prosperity'.[28] One way in which expenses could be minimized was by policing the use of telegraphy and curbing 'verbose and unnecessary telegrams'. Occasionally, these attempts translated into veritable exercises in linguistic condensation and an almost obsessive desire to 'clear' the Indian lines. An exchange in the early 1890s between W. R. Brooke, director general of Indian Telegraphs, and Colonel H. L. Wells, officiating director of the Persian Section of the Indo-European Telegraph Department, illustrates well the drive to reduce both the volume and the length of service messages. In order to impress upon his colleague the importance of the measure, Brooke advised Wells to 'remov[e] every word which is not necessary to convey the meaning of the sender' and to abbreviate words like 'examiner' to 'exr'. He then rewrote some of Wells's telegrams and returned them with a note, indicating in each case how many words he had succeeded in economizing. By one of these exercises, a forty-five-word telegram, originally dated Teheran, 27 May 1891, was returned to its sender from Simla metamorphosed as a twenty-two-word message![29]

Other members of the colonial administration were also keen to cut down on telegraphic costs. In 1878, in a private letter to his friend Roper Lethbridge, the secretary in the Political and Secret Department of the India Office, Owen T. Burne explained why letters remained a preferable alternative to telegrams when communicating with the subcontinent:

> I cannot and do not telegraph to you my dear Lethbridge. My funds are small considering that 4/6 a word soon counts! and I find Colby rather disinclined to shell out funds. Had I the money I could with advantage spend pounds 100 a month in telegrams to you. But it is perhaps an unnecessary expense under present circumstances and I don't want Colby to think I am wasting money.[30]

The hierarchies of telegraphic communication mirrored the hierarchies of the colonial administration itself. In addition to communicating important political decisions, the telegraph was also used for a myriad other, more mundane communications, such as granting furlough, informing superiors of an impending retirement, advertising vacancies, inviting prospective employees to attend an interview, or simply informing one's colleague that a letter was on the way.[31] It was usually this type of exchange that became the target of government scrutiny. In 1862, for example, the chief secretary to the government, T. Pycroft, notified the interested public that officers 'requiring information from Government regarding leave, change of station, and other personal matters of a similar kind' were in future required to shoulder the cost of telegraphic replies.[32]

Access to a rapid, albeit not always reliable, means of communication also raised questions about the changing nature of decision-making processes in colonial India, especially during the Mutiny of 1857, when the government began to order executions by electric telegraph. The first such instance appears to be that of Jemadar Ishwari Pande, sentenced to death for disobeying his superior's order to arrest Mangal Pande. In an unprecedented move, the order to execute the sentence was transmitted by electric telegraph on 20 April 1857, the same day on which Ishwari Pande was hanged. The new procedure appeared to cause some apprehension among the officials involved. But Lord Canning and his close advisor Barnes Peacock, legal member of the Supreme Council, put such concerns to rest when they decided that there was 'no objection' to 'ordering the execution of a sentence of death by electric telegraph'.[33]

If the telegraph could help to seal the fate of some people in such a summary and expedient fashion, it also offered a glimmer of hope to others who tried to contest official verdicts by the same means. Once again, the eventful months of the Mutiny provide a relevant example. The anecdote stands in stark contrast to official reports which emphasized the alleged 'inertia' and reluctance of Indians to use telegraphy, highlighting instead some of the obstacles they had to overcome in order to access these channels of communication, particularly during the turbulent times of the Mutiny. The episode took place in October 1858, when Munshi Anwar Ali's wife filed a complaint against the telegraph master at Meerut. The woman claimed that her husband had been unjustly sentenced to death, despite having saved the life of one Mr Gee, superintendent of the 'Dak company'. When she tried to appeal by telegraph against his death sentence, the officer in charge refused to comply with her request pointing out that it was Sunday.[34] In the course of the ensuing investigation, the officer claimed to have no recollection of the 'native woman', but insisted that no message would have been refused considering the gravity of the situation. The problem, he went on to speculate, was that Indians disregarded the rules of telegraphic communication by attempting to send messages in their own language:

> If the native woman brought a message to be forwarded written in her language, it was of course refused according to the rules of the department. During the period I was in charge at Meerut, I do not remember ever having refused to forward a message that was presented for despatch according to the rules of the department.[35]

The introduction of electric telegraphy to India, like the establishment of the new postal system, was accompanied by the creation of a body of rules which regulated public access to the new technology, eventually leading to the crystallization of new routines and practices of communication. These rules were designed to serve the interests of the colonial government. As such, they could be used to exclude or limit the access to communication of certain individuals or social groups. As the above incident suggests, the rules were also frequently abused.

The new regime of communication required the introduction of 'signs' or instruments of modernity, as Chitra Joshi has pertinently described them.[36] In this respect, Dinshaw E. Wacha's account of early postal services in Bombay is emblematic of other technologies as well. According to him, language was one of the main barriers which prevented the public from understanding the instructions of the post office. This situation usually resulted in 'two or three days preliminary going up and down the Post Office to thoroughly understand the right and proper way of covering the parcel with white oil cloth, sealing it and the rest of the postal abracadabra'.[37] The inability to write letters was overcome by hiring the services of a letter writer, but Wacha claims that even for this category of people, English stationery such as note paper and envelopes 'were taboo'. The usual way of writing letters in India was on thin country paper which was rolled up like a cigar and closely gummed, the address being then written 'with astonishing minutiae'.[38]

Other Contexts of Use

A number of historical sources also provide insights into less-examined contexts of telegraphy use. These included the communication of news about births, marriages, illness, and death, reassuring relatives and friends in the event of a trip or political unrest, the coordination of domestic arrangements, sending money, or conveying congratulations and condolences. Indeed, there was a sense of urgency and importance associated with the arrival of a telegram. An unexpected despatch could become a source of anxiety, especially for those who were not able to read. In Shevantibai M. Nikambe's novel *Ratanbai* (1895), 'the whole house' is thrown into 'a state of excitement and confusion' by the arrival of a mysterious telegram, whose meaning cannot be deciphered by the illiterate mother and aunt of the main protagonist. In the absence of the postman, the only person who can read the message is Ratanbai's father, Vasudevrav Kashinath Dalvi, who reveals the distressing news: 'Brother dangerously ill, come immediately.'[39]

In this particular context, the telegram becomes a tool to advocate the education of upper-caste women, a project to which Nikambe (1865–1930), a native of Poona and a convert to Christianity, was deeply committed. As Ada Harris, wife of Bombay's infamous governor George Harris, also testified in her preface to the novel, Nikambe had been engaged in educational work among 'high caste girls and women in Bombay', first in connection with the Students' Literary and Scientific Society and, since 1890, as manager of her own school.[40] The novel drew on these experiences in its fervent advocacy of women's education as well as its ethnographic approach to the lives of high-caste women in the Bombay Presidency, many of whom were unable to read:

> Just as Anandibai came back the servant walked in with a letter. 'Keep it on the office table, *Bhaya*', said Anandibai to him.
>
> 'Bhai Saheb, it is a telegram,' answered the Bhaya.
>
> At this they were both startled and Kakubai exclaimed, 'Why is there a telegram? Where does it come from and from whom?' They took it in their hands and turned it upside down, and looked it well over; the letters and the address were like Greek to them, they could not make out anything.[41]

A different example comes from Elizabeth Augusta Egerton's diary of residence in India. This contains references to a telegraphic exchange with her former *khansama* (butler) and illustrates both the advantages and the limitations of this medium of communication. While the matter of the former butler joining the family at their new home in Meerut is quickly settled via a lapidary exchange of telegrams, Egerton's curiosity about Pir Baksh's motives in leaving Faizabad is far from being allayed. In fact, rather than bringing resolution to the conversation, Pir Baksh's telegram generates more questioning and speculation, a situation which has parallels in news reporting (see Chapter 5):

> Yesterday I was delighted at getting a telegram from 'Peer Bux, Khansáma. Kindly telegraph if I come'. Peer Bux is our former head butler, the most useful servant we ever had. He is a man of some property at Fyzabad, and in good service there, so I am surprised at his volunteering to come to us here. We telegraphed, 'Come'.[42]

An even more intriguing example comes from Bipin Chandra Pal's memoirs, in which he recollects a particularly arduous journey to Madras. Struggling to survive on the few annas that were still left to him and his wife, Pal was approached by a telegraph messenger at a roadside railway station and handed a telegram and a ten-rupee note. The thoughtful benefactor turned out to be his friend Pandit Shivanath Shastri. As Pal writes, 'The receipt of this money by wire struck me as a direct intervention of Providence', especially at a time (that is, 1881) when there was as yet no postal money-order service in India and the sum had to be ingeniously sent as a prepaid reply for the return message.[43] This was not Pal's last memorable encounter with telegraphy. As it turned out, even blessings could be sent by the telegraph. In another example from 1898, he recounts an exchange with his mentor Bijoy Krishna Goswami, a Brahmo leader and social reformer who resided in Puri at the time. Unable to ask for his blessing before embarking on the trip to England, Pal telegraphed Goswami to express his regret about the situation. The mentor's reply reached him aboard the steamer S. S. Egypt: 'God bless you'.[44]

In Anglo-Indian accounts of life in nineteenth-century India, the telegraph was often predictably associated with the Mutiny of 1857. Its importance as a means of rapid communication was heightened during such moments of crisis, when the spectre of violence rendered both distance and time increasingly relevant. The need to communicate is poignant, with letters and telegrams once again complementing each other. An entry in Georgina Harris's diary, written shortly after her successful escape from Lucknow to Allahabad, reveals that her husband, Rev. James P. Harris, had telegraphed James Colvile, vice-chancellor of the University of Calcutta, asking him to 'write home by the mail which leaves tomorrow, to tell dear mother of our safe arrival here'. As Rev. Harris explains in his own letter to his mother, 'I rushed to the telegraph as soon as we arrived, and sent you a flitting message through Sir J. Colvile, which it is a comfort to us to know will have gladdened your anxious hearts long before you had a real letter.'[45] Similarly, on his departure from Delhi on 21 September 1857, Colonel Keith Young wrote a message to his wife at Simla to inform her that 'I am just going down to the city to the telegraph-office to send off a message to you to say I'm coming, and to ask you to have a pony for me at Syree, where I ought to be, if all goes right, at two or three o' clock.'[46]

The telegraph also emerged as a convenient instrument for conveying congratulations and commiserations. In such situations, telegrams became an expression and a mark of social prestige, especially when messages addressed to public figures were circulated via the newspaper press and reprinted in memoirs and anniversary publications. On the death of Salar Jung, telegrams of condolence 'poured into Haidarabad' from all over India and England, with the viceroy and Queen Victoria being among those who expressed their condolences.[47] Similarly, Queen Victoria's Golden Jubilee in 1887 attracted an impressive number of telegrams from a long list of individuals and associations across the Indian subcontinent. Among these were various *zamindar*s (landlords) in Sylhet, the Behar Landholders' Association, the Upper Assam Sarbajanik Sabha, the Society for Securing the Interests of Native Christians in India, the postal employees and teachers at Hosur, the District Judge at Multan, the Parsi community at Quetta, and officials such as the lieutenant governor of Punjab and the commissioner of the Rawalpindi Division.[48] The experience was repeated a decade later, on the occasion of the Diamond Jubilee, when it became the object of ridicule in some of the vernacular press. In his *Jami-ul-Ulum*, Moradabad-based Amba Prasad chastised the 'Indian flatterers' for the addresses which they 'have been accustomed to present to English officers on various state occasions of joy [when] thanks are invariably offered to the Government for the construction of railways, telegraphs, schools, and hospitals and even the establishment of judicial courts in this country'.[49] Apart from being a pointed nationalist critique of imperial rule, examples like these also demonstrate that the telegraph afforded opportunities for irony and jest. These proved all the more effective when used in highly formalized circumstances.

There were, in fact, many aspects of telegraphic communication which invited criticism, ridicule, and mockery. The substantial literature on 'telegraphic blunders', 'tales of the telegraph', and 'curiosities of the wire' published in Britain and the United States, demonstrates how middle-class commentators used satire as a means to entertain their audiences but also to make sense of and come to terms with social change. Their textual productions often targeted social groups—women, older people—who were alleged to be less technologically savvy and thus liable to commit 'blunders' such as wanting to send food by the wires or to listen in on the messages that travelled along them.[50] Not wishing to undermine or contest the utility of telegraphy, such authors often pointed out that 'the mechanical part rarely fails.... It is the "personal equation" which has to be allowed for.'[51] But not everybody was willing to make such amendments. A much less humorous take on the failings of telegraphy was that of the self-styled 'mercantile communities' of Bombay and Calcutta. Their exasperation with the performance of the telegraph, reflected in the numerous complaints submitted to the colonial government, frequently led them to question the 'overall value and utility' of telegraphy in the 1850s and 1860s.[52]

The comicalities of telegraphic communication often betrayed the precarious condition of British colonizers in India. As Prabhu Mohapatra has remarked in his study of indentured labour in the West Indies, such anxieties resurfaced particularly during public events like the Muslim festival of Muharram, which afforded Indian labourers the opportunity to appropriate otherwise regulated and restricted public spaces.[53] Anxiety was compounded in a town with Mutiny connections like Meerut. As Egerton reminisced two decades after the event, rumours about a potential uprising against the British were 'rife' prior to the festival, constantly reminding people that they 'live on a volcano in India'.[54] The panic took a tragicomic twist when it was revealed that the rumours had originated with the servants of the station-master, who 'had travelled in the train with two Mussulmans, who had said that on the day of the Moharram all the infidels were to be massacred'. The station-master's reaction illustrates the degree of confidence invested in the telegraph, especially in the aftermath of the Mutiny: 'out of his mind with fright', the official turned to the electric telegraph for deliverance and asked his superior to transfer him 'immediately'.[55]

While Egerton could not dismiss the possibility that rumours of revolt might actually materialize, her account can also be read as a subtle criticism of 'official folly' and the dangers of regarding the telegraph as a panacea for all social and colonial problems. Indeed, the episode triggered another recollection, this time about a stationmaster in the Central Provinces, who was alleged to have sent a desperate telegram to his superior in an attempt to save himself not only from 'dangerous natives', but also from the dangers of the Indian environment itself: 'Tiger jumping in station yard. Pointsman unable to go to points through fear. Please arrange sharp.'[56]

The scene might have been fictional; indeed, that is of little relevance here. More important is the fact that such anecdotes belonged to a rich lore about electric telegraphy that was particularly popular in the decades following its introduction, not only in India, but also in other parts of the world. In the colonial environment of India, the role of such narratives was multilayered. On the one hand, they familiarized people with the new technology and chastised those who failed to perform their work or to adapt to the demands of 'modern' life. In doing so, they in fact reminded readers that neither technology nor the people who operated it were infallible. On the other hand, such accounts advocated the utilitarian value of technology and its potential to save lives in situations of crisis. At the same time, they also underscored the precariousness of British presence in India, prompting questions about the ability of telegraphy to save lives in real moments of crisis.

Popularizing Telegraphy

There were other ways in which telegraphy infiltrated public consciousness in the nineteenth century. If the previous sections have tried to balance official records against evidence drawn predominantly from memoirs and (auto)biographies of life in colonial India, in this section I am concerned with how telegraphy featured in the newspaper and the periodical press of the time, both in its popular and more specialized, scientific incarnations. I also consider what this teaches us about the history of electrical science in colonial India, about processes of science-making more generally, and how telegraphy came to be regarded as a panacea for the social and moral 'evils' which allegedly beset Indian society.

By the time the first electric telegraph lines were opened for public use in the Indian subcontinent in 1855, the telegraph was, in many ways, 'old news'. As we have seen in the previous chapter, innovators, projectors, and colonial administrators had been discussing the possibility of building semaphores and shutters in various parts of the Indian subcontinent since the late eighteenth century. Newspapers such as John Francis Sandys' *Calcutta Journal of Politics and General Literature* and Harihar Dutta's *Jam-i-Jahan Numa* followed with interest the latest developments in the field of telegraphic communication, reporting on almost everything from its potential military and naval applications to new 'discoveries', plans of communication, and the advantages of carrier pigeons as a means of conveying information.[57]

In addition, public demonstrations of galvanism such as those conducted in Calcutta in 1794 by the Scottish itinerant lecturer James Dinwiddie demonstrate that colonial science at this time was an affair with utilitarian and entertaining iterations, which depended on both official and public sanction for its success. As Savithri Preetha Nair has argued, late eighteenth and early nineteenth-century Calcutta was a vibrant universe in which 'showmen, ventriloquists, jugglers, magicians, artists, balloonists, model-makers, and mathematical instrument makers vied with each other and traded on the streets and bazaars round Tank Square and Government Place in the heart of the city'.[58] The newspaper press was central to this display of scientific enterprise, providing a medium through which to simultaneously popularize and sell science.

Accounts of 'telegraphic science', as John Macdonald reluctantly called it in 1822, were only the latest expression of an older interest in electricity and galvanism that could be traced back to the eighteenth century, a period in the history of western European science when this was fast becoming a popular field for those with an interest in the study of natural philosophy.[59] Publications about electricity originating in Europe were already circulating in India in the late eighteenth and early nineteenth centuries. As Nair points out, among the more popular titles were James Ferguson's *Introduction to Electricity* (1770), Tiberius Cavallo's *A Complete Treatise of Electricity* (1777), and George Adams's *Essay on Electricity* (1784), all of which included sections on the medical applications of this 'useful science'.[60]

Interest in things electric increased in the course of the next century, as scientists gradually uncovered the 'mysteries' of electricity and practical applications began to multiply, covering almost everything from telegraphy to calico-printing, clocks, medical devices, and even electric whips and hair-dressing machines.[61] But it was the medical applications of electricity which attracted particular attention. Indeed, if we are to believe Michael la Beaume, 'Medical-Galvanist, Surgeon-Electrician, Consulting Ditto to the London Electrical Dispensary', there was not much electricity and galvanism could not cure: from disorders of the digestive organs, of the head and the nervous system, to diseases of the skin, gout, rheumatism, blindness, deafness, and other illnesses 'peculiar' to one of the sexes. In particular, la Beaume was keen to promote galvanism as a safer and more beneficial substitute for mercury-based medical treatments.[62]

Like in other parts of the world such as Europe and Japan, in India the appeal of electricity was partially connected to its alleged healing and rejuvenating properties, a situation which remained unchanged throughout the nineteenth century. At the end of 1836, W. L. M'Gregor 'electrified' Maharaja Ranjit Singh with the help of a self-constructed galvanic battery and an 'electrical apparatus ... supplied from the Agra depot, by order of the late Lord Metcalfe'.[63] While galvanism failed to make an impression upon the maharaja, he agreed to submit himself regularly to electrical shocks, despite his general reluctance towards any medical treatments, be they European or local. The episode is worth quoting at length, for it shows how electrotherapy could also become a way to legitimize power, by testing attributes such as physical and mental strength:

> The machine was set up and the jar charged, but a difficulty arose on the part of His Highness's attendants, who were afraid that the shock might be attended by fatal consequences. At length the Maharajah begged of them to be quiet, and said he would take the *Biglee* [electricity]. We purposely put a small charge in the Leyden phial, and the Maharajah received it without evincing any particular emotion. On witnessing the slight effect on their master, all the courtiers entreated that we would give them a shock; and this time we resolved to give them its full effect! The Minister Dhyan Singh joined hands with Jemadar Khooshyal Singh, and he with others, until a chain was formed of the whole party present in the durbar. The jar being now charged to the full extent, they received a powerful shock, which made them all jump. Not making allowance for the difference in the charge, the Maharajah naturally received the credit of possessing a stouter heart and stronger nerves than any of his suite; and this first trial was satisfactory to all parties. Khooshyal Singh suggested that we should teach someone the art of electrifying the Maharajah, but to this proposal we decidedly objected, though willing to continue our own services as long as they might be required.[64]

Although M'Gregor was protective of his knowledge of galvanism and electricity, this did not prevent Indians from taking up the new 'art' and building their own instruments in the following decades of the nineteenth century. One example comes from the second half of the period when Sitanath Ghosh, a local Brahmo leader from Jessore, used the Hindu Mela, the National Society, and newspapers like *Tattwabodhini Patrika* as a platform for disseminating his ideas and experiments with electricity and magnetism. In the early 1870s, on the occasion of an Agricultural and Educational Fair in his native village of Roygram, Ghosh even constructed a short-distance telegraph from the riverbank to the fair site. Among his other achievements was an electromagnetic healer which he used to treat patients at his medical practice in Calcutta.[65]

The contours of scientific activity changed significantly in the second half of the nineteenth century, as science became increasingly institutionalized and professionalized. Specialist journals began to multiply, but the newspaper press also functioned as one of the main vehicles for the dissemination of information about science, through the publication of regular reports on the latest scientific 'discoveries' and the activity of professional associations and institutions of education. Even more popular were advertisements of electric devices and general news about the development of telegraphic communication, interruptions to the lines, and so on. Browsing through the pages of *Amrita Bazar Patrika*, one can almost create a timeline of the main scientific 'advances' and 'discoveries' of the last decades of the nineteenth century. For example, on 18 July 1878, a correspondent from Lucknow described the telephone experiments between that town and Sitapore (Sitapur), pointing out that not only the voices of the speakers, but also the singing of the canaries was 'distinctly recognizable'. Two decades later, on 30 January 1898, news was published about a 'latest American invention' that enabled the transmission of pictures by the telegraph. The device, as the *Amrita Bazar Patrika* reminded its readers, could be particularly useful in apprehending 'criminals fleeing from justice, by scattering their photographs over the country with the speed of electricity, instead of by the comparatively slow medium of the mails'.

Disseminating information about science was an important brief for many a newspaper in nineteenth-century India, as the numerous articles carrying the headline 'Scientific' suggest. One insight into how editors conceptualized this mission comes from the pages of the *Bombay Times and Journal of Commerce* of 1 December 1841, in which a description of the daguerreotype and the electric telegraph was accompanied by a more general commentary on the role of newspapers in disseminating scientific knowledge:

> The march of invention proceeds at an amazing pace. Scarcely a week elapses without bringing forth some new wonder of this kind, so extremely wonderful that all common terms of admiration become exhausted, and the faculty of the marvellous itself sinks back in a syncope, and refuses any longer to be excited. These wonders are usually reported in the weekly literary journals, and even in the still more familiar news-sheets; yet there must be many who pay little or no attention to them. We have therefore resolved to run lightly over the chief new inventions of the last few months, believing that to most of our readers we shall be giving new ideas, and not mistrusting that even those to whom the ideas are not new will be amused to observe what a few months can bring forth in this land, where business depends intimately on science, and science itself is pursued with all the eagerness of business.[66]

The above paragraph suggests that a transmission view of communication would be inadequate to understand the role of the press in nineteenth-century India. Rather than a vehicle that communicated information to its readers, the newspaper was envisaged more as a mediator between science and the broader public, a vehicle for personal cultivation and a source of inspiration for potential readers-cum-inventors. Significantly, the editor emphasizes the intimate connection between science and commercial enterprise, a message with particular resonance in a commercially vibrant city like Bombay. This is not simply science that serves imperial interest: it is also a science that serves the enterprising projector, the visionary entrepreneur who struggles to succeed against the encroachments of the East India Company and of the state more generally.

The point is also demonstrated by the publication of relevant book excerpts and reviews, such as Charles C. Adley's *The Story of the Telegraph in India*, which received extensive coverage in the pages of the *Englishman* in June and July 1866.[67] A telegraph engineer who had been involved in the construction and supervision of the Burdwan and Raniganj divisions of the Indian railways, Adley was also, as we have seen in the previous chapter, a staunch advocate of the privatization of telegraphs. The publication of the book was timed to coincide with the House of Commons' decision to investigate the state of postal and telegraphic communication between Britain and India. The writer perhaps hoped that increased public pressure would eventually force the Government of India to transfer control of its telegraphs into private hands.[68] The 'public' on behalf of which Adley claimed to speak was a mercantile one, whose relationship with the newspaper press was highly symbiotic. On the one hand, the press represented a channel through which aspiring entrepreneurs and merchants could advance their respective agendas. On the other, the mercantile community itself was often directly involved in the management of newspapers and subsidized the press by subscribing to it and by commissioning advertisements.

Despite the promise of the *Bombay Times* to 'run lightly' over scientific subjects—that is, to report them in a manner which would make them accessible to a wider public—many of the articles published in the newspaper press during this period turned out to be dense in specialist knowledge. Indeed, accounts of telegraphic 'science' ranged from the highly specialized to the more popular and accessible. As Shiju Sam Varughese has observed in relation to the contemporary regional press in Kerala, newspapers provided an 'epistemological cross-space between scientific and popular cultures'.[69] In 1845, debates about the possibility of introducing railways and telegraphs into the subcontinent prompted one correspondent to write a long and detailed letter to the *Englishman*, outlining not only the history of telegraphy, but also the principles of electromagnetism.[70] Similarly, another piece from 1887, which eventually made its way into the *Straits Times* of Singapore, described in specialist detail the 'important telegraphic discovery' of a Mr McGuire from the Ambala Telegraph Office. His idea of disposing with the resistance coils used in duplex telegraphy was alleged to save up to 50 per cent of the electric power necessary to run the telegraph in India.[71]

This also meant that the newspaper press played an important role in evaluating new technologies and innovations. For example, William Haworth's 1845 experiments in Cossipore (Kashipur) were received with a considerable dose of scepticism. While the editor did not dismiss the public utility of an invention which claimed to apply galvanism to horticulture, he nevertheless criticized the inventor for not providing enough information 'as to the mode in which the galvanic influence [had been] applied' to grow potatoes.[72] By reporting on such topics, the press became a platform for the validation and popularization of scientific enterprise.

In the particular field of medicine, this generated numerous debates about the meaning of professionalism, particularly with regard to the practice of advertising new 'inventions' and devices. One notable example was that of Isaac Louis Pulvermacher's galvanic appliances, especially his 'patent galvanic chain-bands, belts, and batteries'. The global circulation of his devices is also demonstrated by the advertisements featured in the *Times of India* in the second half of the nineteenth century.[73] Originally from Kempen, in Prussia, Pulvermacher was an electric engineer with experience in the field of telegraphy. His travels took him to London by way of Vienna, Prague, Breslau, Berlin, and Paris, in the process also prompting him to shift his attention to the field of electrical medicine.[74] His electric belts, which claimed to cure rheumatism, neuralgia, and 'nervous & functional disorders', were only one example of the myriad electrical devices invented in the course of the nineteenth and early twentieth centuries (another was Overbeck's rejuvenator, which also received conspicuous publicity in the pages of the *Times of India* at the beginning of the twentieth century).[75] Pulvermacher and Overbeck's careers are interesting examples of how patenting and advertising were harnessed for commercial profit. They demonstrate the blurred boundaries between professional medicine and quackery in the nineteenth century, as social actors pondered their allegiances, struggled to balance financial gain against institutional prestige, and debated the relationship of advertising to professional medicine.

In the nineteenth century, the electric telegraph also became an important subject of news and views, all the more so since the newspaper press was one of the main beneficiaries of this new medium of communication. The news value of telegraphy-related stories was high not only on account of the novelty of telegraphy, but also because disruptions to telegraphic traffic had the potential to impact significantly on the conduct of business and the administration of the British Empire. It is not surprising therefore that one of the most common ways in which the press monitored the state of telegraphic communication was by reporting regularly on interruptions to traffic caused by technical failures, natural factors, and human tampering. Like intelligence about the arrival and departure of ships, reports about the state of the lines became a regular feature in the pages of many nineteenth-century newspapers, appealing not only to speculators and other members of the mercantile community, but also to the wider reading public.

In addition, the newspaper press followed keenly the 'progress of telegraphy' in India and the rest of the world. The publication of Adley's book discussed earlier also coincided with the successful laying of the transatlantic cable in 1866. This event helped to overcome initial scepticism about the viability of submarine telegraphy and opened the road to future achievements in this field, most notably the completion of the Red Sea line in 1870 and the gradual expansion of the cable to East Asia and Australia in the following year. Achievements like these were not only newsworthy events, but also occasions to revel in the engineering marvels of the Victorian age. The progress of the *Great Eastern*, the sailing vessel which laid the transatlantic cable, received wide coverage both in India and other parts of the world.[76]

Similarly, the completion of the Indo-European route in 1865 and the opening of the Red Sea line in 1870 became perfect displays of the 'triumphs' of Western science. International and domestic reports about the opening of the Red Sea line and the 'telegraphic soirée' organized by the famous cable magnate John Pender to celebrate the occasion provide a vivid illustration of this.[77] An article published in the *Daily Telegraph* spoke of jubilant guests gathered at Pender's residence in London—including such high-profile personalities as the Prince of Wales—and tapped into underlying public anxieties to reiterate the manifold benefits of telegraphy in India. Among these were the ability to 'preserve our empire by warning us of mutiny', to 'outstrip the passage of the storm and save whole navies and flotillas', to 'bring to our breakfast-table news from all regions of the earth', and, more generally, to 'telegraph [time] out of existence'.[78]

The event attracted global attention, with newspapers such as *The Times*, the *Observer*, and the *New York Herald* also joining in the celebration.[79] In India, the *Madras Times* dedicated a whole column to the coverage and published some of the telegraphic despatches exchanged between Lord Mayo and President Ulysses S. Grant by means of an ad-hoc line that connected Pender's house to the London office of the British Indian Submarine Telegraph Company.[80] The spectacle of colonialism, which enabled the appropriation of science for both imperial and national purposes, drew on familiar and easily recognizable tropes. The two leaders congratulated each other, expressing their hope for a telegraphy-mediated 'union' between the eastern and the western hemispheres.

As Thomas R. Metcalfe has argued with regard to durbars, occasions like these helped to mark the difference between colonizers and colonized, but were also riddled with contradictions and uncertainties.[81] Indeed, the celebrations at Pender's house also exposed the Indian government to criticism from the newspaper press. The logic of speed guided the celebrations to such an extent that a record was kept of the transit time of telegrams. Urgent messages were exchanged between various parts of the world with a view to demonstrate the efficiency of the new system of communication. One message read: 'The Press of India sends salaam to the Press of America. Reply quickly.'[82]

Yet, at the level of everyday life, the intrusion of modernity was not always welcome. Much to the dismay of the reporters, Lord Mayo failed to 'reply quickly', being 'in bed' at the time when President Grant engaged him in telegraphic conversation. The press frowned upon the viceroy's insistence on discharging official duties at his own convenience, instead of adapting to the rhythm of the telegraph. His conduct provided yet another opportunity to criticize the Government of India. One male reporter expressed his outrage through the medium of an imaginary female audience: 'Why Sir Seymour Fitzgerald and Lord Mayo went to bed when it was known in India that this particular *soirée* was about to take place, was another question which agitated the female mind.'[83]

Education and Professionalization

The newspaper press was not the only medium which helped to disseminate information about telegraphy and electricity in nineteenth-century India. Another important genre was that of scientific periodicals. Despite the public appeal of subjects such as electricity and telegraphy, we must remember that electrical engineering in general occupied a relatively minor position in the pages of emerging scientific periodicals in colonial India, especially prior to the 1860s and by comparison with other fields like astronomy, geology, archaeology, meteorology, and medicine. The predilection for the latter areas of investigation stemmed from a combination of factors, most conspicuously the lingering influence of an early orientalist preference for the study of subjects connected with natural history, and the colonial government's own reluctance to promote the education of Indians in the field of engineering and technology.[84]

The gradual expansion of roads, canals, railways, and telegraphs in the second half of the nineteenth century created an acute need for a qualified body of engineers, surveyors, and other personnel, which was only partially met by the establishment of the civil engineering colleges at Roorkee (1847) and Madras (1859). Colonial rhetoric often emphasized the lack of local interest in 'mechanical science' and the fact that Indians, in particular Bengalis, were 'naturally' inclined to devote their attention 'almost exclusively to the pen'. This argument became the target of nationalist critique and contestation. Public figures like the journalist Moti Lal Ghosh contested the widespread notion that Bengalis were not interested in technical education, pointing out that it was not the 'defects of national character', but the lack of any viable avenues of employment and the discriminatory policies of the colonial government which rendered engineering unappealing to many young Bengalis.[85]

Indeed, colonial accounts often ignored or misrepresented local engagement with technology, conveniently dismissing the importance of scientific education in indigenous projects of modernity, the proliferation of vernacular publications in this field, or Indian experiments with electricity and magnetism. As Indira Viswanathan Peterson has argued in her study of Serfoji II of Tanjore, the Raja's public education project in the early nineteenth century 'reflect[ed] his appreciation of the value of educational modernity as a kind of social and political capital'. His initiative to transform the Tanjore court into a 'disseminator' and not a mere 'receiver' of modern knowledge extended to electricity as well. Accordingly, in 1810 Serfoji II instructed his court officer Soob Row to join Dr Klein and Rev. C. S. John at their Tranquebar mission in order to learn about electricity and pneumatics.[86]

Another example comes from Ulrike Stark's work on Raja Shivaprasad's project of rural education in the Benares Circle in the 1850s, which highlights the hybrid nature of this enterprise in which scientific education became an instrument both for the 'moral and material uplifting of the masses' and for their 'empowerment'.[87] In this context, scientific experiments, such as those conducted with instruments imported from London, which were used to demonstrate the principles of magnetism, became particularly important. In fact, they proved more successful than text-based education on subjects like electroplating, vaccination, and so on.[88] 'Educational modernity' thus represented an important source of social capital for prospective students, who were already keen to take up new and potentially lucrative areas of study in the first decades of the nineteenth century. In 1839, a report of the Bombay Native Education Society shows that two students from the Division of West Scholars, Dhondoo Janardhunjee and Narayen Shewshunker, were examined on the subjects of electricity and medical mechanics, respectively, at the annual meeting.[89]

Things changed during the second half of the nineteenth century, when the gradual crystallization of a professional ethos witnessed the emergence of societies and journals dedicated exclusively to engineering.[90] In 1872, the *Amrita Bazar Patrika* reported the establishment of the Indian Engineers' Association, pointing out that among the papers read before the society were Madhub Chundra Roy's contributions on the history of the steam engine and the 'electro-magnetic engine'.[91] With regard to journals, popular titles included Adley's own *Engineers' Journal and Railway and Public Works Chronicle of India and the Colonies*, founded in Calcutta in 1858. The first journal dedicated to electric science was the bimonthly *Indian Telegraphic Journal* published in Lahore (1875–?), followed by the *Indian Telegraphist* of Allahabad (1893–1913).[92]

Electrical Science in the Vernacular

Needless to say, English was not the only medium of scientific activity and communication in nineteenth-century India.[93] On 1 January 1854, Henry Carre Tucker, chief commissioner of Benares and writer and trustee for the Church Missionary Society, gave a talk on the 'Electric Telegraph' at the Benares School, which was accompanied by a practical demonstration. Babu Sheo Prasad translated the lecture for the audience.[94] Furthermore, by mid-century, scientific periodicals as well as books about telegraphy and electricity were available in the vernaculars.[95] In 1855, Kalidas Maitra published in Serampore his Bengali-language *The Electric Telegraph or The Telegraph Office Assistant's Manual*, claiming that his was the first book on electricity authored by an Indian. As D. K. Lahiri Choudhury has discussed, apart from providing an overview of magnetism and O'Shaughnessy's single-needle signalling instrument which was in use in India at the time, Maitra's *Manual* presciently discussed the possibility of transmitting messages in languages other than English. To this end, he produced charts to illustrate a system of communication in Bengali,

Hindustani, and Persian, pointing out that 'signals are arbitrary … therefore similar to how information arrives in the English alphabet, news can come in Bengali or Persian or other languages'.[96]

Maitra's book was not the only publication on electric telegraphy. The same year also witnessed the publication of a book in Gujarati, which had been prepared by Karsondas Mulji and Rav Saheb Mohanlal Ranchoddas, members of the managing committee of the Bombay Vernacular Society.[97] A few years later, Ganpat Krishnaji's Press, the same establishment which had printed Mulji and Ranchoddas's book, brought out another publication on electricity authored by Krishna Sastri Bhatavadekar.[98]

As Veena Naregal has pointed out, Krishnaji was the first commercial printer-publisher in Marathi, whose range of publications exceeded the usual official and pedagogical works to include a wide variety of material of both religious and popular nature. Her point that Krishnaji's 'modern ideas of literacy' might be traced back to missionary influence is significant in light of the fact that Maitra's own *Manual* was published in a place with strong missionary connections. The Baptist missionaries of Serampore were well known for their efforts to diffuse Western scientific knowledge through vernacular translations. Maitra himself had been a student of John Mack, a long-time professor of mathematics and natural sciences at the Serampore College and author of the first book of chemistry in Bengali.[99] This suggests that early vernacular publications on electricity and telegraphy were, partially at least, an offshoot of missionary efforts to educate the Indian public by making available in vernacular languages various works on 'useful' sciences such as anatomy, mathematics, and geography. Such publications would have been of interest to members of the public involved in business and trade, especially in places like Bombay and Calcutta, where merchants actively promoted the development of telegraphic communication in India. But they would have also appealed to young men who aspired to expand their knowledge of telegraphy and electricity and perhaps to secure a job in a related field. Although, as we have already seen, colonial regulations during this period restricted the employment of 'native' telegraph personnel, preferring to hire Indians for menial jobs such as peons, *jemadar*s (here, chief peons), and sweepers, a limited number of Eurasians and Indians did work for the Telegraph Department as signallers or artificers.[100]

The Telegraphic Imaginary: Speed, Progress, and the Technologies of Modernity

As this chapter has discussed so far, the telegraph was put to a variety of uses in nineteenth-century India. Interest in telegraphy and things electric found expression in a number of print genres, ranging from the popular and scientific press to handbooks and histories of telegraphy, memoirs of engineers, and accounts of telegraphic expeditions. But how did telegraphy feature in the cultural imaginary of nineteenth-century India? How did people respond to the new technology and to the ways in which it was infiltrating not only their communication practices but also their socio-economic and political life and, via the materiality of telegraph poles and wires, even their natural environment? Finally, how did the telegraph become such a potent symbol of imperial rule?

There was a palpable fascination with the 'new' and the 'modern' in the nineteenth century which transcended geographical and social boundaries.[101] That fascination was compounded when the 'new' took the form of mysterious electric devices which held the promise of regenerating the human body or rendering both time and distance irrelevant. Not infrequently, the colonizers and the colonized were united in their appreciation of the potential of electricity and technology in general to transform individuals and societies. Indeed, the telegraph inspired surprisingly similar cultural representations across geographic, social, and political divides. Despite such similarities, the actual experiences of telegraphy were far from universal. In this respect, the telegraph proved to be a mixed blessing for many nineteenth-century observers: fascinating and useful, yet also unsettlingly disruptive and divisive.

Admittedly, most of the practices and attitudes towards telegraphy I was able to recover originated with literate, elite groups of both Europeans and Indians. This is in sharp contrast to the mass of the Indian population, about which we have little documentary evidence that would allow us to ascertain not only their attitudes towards this technology, but also the extent to which they used it in the nineteenth century. It is a familiar complaint which might be partially overcome through the use of oral sources, themselves mediated by a textual record for the period of time covered in this book.

We should begin by pointing out that there were, arguably, plenty of people in nineteenth-century India who did not actually use the telegraph. In the absence of evidence related directly to this period, we can refer here to the research of anthropologist Verrier Elwin, well known for his work with the Agaria, who remarked in the early 1940s that many of his interlocutors were fascinated with trains, telegraphs, and gramophones, yet very few had actual experiences of using these technologies.[102] This being said, inability to own or use technology did not necessarily translate into a lack of engagement with technology, which remained possible most notably through acts of seeing and hearing. People with no experience of rail journeys could still partake in the experiences of others through the medium of folk songs. Elwin identified only one Agaria man who had travelled by train. Yet, the experience was memorialized in a song and shared widely with his fellow villagers:

> *Hai re*! The train whistles, it is leaving Bilaspur.
> In front is the train, behind is the signal.
> The villagers leave their work and run to see it.
> At every station the engine takes coal and water.
> In front runs the wire to give the news.
> Behind, we sit clutching our tickets in our hands.
> In front goes the motor,
> Behind goes the cycle.
> Leaving their food, the children run to see.[103]

The scene is familiar. One of its best-known visual representations, which has remained imprinted on the retina of generation of viewers, can be found in Satyajit Ray's masterpiece *Pather Panchali*, in which the children, Durga and Apu, rush to get a glimpse of a passing train. The noisy progress of the train disturbs for a moment the serene atmosphere of the countryside, leaving behind not only a trail of smoke, but also a trail of memories, to be remembered in later life. Indeed, the impact of such experiences with technology on the psychology of children is often remarkable. Consider, for example, Rabindranath Tagore's recollections of the scientific experiments conducted by his teacher Sitanath Ghosh at their house in Jorasanko.[104] Or Dinshaw Edulji Wacha, the famous Parsi politician, who was barely a child of 10 when the first telegraph lines were opened in India in the 1850s:

> I remember our elders of the family conversing on the subject and recalling the legendary lore of Hindu and Persian mythology just as much as previously in reference to the first balloon in which that intrepid aeronaut, Mr. Kyte (a suggestive name) flew. He was called in Gujarati the modern 'Pavan Pavri', that is, he who in the legendary lore of the Aryans

was known to achieve miracles by flying from the heavens to the earth in the twinkling of an eye.[105]

The association of telegraphy and electricity with religion and the supernatural is far from unusual. If anything, in the nineteenth century this type of discourse was surprising in its frequency. Across barriers of geography, social status, age, and gender, we find numerous examples of people for whom technology was nothing less than a symbol of life; electricity, in particular, was an incarnation of the supernatural and a vehicle of communication with the invisible world. In the United States, telegraphy provided inspiration for spiritualism, a system of belief which emphasized the duality of human beings and the possibility of communication with departed souls through a 'medium'; the telegraph, by using electricity which originated 'in the heavens', was regarded as the perfect channel of communication with that world.[106] In a similar vein, steam and trains also became a symbol of life and activity. In an evocative piece, a writer for the American edition of *Blackwood's Magazine* contrasted the stillness of a cemetery surrounded 'on either side by one of those gigantic achievements of modern science—a railway', with the 'noise, the hurry, and the whirl of life' which the passing of the train created.[107]

For the Agaria themselves, technologies such as trains were not simply inanimate objects, but had their own *jiv* (soul).[108] Yet, despite the fact that by the last decades of the nineteenth century such technologies had become familiar sights of the Indian landscape—in *The Poison Tree*, Bankim Chandra Chatterjee writes evocatively about the 'telegraph wires [which] by the wayside hummed in the wind'—such technologies always remained to a certain extent foreign, their presence a stark reminder of the political realities of colonial India.[109] The telegraph and the railways were foreign 'inventions', which had come to India together with British rule; as such, their presence also spelt disruption and alienation. In a conversation with Elwin, one Agaria man pointed out that it was the British who 'create[d] the *jiv*' like trains and gramophones. Similarly, the singer Rupchand Pakshi lamented the ways in which machines were undermining the fabric of Indian society and promoted the onslaught of a foreign culture:

> Steam-vessel and railway are so strong by the way
> That the Vedas and Brahma
> Have given up their karma
> And on fire, water and air have run away.[110]

The onslaught was not only cultural and spiritual, as also demonstrated by missionary belief in the ability of railways and telegraphs to promote conversion to Christianity among colonized peoples, but also ecological.[111] The new technologies altered the physical environment in significant and visible ways. If, for people like Egerton, the telegraph wire between Landour and Simla was 'the only visible sign of civilization', which 'bridg[ed] … precipitous valleys, taking a leap of 500 yards from one hill to the next, and suspended 1,000 feet in the air' as it carried along 'some message "big with fate"', for others the seeming 'conquest' of nature was something to be deplored, not celebrated.[112] The massive destruction of the gutta-percha trees in Southeast Asia has already been mentioned. A similar example comes from rural Ceylon, where jack trees were often sacrificed in order to construct telegraph lines. Thomas Steele, a member of the Ceylon Civil Service, provided a rare glimpse into the impact of this process on the lives of Sinhalese villagers:

> It [the jack tree] is highly thought of by Sinhalese villagers, one of whom (two of his jak-trees having been cut down to admit passage of the telegraph wire, some years ago, when Ceylon was first put in connection with the Indian telegraph system) characteristically told the writer that the loss of each was to him almost as great a bereavement as the death of a child, indeed, in some respects, rather more so, as other children might be born to him in his lifetime, but such stately trees as he had been deprived of could not possibly grow up before he died.[113]

Technologies like the telegraph and the railways generated significant political, economic, and cultural power for the British colonizers, a topic with which many Indian commentators engaged. Amba Prasad, for example, was indicting in his diagnosis of the role of technologies of communication and their impact on Indian society. To those who argued—like many contemporary observers still do—that the British had brought the railways and other 'modern' technologies to the Indian subcontinent, Amba Prasad replied,

> The original object of Government in constructing railways in this country was to afford facility in traveling to its civil and military employés and thereby effect economy in its expenditure, so that the benefit which the Indians derive from them is only indirect. Properly speaking the railway has done rather harm than good to India. It has, in the first place, deprived millions of natives of their employment. Secondly,

> had it not been for the railway, no such wide-spread famine as the prevailing one could have been possible in this country, for food grains could not then be exported to foreign countries with so much ease as now. Again, in former times if one part of the country was affected with famine, food-grain came from other parts where it was cheap. But in these days of easy transportation, the prices of food-grains are the same everywhere, and famine, whenever it occurs, seizes almost every part of the country. Even in these days food-grains are much cheaper in such parts of the country where the accursed railway does not exist yet. The telegraphs too like the railways were really constructed for the benefit of the Government and its officers.[114]

Prasad thus questioned the benefits of 'modern' technologies for Indian society. For him, improved means of communication did not necessarily translate into material improvement for the colonized. On the contrary, they generated new opportunities for exploitation, by making India vulnerable to crises that were not necessarily of its own making.

Apart from the very practical ways in which technologies like the railways and the telegraph served the military, administrative, and commercial activities of the colonial government, the telegraph also became amenable to the imperial project through its association with speed. As Marian Aguiar points out in a recent study of cultural representations of India's railways, 'Modernity has often been allied with mobility through representational forms—textual, spatial and temporal.'[115] The telegraph did not offer the same opportunities for mobility that the railways and steamers did, as they facilitated the movement of people, goods, and ideas across the Indian subcontinent and, indeed, the world. Instead, it made possible what I would like to call, drawing on Roland Wenzlhuemer's work, a dematerialized mobility, in which information no longer moved physically through space together with its material carriers, but was transmitted as electric signals along wires that spanned the world.[116]

There were many remarkable dimensions that characterized electric telegraphy, but perhaps none received so much attention as the fact that it was able to transmit information rapidly. It is no exaggeration to say that the telegraph became a metonym for speed, as demonstrated by the commonly encountered trope that it had 'annihilated' both time and space. The notion gained even more notoriety after the publication of Marx's *Grundrisse*, in which he argued that fast and cheap communication was central to capitalist enterprise.[117] Indeed, as John Tomlinson has pertinently remarked, 'Acceleration rather than deceleration has been the constant leitmotif of cultural modernity.'[118] As a technology which had accelerated communication more than any other previous invention, the telegraph became a particularly pertinent symbol of progress and modernity.

The association between media of communication, progress, speed, and modernity deserves some elaboration. To begin with, the idea that means of communication could be regarded as an index of a people's degree of progress had a long pedigree in European thought. For example, during the Enlightenment, philosophers like Rousseau and Condillac had posited a link between writing and civilization. Indeed, as Peter Simonson and others have remarked, it is in Enlightenment thinking that we can find 'the modern origins of grander narratives of communication in history, fuelling more-or-less ethnocentric progress tales of civilization and its media, and underwriting a reform-minded and forward-looking liberal politics with both individualistic and communitarian iterations'.[119] Such ideas survived in the nineteenth century, when the semantic repertoire of the word 'communication' itself expanded considerably to accommodate contemporary technological developments in the form of roads, canals, railways, and telegraphs.[120] In political economy, in particular, expressions such as 'lines of communication' and 'system of communications' became increasingly common, and were used alongside other idioms—'we had a communication from…'—which referred specifically to the act of exchanging information with the help of media like letters and telegrams.[121] As understood during this period, communications referred both to transport (public works) and to the interactions they facilitated.

The scientific developments of the nineteenth century propelled technology to the centre of much intellectual thinking about progress and human society, prompting questions about the role of technology in effecting social change. For Charles Babbage, material and social improvement 'ever follow[ed] new and cheap communications'. Machines, as opposed to tools, were an index of a country's progress towards civilization, whose application in processes of manufacture economized both time and labour.[122] Similarly, for the German economist Karl Knies, railways and telegraphs stood at the apex of industrial development.[123]

Perhaps the best illustration of this mode of thinking, for the purposes of this book, comes from the work of John Stuart Mill, for whom the diffusion of property and intelligence and the power of cooperation were the most significant markers of a civilized state. In this context, reading, newspapers, and, more generally, 'the increase of the facilities of human intercourse', represented not only instruments for the physical and mental cultivation of the 'masses', but also vehicles through which to mobilize and homogenize public opinion for the purposes of creating a democratic government. As Mill put it,

> The newspaper is the telegraph which carries the signal throughout the country, and the flag round which it rallies. Hundreds of newspapers speaking in the same voice at once, and the rapidity of communication afforded by improved means of locomotion, were what enabled the whole country to combine in that simultaneous energetic demonstration of determined will which carried the Reform Act [of 1832]. Both these facilities are on the increase, every one may see how rapidly; and they will enable the people on all decisive occasions to form a collective will, and render that collective will irresistible.[124]

Mill understood communication as a top-to-bottom project, in which the lower classes (workers) and 'uncivilized societies' (like India) were reformed, both physically and morally, through training and education.[125] The newspaper and the telegraph were crucial to his project: they enabled people to communicate more rapidly and more effectively with each other, while also educating them and helping to build a consensus of opinion.

Seen against this background, it is hardly surprising that the telegraph—and other technologies like the railways—should have been widely regarded as vehicles for 'universal brotherhood' and, later on, nation-building. Indeed, Mill's ideas were shared by many of his contemporaries and found expression in numerous other outlets. Lord Dalhousie, for example, referred to the telegraph as one of the 'three great engines of social improvement', along with railways and a uniform postal system.[126]

In addition to being a rapid means of communication, the telegraph also became particularly amenable to the imperial project through its association with electricity, as a member of the 'highly scientific galvanic family'. Accounts of life in nineteenth-century India often emphasized the fact that this was a land ridden with disease and that climate impacted not only on the physical and mental well-being of its inhabitants, but also on the moral fabric of the society.

With the possible exception of a number of designated 'martial races', the inhabitants of India were often described as suffering from an 'innate apathy and inertness'.[127] Europeans themselves degenerated under the influence of India's climate. Mark Harrison has pointed out how eighteenth-century 'guarded optimism' about the possibility of European acclimatization faded away in the first decades of the next century, as the emerging field of statistics began to lend scientific currency to such opinions.[128] In this context, science and technology offered a ray of hope, both for Indians and Europeans. According to some contemporary commentators, what was needed was a surgical procedure, 'a great and scientific operation which was to arouse all India from its torpor, and impart to the lethargic fluid flowing in its veins vital speed and activity'.[129]

Medical metaphors were common in the nineteenth-century iconography of electricity. As Graeme Gooday has also pointed out, much like steam before it, electricity was often represented in Victorian Britain and the United States as an 'autonomous agent of social transformation'.[130] As an electrical device par excellence, the telegraph became one of the 'surgical instruments' which was going to effect the desired transformation in the Indian character. It was British benevolence that had brought such technologies to India, as one Victorian periodical suggested: 'Dr. O'Shaughnessy leads the van with the lightning wires of the electric telegraph, whilst railroads will grow and increase yearly, and steamers ply rapidly up and down the Ganges canal.'[131] But, the writer went on to claim, the onus of the choice for the 'modern' was on the Indians themselves: 'So much for the effect of electricity upon the Indian community. They have been aroused, and they will further begin to feel that unless they keep pace with the growing improvements around them, they may make up their minds to starve and die in abject poverty.'[132]

As John Tomlinson has argued, the ideology of progress 'forces a choice for the modern upon us—a choice that cannot be refused without seeming irrational or deliberately obtuse'.[133] This was all the more so with a technology such as the telegraph which liberated people not only of effort, but also of time. This utilitarian dimension of telegraphy, as Tomlinson reminds us, was one of the factors which, together with the 'quasi-moral' association between dynamism and 'visions of human good', made the ideological link between speed and progress possible.

Memorializing the Telegraph

The idea that technology—more specifically, improved means of communication—would mediate a consensus of opinion between the colonizers and the colonized was severely put to trial during the Mutiny of 1857, an event in the history of colonial South Asia with which the telegraph is most often associated. As Rudrangshu Mukherjee and others have shown, controlling the routes and means of communication during the Mutiny was an important preoccupation not only for the British, but also for the mutineers. Thus, the Grand Trunk Road 'became the site for a battle to keep the *dak* running', while Khan Bahadur Khan instructed the rebels to intercept the communications of the British and 'cut up their daks and posts'. Technologies of communication like the telegraph also became targets of violence through the 'logic of association' with British rule.[134]

The role of the telegraph in suppressing the unrest has been the subject of much debate, with some scholars echoing the words of Robert Montgomery, former lieutenant governor of the Punjab, who famously proclaimed that 'The Electric Telegraph has saved India,' and others insisting that 'The telegraph did not save India, rather India saved the telegraph and the Uprisings of 1857 saved the telegraph in India.'[135] In this final section, I do not wish to revive that familiar debate, but rather to use it to demonstrate how technology was enlisted to support the imperial project in South Asia. The discussion focuses on a key episode of the Mutiny, namely the transmission, on 11 May 1857, of the famous 'fateful message' to Ambala that alerted the authorities in the Punjab about the revolt in Delhi.

As one of the most disruptive events of British colonial rule in South Asia, the Mutiny provided ample opportunities for myth-making. Indeed, the nineteenth century alone saw the publication of an impressive number of accounts in which reality and fiction were woven together to create heroic narratives of British bravery and determination.[136] One of the most familiar examples was that of the signaller at the Delhi Telegraph Office allegedly killed while sending one last telegram to Ambala. The earliest example of this type of account I was able to identify comes from F. H. Cooper's *Handbook for Delhi* (1865), which contains the following passage: 'The young assistant at the telegraph office who had taken Mr. Todd's place and whose last message electrified and warned the Punjab, was cut down with his hand on the signalling apparatus.'[137] From here, the episode seems to have taken on a life of its own, travelling through the available oral and print media channels. For example, Flora Annie Steel's late nineteenth-century work *On the Face of the Waters* contains a strikingly similar scene in which a 'young telegraph clerk' is murdered by 'some ruffians [who] rushed in and sabred him with his hands still on the levers'.[138]

The scene, as we now know, was partly real and partly fictitious: of the three signallers, only Charles Todd was killed during the Mutiny. Significantly, however, he was not murdered in the telegraph office, but while crossing the Yamuna River in an attempt to restore communication with Meerut. The other two, William Brendish and J. W. Pilkington, passed away in 1867 and 1907 respectively.[139]

Less known, perhaps, are a number of late nineteenth- and early twentieth-century attempts to correct this widespread myth of the heroic telegraphist, one of which originated with P. V. Luke, deputy director general of Indian Telegraphs. A man with extensive experience in the Indian subcontinent, Luke had joined the Telegraph Department in 1868 and served as a telegraph officer with the Peshawar Field Force (1878) and Northern Afghanistan Field Force (1878–9) before being appointed as head of the telegraph establishment.[140] A keen writer and photographer, he was the author of a suggestively titled essay, 'How the Electric Telegraph Saved India' (1897), in which he dismissed the accounts of murder in the Delhi Telegraph Office as 'touching and exciting … but unfortunately not quite true, as the signaller in question [William Brendish] is still alive, and able to recollect what really did happen, which, stirring enough in all conscience, lacked the final tragedy of the popular version'.[141]

Luke's account, based on first-hand evidence provided by Brendish himself, illuminates some of the everyday practices which surrounded the use of telegraphy in mid-nineteenth-century India. Writing about the role of the telegraph in the Indian Mutiny, Lahiri Choudhury has convincingly argued that in 1857 the telegraph network was beset with 'severe structural and spatial flaws', such as faulty insulation, the absence of duplex lines, and the actual choice of telegraphic routes.[142] Luke's account reinforces this position, suggesting that communication was also impeded by more mundane circumstances, like the rule of the Indian Telegraph Department to close all telegraph offices on Sundays between 9 a.m. and 4 p.m. It was this regulation, Luke argued, together with British confidence in their position in India, which was responsible for delaying the communication of news about the outbreak to Delhi:

> The exaggerated gossip which passed over the telegraph-wire only emphasizes the indifference engendered by confidence in the large force of European soldiers stationed at Meerut, or by ignorance of the widespread feeling of discontent that prevailed in the Native army, and makes it the more extraordinary that, notwithstanding the excitement and possible danger, the telegraph-offices both at Delhi and Meerut were closed as usual at nine o'clock. One would have thought that, considering the grave condition of affairs, the authorities at Meerut and Delhi would have desired to keep in touch with each other; but such was not the case, and the same spirit which actuated those who attended morning church at Meerut, or went for their afternoon drive as usual, led to the customary Sunday routine being carried out, and consequently to nothing being known that day in Delhi of the terrible events at Meerut. For when the Delhi office was opened in due course at four o'clock in the afternoon, communication with Meerut was found to be interrupted. As a matter of fact, the telegraph-wire was cut by the mutineers near Meerut some time in the afternoon, though of course this was not known at Delhi.[143]

According to Luke, on 10 May 1857 Brendish and Pilkington went across the Yamuna to check the telegraphic connection with Meerut and their own office in Delhi. In this way, they established that no messages could be sent to the former location, while the latter section was still in working order. The next morning, Charles Todd travelled across the river in an attempt to restore communication and disappeared shortly thereafter.[144] Brendish and Pilkington eventually found out about the mutineers' attack on Delhi from the telegraph messenger boys regularly posted by the *Delhi Gazette* at the telegraph office. They passed this information on to Ambala *unofficially*, as part of the telegraph 'chatter' in which signallers often engaged as a pastime. Brendish's last message 'and now I'm off', often represented as his last words before being murdered, were sent to indicate that he and Pilkington were leaving the office and taking refuge at Flagstaff Tower, together with Todd's wife and infant child.[145]

It was only after reaching Flagstaff that a military officer came and handed Pilkington an official telegram, asking him to return to the telegraph office with an escort of sepoys. Brendish believed that Pilkington sent the official telegram, which contained details about the number of mutineers, the refusal of the 54th Native Infantry to defend Delhi against them, and the losses on the European side. He also claimed that officials failed to act promptly due to their unshaken belief in the arrival of the British troops from Meerut. For his part, Luke interpreted this as a direct outcome of the absence of a centralized system of administration and the fact that in 1857 the telegraph was a relatively new technology in India.[146] According to his interpretation, lack of familiarity with the new technology was compounded by the failure to appreciate the gravity of the situation. The next day, both Brendish and Pilkington succeeded in making their way to Ambala, where they were received with much surprise by fellow operators who thought they had been all killed. As Luke concludes,

> It appears that late in the afternoon of the 11th there were movements on the needle at Umballa as if someone at Delhi was trying to signal, but as no answer came to the usual question, ('What is your name?') they suspected that it was somebody unfamiliar with the apparatus, and that all the staff had been murdered. The telegraph-office at Delhi shared the fate of most other European houses and was burned, but it is not known how long after the despatch of the last message which Pilkington was sent back to signal.[147]

We can assume that rumours about the Mutiny spread among the operators of the Telegraph Department in the same manner as other information spread, as telegraphic 'chatter'.[148] Some of these stories became part of a colonial rhetoric of bravery and sacrifice, a perfect illustration of the way in which history was selectively appropriated for imperial purposes. At the beginning of the twentieth century, an obelisk was erected to commemorate the services of the staff of the Telegraph Department during the Indian Mutiny. The Mutiny Telegraph Memorial (see Illustration 2.1), as it was known, was unveiled on 19 April 1902 in the presence of Lord Curzon and other officials, on the exact site from where Brendish, Pilkington, and Todd were believed to have sent the message to Ambala warning the Punjab government of the rebellion.[149]

Against the background of an increasing nationalist agitation in India, the founders of the Telegraph Memorial negotiated Britain's imperial history by glorifying the deeds of the three telegraph operators. The inscription on the rear of the monument mentions that Pilkington 'returned to Telegraph Office from Flag Staff Tower, and signalled despatch to Commander-in-Chief, containing full report

Illustration 2.1 Delhi Telegraph Memorial, 2010
Source: Author's collection.

of Mutiny'.[150] One mystery remains, however. The monument mentions—incorrectly, if we are to believe Brendish's testimony—that Pilkington was taken prisoner and managed to escape.

Remarkably, Brendish was among those present at the unveiling of the Mutiny Telegraph Memorial. Lord Curzon bestowed upon 'the retired veteran' the Victorian Order, 'in public recognition of deeds in which he bore a share when a boy'.[151] In his speech, Curzon commended the bravery of Delhi's telegraph staff and advocated a vision of India's past in which violent events, such as the Mutiny, were only 'stepping-stones' towards a 'better understanding' and 'truer union' of colonizers and colonized in India:

> I think that this view becomes even more important and true when we remember that, in many of these cases, it was not the white men on one side and the Indians on the other. In the Mutiny, as is well known, there was no such general division. In the Telegraph Department, as elsewhere, there were many of the Native clerks who stood loyally to their service and their masters in those terrible days.... Similarly, in the present case, I learn that among the subscribers to this memorial have been more than 300 Natives of India, at present connected with the Telegraph Department. This shows that their views are identical with those which I have expressed, and that they are as proud of the deeds of the Delhi European Telegraphic Staff of May 1857 as any Europeans can be. Should the occasion ever arise, I doubt not that many of them, at the risk of life, would be ready to follow the same example.[152]

The individual actors of this drama, temporarily rescued from oblivion by the unveiling of the monument, vanished again in the highly politicized maze of memory and forgetting. But some of the myths associated with the Indian Mutiny proved enduring.[153] Now and then, efforts were made to set the record straight, at least as far as the fate of the three signallers at the Delhi Telegraph Office was concerned. In 1922, a letter from India signed by F. B. Brendish, son of William Brendish, arrived at the office of the *Children's Newspaper*, a highly popular weekly established in Britain in 1919. Its purported aim was to correct a mistake which had crept into the *Children's Encyclopedia* regarding the death at Ambala of his father and his fellow signaller Pilkington. The letter told of the former's service with the Telegraph Department until his retirement in 1897, of his participation in the unveiling of the Telegraph Memorial, and his death in 1907, survived by his wife.[154]

The Telegraph Memorial's upright form continues to pierce the Delhi sky, its existence all but forgotten by the locals themselves. Nobody seems to remember its significance, nor, indeed, its name; its inscription, hardly legible due to the passing of time is, like the monument itself, at best anachronistic. The narrative of history it embodies has since been replaced with another, which requires different images and symbols. As the account of the Mutiny immortalized at Gandhi Smriti in Delhi demonstrates, nationalist narratives, just like imperial ones before them, can be equally selective in their interpretations and representations of history.

***

This chapter has examined the wide range of practices and discourses associated with the introduction and use of electric telegraphy in nineteenth-century India. In the process, it has also engaged with some of the meta-narratives which have surrounded this technology of communication and questioned their usefulness as analytical tools for examining the history of telegraphy.

Rather than taking for granted the idea that telegraphy 'annihilated time and space' or 'saved' India for the British in 1857, my aim was to rethink the ways in which we evaluate the history of telegraphy by pondering what fuelled such narratives and what is marginalized, ignored, or erased from the historical record when we privilege the frameworks of interpretation they suggest. Being sensitive to the wide variety of discourses, contexts, and practices associated with electric telegraphy in colonial India enables us to achieve a better balance between the macro and micro levels of the history of technology. To this end, the chapter has examined simultaneously the practices and discourses of telegraphy across a variety of socio-economic and political contexts, ranging from imperial administration to the less visible and hitherto little-explored domains of 'work, lived practice, and everyday experience' and their role 'in shaping visions of modernity'.[155]

In pursuing this line of investigation, my intention is not to deny the role of telegraphy as an instrument of imperial rule—indeed, Chapter 4 engages with this topic in detail—but to contextualize it in relation to other sites of use and discourses of telegraphy. Furthermore, I want to expose the tension, identified by Manu Goswami in her discussion of Indian railways, between the 'simultaneous homogenization and differentiation of social relations' promoted by the use of telegraphy and to consider how this was reflected in contemporary discourses and practices of technology.[156] At its heart, this is a question about evaluating the role of technology as an instrument of (colonial) modernity in the nineteenth century. I have tried to understand how this ambivalence about technology was connected to the socio-economic and political conditions which shaped technology use as well as the social realities of individual actors. It is a topic I continue to explore in the next chapter, this time with a focus on journalism and news reporting.

Notes

1. Jean de Pontevès-Sabran, *L'Inde à fond de train* (Paris: Alphonse Lemerre, 1887), p. 193; my translation. Pontevès-Sabran (1851–1912) was a French nobleman and military officer who travelled through India and Ceylon with a friend in 1884–5. This humorous episode describes their attempt to contact the police authorities by telegraph after discovering that their servants had absconded with their luggage.
2. Dionysius Lardner, *The Electric Telegraph Popularized* (London: Walton and Maberly, 1855), p. 118.
3. Iwan R. Morus, '"The Nervous System of Britain": Space, Time and the Electric Telegraph in the Victorian Age', *British Journal for the History of Science* 33, no. 4 (2000): 455–75, at 455.
4. The expression is Daniel R. Headrick's. See his work, *The Tools of Empire: Technology and European Imperialism in the Nineteenth Century* (New York: Oxford University Press, 1981).
5. 'The Three Great Indian Physicians; or, Railways, Canals, and Telegraphs', *Leisure Hour*, 147 (1854): 663–6.
6. D. K. Lahiri Choudhury, *Telegraphic Imperialism: Crisis and Panic in the Indian Empire, c. 1830* (Basingstoke: Palgrave Macmillan, 2010).
7. *Administration Report of the Telegraph Department for the Years 1862–6*, V/24/4284, pp. 7, 13, 16, IOR.
8. *Administration Report of the Telegraph Department for the Year 1890–1*, V/24/4287, p. 25, IOR.
9. 'Indo denshin' [The Indian telegraph], *Denshin kyōkai kaishi*, 5 (1897), pp. 44–5. Translations from the Japanese are my own.
10. *Times of India*, 20 September 1861.
11. The main problem was how to balance the charge and discharge of the line in order to ensure a constant supply of electric current and how to improve receiving instruments. Louis Schwendler, 'On the General Theory of Duplex Telegraphy', *Journal of the Asiatic Society of Bengal* 43 (1874): 1–21, at 4. Duplex telegraphy was first patented in the United States in 1872 by Joseph Stearns. Two years later, Thomas A. Edison and George B. Prescott designed the 'double duplex', also known as the quadruplex. See Charles Thom and W. H. Jones, *Telegraphic Connections: Embracing Recent Methods in Quadruplex Telegraphy* (New York: D. van Nostrand Company, 1892), p. 19; also Roland Wenzlhuemer, *Connecting the Nineteenth-Century World: The Telegraph and Globalization* (Cambridge: Cambridge University Press, 2012), p. 76.

12. *Administration Report of the Telegraph Department for the Year 1879–80*, V/24/4286, p. 7, IOR; *Administration Report of the Telegraph Department for the Year 1900–1*, V/24/4288, p. 21, IOR.
13. *Administration Report of the Telegraph Department for the Year 1900–1*, V/24/4288, p. 13, IOR; F. J. Goldsmith, *Telegraph and Travel: A Narrative of the Formation and Development of Telegraphic Communication between England and India, etc.* (London: Macmillan, 1874), p. 121.
14. According to John Tully's estimate, by the end of the nineteenth century, 88 million trees had been cut to insulate telegraph cables worldwide. John Tully, 'A Victorian Ecological Disaster: Imperialism, the Telegraph, and Gutta-Percha', *Journal of World History* 20, no. 4 (2009): 559–79, at 575.
15. 'The Exhaustion of Gutta-Percha', *Engineer*, 86 (1898), p. 646; 'Gutta-Percha Manufactures', *Manufacturer and Builder*, 2 (1870): 174–5.
16. Richard B. Evans, *In Defence of History* (London: Granta Books, 1997), p. 109.
17. This is particularly relevant in the context of ongoing debates about the 'agency' of technology. Here, I draw on John Tomlinson's work, who argues that we need to pay attention to the various contexts in which technology was used and 'the lived experiences of ordinary people in their everyday interactions with technologies'. John Tomlinson, *The Culture of Speed: The Coming of Immediacy* (London: Sage Publications, 2007), pp. 11–12.
18. Partha Chatterjee, 'Our Modernity', SEPHIS/CODESRIA Lecture, 1997, p. 10, available at: http://ccs.ukzn.ac.za/files/partha1.pdf (accessed 14 March 2016). The topic has remained relevant, as demonstrated by contemporary debates about the democratizing potential of the internet, its contribution to alleviating poverty, empowering individuals, and so on. See, for example, Manuel Castells, *Communication Power* (Oxford: Oxford University Press, 2009); Indrajit Banerjee (ed.), *The Internet and Governance in Asia: A Critical Reader* (Singapore: Asian Media Information and Communication Centre, 2007).
19. In nineteenth-century Britain, some medical practitioners and members of the public considered railway travelling detrimental to 'persons of a nervous temperament' and claimed that it could lead to 'paralytic seizures' and 'railway spine'. Many telegraphists, especially those who worked with Morse instruments, were also reported to suffer from a type of repetitive strain injury known as 'telegraphists' cramp'. In Britain, this condition was recognized as compensable under the Workmen's Compensation Act, 1908. See H. W. Porter, 'On the Influence of Railway Travelling on Public Health', *Assurance Magazine, and Journal of the Institute of Actuaries*, 11 (1863): 152–71, at 156–7; R. Harrington, 'The Railway Accident: Trains, Trauma, and Technological Crises in

Nineteenth-Century Britain', in *Traumatic Pasts: History, Psychiatry and Trauma in the Modern Age, 1870–1930*, edited by M. Micale and P. Lerner (Cambridge: Cambridge University Press, 2001); H. T. Thompson and J. Sinclair, 'Telegraphists' Cramp', *Lancet* 179 (1912): 888–90.

20. Line riders restored communication in the event of an interruption to the line.
21. *Administration Report of the Telegraph Department for the Years 1862–6*, V/24/4284, p. 47, IOR.
22. *Administration Report of the Telegraph Department for the Years 1862–6*, V/24/4284, p. 3, IOR.
23. Paul Fletcher, 'The Uses and Limitations of Telegrams in Official Correspondence between Ceylon's Governor General and the Secretary of State for the Colonies, circa 1870–1900', *Historical Social Research* 35, no. 1 (2010): 90–107.
24. Sayagi Rao Gaekwar, 'My Ways and Days in Europe and India', *Nineteenth Century and After* 49, no. 288 (1901): 215–25, at 221–2.
25. Duke of Argyll to the Governor General of India, 20 January 1869, Home Department, Public Branch A, 6 March 1869, No. 131, NAI.
26. *Administration Reports of the Indian Telegraph Department*, various years between 1867 and 1877, V/24/4284, IOR.
27. *Bombay Times and Journal of Commerce*, 4 August 1855.
28. *Administration Report of the Telegraph Department for the Year 1873–4*, V/24/4284, p. 2, IOR.
29. Verbose and unnecessary telegrams, 25 May 1891 and 29 May 1891, L/PWD/7/1163, File 458 I.E., IOR.
30. O. T. Burne to R. Lethbridge, 15 November 1878, Lethbridge Papers, MSS.EUR B 182, IOR.
31. For his job in the Meteorological Department, Ruchi Ram Sahni was 'telegraphically asked to see Mr. A. S. Hill, Professor of Physics at Central Muir College, Allahabad'. N. K. Sehgal and S. Mahanti (eds), *Memoirs of Ruchi Ram Sahni, Pioneer of Science Popularisation in Punjab* (New Delhi: Vigyan Prasar, 1994), pp. 4–5.
32. 'Communication by Telegraph', *Madras Quarterly Journal of Medical Science*, 4 (1862), p. 218.
33. Henry W. Norman and Mrs Keith Young (eds), *Delhi 1857: The Siege, Assault, and Capture as Given in the Diary and Correspondence of the Late Colonel Keith Young* (London and Edinburgh: W. & R. Chambers, 1902), pp. 6–7. See also Rosie Llewellyn-Jones, *The Great Uprisings in India, 1857–58: Untold Stories, Indian and British* (Woodbridge: Boydell Press, 2007), pp. 34–5.
34. Abstract translation of a petition from the wife of Unwur Allee, Moonshee, Post Office, Meerut, 6 October 1858, India Telegraph Consultations, P/189/10, IOR.

35. H. V. Walton to H. B. Harrington, 18 January 1859, India Telegraph Consultations, P/189/10, IOR.
36. Chitra Joshi, 'Dak Roads, Dak Runners, and the Reordering of Communication Networks', *International Review of Social History* 57, no. 3 (2012): 169–89, at 174.
37. D. E. Wacha, *Shells from the Sands of Bombay: Being My Recollections and Reminiscences, 1860–1875* (Bombay: Bombay Chronicle Press, 1920), p. 233.
38. Wacha, *Shells from the Sands of Bombay*, pp. 230–2.
39. Shevantibai M. Nikambe, *Ratanbai: A Sketch of a Bombay High Caste Hindu Young Wife* (London: Marshall Brothers, 1895), p. 32.
40. Nikambe, *Ratanbai*, p. vi.
41. Nikambe, *Ratanbai*, p. 32. For an analysis of *Ratanbai*, see M. R. Paranjape, *Making India: Colonialism, National Culture, and the Afterlife of Indian English Authority* (Dordrecht: Springer, 2013), pp. 116–20.
42. Mrs Robert Moss King, *The Diary of a Civilian's Wife in India, 1877–1882*, vol. 1 (London: Bentley and Son, 1884), pp. 29–30.
43. Bipin Chandra Pal, *Memories of My Life and Times*, 2 vols (Calcutta: Bipinchandra Pal Institute, 1973), p. 325.
44. Pal, *Memories of My Life and Times*, p. 549.
45. Mrs James P. Harris, *A Lady's Diary of the Siege of Lucknow, Written for the Perusal of Friends at Home* (London: John Murray, 1858), pp. 190, 203.
46. Norman and Young, *Delhi 1857*, p. 300.
47. S. H. Bilgrami, *A Memoir of Sir Salar Jung* (Bombay: Times of India Steam Press, 1883), p. 131.
48. Her Majesty's Jubilee; Re telegrams of congratulation from authorities and persons in India, 8 Mar 1887, L/PJ/6/198, File 557, IOR.
49. *Jami-ul-Ulum*, 14 April 1897, *Native Newspaper Reports* (henceforth *NNR*), North-Western Provinces & Oudh, No. 16 of 1897, pp. 276–7.
50. 'Tales of the Telegraph', *Chambers's Journal of Popular Literature, Science and Arts*, 843 (1880): 126–8; 'Curiosities of the Wire', *Times of India*, 18 October 1876. The latter article was originally published in *Chambers's Journal*.
51. 'Freaks of the Telegraph', *Blackwood's Edinburgh Magazine*, 129 (1881), p. 468.
52. See, for example, Appendix F in *Report of the Committee of the Bengal Chamber of Commerce from 1 May 1861 to 31 October 1861*.
53. Prabhu P. Mohapatra, '"Following Custom"? Representations of Community among Indian Immigrant Labour in the West Indies, 1880–1920', *International Review of Social History* 51, supplement S14 (2006): 173–202.
54. King, *The Diary of a Civilian's Wife*, p. 41. On the role of rumours in the Indian Mutiny, see Rudrangshu Mukherjee, *Awadh in Revolt, 1857–1858* (New Delhi: Permanent Black, 2001), pp. 72–3.

55. King, *The Diary of a Civilian's Wife*, pp. 41–2.
56. King, *The Diary of a Civilian's Wife*, p. 42.
57. Signum Fero, 'Semaphoric Telegraph', *Calcutta Journal, or Political, Commercial and Literary Gazette*, 1 March 1821, p. 185; 'Pigeons and Telegraphs', *Calcutta Journal of Politics and General Literature*, 1 October 1822, p. 414; 'Native Papers', *Calcutta Journal of Politics and General Literature*, 14 May 1822, p. 196.
58. Savithri Preetha Nair, '"Bungallee House Set on Fire by Galvanism": Natural and Experimental Philosophy as Public Science in a Colonial Metropolis (1794–1806)', in *The Circulation of Knowledge between Britain, India and China: The Early-Modern World to the Twentieth Century*, edited by B. Lightman, G. McOuat, and L. Stewart (Leiden: Brill, 2013), p. 46.
59. Macdonald's objection was that the 'imperfect … state' of knowledge in the field of telegraphy did not really warrant the use of the term 'science'. See John Macdonald, *A Treatise Explanatory of a New System of Naval, Military and Political Telegraphic Communication* (London: T. Egerton's Military Library, 1817), p. 1.
60. Nair, 'Bungallee House Set on Fire', p. 51.
61. 'Some New Uses of Electricity', *Manufacturer and Builder* 9 (1877), p. 159.
62. Michael la Beaume, *On Galvanism, with Observations on Its Chymical Properties and Medical Efficacy in Chronic Diseases* (London: Highley, 1826), p. 199.
63. W. L. M'Gregor, *The History of the Sikhs,* vol. 1 (London: James Meaden, 1846), p. 275. The galvanic current was produced in a Leiden jar as a result of a chemical reaction.
64. M'Gregor, *The History of the Sikhs*, pp. 275–6, italics original. M'Gregor also mentions that Ranjit Singh appeared sceptical about the possibility of harnessing 'the wonderful rapidity of electricity' to 'communicate … in an instant of time, with the most distant parts of the kingdom'.
65. Chittabrata Palit, *Scientific Bengal: Science Education, Technology, Medicine and Environment* (Delhi: Kalpaz Publications, 2006), pp. 77–83.
66. 'Scientific: Recent Wonders of Invention', *Bombay Times and Journal of Commerce*, 1 December 1841.
67. *Englishman*, 28 June and 2 July 1866.
68. Charles C. Adley, *The Story of the Telegraph in India* (London: E. & F. N. Spon, 1866), pp. v–vi.
69. Shiju Sam Varughese, 'Media and Science in Disaster Contexts: Deliberations on Earthquakes and in the Regional Press in Kerala', *Spontaneous Generations: A Journal for the History and Philosophy of Science* 5, no. 1 (2011): 36–43, at 40.

70. Hospes, 'Electric Telegraphs', *Bombay Times and Journal of Commerce*, 27 August 1845. Other interesting examples include articles on the electromagnetic printing telegraph (*Bombay Times and Journal of Commerce*, 6 October 1841) and on electricity and magnetism (*Bombay Times and Journal of Commerce*, 8 July 1840).
71. 'An Important Telegraphic Discovery', *Times of India*, 22 January 1887; 'An Important Discovery in Telegraphy', *Straits Times*, 21 February 1887.
72. W. Haworth, 'Application of Galvanism to Horticulture', *Bombay Times and Journal of Commerce*, 2 July 1845.
73. See, for example, *Times of India*, 6 January 1853, for the 'portable hydro-electric chain'; *Times of India*, 22 March 1871, for the 'galvanic chain-bends, belts, and pocket-batteries'; *Times of India*, 17 November 1891, for the 'world-famed galvanic belts'.
74. Robert K. Waits, 'Gustave Flaubert, Charles Dickens, and Isaac Pulvermacher's "Magic Band"', in *Literature, Neurology, and Neuroscience: Historical and Literary Connections*, edited by A. Stiles, S. Finger, and F. Boller (Amsterdam: Elsevier, 2013).
75. James Stark, '"Recharge My Exhausted Batteries": Overbeck's Rejuvenator, Patenting, and Public Medical Consumers', *Medical History* 58, no. 4 (2014): 498–518. For an elaborate ad of the rejuvenator, including Overbeck's portrait, see *Times of India*, 23 February 1929.
76. See, for example, the *Times of India*, 9 May, 19 June, 27 July, and 15 August 1866. The successful laying of the cable was reported on 10 August 1866, through the publication of a Reuter telegram dated London, 27 July [1866]: 'The *Great Eastern* has arrived safely at Trinity Bay, having successfully laid the new Atlantic Cable.' This telegram was followed by a longer report by overland mail which was published in the issue of 25 August 1866. The *Madras Times* also announced the completion of the Atlantic cable, but its telegraphic news was five days older than that of the *Times of India*.
77. John Pender, described by Winseck and Pike as 'the world's most prominent cable baron', was at the time chairman of the British Indian Submarine Telegraph Company, one of the ventures established for the purpose of linking Britain with India by submarine cable. See Dwayne R. Winseck and Robert M. Pike, *Communication and Empire: Media, Markets, and Globalization, 1860–1930* (Durham and London: Duke University Press, 2007), pp. 21–30.
78. *Daily Telegraph*, 24 June 1870, quoted in *Souvenir of the Inaugural Fete [held at the House of Mr. John Pender] in Commemoration of the Opening of Direct Submarine Telegraph with India, June 23rd 1870* (London, 1870), pp. 46–50.
79. *Souvenir of the Inaugural Fete*, pp. 43–64.
80. *Madras Times*, 2 July 1870.

81. Thomas R. Metcalf, *Ideologies of the Raj* (Cambridge: Cambridge University Press, 1995), pp. 51, 195.
82. *Souvenir of the Inaugural Fete*, pp. 50–2.
83. *Souvenir of the Inaugural Fete*, pp. 50–2, italics original.
84. As Dhruv Raina has shown in his bibliometric survey of the *Indian Journal of History of Science*, this trend continued well into the twentieth century, when only 5 per cent of the articles published between 1966 and 1994 were in the field of technology. Dhruv Raina, *Images and Contexts: The Historiography of Science and Modernity in India* (New Delhi: Oxford University Press, 2003), pp. 109–15.
85. *Amrita Bazar Patrika*, 21 March 1872.
86. Indira Viswanathan Peterson, 'The Schools of Serfoji II of Tanjore: Education and Princely Modernity in Early Nineteenth-Century India', in *Trans-colonial Modernities in South Asia*, edited by M. S. Dodson and B. A. Hatcher (Abingdon: Routledge, 2012), see pp. 24, 27.
87. Ulrike Stark, 'Knowledge in Context: Raja Shivaprasad as Hybrid Intellectual and People's Educator', in *Trans-colonial Modernities in South Asia* (Abingdon: Routledge, 2012), p. 79.
88. Stark, 'Knowledge in Context', p. 79.
89. *Bombay Times and Journal of Commerce*, 19 January and 2 February 1839.
90. B. K. Sen, *Growth of Scientific Periodicals in India (1788–1900)* (New Delhi: Indian National Science Academy, 2002), pp. 34–5, 54. Arun Kumar, 'Thomason College of Engineering, Roorkee, 1847–1947', in *History of Science, Philosophy, and Culture in Indian Civilisation*, vol. 15, part 4: *Science and Modern India: An Institutional History, c. 1784–1947*, edited by D. P. Chattopadhyaya (New Delhi: Centre for Studies in Civilizations, 2011). For a history of science education in India see Kumar, *Science and the Raj*, especially pp. 113–50.
91. *Amrita Bazar Patrika*, 21 March 1872.
92. For an overview of scientific periodicals in India, see B. K. Sen's excellent *Growth of Scientific Periodicals in India*, especially pp. 17–18, 62, 88.
93. Nor was prose, as Indira Viswanathan Peterson has pointed out in her discussion of Serfoji II, for whom poetry was the 'preferred medium' of learning, even when that learning pertained to science. Peterson, 'The Schools of Serfoji II of Tanjore', p. 34.
94. K. Sajan Lal, 'The Omdat-ul-Akhbar of Bareilly', in *Indian Historical Records Commission: Proceedings and Meetings*, 24th Session (Jaipur: 1948), p. 103.
95. The periodicals were *Pasvavali* (1822), published by the Calcutta School Book Society, *Vijnan Sebadhi* (1832), and *Vijnan Sar Sagraha* (1833), all in Bengali. Sen, *Growth of Scientific Periodicals in India*, pp. 31–2.

96. Lahiri Choudhury, *Telegraphic Imperialism*, p. 26; A. Ghosh, 'Some Eminent Indian Pioneers in the Field of Technology', *Indian Journal of History of Science* 29, no. 1 (1994): 63–75, at 66; K. Maitra, *The Electric Telegraph or The Telegraph Office Assistant's Manual* (Serampore: Tomohur Press, 1855). Rev. James Long also mentions one book on the 'electric telegraph' as having been published in the Bengali language in 1856, which is most likely Maitra's *Manual*. See Rev. James Long, 'Returns Relating to the Publications in the Bengali Language, in 1857, to which is added, a list of the Native Presses, with the Books Printed at Each, their Price and Character, with a Notice of the Past Condition and Future Prospects of the Vernacular Press of Bengal, and the Statistics of the Bombay and Madras Vernacular Presses', in *Selections from the Records of the Bengal Government*, no. 32 (Calcutta: General Printing Department, 1859), VII.
97. A. Grant, *Catalogue of Native Publications in the Bombay Presidency up to 31st December 1864* (Bombay: Education Society's Press, 1867), p. 200. The title of the book, as recorded by Grant, was *Vijlíná Tárvis´e* [About electric telegraphs]. See Maitra, *The Electric Telegraph*.
98. Grant, *Catalogue of Native Publications*, pp. 104, 200. As far as Hindustani is concerned, two books on electricity also deserve notice: Anwar Ali, *A Dialogue between a Master and His Pupil on Electricity* (1872) and *A Treatise on Electricity* (1876), both mentioned in J. F. Blumhardt, *Catalogue of Hindustani Printed Books in the Library of the British Museum* (London: Longmans and Co., 1889), p. 35.
99. V. Naregal, 'Vernacular Culture and Political Formation in Western India', in *Print Areas: Book History in India*, edited by A. Gupta and S. Chakravorty (New Delhi: Permanent Black, 2004), p. 153; D. Bhattacharya, R. Chakravarty, and R. D. Roy, 'A Survey of Bengali Writings on Science and Technology, 1800–1950', *Indian Journal of History of Science* 24, no. 1 (1989): 8–66, at 12, 15.
100. For the upper ranks of the department, the proportion was considerably lower. See *Administration Report of the Telegraph Department for the Years 1862–6*, V/24/4284, p. 47 and Appendix D, IOR.
101. In Bengal, for example, the word used to describe such developments was *nabya* or 'new' (as opposed to the contemporary *adhunik* or 'modern'). See Chatterjee, 'Our Modernity', p. 4.
102. The Agaria were not alone in voicing their fascination with railways and telegraphs. Consider, for example, Govind Narayan's 1863 account of Bombay, *Mumbaiche Varnan*, in which he exclaims, referring to the telegraph: 'How can one not be stunned by the manner of the English people in running their Empire!' See M. Ranganathan (ed. and trans.), *Govind Narayan's Mumbai: An Urban Biography from 1863* (London: Anthem Press, 2009), p. 190. For a discussion of such responses in

a European and American context, see Wolfgang Schivelbusch, *The Railway Journey: Trains and Travel in the 19th Century* (New York: Urizen Books, 1979).

103. Verrier Elwin, *The Agaria* (London: Oxford University Press, 1942), p. 15.
104. Palit, *Scientific Bengal*, p. 79.
105. Wacha, *Shells from the Sands of Bombay*, pp. 433–4, 550–61. According to Wacha, Kyte was the first person to carry out a balloon flying demonstration in Bombay in the 1850s. He set off in a gas balloon at Byculla under the entranced gaze of hundreds of spectators and is believed to have landed near Thana or Uran.
106. J. H. McCormack, 'Domesticating Delphi: Emily Dickinson and the Electro-Magnetic Telegraph', *American Quarterly* 55, no. 4 (2003): 569–601, at 584.
107. 'Post-mortem Musings', *Blackwood's Magazine*, 48 (1840), p. 834.
108. Elwin, *The Agaria*, p. 16.
109. Bankim Chandra Chatterjee, *The Poison Tree: A Tale of Hindu Life in Bengal*, translated by Miriam S. Knight (London: T. Fisher Unwin, 1884), p. 244.
110. Utpal Datta, *Girish Chandra Ghosh: Makers of Indian Literature* (New Delhi: Sahitya Akademi, 1992), p. 9. Many years later, author Gita Mehta wrote in similarly evocative language that it was the British who brought 'those gods of progress, the machines of the Industrial Revolution, into India'. See Gita Mehta, *Snakes and Ladders: A View of Modern India* (London: Minerva, 1997), p. 52.
111. See, for example, the discussion of David Livingstone's ideas regarding Christian conversion in Africa, in M. Adas, *Machines as the Measure of Men: Science, Technology, and Ideologies of Western Dominance* (Ithaca and London: Cornell University Press, 1989), p. 206.
112. King, *The Diary of a Civilian's Wife*, pp. 148–9.
113. Thomas Steele, *An Eastern Love-Story: Kusa Jātakaya, a Buddhistic Legend* (London: Truebner & Co., 1871), p. 217.
114. *Jami-ul-Ulum*, 14 April 1897, *NNR*, North-Western Provinces & Oudh, No. 16 of 1897, pp. 276–7.
115. Marian Aguiar, *Tracking Modernity: India's Railway and the Culture of Mobility* (Minneapolis: University of Minnesota Press, 2011), p. 2.
116. On telegraphy and dematerialization, see Wenzlhuemer, *Connecting the Nineteenth-Century World*, pp. 30–7.
117. Marx argued that capital, in its drive to overcome 'every spatial barrier', was dependent on ever improved and cheaper means of communication and transport that would ensure the 'annihilation of space by time'. See Karl Marx, *Grundrisse: Foundations of the Critique of Political Economy* (London: Penguin Books, 1973), p. 459; Tomlinson, *The Culture of Speed*, p. 17.
118. Tomlinson, *The Culture of Speed*, p. 1.

119. Peter Simonson, Janice Peck, Robert T. Craig, and John P. Jackson, Jr., 'The History of Communication History', in *The Handbook of Communication History*, edited by Peter Simonson, Janice Peck, Robert T. Craig, and John P. Jackson, Jr. (New York: Routledge, 2013), p. 18.
120. Raymond Williams, *Keywords: A Vocabulary of Culture and Society* (London: Fontana Paperbacks, 1983), s.v. 'Communication', p. 72.
121. See, for example, A. Cotton, *Public Works in India: Their Importance* (London: W. H. Allen, 1854), pp. 277–88.
122. Charles Babbage, *On the Economy of Machinery and Manufactures* (London: Charles Knight, 1832), pp. 6, 188.
123. Karl Knies, *Der Telegraph als Verkehrsmittel* [The telegraph as a means of communication] (Tübingen: Laupp & Siebeck, 1857). I thank Dominik Schieder for help with the German translation. For a discussion of Knies' ideas about technologies of communication and news journalism, see Hanno Hardt, *Social Theories of the Press: Early German & American Perspectives* (Beverley Hills and London: Sage Publications, 1979), pp. 75–97.
124. John Stuart Mill, 'Civilization' (1836), in *Essays on Politics and Society*, vol. 18, edited by J. M. Robson (Toronto: Routledge & Kegan Paul/University of Toronto Press, 1977), pp. 124–5.
125. By positing a connection between communication media and forms of government, Mill also provided a research agenda for future historians of communication. The best illustration of this comes from Harold Innis's work on the spatial and temporal 'bias' of communication media. See Harold Innis, *The Bias of Communication* (Toronto: University of Toronto Press, 1951).
126. Adas, *Machines as the Measure of Men*, p. 225.
127. 'The Three Great Indian Physicians; or, Railways, Canals, and Telegraphs', *Leisure Hour*, 147 (1854), p. 663.
128. Harrison also points out that the statistics were unreliable. Mark Harrison, *Public Health in British India: Anglo-Indian Preventive Medicine, 1859–1914* (Cambridge: Cambridge University Press, 1994), pp. 59, 232.
129. 'The Three Great Indian Physicians', p. 664.
130. Graeme Gooday, *Domesticating Electricity: Technology, Uncertainty and Gender, 1880–1914* (London: Pickering & Chatto, 2008), p. 40.
131. 'The Three Great Indian Physicians', p. 666.
132. 'The Three Great Indian Physicians', p. 665.
133. Tomlinson, *The Culture of Speed*, pp. 21–2.
134. Mukherjee, *Awadh in Revolt*, pp. ix, xvi, 108–9. See also Harris, *A Lady's Diary of the Siege of Lucknow*, pp. 1–70, who anxiously monitors the state of communication by post and telegraph.

135. See, for example, Shridharani's claim that the electric telegraph played a 'strategic role' in the uprisings and his illustration of this claim with excerpts from the newspaper press. K. Shridharani, *Story of the Indian Telegraphs: A Century of Progress* (New Delhi: Government of India Press, 1953), p. 63; Lahiri Choudhury, *Telegraphic Imperialism*, p. 49.
136. But see Projit Bihari Mukharji's discussion of how other nationalist projects in Victorian Britain shaped the 'memorialization' of the Indian Mutiny. Projit Bihari Mukharji, 'Jessie's Dream at Lucknow: Popular Memorializations of Dissent, Ambiguity and Class in the Heart of Empire', *Studies in History* 24, no. 1 (2008): 77–113, at 84. For an analysis of historical accounts of the Mutiny produced in the Victorian era see Michael Adas, 'Twentieth-Century Approaches to the Indian Mutiny of 1857–58', *Journal of Asian History* 5, no. 1 (1971): 1–19.
137. F. H. Cooper, *The Handbook for Delhi* (Lahore: Lahore Chronicle Press, 1865), p. 137.
138. Flora Annie Steel, *On the Face of the Waters* (London: William Heinemann, 1897), p. 217.
139. See also Louis Tracy, *The Red Year: A Story of the Indian Mutiny* (New York: Edward J. Clode, 1907), p. 46. Tracy claims, on the authority of Holmes's *History of the Indian Mutiny* (1898), Cave-Browne's *The Punjab and Delhi in 1857* (1861), and *The Punjab Mutiny Report* (1881), that '[i]n the telegraph office a young signaller was sending a thrilling message to Umballa, Lahore and the north. "The sepoys have come in from Meerut," he announced with the slow tick of the earliest form of the apparatus. "They are burning everything. Mr. Todd is dead, and, we hear, several Europeans. We must shut up." That was his requiem. The startled operators at Umballa could obtain no further intelligence and the boy was slain at his post.' Other accounts of the Mutiny include Norman and Young, *Delhi 1857*; A. R. D. Mackenzie, *Mutiny Memoirs: Being Personal Reminiscences of the Great Sepoy Revolt of 1857* (Allahabad: Pioneer Press, 1892); Steel, *On the Face of the Waters*.
140. *Times of India*, 17 March 1897.
141. P. V. Luke, 'How the Electric Telegraph Saved India', *Macmillan's Magazine*, 76 (1897), p. 402.
142. Lahiri Choudhury, *Telegraphic Imperialism*, pp. 31–49.
143. Luke, 'How the Electric Telegraph Saved India', p. 403.
144. Luke, 'How the Electric Telegraph Saved India', pp. 403–4.
145. Luke, 'How the Electric Telegraph Saved India', pp. 404–5.
146. Luke, 'How the Electric Telegraph Saved India', p. 405.
147. Luke, 'How the Electric Telegraph Saved India', p. 406.
148. Signallers were sometimes suspected of spreading gossip. In the aftermath of an earthquake, one correspondent from Rawalpindi dismissed

as 'gup' a signaller's report that several houses had collapsed at Lahore and Attock (now in Pakistan). *Bombay Times and Journal of Commerce*, 12 July 1856.

149. *Administration Report of the Indian Telegraph Department for 1902–3*, V/24/4288, p. 5, IOR.
150. The inscription on the monument is written in a telegraphic style. The text, now barely legible, was reproduced in H. C. Fanshawe, *Delhi Past and Present* (London: John Murray, 1902), p. 331.
151. T. Raleigh, *Lord Curzon in India: Being a Selection from His Speeches as Viceroy and Governor-General of India, 1898–1905* (London: Macmillan, 1906), pp. 439, 442.
152. Raleigh, *Lord Curzon in India*, p. 441.
153. The New York–based *Telegraph Age* also published a version of Luke's story in 1902. Intriguingly, the date of the episode was given as 11 May 1866! See 'The Man Who Helped to Save the Punjab', *Telegraph Age*, 19 (1902), p. 231.
154. 'Telegraphist of the Mutiny', *Children's Newspaper*, 28 January 1922, p. 3.
155. Stark, 'Knowledge in Context', p. 69.
156. Manu Goswami, *Producing India: From Colonial Economy to National Space* (Chicago: University of Chicago Press, 2004), p. 104.

3 Journalists and Journalism in Nineteenth-Century India

> The fortunes of a newspaper in this country are often influenced by rare accidents. An exclusive telegraphic despatch, a well-timed leading article, the introduction and original treatment of a social subject in which the public takes a deep interest, may at any moment impart a wonderful momentum to circulation; and if those persons who had never seen the paper before, seek its pages for the sake of a special object of attraction, and find it possesses enduring claims to respect, they are likely to adopt it in perpetuity. One such accident was of amazing service to the *Englishman*.
>
> —J. H. Stocqueler, *The Memoirs of a Journalist* (1873)

In the previous chapter, we examined the discourses and practices that surrounded electric telegraphy in nineteenth-century India, arguing for a reconceptualization of the telegraph as a technology which was used in various contexts and engendered a multitude of often diverging and contradictory responses. Rather than focusing narrowly on the usual sites of investigation, the military and administrative affairs of the colonial state, I have attempted to expand the scholarly repertoire of telegraphy by identifying and discussing other sites and purposes of use. In doing so, my aim was not to draw superficial distinctions between various domains of technology use, but rather to suggest that each has something meaningful to contribute to our understanding of the history of telegraphy in the subcontinent. In addition, these sites of telegraphic practice were interconnected and interdependent. Indeed, as the engineer Charles Bright remarked at the end of the nineteenth century, journalism, politics, and commerce were interrelated spheres of activity as far as telegraphy was concerned.[1]

In this and the following chapters, I continue this discussion by focusing on the nexus of technologies of communication and journalism. To this end, I examine some of the contexts of news reporting in colonial India, focusing on some of the actors who wrote for and about the newspaper press, especially in relation to technologies of communication like the telegraph, but also considering the role of such technologies in the practice of journalism. The chapter is structured into several sections which reconstruct the production and dissemination of news in the nineteenth century from a number of complementary angles: perceptions of journalism and news reporting in colonial India; the socio-economic background of journalists; and the processes of collection, transmission, and publication of news as well as its eventual return into the public domain via subscription, distribution, and reading practices. The overall aim of the chapter is to examine telegraphy as part of a broader process of communication in which journalists drew on multiple social networks and media of communication in order to obtain and disseminate intelligence.

Journalism in Colonial India

Journalism was not a profession in nineteenth-century India, at least not in our current understanding of the word. It was at best an occupation, and not a highly reputable one at that. This was particularly the case in the late eighteenth and early nineteenth centuries, when people who wrote for the press were often dismissed as peddlers in gossip, calumny, and scandal.[2] This unfavourable image was, partly at least, a by-product of the fraught relationship between the press and the Company Raj. Succeeding generations of journalists and commentators usually responded to this perception by distancing themselves from the 'scandalous' journalism of the earlier decades. Subscribing to what later historians would call the 'Whig model' of interpretation, they explained the history of journalism as progressing linearly towards professionalization and a more responsible and independent style of reporting. A fairly typical example was that of Siddha Mohana Mitra, editor of the *Deccan Post*, who at the beginning of the twentieth century described James Augustus Hicky, the troubled editor of India's 'first' newspaper, as an 'illiterate man' and his newspaper, the *Bengal Gazette*, as being 'at first dull and vulgar, and on the whole harmless, [until] it descended to indecency, personalities, and scurrilous attacks'.[3] In a similar vein, Douglas Dewar, a British civil servant in India, also commented in 1922 that '[i]n the days of the Company, the average editor of an English newspaper in this country was a rolling-stone, an adventurer possessed of more or less literary ability, who in the course of a chequered career had tried his hand at most things.'[4] A second reaction, of a more nationalist bent, was to revalorize these early exponents of journalism as outspoken, courageous characters who fought for freedom of speech and expression against the increasing encroachments of a despotic colonial rule.[5]

The history of the early press in colonial South Asia has been the object of much study and comment. One aspect which deserves more emphasis, from the perspective of this study, is the fact that the style of journalism practised by people like James Augustus Hicky was very much a product of its own time, an offshoot of the polemical journalism of the eighteenth century which was far from peculiar to the environment of Calcutta. One need only remember the fate of the British printer Nathaniel Mist who was prosecuted for libel at the beginning of the eighteenth century for publishing his allegorical 'Persian Letter'—not dissimilar to Hicky's 'Japan Journal'—in which he criticized a usurper king for the condition of his country.[6] In fact, as one candid commentator remarked in the mid-twentieth century, 'The manner of writing in much of the British journalism of his time was less remarkable for restraint than in these days, and Hicky did little more than add spice to a style common elsewhere.'[7]

This is not to suggest that the conditions under which journalism operated in Britain and India were identical. Nor is this merely an example of the 'diffusion' of journalistic norms and trends from metropole to colony. If anything, it is proof of the interconnected development of journalism as an enterprise which depended, quite literally, on the circulation of newspapers, news, and views between multiple geographical locations which came to span the world, not only Britain and India. One example is that of foreign telegrams published in newspapers in India and Japan, usually sent through the agency of Reuters, whose format and content was often highly similar if not entirely identical. The issue of 11 June 1880 of the *Amrita Bazar Patrika* contained a despatch from Paris, dated 2 June, which reported that 'Rochefort has been severely wounded in a duel.' Almost a month later, the *Japan Times* of 5 July 1880 featured a similar telegram from Paris, dated 1 June, which announced that 'Comte Rochefort has been severely wounded in a duel.' Another telegram sent from Constantinople on 2 June 1880 and published in the same issues of the two newspapers reported that 'Midhat Raschid Pasha has tendered his resignation to the Sultan, but it has not yet been accepted' (in this connection see also the discussion in Chapter 5).

The extent of circulation of news and newspapers in the nineteenth century is demonstrated by another example, a report originally penned by the Simla correspondent of the *Englishman* which described the death of one Captain Boydell. While hunting in Nahan (present-day Himachal Pradesh) with his *shikaree* (Indian hunter), Boydell was attacked by a tiger, who bit him on the shoulder and his knee. His Indian companion managed to fend the tiger off, but the unfortunate officer did not survive the attack and eventually died in hospital the next day.[8] The piece of news proved interesting enough to be published, more than a year later, in *Albina Carpaţilor* (The Carpathian Bee), a weekly journal of science and literature published in Sibiu (present Romania). The gist of the event—the death of Captain Boydell—remained identical, but the circumstances surrounding the incident were changed to construct a narrative of British heroism in the face of India's adverse natural environment. Romanian readers, presumably less familiar with South Asia, were first told that 'Simlah' was 'the summer residence of the English viceroy in the Oriental Indies'. In the original report published by the *Englishman*, Boydell had been out 'shooting' when tragedy struck. In the Romanian version, the 'brave officer', accompanied by an 'Indian hunter', was alleged to have gone in search of the tiger, who had already carried away 'a number of domestic animals'. The tragedy also culminated in his instantaneous death at the hands of the wounded animal.[9]

The specific historical circumstances of the Indian subcontinent made the experience of producing a newspaper different from the one in Britain or the United States. But ideas about how journalism should be conducted circulated just as much as news did, and the questions that faced journalists in nineteenth-century India were not entirely dissimilar from those faced by journalists elsewhere. They revolved, for example, around freedom of speech and the relationship with the state, the need to secure subscriptions and advertisements as well as access to postal and, later, telegraphic communication, the role of journalism in society and the meaning of 'good' journalism, the increasing drive towards professionalization, and so on.

In this respect, Hicky's own style of journalism was shaped by his experiences in two specific environments, those of Hastings's and Elijah Impey's Calcutta, and of Georgian Britain, in which newspapers did not shy away from publishing similarly 'scandalous' items.[10] As a number of authors have pointed out, the rise of radical journalism in eighteenth- and early nineteenth-century Britain was connected to the diversification of readership as a result of the Industrial Revolution, the influence of the American and French revolutions, as well as the 'popular agitational journalism' advocated by Thomas Paine since the 1770s.[11] In this context, newspapers and print more generally became 'a publicly accessible and accountable medium of communication, not a tool under the monopolistic control of government, journalists or printers'.[12]

Like the press in Britain, the press in colonial India was also a stratified and multilayered entity. However, unlike Britain, where distinctions were usually drawn between metropolitan and provincial newspapers, in India the most conspicuous divisions ran along the lines of race and language, as betrayed by the multitude of categories used to describe newspapers and periodicals: 'Anglo-Indian press', 'Indian press', 'native press', 'vernacular press', 'native Indian press', and so on.[13] Comparisons were made not only between various sections of the press in India, but also between South Asian and metropolitan newspapers in Britain. As William Knighton pointed out in mid-century, circulation and the volume of information published were two aspects which usually distinguished dailies in Calcutta from their London counterparts. For the former, a circulation figure of a thousand subscribers was considered large (by contrast, *The Times* had an estimated circulation of approximately 60,000 subscribers in the 1860s). Furthermore, it was estimated that newspapers like the *Englishman* and the *Hurkaru* published only a tenth of the amount of information which usually appeared in the pages of *The Times*.[14]

The purpose of these comparisons was to establish hierarchies between the various sections of the press. For example, there was a widespread view that the 'Indian press', whether understood narrowly as newspapers and periodicals published by Indians, or more inclusively as all the newspapers published in the Indian subcontinent, lacked the qualities of penmanship of the press 'at Home'. Anglo-Indian journals were found lacking in the quality of the paper on which they were printed, the subjects they treated, or the editorial style.[15] But perhaps no charge was more damning than the accusation that these newspapers, like other similar publications produced in the various corners of the empire, were plagued by provincialism and were in danger of losing 'caste':

> Colonialism is, of course, much the same as provincialism, as far as the Press is concerned; and even the 'editor from London', who goes out to Australia or India to conduct the *Bendigo Gully Universal Intelligencer*, or the *Mozuffurnugger Pukka Gudha*, soon loses caste when it is found that he is not so very different from the local people; and in the course of time he naturally becomes a 'local' himself.[16]

Other commentators held more nuanced views. In an article published in the *Calcutta Review* in March 1856 and attributed to William D. Arnold, the author conceded that newspapers in India could not 'secure the same galaxy of talent or the same universality of information as are concentrated on the London *Times*'. But he went on to add that there were 'other more serious obstacles to newspaper success in this country than the absence either of efficient reporting or literary ability'.[17] The main problem, according to Arnold, was that free debate about political affairs was impossible in India. Rather than blaming the government directly for this state of affairs, he pointed out that lack of anonymity prevented journalists from writing freely. In India, he argued, readership was limited to the civil and military ranks of the Anglo-Indian population. Journalists could hardly be protected in a community where most people were usually familiar with each other.[18] Impersonality, the norm in much Victorian journalism, was regarded as a guarantee of 'collective authority and encouragement of judicial impartiality'.[19] Indeed, as Arnold put it, 'It is a matter of common consent that the power of a newspaper consists in the combination of secrecy and publicity; the incognito of the writer, the multiplication of the readers.'[20] The government, for its part, disagreed with this stance, especially when its own servants were associated with the press. Sir Steuart Bayley, member of the Governor General's Council, summarized the main objections against anonymity in journalism: '[W]e could not control anonymous publication, and a man writes much more soberly and temperately under the check of publishing his name than he does so anonymously; and if he is in a position to write from personal knowledge, his writings have much more weight.'[21]

Predictably, language and the style of writing also became important targets of scrutiny when discussing the press conducted by Indian journalists. Some commentators found fault with the 'hyperbolic' language which allegedly characterized this section of the press. William Digby, editor of the *Madras Times*, drew attention to the 'grandiose titles' of many a vernacular journal, referring specifically to publications like *Samachar Chandrika*, *Bhagvat Tatwa Bodhika*, *Santi Prodaini*, and *Biswa Duta*.[22] Ironically, the devaluation of the vernacular press occurred despite occasional recognition from such writers that Europeans in India usually lacked the language skills necessary to access these publications. In the words of Arnold Wright, '[T]he strictly vernacular Press is a sealed book to most Europeans.'[23] Some allowance was made for newspapers published in English by educated Indians: this was 'the better class' of the native press, represented by a handful of papers such as the *Hindoo Patriot* (Calcutta), the *Indian Spectator* (Bombay), and the *Hindu* (Madras), which were described as 'the chief organs of native opinion'.[24] Of all the English-language newspapers conducted by Indians, Bengali publications were considered the most satisfactory with regard to language skills. Press Commissioner Roper Lethbridge attributed this situation 'to the fact that the best literary talent of Bengal is devoted to the cultivation of English literature'.[25]

The problem, of course, was not simply linguistic or stylistic. Indian newspapers, especially vernacular publications, had long been identified as potential vehicles of anti-colonial dissent and criticism. This was particularly the case during the last decades of the nineteenth century, when the passing of a number of controversial items of legislation by the colonial government—among them the Vernacular Press Act of 1878, which will be discussed in the next chapter, and the Ilbert Bill of 1883—helped transform some of the Indian newspapers, both English-language and vernacular, into important media of anti-colonial and nationalist agitation.[26] While this story is familiar to scholars of South Asia, less known is the fact that fear of the 'seditious' activities of the Indian press went hand in hand with the devaluation of Indian newspapers as 'respectable' organs of public opinion and a general bias against the type of journalism they practised.

It was against this background that an increasing number of writers attempted to dissect and evaluate the 'character' of the Indian press.

S. Wheeler, for example, wrote, 'The peculiar stridency of the native Press of India is in marked contrast to the simple mechanism of this organ of public opinion. Like the cicada, a native newspaper makes a noise out of all proportion to its size and consequence.'[27] In a similar vein, G. M. Chesney claimed that the reason the vernacular press devoted so much attention to criticizing the colonial government was because the Indian public had no interest in other types of news, such as that pertaining to foreign politics, sport, social amusements, drama, literature, science, art, or travel.[28] Thus, together with press regulations which aimed to crack down on 'seditious literature', arguments about journalistic language, style, and the content of reporting were useful in undermining the credibility of Indian journalism by representing it as poorly conducted, biased, and associating it with a style of writing that emphasized description at the expense of the 'objective', concise presentation of 'facts'. The identity of a newspaper in colonial India came to be defined predominantly in terms of the national background of its owners/editors, while other factors which shaped journalism during this period were usually ignored.

One such element was the development of a growing professional ethos in nineteenth-century journalism. As Brake and Demoor have pointed out for Britain, throughout the nineteenth century, journalists 'struggled to achieve recognition as members of a legitimate profession'.[29] A foundational step in this direction was taken in 1887, when David Anderson, a leader-writer for the *Daily Telegraph*, founded the first British school of journalism at Fleet Street. Previously, aspiring journalists had acquired the skills of their trade exclusively through apprenticeships in newspaper offices, but Anderson's initiative offered a more systematic and theory-grounded training for this avenue of employment by teaching students libel law, interviewing techniques, and how to use reference books and news agency wires.[30] Aspiring journalists in nineteenth-century India also learned their trade on the job. William Knighton admitted to being 'totally ignorant about the "mysteries of printing"' when he joined the *Ceylon Herald*:

> ... innocent of the difference between a composing-stick and a galley, between Great Primer type and Diamond—I seated myself at the little table in the mysterious office, sole manager and director, editor, corrector of the press, accountant, cashier, treasurer, and letter-writer, of the newspapers and of the printing office.[31]

Writing about his work on the short-lived but successful Bengali weekly *Paridarshak*, published in Sylhet in 1880, Bipin Chandra Pal described a similar experience in a town where there were few qualified printers, compositors, and pressmen. Since the available men were already employed by the other printing establishment in Sylhet, the Shrihatta Prakash Press, help had to be brought in from Calcutta or Mymensingh to work the hand press on which the newspaper was printed.[32] To overcome this difficulty, Pal and his friends decided to 'master the printer's work, setting up matter, correcting proofs and even working the printing machine', an experience that enabled them to become more independent as journalists and prospective employers.[33]

Editing, reporting, and printing became increasingly separated from each other as the century advanced, but, in practice, financial constraints continued to blur the boundaries between these fields of newspaper production. While certain features of professionalization were already visible in the nineteenth century—most notably in the way in which journalists spoke about themselves as a distinct occupational group—others, such as specialist education, did not appear until the twentieth century. The first attempts to teach journalism in India that I was able to identify date to the 1920s and originated with the National University at Adyar. Founded by Annie Besant in 1918, this institution offered instruction about the history of journalism, press laws, newspaper management, and editorial practice as part of its Department of English.[34] Organizations like the Indian Journalists' Association in Calcutta also sponsored training courses for future practitioners, while Aligarh University offered a diploma programme in journalism for a brief period (1938–40), managed by the English- and Urdu-language journalist Ram Ali-ul-Hashmi. The first Department of Journalism proper was established in 1941 at the University of the Punjab in Lahore, under the guidance of Professor Prithvi Pal Singh, a graduate of the University of Missouri who had worked for the International News Service and the *Pioneer*.[35]

Journalists in Nineteenth-Century India

Although it is difficult to know with any degree of precision how many people worked as journalists in colonial South Asia, it is safe to say that, compared with Robin Jeffrey's estimate that there were 25,000 journalists in India in the 1990s, nineteenth-century journalism was a fairly small-scale affair.[36] C. E. Buckland's *Dictionary of Indian Biography* (1906) lists more than a hundred names of Anglo-Indians and Indians who worked for newspapers as editors, proprietors, correspondents, or contributors between 1750 and 1900.[37] The data is, of course, far from exhaustive: Indian journalists were visibly under-represented by comparison with their Anglo-Indian counterparts—the ratio was one to three—and one suspects that personal bias, apart from considerations of time, space, and personal merit, were among the criteria which guided the process of selection. One conspicuous absence from the pages of the *Dictionary* is the name of Robert Knight, the founder of two of India's most successful newspapers, the *Times of India* and the *Statesman*, a situation that biographer Edwin Hirschmann puts down to a 'case of personal spite'.[38]

The word 'journalist' had been in use in Europe since the late seventeenth century. It was an umbrella term which incorporated a number of other, much more common occupational denominations, like editors, subeditors, or correspondents.[39] In nineteenth-century India, while it is possible to speak about the existence of an overarching identity as 'journalists', especially during the later decades of the century, the boundaries between journalism and other occupations were flexible. As many contemporaries observed, especially during the first half of the nineteenth century, almost anybody who was overcome by *furor scribendi* or *cacoethes scribendi* (rage or itch for writing) could 'dabble' in journalism.[40] Indeed, as Sidney L. Blanchard wrote in 1867, 'many [Anglo-Indians] attach themselves to more direct literary pursuits, and, besides producing independent works in various departments, including, of course, fiction, contribute extensively to the periodical press, from quarterly reviews to daily newspapers'.[41]

One important difference was between those who engaged in journalism only occasionally and those for whom it was their main occupation. Overall, relatively few people were able to derive their livelihoods exclusively from writing for newspapers. Major dailies offered more attractive salaries than smaller publications, which usually struggled to survive. A proud Stocqueler claimed to have drawn an impressive salary of Rs 1,000 per month as the editor of the *Bombay Courier* in the late 1820s. If true, this would have been exceptional, considering the privileges the newspaper enjoyed due to its monopoly on government advertising and printing, which according to the editor generated a handsome profit of Rs 40,000 per year.[42] By contrast, in 1884, as a subeditor at the *Bengal Public Opinion*,

Bipin Chandra Pal was drawing a monthly salary of Rs 70, a sum he complemented by contributing to other newspapers like the *Bharat Mihir* and *Bangabasi*. The former brought him an additional income of Rs 20 to 25 a month, while the *Bangabasi* 'paid … liberally according to the standard of those days'. However, *Sanjibanee*, the other newspaper for which Pal wrote occasionally, 'paid nothing to its contributors, pleading poverty'; unlike the *Bangabasi*, it also interfered with the content of his writing. Three years later, as subeditor of the *Lahore Tribune*, Pal received Rs 150 a month, a sum he found sufficient to maintain his family.[43]

Some of those who worked for the press in India, especially in the first seven decades of its existence, belonged to an earlier generation of printer-journalists. Men like James Silk Buckingham, Rev. William Ward of the Serampore Mission, or Matthias Mull of the *Bombay Times and Standard*, were involved with the press in multiple qualities—as printers, compositors, editors, or proprietors—either in Britain or in India. A similar example is that of Syed Muhammad Azim who, after being educated at the Delhi College and in England, became a compositor in the Delhi Gazette Press. He went on to establish the *Lahore Chronicle* in 1849, the first English-language newspaper published in the Punjab, strategically locating his press in the Naulakha area, 'near the future railway station'. Azim also hired Henry Hope, former editor of the *Delhi Gazette*, and other staff from Sikandarabad to work on his newspaper.[44]

In addition to these examples, the ranks of nineteenth-century 'journalists' also included a rather prominent group of 'elite' practitioners—elite by virtue of their association with the colonial administration—who wrote for the newspaper press either habitually or occasionally. Indeed, the overwhelming majority of 'journalists' recorded in Buckland's *Dictionary* pursued careers as magistrates, secretaries to the various branches of government or the Chambers of Commerce, translators, teachers, medical doctors, soldiers, barristers, engineers, merchants, postmasters, and so forth.[45] For example, in the 1780s, Hugh Boyd, secretary to the Government of Madras, conducted the *Madras Courier* and also contributed to the *Indian Observer* and the *Hircarrah*.[46] Dr John Grant, a Scotsman working for the Bengal Medical Board, edited the *India Gazette* between 1822 and 1828, after which he 'transferred his services to the Government Gazette'.[47]

So widespread was the practice of government servants becoming involved with the press that in 1826 the Court of Directors of the

East India Company prohibited them from owning and editing journals.[48] As a result of this regulation, many officials-cum-proprietors were forced to sell their shares in newspapers. But as far as writing for the press was concerned, as the *Calcutta Monthly Journal and General Register* also remarked, the order was 'a complete dead letter', since 'the civil service, on this side of India especially, have never ceased, to adorn the papers with the fruits of their experience and the offspring of their talent'.[49] For the colonial government, the association of its servants with the press remained a thorny issue during the nineteenth century, for reasons which are easy to surmise. On 4 June 1886, Sir Steuart Bayley pointed out in a confidential note that the government, while not expressly prohibiting its servants from contributing to the press, did not particularly welcome their involvement as editors, except when they contributed to publications of a 'purely literary or scientific class'. The disclosure of official information and criticism of the government, as in the case of Mr Geddes's 1874 attack on the financial policy and Robert Knight's 1875 criticism of Lord Northbrook, were not tolerated. Overall, government servants were expected to conduct themselves 'within the limits of temperate and reasonable discussion'.[50]

Like many of their contemporaries who had left their homes in search of opportunities in Britain's vast empire, journalists were also a highly mobile group, often relocating between cities and countries. One example was that of William Duane, the American editor of the Calcutta journal *Indian World* and the first journalist to be deported from India on account of his publications.[51] Another was William Ward, who belonged to the early generation of missionaries-cum-journalists, who had worked as an editor for no less than three British newspapers—the *Derby Mercury*, the *Hull Advertiser*, and the *Stafford Advertiser*—before moving to India.[52] Similarly, William Knighton began his career as an editor for the *Ceylon Herald*. He eventually moved to Calcutta, where he contributed articles to the *Calcutta Review* ('about Confucius and Lord Wellesley'), the *India Sporting Review* ('about the bagging of alligators and elephants'), and for another daily ('about politics and the Sikh war'), before being offered the editorship of a daily newspaper.[53]

Developments in means of transport and communication in the course of the nineteenth century made it increasingly convenient for people to travel and relocate, but also shaped the practice of journalism in other important respects. The speed and the volume of information exchange increased, and journalists were able to forge links with newspapers in India, Britain, and other parts of the world, often acting as correspondents and occasional contributors.[54] Correspondents were essential in facilitating a newspaper's access to news. The extent of a paper's networks of information depended on a number of factors, such as financial resources and the symbolic capital of its editor and proprietors. Some correspondents wrote regularly from key locations like London and Paris, while others were dispatched to report on wars and military campaigns. One of the pioneers in this field was the famous William Howard Russell who, after reporting the Crimean War, was sent to India by *The Times* to cover the Mutiny.[55] Towards the end of the century, topical correspondence also became increasingly common, with the *Times of India* employing a 'sporting correspondent'.

Many of those who acted as correspondents for newspapers in India and Britain were themselves in charge of newspapers. William Martin Wood was a leader-writer on the *Lancaster Guardian*, and its London correspondent until 1864. After moving to India and assuming the editorship of the *Times of India*, he contributed to various publications in the subcontinent and to *Vanity Fair*, a popular 'society journal' from London. Later on, he became the proprietor and editor of the *Bombay Review* and *Indian Advertiser*, while in 1875, during the Baroda state trial, he acted as *The Times*' correspondent in India.[56] Occasionally, trips to Britain or India also provided opportunities to send back reports of events. This was the case of Surendranath Banerjea, who acted as a correspondent for the *Hindoo Patriot* during his stay in London in 1874–5.[57] In 1877, Banerjea was also present, in the same capacity, at the Delhi Durbar.[58]

In addition to appointed correspondents, members of the general public also contributed intelligence to newspapers, a situation which underscores the collaborative nature of journalism as an enterprise that depended, in the nineteenth century as nowadays, on the larger public for the supply of its news. Before deciding, at the age of 21, to trade 'the prospect of a fortune' in coffee cultivation for the editorship of the *Ceylon Herald*, William Knighton seemingly sent 'letters from the jungle' to newspapers in Colombo, which 'always appeared in conspicuous positions in the Colombo papers'.[59] In her diary of life in Meerut, Elizabeth Augusta Egerton also recollected how she shared with the press an account of a 'most singular phenomenon' which she and her Indian servants had witnessed on 20 August 1878.

In the aftermath of a heavy bout of rain, the party walked out to discover a 'large shoal of little fish' in their compound. Unable to find a rational explanation for the presence of the fish, yet unwilling to admit publicly the possibility of a 'miracle in these days of newspapers, telegraphs, and scientific men', Egerton decided to share the unusual details of this incident with the public so that readers could decide for themselves how to interpret it.[60] The newspaper, as this episode suggests, was a forum for the publication of unusual occurrences, but the standards of 'respectable' journalism rejected indulgence in sensationalism and superficiality. Instead, such incidents were to be reported in the detached language of the rational observer.

Many of the newspapers published in the nineteenth century were established with meagre resources, often for the purpose of promoting social, political, and religious reform among various sections of the Indian society. They were usually produced by a limited number of people, who combined responsibilities as editors, subeditors, leader-writers, and even as compositors and printers. The example of Bipin Chandra Pal who, together with three of his Brahmo friends, Brajendra Nath Sen, Raj Chandra Chaudhury, and Radhanath Chaudhury, published *Paridarshak* from the first floor of their house in Sylhet has already been mentioned.

But there was also an important connection between journalism and commercial enterprise, which was reflected not only in the shipping and commercial intelligence published by the newspaper press (see Chapter 5), but also in the crucial role played by the mercantile community in India in the establishment and development of the press. The Parsi community of Bombay was prominent in this regard: its members were instrumental in providing financial support to many a newspaper enterprise, while also distinguishing themselves as journalists. The first Gujarati newspaper, *Bombay Samachar*, was established by Fardunji Marzbanji, whose son went on to edit Dadabhai Naoroji's *Rast Goftar* and to become the proprietor of the Daftar Ashkara Press.[61] Similarly, Robert Knight's *Times of India* was partially owned by Parsi businessmen.[62] While these are relatively familiar examples, less known is the activity of people like Darashah Dorabji Reporter, whose career as a journalist in Bombay spanned an impressive five decades. At the celebrations marking the anniversary of his six-decade-long association with the press, the veteran journalist spoke about his early fascination with this 'profession', which had led him to join the press as a reporter for the *Bombay Times* in 1855, even acting as its subeditor during the time of Robert Knight's illness in the second half of 1859. He continued to work as a reporter for this newspaper after its incorporation into the *Times of India*, while also editing the *Indian Banner* in 1860 'during his leisure hours'. After sixteen years at the *Times of India*, 'Mr. Darashah' left this newspaper to work as a reporter for the *Bombay Gazette* for another thirty-four years.[63]

The Parsi community was also conspicuous in the field of printing. In 1897, 25 per cent of the English-language newspapers and periodicals recorded in the Bombay Presidency were printed by Parsis, including the *Times of India* and the *Indian Spectator*, a newspaper owned and edited by Behramji Merwanji Malabari.[64] The mercantile pursuits of the community were also reflected in the type of periodical publications they owned, edited, or published, many of which were commercial journals containing market information, such as the Chamber of Commerce's *Daily Arrivals of Cotton, Wheat and Seeds*, *Daily Trade Return* or the *Daily Commercial Sale Report*, and the *Daily Telegraph* and *Deccan Herald*.[65] Such publications were particularly dependent on access to the latest telegraphic intelligence. In what follows we will examine how journalists and other contemporary observers responded to the introduction of telegraphy in the Indian subcontinent and discussed its role in news reporting.

Discourses of Telegraphy and Journalism

The newspaper press in India was among the earliest and most enthusiastic beneficiaries of electric telegraphy. In his first report on the operations of the Electric Telegraph Department, W. B. O'Shaughnessy remarked that newspapers were regularly using the telegraph to transmit news and claimed that the popularity enjoyed by the telegraph with the editors of the *Delhi Gazette* and *Lahore Chronicle* was partly responsible for the high receipts of the department in these two towns.[66] So eager were the representatives of the press to make use of the new technology that Lord Dalhousie's decision to open the telegraph lines only when they were fully completed and in working order became the object of ridicule in the press. On 8 January 1855, the Calcutta correspondent of the *Delhi Gazette* criticized the governor's decision saying that 'because the Railway is not finished as far as Delhi, no body [*sic*] should be permitted to travel by it to Burdwan, to which place it *is* finished'.[67] When the telegraph was eventually opened on 1 February 1855, the correspondent was among the great number of people present at the telegraph office. His account of the day's events makes for captivating reading:

> I sent you a brief message by the Electric Telegraph on the day it opened, to say it was opened, and I hope it reached you in due course and in a correct form, as I have no doubt it did, as the number of words was *just sixteen and no more*. There was a great rush that day at the Telegraph Office, and an extraordinary flight of messages for all parts of the country, and as the thing was quite a novelty to every one [*sic*], there was the proper amount of confusion and I fear also mistakes. I am told that up to 10 A.M. that first day, the Telegraph received more than a hundred rupees for the transmission of private messages. While I was there, a Parsee paid down a large heap of silver for a single message to Bombay, and you may depend upon it there was no trifle at stake which called forth that message.[68]

Like in other domains of activity discussed in Chapter 2, the trope of 'revolutionary' transformation also enjoyed currency in discussions about the effects of telegraphy on journalism. Some of the most enthusiastic proponents of this strand of opinion were the telegraph engineers themselves. In his discussion about the effects of submarine telegraphy on the 'world's progress', Charles Bright, son of the celebrated engineer Charles Tilston Bright, included the 'dissemination of news' among the spheres of activity affected by this 'great revolution' in communication, alongside diplomacy and commerce. Bright credited the telegraph with enlarging the area of circulation and the speed of transmission of 'war and sensational news', which now enjoyed a 'phenomenally rapid dissemination in all quarters of the world'. He also underlined the utility of telegraphy in times of war and its potential to act as a vehicle for peace:

> In old times it sometimes happened that battles were fought in ignorance of the fact that a treaty of peace had already been formally signed between the contending parties—sometimes long after it. Now, thanks to the telegraph, such dreadful mistakes would be impossible. The influence of this early news upon the policies of nations and the financial and commercial operations of individuals, upon the fortunes—indeed, very existence—of a great portion of the daily press of modern times, is incalculable. Thus, during the Afghan campaigns of 1878, 1879, and 1880, the Indian authorities and our own made large use of the telegraph cable and wires, thereby incidentally enabling the public at home

> to read full details of every action almost as soon as it took place. On the other hand, the disaster of Isandula, South Africa, in January 1879, was not known in this country until some weeks after, owing to the absence of telegraph communication.[69]

Bright's views, which were shared by many of his contemporaries, were not necessarily new. Rather, they espoused older ideas about the potential of technology-mediated communication to promote peace, and regarded wars as the direct outcome of a lack of communication. Individuals and countries were unable to reach consensus either because they lacked the means to communicate with each other, or because communication was sparse and irregular. It followed from this that sustained and regular exchange of information would promote mutual understanding and consensus, as various parts of the world were brought 'in continual contact with each other through the telegraph and its powerful ally the Press'.[70] The outcome was a utopian community, in the form of a 'Pan-Britannic Zollverein or Customs Union between the United Kingdom, its self-governing colonies and India' or indeed, a 'new nation', in the shape of a 'Pan-Anglican Federation'.[71]

As Ralph O'Connor and others have pointed out, during the nineteenth century, 'Electricity provided a widely exploited and largely positive focal point for speculations about technology's potential to transform the social order, and fantasies of an electrified future were produced by novelists, journalists and the electrical entrepreneurs themselves.' Such speculations also enabled engineers and entrepreneurs to fashion themselves as 'authoritative "wizards" or "magicians" of the modern age'.[72] But Bright's triumphalist account of the value of submarine telegraphy was also a nostalgic celebration of past achievements at a time of visible change. The late nineteenth and early twentieth centuries were marked by a strategic reorientation of British imperial policy, most notably under the influence of Halford Mackinder's ideas about the emergence of a new geopolitical order, in which renewed emphasis was placed on land as opposed to the sea. In this context, people like Henniker Heaton, well known for his campaigns for cheap imperial communications, also advocated the importance and cost-effectiveness of land telegraphs.[73]

For their part, journalists hailed the utilitarian value of telegraphy, but their position at the heart of processes of news production and circulation also offered unique 'insider' perspectives into the world of journalism, which qualified and complicated the predominant narratives of 'acceleration' and 'shrinkage'. Writing in 1855, William Knighton captured the mood of the time when he anticipated that his account of 'newspapers and their offices' might soon be rendered obsolete by the 'complete revolution [produced] in the ordinary routine of Indian existence' by the telegraph, the railways, and the civil service.[74] Yet, his account of editorial work in Colombo also suggested that the 'rush for news' was more than just a by-product of telegraphy. In a scene more often associated with press telegrams, the arrival of the English mails also saw newspaper clerks, aide-de-camps, and editors competing with each other at the post office for the privilege of being 'the first with the news':

> The aide-de-camp of the governor swears terribly because he is kept waiting for his own and the governor's letters and newspapers—the clerks from the various offices more mildly discuss the chances of speedy departure in English, in Portuguese, and in Singhalese—the two newspaper editors, having hastened to the assistance of their clerks, drawn to the post-office by the delay, stand, most eager and most anxious, side by side, the [*Colombo*] *Observer* and the [*Ceylon*] *Herald*, the *Herald* and the *Observer* in friendly rivalry, polite and affable to each other, strange though it may appear, yet each intensely desirous of receiving his papers and having his *Extraordinary* first out.
>
> 'Hot work,' observes the *Observer*, as he casts an anxious glance into the mysterious chamber, vainly essaying to catch the post-master's eye, and with a glance assure him that old animosities, for the time being, are ended. 'The newspapers certainly ought to be supplied first,' replies the *Herald*, 'because they are supplied *pro bono publico*.'
>
> … At length the desired newspapers are found; *Observer* and *Herald* are supplied *simultaneously*, that there may be no imputation of unfair play or favouritism.[75]

As Terhi Rantanen has pointed out, the telegraph facilitated the 'global mass production of news' by enabling the simultaneous transmission of messages to a number of locations and thus contributing to their multiplication.[76] For a journalist like Alexander Sinclair, who started working as a boy clerk for the *Glasgow Herald* in 1845 and eventually rose up the ranks to become a managing partner, one of the main merits of telegraphy was that it enabled provincial newspapers with limited or no access to non-local news to obtain intelligence in a timely manner, while also facilitating the global circulation of information, to the benefit of business enterprises and the general public.

However, as Sinclair also pointed out, access to telegraphic intelligence was shaped by considerations of cost and was hindered by high prices until the last two decades of the nineteenth century. Furthermore, the use of the telegraph 'disturbed' extant 'ways of reckoning the time', a situation which sometimes resulted in 'amusing paradoxes, such as that [of] the birth of the present Emperor of Germany in Berlin [being] announced to the Queen 53 minutes by the clock before it occurred'.[77]

Sinclair's account suggests that change in the field of journalism was gradual, piecemeal, and unequally distributed. Overall, he remained enthusiastic about the general benefits of telegraphy. Other commentators, however, were more ambivalent. In fact, telegraphy also generated a substantial discourse of loss, with many journalists lamenting the decline in the literary quality of journalism and transformations in their own working routines. Such themes found expression in a number of literary works, which questioned the meaning of 'news' at a time when intelligence became not only more timely and diversified, but also more 'condensed'. At the heart of these discourses were growing concerns about the value of telegrams as a means of reporting events. Emily Dickinson's poem 'Myself Can Read the Telegrams' captured these anxieties well. Apart from illustrating the 'verbal condensation' characteristic of her verse, the poem also suggests a refined awareness of the ways in which telegraphy made possible new modes of experiencing time, place, and news:

> Myself can read the Telegrams
> A Letter chief to me
> The Stock's advance and retrograde
> And what the markets say
>
> The Weather—how the Rains
> In Countries have begun.
> 'Tis News as null as nothing
> But sweeter so than none.[78]

Similarly, for one contributor to the *Chambers's Journal of Popular Literature, Science and Arts*, a prominent London magazine which aimed to educate its readers through articles on history, science, and religion, telegrams were not really news, but merely a 'counterfeit'.[79] The 'real' news was elaborate and meaningful; it arrived by post in more-or-less regular instalments and was penned by men well versed in the craft of writing.

As Laurel Brake and Marysa Demoor have pointed out, the association between literature and journalism was not unusual in the nineteenth century, with the two often being regarded as overlapping domains of activity.[80] Telegrams failed to meet the exigencies of 'good' journalism, not only on account of their lack of literary merit, but also because they contained information which was not always interesting or useful to the reader. Like Dickinson, who wrote that telegraphic news was 'as null as nothing', the *Chambers's* contributor also associated the growing popularity of telegrams with superficiality, sensationalism, and even inaccuracy. Telegrams were a sign of the time, a symptom of the Victorian age's increased obsession with speed. And speed in journalism was a metonym for superficiality and sensationalism:

> Those 'sensation paragraphs' [telegraphic news] to which nine-tenths of us turn as naturally as the compass points to the north, are not of very ancient pedigree. They made a feeble beginning in the days of the Irish famine and the Anti-corn law meetings, but the year 1848 forced them into tropical luxuriance. Then we first began to think a paper tame and dull unless it could announce in huge letters the toppling of thrones, the flight of kings, here a massacre, there a bloodless revolt, elsewhere a desperate strife across barricades. When revolutions were replaced by wars, we came to enjoy our battles, carefully seasoned for our taste by the purveyors of telegrams, and to the present day, these headings in big staring letters form the main attraction of a newspaper in most eyes. There is a peculiar knack in the construction of these startling paragraphs. They are generally sonorous, and adapted to rivet the attention, but will not always bear analysis. They do not invariably convey news, but sometimes merely the counterfeit of news. Such paragraphs are wooden nutmegs, not genuine literary spice; and yet even they serve to illustrate the depth and breadth of the almost universal craving for news.[81]

The effects of speed were even registered on the body. Like colonial administrators, journalists in India also lamented the ways in which the telegraph had helped to upset the balance between work and rest, reconfiguring notions of time in relation to work. Kipling's short story 'The Man Who Would Be King' offers interesting insights into the work associated with the production of a daily newspaper in late nineteenth-century India. The story draws on his own experiences as an editor in the subcontinent. The narrator is a journalist based in Lahore, who recounts his encounter with two British adventurers, soon to become kings of Kafiristan, and occasionally muses on the circumstances of journalistic work. In one scene, we find the editor and the composers of the newspaper staying awake all night and postponing printing until the very last moment, in the hope of catching that elusive telegram from the other side of the world:

> A King or courtier or a courtesan or a Community was going to die or get a new Constitution, or do something that was important on the other side of the world, and the paper was to be held open till the latest possible minute in order to catch the telegram.... I drowsed, and wondered whether the telegraph was a blessing, and whether this dying man, or struggling people, might be aware of the inconvenience the delay was causing.[82]

Kipling's rhetorical remark points to an expectation on the part of the journalists and the public that the latest news should be available almost around the clock. This was particularly the case with daily journalism, which was much more dependent on timely intelligence than other, less frequent types of publications like bi-weeklies or weeklies. The journalist was now expected to organize his working routine around the rhythm of the telegraph. Indeed, it is worth remembering here that press telegrams were usually transmitted during the night, when the lines were not used for state business or for the general public.[83] It is to this topic of transmission that we now turn our attention.

Transmitting the News

For the sake of analysis, news published in nineteenth-century newspapers can be divided into two main categories: foreign, that is, news which originated outside South Asia, and domestic. This distinction is used here merely to indicate the place of origin of intelligence and thus to facilitate discussion about its means and routes of communication, not to suggest that news from London or pertaining to the British Empire more generally was regarded as 'foreign' in the same way that American or German news was. Indeed, there were various levels of geographical aggregation of news: local news pertained to the particular locality where the newspaper was published (Calcutta, Bombay, Lahore, Madras, and so on), regional news could refer to one of the presidencies or princely states, Indian news pertained to the whole subcontinent, imperial news reported more generally about the British Empire or a certain part of it, while international news could refer to other parts of the world which were outside Britain's imperial remit.

The data available allows us to reconstruct in some detail the process of transmission of news from Britain to India by means of post and telegraph. The former type of intelligence was transmitted via correspondents' letters, overland summaries, and newspapers. Newspapers containing summaries of European intelligence emerged as an important medium for the communication of the latest news to readers in the Indian subcontinent. They also provided important business opportunities for many publishers and booksellers. One familiar example was that of the *Home News*, published by Grindlay & Co. on the 10th and 26th of each month and sent to all stations in India and China for an annual subscription fee of 18 shillings, in addition to a 6-shilling fee for the postage via Marseilles. In the 1850s, the journal was edited by Charles William Shirley Brooks, well known for his contributions to the *Punch*, and promised to deliver 'all news of interest for the reader in India … brought down to the latest hour'.[84]

The same firm also supplied the British public with newspapers from India. The East India Reading Rooms at Charing Cross offered a wide selection of titles from across the subcontinent, including the *Bengal Hurkaru*, the *Bombay Government Gazette*, the *Bombay Gazette*, the *Bombay Telegraph*, the *Bombay Herald*, the *Bombay Guardian*, the *Calcutta Government Gazette*, the *Englishman*, the *Eastern Star*, the *Mofusilite*, the *Ceylon Observer*, the *Colombo Observer*, the *Delhi Gazette*, the *Madras Government Gazette*, the *Madras Morning Chronicle*, and the *Kurrachee Advertiser*.[85] The traffic of newspapers was indeed impressive if we consider the estimates based on official stamp returns issued in connection with Her Majesty's and the East India Company's Services in 1854: *Home News* (fortnightly, 131,000); *Indian News* (fortnightly, 35,000); *Allen's Indian Mail* (fortnightly, 27,000); *United Service Gazette* (weekly, 106,086); *Civil Service Gazette* (weekly, 83,000); and *Naval and Military Gazette* (weekly, 73,075).[86]

Intelligence was sent to India by a combination of means of transport and routes of communication, the contours of which have been outlined in Chapter 1. Here, I will focus on the actual mechanisms of transmission. William Acworth, a noted railway economist and politician, provided a first-hand account of the progress of the Indian mail from London to Brindisi: the 'distinguished service', as it was known amongst railways and steam officials. In 1888, Acworth visited the GPO at St Martin's-le-Grand to witness the preparations for one of the weekly mail dispatches which left London each Friday at 8 p.m. Unlike the usual mails, which were sorted aboard the train, mails for India had to be sorted and sealed before the departure of the train for Dover. As Acworth writes,

> Perhaps in all England there is no better specimen of work done at high pressure than may be seen at St. Martin's-le-Grand any evening from 6 P.M. till 8 P.M. But if any one wishes to see the rush at its very fiercest, let him choose Friday for his visit. As the present writer saw it on April 13th, the entire mail that left Calais consisted of 871 sacks, filling seven luggage vans, or *allèges*, to use the French technical term. Out of this number, however, 319 had been sent on to Dover in the course of the previous week, and 28 more on the Friday morning; the rest went down on Friday night.[87]

A large proportion of the mail bags was sent to Australia. India followed closely with 284 bags, while 30–50 bags each were destined for Hong Kong, Ceylon, and Singapore; lesser numbers travelled as far as Fiji and Yokohama in Japan.[88] The bulk of the postal matter only reached the GPO on Friday afternoon, a situation which created the surge of activity reported by Acworth. Letters and newspapers poured in from all over the country, not only from London: the Irish train pulled into Euston at 5:45 p.m., followed shortly by the West mail; at 7 p.m. the mails from Liverpool and Manchester arrived, while the mail from West Riding did not reach until 6:50 p.m. Although this incoming postal matter had already gone through one round of sorting by the time it reached the GPO—the letters for non-European destinations now carried a pink label—they still required additional work in order to be ready for the 8:13 p.m. departure of the train to Dover.[89]

The process of sorting was demanding and required the mobilization of an additional workforce of 200 sorters on Fridays. The work took place in the Foreign Department of the GPO and consisted of several rounds of sorting, with newspapers, letters, and books being handled separately. In the first stage, postal matter travelling via Brindisi was separated from that travelling via Southampton or

Ostend. Then, Indian mail was separated from mail sent to other parts of the world, after which it was further subdivided according to the particular division in the subcontinent to which it was sent. Business and official correspondence usually incurred higher postage fees than normal letters. As Acworth noted, the dispatch of newspapers also generated considerable expense for their proprietors:

> The proprietor of two leading trade journals states that his postage via Brindisi costs him between £1,000 and £2,000 per annum. Of one issue this spring he sent close upon two tons to the East, but a certain proportion of the copies of this particular number were forwarded as freight. This is a custom that, as we were told, is more and more being adopted in the case of special publications, such as for instance the Christmas numbers of the illustrated journals.[90]

Once the sorting was completed, the bags were transported across the road to Cannon Street to be loaded onto the train for Dover and thence sent by ship to Calais. At this latter point, the mail bags were handed over to another officer who accompanied them on the special train to Brindisi. Acworth criticized the extant postal arrangements, which prevented British boats from carrying European mails to the continent, with the exception of half of the French mails.[91] According to him, the British were forced to pay 'extortionate' fees to the French for the carriage of their mails by the special train, despite the fact that the French mails were also carried on this service and amounted to a mere 70–80 bags, as opposed to the 800–900 bags sent from London.[92] Indeed, the only thing which seemed to please him about this arrangement was the punctuality of the French railways!

A similar account published in the British periodical *Leisure Hour* at the beginning of the twentieth century enables us to reconstruct the transmission of telegraphic intelligence from London to Bombay via the Red Sea route. The first stage involved sending messages over the land cables from London to the Eastern Telegraph Company's station at Porthcurno in Cornwall. This was done by operating instruments manually or by inserting a punch slip into a Wheatstone automatic telegraph that was capable of transmitting 300–400 words per minute.[93] At Porthcurno, the message was read by a siphon recorder, in which the humps represented dots and the depressions represented dashes (see Illustration 3.1). The message was then re-punched for transmission to Gibraltar, where an operator acting as a 'human

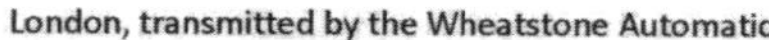

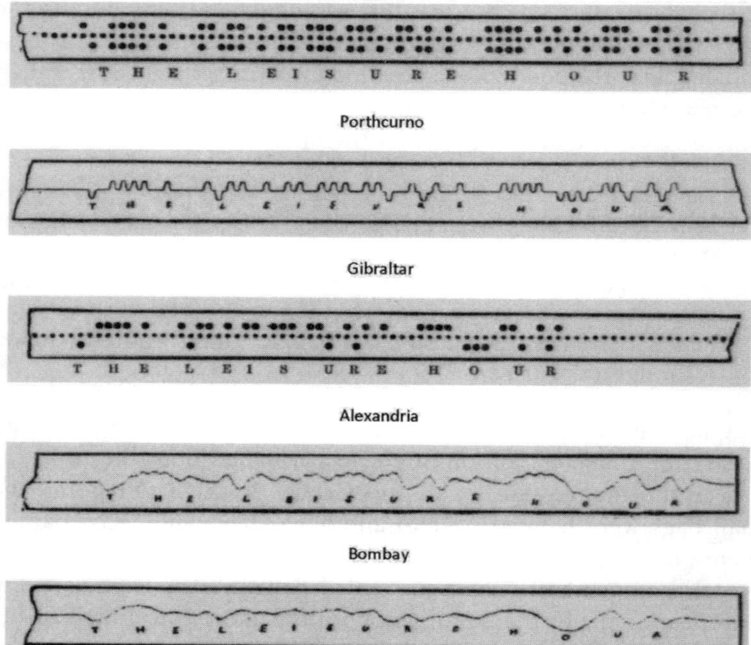

Illustration 3.1 Telegraphic news on its journey from London to Bombay, *The Leisure Hour*, 1901
Source: Author's collection.

relay' simultaneously read and re-sent it to Alexandria via Malta (at Malta, the cables connecting this place to Gibraltar and Alexandria were merged to form one continuous line). The next point at which the message appeared was at Alexandria. Here, it was written on slips of paper and retransmitted over land cables to the Suez, along a route which followed roughly the railway line. From Suez, the message was forwarded to Aden, where a clerk acted once again as a 'human relay', helping it on its final journey over the 2,000-mile submarine cable that connected this place with Bombay.[94]

Illustration 3.1 enables us to 'visualize' the telegraphic message, now encoded as dots and dashes, on its journey from London to Bombay. As we can easily observe, the impressions on the slip faded as the distance between stations increased. Both accuracy and speed were affected in this process, usually as a result of electrical disturbances and earth currents. As the contributor to the *Leisure Hour* put it,

> The strength of the chain is the strength of its weakest link, and so in the chain of cables between England and India the speed of transmission is the speed of the slowest section. Although a speed of 300 or 400 words a minute can be readily obtained on the land wires in England and Egypt, the speed of the very best cables is only a tenth of this, and the longer the cable the slower the speed, the longest cable working up to four or five words per minute only.[95]

Once overseas news reached India, the next stage was to ensure its rapid distribution to various parts of the country. In the 1850s, the Telegraph Department regularly sent 'news bulletins' to the local governments upon the arrival of overland mails at Calcutta and Bombay. The bulletins were published for free at the principal centres of telegraphic communication—Calcutta, Madras, Agra, and Lahore, as well as the repeating stations of Benares, Indore, and Bangalore.[96] A regular weekly message from Calcutta was also provided.[97]

Joseph Archer Crowe was one of the people responsible for preparing telegraphic summaries for transmission to other parts of India, a position he occupied until January 1858, when it was decided that summaries of 'Home news' would be prepared in London.[98] A correspondent with the *Illustrated London News* during the Crimean War and with *The Times* during the Austro-Prussian War, Crowe was in Bombay during the Indian Mutiny. Here, he juggled an impressive number of jobs, including that of correspondent for the *Daily News*, *The Times*, and a French news company whose name he does not disclose but which might have been Havas. In addition, he acted as editor of the *Bombay Gazette*, secretary to the Bombay Chamber of Commerce, and telegraphist to the government. In this latter position, Crowe was responsible for sending a telegraphic summary of the Home news to government officials in various parts of India upon the arrival of the mail at Bombay. The summary was also published in the newspaper press ahead of the full reports which arrived by post. As Crowe recalls,

> There was now [1857] more Indian news than ever to communicate to friends in Europe, and I worked with renewed vigour at my correspondence. But home news had at the same time acquired fresh interest, and people awaited eagerly the moment when a mail steamer should enter

> the bay. I knew to an hour when to expect its arrival. I could see from the club windows the signal staff, on which the number of the ship must be hoisted. I watched the signal as it was made, and when the number was shown I drove to the fort and within the hour a summary, signed with my name, was telegraphed over all India, wherever the wires carried and had not been broken by the mutineers.[99]

In those early days of electric telegraphy, monitoring the time of dispatch was crucial in assessing the performance and efficiency of the telegraph. It was only by recording the exact time of dispatch above each telegram that the telegraph staff could track down errors in transmission.[100] Along with brevity, this feature of telegraphic messages came to distinguish them from other types of news items. Once the telegrams were published in newspapers in this format, the time of dispatch became an important indicator of timeliness. In his official reports of the Telegraph Department, O'Shaughnessy invariably prided himself on the speedy delivery of the bulletins of overland news:

> We have repeatedly sent the 1st Bulletin of Overland News in 40 minutes from Bombay to Calcutta, 1,600 miles. We have delivered despatches from Calcutta to the Governor General of India at Ootacamund during the rainy season in three hours, the distance being 200 miles greater than from London to Sebastopol. We have never failed for a whole year in delivering the Mail News from England via Bombay within 12 hours, while I have positive information that Indian News sent the same distance from Trieste to London has, often during the same year, been double that time in transit.[101]

At the beginning of 1858, it was decided to telegraph the mail news which arrived at Madras to Calcutta and Bombay, while in October 1858, at O'Shaughnessy's suggestion, the Government of India reissued instructions for the delivery of Bombay mail news to Calcutta.[102] The order in which items were to be telegraphed was scrupulously prescribed, a fact which testifies to the hierarchical nature of news under the colonial administration. The heads of intelligence of Home news were to be followed by the 'commercial intelligence', the 'mercantile messages' and, finally, by the details of intelligence prepared at Bombay and Madras. Telegrams were limited to 400 words. In addition, it was decided that the mail news should be delivered free of charge to all stations in which the Morse instruments were in use.

This decision led to a further increase in the number of stations with access to free news bulletins.[103] Nevertheless, the main port cities of Calcutta, Bombay, and Madras, also key nodes of telegraphic communication, occupied a privileged position in the exchange of intelligence by telegraph.

After O'Shaughnessy's departure, his successor in the Telegraph Department began to change the practice regarding the transmission of overland news by telegraph. Eager to cut costs, Major C. Douglas issued a circular on 18 August 1860 prohibiting the repetition of such messages at the request of any intermediary offices in the telegraphic network. Douglas claimed that the confirmation of unintelligible messages placed an unnecessary burden on the lines since 'the news, either corrected by guess or with the doubtful parts omitted, has been in circulation many hours before the correction by repetition can reach'.[104] Only the heads of the main telegraphic offices at Calcutta, Madras, and Bombay were entitled to ask for repetitions. The practice of intimating by telegraph the time of passing through offices of the mail bulletins was also discontinued, and Douglas issued instructions regarding the transmission of news to Calcutta and Bombay for inclusion in the outward mail to Britain. His instructions demonstrate how important chronology was to the utility of telegrams as conveyors of intelligence:

> I request you will invariably Telegraph as Public News and address to the Assistant in Charge of each of the three Presidency Offices the Office date of that Message which was received last in time for the outward Overland Mail Steamer. It is obvious that to admit of this information being of any use, the strictest attention must be given to ensure the transmission of such Messages by intermediate Offices in order of their Office dates. Should a portion of the Mail Messages have been sent by other than the direct route owing to an interruption in the latter, then the latest Office date of Messages in time by each route should be reported.[105]

While the telegraph helped to widen the network of locations with rapid access to the latest intelligence, the new system of communication was not devoid of hierarchies and limitations. Indeed, the mail bulletins containing European intelligence were delivered free of charge only to those newspapers published at the principal telegraphic stations which were 'of sufficient standing and circulation to render the communication of intelligence to them a real convenience to the community'.[106] Newspapers published at minor stations or stations that were not on the telegraph line were provided only with the heads of intelligence. Furthermore, the language of telegraphic news was limited to English.

From the 1860s onwards, the telegraphic news transmitted by the Indian Telegraph Department was usually classified under two main categories: 'news-free' messages, that is, telegrams which were sent free of charge because they were considered to be of public interest, and 'press telegrams', which were sent for concessional rates by news agencies like Reuters and, later, the Indian News Agency as well as various newspapers in India. News-free messages consisted mainly of meteorological reports and mail-steamer reports which were circulated to a large number of stations and publicized through the press.[107] Since they were transmitted free of charge, the government regarded them as a burden on its finances and constantly attempted to reduce costs by redefining the notion of 'public news'. In 1880, for example, it was decided to remove the meteorological reports of the Government of India and the Government of Bengal from the list of news-free telegrams, a move which suggested that mail steamer reports were now believed to be of more interest to the 'public' than meteorological reports.[108] Although, as Table 3.1 shows, the number of news-free messages decreased considerably as a result of this measure, the expected decrease in expenditure did not materialize because mail reports increased in length.[109] Even more puzzling was the decision to include Reuter's government news messages in the list of news-free telegrams in 1893.

Ruchi Ram Sahni, who worked with the Indian Meteorological Department from 10 January 1885 until the end of March 1887, left an account of how the meteorological reports were compiled. Employed as a second assistant meteorological reporter to the Government of India on a salary of Rs 100–150, he was posted at Simla to work under the supervision of Henry Francis Blanford, India's first meteorological reporter, and the first assistant, Mr W. H. Dallas. While the latter was in charge of the logbooks of ships passing through the Indian Ocean—these were used to collect meteorological observations—Sahni was entrusted with the compilation of the daily and monthly weather reports.[110] The office, located on the top floor of the Government of India buildings, was manned by approximately a dozen clerks and computers, some of whom had been temporarily relocated from Calcutta.

Table 3.1 Traffic of news-free messages, 1867–1900

Year	Mail steamer reports, meteorological reports, and so on	Reuter's government news messages	Total no. of news-free messages	Remarks
1867–8	8,199		8,199	Until 1880–1, the list of news-free messages included mainly steamer reports and meteorological reports.
1868–9	6,690		6,690	
1869–70	3,595		3,595	
1870–1	3,873		3,873	
1871–2	3,769		3,769	
1872–3	5,008		5,008	
1873–4	5,777		5,777	
1874–5	7,365		7,365	
1875–6	7,611		7,611	
1876–7	7,307		7,307	
1877–8	7,358		7,358	
1878–9	7,591		7,591	
1879–80	7,396		7,396	
1880–1	2,417		2,417	
1881–2	746		746	From 1881 until 1893, the list of news-free messages included mainly mail steamer reports.
1882–3	895		895	
1883–4	748		748	
1884–5	681		681	
1885–6	788		788	
1886–7	823		823	
1887–8	933		933	
1888–9	754		754	
1889–90	857		757	
1890–1	806		806	
1891–2	706		706	
1892–3	681		681	
1893–4	585	377	962	From 1893, Reuter's government news messages were transmitted as news-free telegrams.
1894–5	604	751	1,355	
1895–6	552	799	1,351	
1896–7	370	801	1,171	
1897–8	332	847	1,179	
1898–9	313	871	1,184	
1899–1900	268	1,162	1,430	

Source: Compiled from *Administration Reports of the Indian Telegraph Department*, various years, 1867–1901, V/24/4284–4288, IOR.

Using the meteorological observations recorded at the 120 stations in India and Burma and transmitted to Simla telegraphically each morning, Sahni prepared the daily weather report, which was then wired simultaneously to the Government Press at Simla and all the daily newspapers.[111] In 1884, for example, the *Times of India* published such telegrams together with weather charts that contained information about rainfall, the direction and velocity of the wind, the quantity of clouds, humidity, variations in temperature, and barometer. The stations from which intelligence was published ranged from Karachi to Bombay, Hyderabad, Indore, Darjeeling, and Chittagong. By contrast, the *Bharat Jiwan* did not publish such detailed weather news; the most conspicuous difference was the absence of numerical data. For example, a piece of intelligence published on 7 July 1884 announced, 'In Agra, rainfall has increased; in Etmadpur, there is nothing.'[112]

The widespread public relevance of meteorological reports is demonstrated by an episode which Sahni was to describe in his memoirs as 'the most important event of my career in the Weather Office'.[113] This involved the transmission of news about the False Point Cyclone, a powerful storm which swept across Orissa (then part of Bengal) between 19 and 23 September 1885.[114] Sahni's account of the day's events are worth quoting at length, as they provide a fascinating insight into the workings of the Meteorological Department and the way in which telegraphy was used to disseminate vital meteorological information, a topic little explored in previous literature:

> On going to office in the morning, I called for as usual such of the weather reports as had been tabulated. On examining them, I noticed that Diamond Harbour had reported an unusually rapid fall of atmospheric pressure. There was nothing in the reports from the surrounding stations to explain or support this. I was alone at Simla at the time, both Mr. Blanford and Mr. Dallas having gone down to Calcutta. I had an urgent telegram sent to the 'Observer' at Diamond Harbour asking him to send me a fresh report of the latest readings. This report confirmed my original suspicion that a big storm was approaching. I then asked him not to leave the observatory till further orders, and keep sending me half hourly reports of the weather. A little later, I asked two or three of the other neighbouring stations also to do the same. Meanwhile, I was up fuller also making a hurried study of the reports of previous big storms. It was only when I was quite convinced in my mind that a big storm was approaching the coast that I issued the immediate danger signals.

> This done, I sent a long wire to my Chief at Calcutta informing him of what I had done and reproducing the important features of the special reports that I had obtained. I afterwards learnt from the office men at Calcutta that for a few minutes after the receipt of my telegram, Mr. Blanford felt seriously perturbed and upset. He at once ran to Professor Pedler and asked him if he knew anything of a big storm in the Bay. Professor Pedler was Provincial reporter for Bengal. In this capacity he used to get all the reports of the Bengal stations which were nothing but duplicates of the morning reports that were sent to Simla for the 'daily weather report'. Professor Pedler knew nothing of the storm.... On the suggestion of Mr. Blanford, Professor Pedler sent out orders to the affected stations to repeat the telegrams they had been sending to me.[115]

Despite Sahni's accurate prediction, there was little at the time that could be done to prevent the devastating effects of the storm. A telegram from Cuttack to the *Englishman* dated 30 September 1885 reported that the Telegraph Department had sustained considerable losses, with the lines between Cuttack and Balasore, Cuttack, Kendrapara, and False Point, and Bhadrak, Chandabali, and Puri 'completely wrecked'. The office at False Point was also 'completely destroyed'.[116] The plight of the local inhabitants was dramatic. According to newspaper coverage, the storm travelled inland as far as the Brahmani River, submerging 500 villages on its way and drowning all the inhabitants. At False Point, the houses were levelled and the port officer, one Captain Douglas, together with his wife, three children, and nine other people lost their lives. As one reporter dramatically put it,

> ... the settlement on the island of Hookeetollah [Hukitola] has been entirely washed away, houses and trees are levelled to the ground, except the refuge house, which is, however, in a very shaky condition, and on the top of which were found the only persons that were saved—eight natives, two of whom have since died from exhaustion. The beach is strewn with numberless dead bodies of Europeans and natives and cattle, also a good many deer and fish.[117]

As far as press telegrams were concerned, on 1 January 1872 the government introduced a concession by which bona fide press messages could be transmitted at reduced rates.[118] Despite the new concessionary rates, the increase in the number of press telegrams sent during the decade 1870–80 failed to meet the expectations of the

Table 3.2 Traffic of press telegrams, 1873–1900

Year	Number	Value (in Rs)
1873–4	2,375	11,536
1874–5	4,206	17,820
1875–6	5,807	24,141
1876–7	5,707	22,905
1877–8	7,537	40,511
1878–9	7,397	47,929
1879–80	7,350	51,497
1880–1	8,198	46,772
1881–2	7,941	40,975
1882–3	10,832	40,553
1883–4	10,750	39,593
1884–5	13,873	53,285
1885–6	16,150	69,427
1886–7	17,036	69,740
1887–8	17,864	72,538
1888–9	26,988	92,473
1889–90	28,013	97,388
1890–1	25,397	82,393
1891–2	29,149	113,279
1892–3	29,095	112,942
1893–4	29,595	118,722
1894–5	29,296	121,482
1895–6	28,314	116,032
1896–7	30,063	121,269
1897–8	41,188	171,737
1898–9	42,597	164,377

Source: Compiled from *Administration Reports of the Indian Telegraph Department*, various years, 1873–1901, V/24/4284–4288, IOR.

government (Table 3.2). According to D. G. Robinson, director general of Telegraphs in India, the low traffic was indicative of the differences in news reporting between the British and the Indian press:

> The whole press of India spent only Rs. 14,729, in the year in obtaining early information on subjects of general interest. The London *Daily*

> *News* paid in one day Rs. 1,400 for one telegram containing intelligence from the famine districts.
>
> Undoubtedly, in India, there is a lack of sensational occurrences interesting to its residents, and an absence of that perhaps unhealthy impatient curiosity, of that competition and of those press associations that exist in Europe and America, but something more than the meager information communicated by Reuter might be culled from the newspapers received weekly at various ports from Australia, China, Europe and America, something worth communicating two or three days earlier than is possible by post, with advantage to the readers, and, I would hope, of the press proprietors. The number of both is certainly far greater in England and America. But how much larger is the area of India and how slow, comparatively, the communication by post. It pays in England and in America to forestall the post by a few hours, but in this country a few days appear to be of little consequence.[119]

Notwithstanding Robinson's dismissive comments, it was primarily the price of telegraphic communication which discouraged newspapers from making greater use of this technology. As the officials of the Telegraph Department themselves remarked, traffic was usually focused around important political and military events and natural calamities, a conclusion borne out by the data in Table 3.3, which suggests an increase in the number of press telegrams sent by associations other than Reuters and individuals on the occasion of the visit of the Prince of Wales to India in 1874.[120] This led R. Murray, officiating director general of Indian Telegraphs, to declare in 1875 that 'the special advantages afforded by the Press rules are beginning to be known and appreciated.'[121]

A further reduction of the tariff for press messages was introduced on 1 April 1880, when the price became Re 1 per 24 words during daytime and Re 1 per 36 words during nighttime. The new rules also allowed for an increase in the maximum length of press messages from 200 to 500 words.[122] As Table 3.2 demonstrates, the traffic of inland press messages continued to increase gradually in the 1880s.[123] The officials of the Telegraph Department also recorded an increase in the number of messages that reported on military events, more specifically on the military operations in Afghanistan which 'gave an abnormal impetus to lengthy News messages'.[124] As we will see in Chapter 5, these trends were reflected in the pages of the newspapers themselves.

Table 3.3 Abstract of press messages sent by Reuters and other associations and individuals, 1873–9

Year	Sent by Reuters		Sent by other associations and individuals	
	No. of telegrams	Value (in Rs)	No. of telegrams	Value (in Rs)
1873–4	1,672	9,903	703	1,633
1874–5	1,047	8,291	3,159	8,829
1875–6	1,531	12,640	4,276	11,501
1876–7	1,811	12,580	3,896	10,325
1877–8	2,695	13,620	4,842	26,891
1878–9	2,621	20,900	4,776	27,029

Source: Compiled from *Administration Reports of the Indian Telegraph Department*, various years, 1876–80, V/24/4285–4286, IOR.

On 1 July 1886, the director general of Indian Telegraphs announced a reduction in the rates for foreign press telegrams, which could now be sent for 16 pence per word via the Suez route from London to India, and 15 annas per word from India to London. Messages had to be addressed to a newspaper office and written in 'plain English'. The use of code words was prohibited, as was 'selling, distributing, or communicating such telegrams to clubs, exchanges or news rooms'. Once sent, the messages had to be published, otherwise the newspaper was liable to pay the full charge. The measure was received with scepticism, with the *Times of India* pointing out that Reuters, who possessed 'an extremely valuable and ingenious code', was likely to be severely affected. Although the editor estimated that the new rule was likely to benefit his newspaper, he criticized official designs to render private codes, such as those used by the *Times of India* and the *Pioneer*, 'useless'.[125] The government, this episode shows, was more concerned with controlling the content of intelligence rather than encouraging its circulation.

Newspaper Circulation

During the nineteenth century, newspapers circulated both ways between Britain and India, together with mail, passengers, and cargo. They could be individually subscribed to, read in local libraries or clubs; the agents who traded general printed matter such as books and almanacs were often the same people who distributed newspapers as well. They advertised their business through the medium of newspapers. In 1855, for example, an advertisement in the *Bombay Quarterly Review* announced that Smith, Taylor, & Co. delivered newspapers and periodicals published in England, France, and Germany and forwarded them by post to India on the day of publication.[126]

Statistics about the press offer useful insights into the extent of circulation of newspapers. One of the earliest sets of data was compiled in response to an inquiry initiated by Governor General William Bentinck shortly after his arrival in Calcutta in 1828. Against the background of an ongoing controversy about the desirability of a free press in the subcontinent, fuelled by occasional expulsions of editors from India—the case of James Silk Buckingham of the *Calcutta Journal* being the most notorious—circulation numbers came to be regarded as an important index by which to judge the potential influence of the press on the public mind.[127]

Based on the circulation figures of newspapers delivered through the post office during the period 16–26 September 1828, Postmaster General G. Stockwell reported the existence of five English-language papers in Calcutta: two dailies, *John Bull* (1,432 subscribers) and the *Bengal Hurkaru* (1,089 subscribers); and three bi-weeklies, the *Government Gazette* (595 subscribers), the *India Gazette* (561 subscribers), and the *Calcutta Chronicle* (397 subscribers).[128] One Persian weekly, later identified as the *Jam-i-Jehan-Numa*, was also recorded with 26 copies per issue. Seven copies of the *Government Gazette* were sent to Indian subscribers in Lucknow, Chandernagore, Burdwan, Kanpur, Santipur, and Murshidabad, while the *India Gazette* was distributed as far as Bombay. In addition, some of the copies destined for British officials—for example the political agent at Bundelkund—were believed to be for independent rajas.[129]

Stockwell's data only included newspapers which circulated through the post office. In response to Bentinck's inquiry, the Persian secretary to the governor general, A. Stirling, also reported the existence of six vernacular papers in Calcutta in 1824–6, that is, three in Bengali, two in Persian, one in Hindi, as well as one newspaper each in Persian and Bengali at the Serampore Mission.[130] Although Stirling did not submit any circulation data, he claimed that such publications enjoyed only a limited distribution 'beyond the limits of Calcutta', and that they were inoffensive in 'tone'.[131] His data provides an early example of how statistics about the press in the colonial period were not simply bureaucratic exercises in quantification: they were also attempts to diagnose the character of the press, especially, though not exclusively, of the vernacular press.

During the days of James Silk Buckingham, the English-language newspapers of Calcutta had a limited circulation outside the town proper, and the *Government Gazette* seems to have been the most popular paper with Indian subscribers, probably because it offered access to official intelligence and provided lower rates of advertising.[132] The overwhelming majority of subscribers were drawn from the ranks of the Anglo-Indian population or, as James Silk Buckingham wrote, 'the civil and military servants of the East India Company, the officers of His Majesty's army, and the respectable English merchants settled in India'.[133] The acknowledgements lists regularly published in the early newspapers, such as the *Delhi Gazette*, also support this conclusion. Furthermore, they highlight the importance of institutional subscribers such as book clubs, libraries, and assembly rooms in providing access to the press.[134]

By mid-century, according to the statistics compiled by Rev. James Long, the main vernacular dailies and tri-weeklies of Calcutta had an average circulation of 600 and 300 copies respectively, with some newspapers travelling well beyond the confines of their place of publication. For example, *Bhaskar*, a tri-weekly newspaper from Calcutta, had subscribers in the Punjab and 'even in England among Europeans who wish to keep up their acquaintance with the Native press'.[135] By the last decade of the century, the vernacular dailies of Calcutta had reached an average circulation of 600 to 775 copies, while some of the weekly newspapers surpassed 1,500 copies.[136]

During the second half of the nineteenth century, the place of publication of most newspapers had also shifted from Calcutta proper to the mofussil, where approximately 58 per cent of all vernacular papers were produced.[137] While dailies continued to be an exclusive product of the former locality, weeklies dominated the newspaper press of the mofussil. Furthermore, bi-weeklies and tri-weeklies had been replaced with a new type of publication, the fortnightly, which was published exclusively outside Calcutta. The linguistic diversification of the newspaper press also deserves emphasis: although the overwhelming majority of newspapers were monolingual, they were published in languages as diverse as Bengali, Hindi, Urdu, Persian, and Oriya; the only bilingual paper was the *Dacca Gazette*. Finally, although the average circulation of daily newspapers had not increased considerably since the mid-century, the average circulation of weeklies showed a remarkable increase in number from approximately 200 to 1,775 copies.[138]

The major English-language dailies fared better, as official reports demonstrate. In a confidential statement prepared for the government, G. M. Sathe recorded the existence of thirty newspapers whose language of publication was English in the Bombay Presidency in 1897.[139] Weeklies and dailies were the most popular types of newspapers published at the time, with the former being twice as numerous as the latter. The number of biweeklies was insignificant, although both the *Bombay Gazette* and the *Times of India*, two of the leading newspapers at the time, published biweekly editions as well. As far as management and editing was concerned, more than 50 per cent of the newspapers were managed by Anglo-Indians, approximately 36 per cent by Indians, while the remaining 10 per cent were mixed. In Bombay, for example, the *Times of India* had a circulation of 4,300 in 1897, followed by the *Bombay Gazette* with 2,500 and the *Advocate of India* with 2,000. In fact, at the end of the nineteenth century, the *Times of India* was not only the newspaper with the highest circulation in Bombay, but also in India, being challenged only by the *Statesman* of Calcutta. With the exception of the *Daily Telegraph* and *Poona Observer*, both published in Poona, all the other newspapers which enjoyed a high circulation were published in the city of Bombay and most of them were dailies. Only one daily was published outside Bombay, the *Kathiawar Times* of Rajkot, which featured news about the native states in Kathiawar and had a circulation limited to seventy-five copies.

Reading the Newspapers

Many scholars have pointed out that statistics about the circulation of newspapers in colonial South Asia are unreliable indicators of the actual number of readers. Collective reading was considered particularly widespread among Indians due to the high rate of illiteracy—according to the Census of 1901, the literacy rate for males was around 9.8 per cent, while for females it was only 0.7 per cent—and the importance of oral traditions in India.[140] During the nineteenth century, officials in

India also remarked that it was extremely difficult to compile accurate circulation figures for newspapers, especially with regard to the vernacular press. As William Digby, editor of the *Madras Times*, wrote, '[A] native paper in India has many readers … a case, which is but a sample of many, is on record where a single newspaper served a whole village. When the copy was received the people were called together, its contents read, explained, and discussed.'[141]

Collective reading became particularly important when the newspaper acted as a medium for the communication of very personal news, as Shevantibai M. Nikambe's novel *Ratanbai* (see Chapter 2) suggests. Although frustrated in her own educational endeavours by an unsupportive mother-in-law, the protagonist Ratanbai directs her energies towards her husband and his examination at Wilson College. The joy of his success is compounded by the ability to share the news with her friends and by reading together the list of successful candidates published in the *Times of India*:

> Ratanbai quickly glanced down the list, and came to the name which, according to custom, never passed her lips except in a song or a rhyme. She burst out laughing to her heart's content, as half-a-dozen young wives repeated the name *Pratap Harishchandra Khote* aloud. She again took the paper, and read aloud the two or three names of the husbands of her friends who were among the successful candidates of some examination.[142]

Further insight into the reading practices of the Indian public at the end of the nineteenth century comes from A. R. Iyengar, who reminds us that even newspaper reading was marked by its own hierarchies, according to the social status of the reader:

> In the days of my boyhood, it was a familiar sight to see the circulation-peon of the local reading room quickly pacing the streets of a mofussil station to complete the luxury of taking the newspaper of the day to the houses of first class members in circulation so that he may place it on the table of the reading room in time for the second and third class members to peruse. At the table, the newspaper got analysed by sheets, sometimes by half-sheets, when exciting news came in, and the contents were pored over by many members putting their heads together or, later, a loud-throated member would read out the finished periods of a Congress orator or the sententious comments of a great Editor.[143]

There is no reason to believe that collective reading was restricted to the Indian population, especially since this practice did not necessarily depend on the presence or absence of literacy. William Digby, an editor with extensive experience in India and Ceylon, remarked that collective reading was a practice which had existed in Britain as well 'in times not yet ancient'.[144] Indeed, recent scholarship shows that at least before mid-century, 'newspaper reading was often a communal rather than an individual activity', and that newspaper ownership itself was collective.[145] In colonial India as well, newspapers could be read and discussed together with friends at the various European clubs or in the confines of the home, with other members of the family. For Captain G. F. Atkinson of the Bengal Engineers, the coffee shop in their fictional village of Kabob was the place where 'we read the newspapers, expatiate on affairs in general, discuss the state of parties (dinner and musical), traffic in ideas, and while away an hour or two from the day's dull monotony, by mutual interchange of generous sentiment'.[146]

Nevertheless, it must be remembered that in view of the low literacy rates mentioned above, newspaper reading remained largely a class-based activity and the number of active readers represented but a small category of the total population of India. In this context, newspapers also came to be regarded as a vehicle for education, not only as a means of disseminating information. They were valued both for their informational content and their 'criticisms' on various matters of contemporary relevance. Regular access to newspapers, especially to those published in Britain, was an important part of the English-language education imparted to Indian students. In the 1850s, at the Elphinstone College in Bombay, students could read 'the best London weeklies' such as the *Evening Mail*, the *Edinburgh*, the *Quarterly*, and the *Westminster*. According to Dinshaw E. Wacha, a reading room was established for this particular purpose by one of the teachers of the college who also provided the costs associated with it.[147] Newspapers also represented staple reading in the education of affluent Indian women. For example, Maharaja Sayajirao Gaekwar of Baroda documented his wife's reading habits for the British public, not forgetting to point out that 'the English and Indian newspapers invariably form part of her reading'.[148]

For some commentators, however, the situation was far from satisfactory, especially since education via the medium of newspapers failed to reach the lower strata of society. As Surendranath Banerjea remarked at the end of the century, 'We have not yet reached that state of blessedness, devoutly to be wished for, when the Bengal ploughman may be seen ploughing with one hand and holding the *Sulav Samachar* in the other.'[149] Similarly, Digby wrote that the vernacular newspapers reached 'the directing, active sections of the population, those who bear the burden and heat of the day in the machinery of social life as distinguished from those who are the actual busy bees working in the hive—the artisans and the labourers'.[150]

Yet other commentators considered that there were limitations to the value of newspapers as sources of personal cultivation. The ephemeral quality of newspapers, as opposed to other printed forms like books, was considered responsible for this situation. As N. J. Ratnagar, former editor of the *Hindu Reformer*, wrote in 1879 in a collection of essays designed to be used by matriculation candidates,

> … to confine ourselves to newspaper reading and nothing more is not safe at all, as a newspaper after all is a hasty production, and wanting in that finish which is the work of time; although there are numerous papers in England, not one of them can be said to be uniformly brilliant. A brilliant book written by a true artist is more useful and may contain more valuable matter than a large load of any of the newspapers of the world. In the daily newspapers there is a sameness of style and a conventional form of style which, if we confine ourselves exclusively to it, is likely to do us harm, unless a continual addition to our knowledge is made by the study of the best writers. Every editor has been surpassed in the treatment of political and economic questions, and in purity and energy of style by William Cobbet, yet his Political Register contains in almost every page unmistakable marks of haste, and in grace and finish cannot be compared to the finished productions of many writers who have never been in the journalistic line, and who were not under the necessity of writing anything within a specific time.[151]

It is difficult to say whether the readers themselves endorsed this opinion, although occasional records provide some hints. For example, in her important study of the Naval Kishore Press, Ulrike Stark shows that readers of the *Avadh Akhbar* were particularly enthusiastic about the newspaper's commitment to the publication of a great diversity of foreign and domestic news, and they appreciated the timely manner in which it was delivered.[152]

Other members of the public, like India's self-styled mercantile community, proved notoriously vocal in their determination to secure access to the latest intelligence. The Chambers of Commerce of Bengal and Bombay did not only petition the government with requests to be granted preferential treatment for the transmission of their commercial intelligence, but also took it upon themselves to police the access to news of their potential adversaries.[153] For example, in the 1860s, the secretary to the Bombay Chamber of Commerce, James Taylor, accused Bombay newspapers of abusing their press privileges by selling their press telegrams. Taylor was referring specifically to a controversy involving the *Bombay Gazette* and the *Times of India* in which the two newspapers had blamed each other of trafficking telegrams. According to Taylor, this practice existed among the 'native' newspapers as well, especially some Gujarati dailies whose editors received bribes from private persons to send telegrams at the discounted rates afforded by the press-message privilege.[154]

By contrast, other evidence suggests the existence of alternative perceptions. In his autobiography, Surendranath Banerjea points out that the craving for timely news in nineteenth-century India was far from universal. Whether his account should be interpreted as a true reflection of popular attitudes towards news or an expression of his own middle-class disappointment with the state of the press and literacy in India, is a matter for debate:

> The craving for fresh news was then not general; and Indian readers for the most part were content to have a weekly supply of news and comments thereon. I remember speaking at the time to the head master of a Government high school, a man of education and culture, who said to me that it took him a week's time to go through the *Bengalee* (then a weekly paper), and that if it were a daily paper he would not know what to do with it. That represented the temper of the *Bengalee* mind, say, thirty years ago [1879]. The daily paper is a more recent development, but it has so completely superseded the weekly that the latter has no chance of a wide circulation except as an adjunct to a daily paper.[155]

At the very least, we might assume that not everybody shared the same news values. An item of intelligence like 'William Fraser Sahib Bahadur enjoying [*sic*] his work in his department', published in the akhbarat of 1830, was unlikely to interest a large audience (nor, indeed, was the news intended for an audience other than Akbar Shah II, the British resident at Delhi, and, possibly, a few other British officials).[156] The same cannot be said about a piece of news pertaining to disease and famine, which was likely to have a wider social impact and, therefore, to interest a wider audience.

Many people greeted news from abroad with eagerness, curiosity, and anticipation. Such reactions are usually recorded in the early decades after the introduction of new technologies of communication in the form of steamers and telegraphs. Think, for example, of Govind Narayan's account of Bombay, in which he recollects the day—28 April 1837—when the new paddle steamer *Hugh Lindsay* docked in the port, bringing along passengers and a 'post of 3,463 letters and newspapers':

> When our people witnessed for the first time that the post and passengers had arrived in a month's time, they were amazed. While it took old ships with masts almost six months to make this journey [around the Cape], the steamship took only a month and its speed led many of the simple folk to believe that its Captain must be the son of the god of winds, Vayu.[157]

While news about the arrival of steamers was regularly published in the newspaper press, it also circulated, arguably more rapidly and extensively than telegraphic despatches, via word of mouth and local channels of communication. Domestic servants were often an important source of information about the latest news in town. Albert Fenton, a cadet stationed in Calcutta in the early decades of the nineteenth century, began his morning routine by asking his *sircar* (house steward) a familiar question: 'Any news today?' The news, as he learned, was, 'One very great ship is arrived at Saugor from England.'[158]

News, whether published in newspapers or written down in letters, provided an important link to the surrounding world. Ghalib likened the receipt of letters to the visit of a friend, recollecting that on some days he received two letters by each of the morning and afternoon posts. When his friend Tufta failed to write, the poet was quick to admonish him:

> Why is it that for ten and twelve days together you haven't written—that is haven't been to see me? Write to me, Sahib. Write why you haven't written. Don't grudge the half-anna postage. And if you're *so* hard up, send the letter unstamped.[159]

During her travels to Jammu and Kashmir in 1881, Elizabeth Augusta Egerton also recollected visiting the post office in the former locality to collect seventeen newspapers and 'a great budget of letters'. As she confessed, '[I]t is nineteen days since we have heard a word of the outer world, but no kings or emperors seem to have been made or unmade during the time.'[160] Not all news instilled the same degree of interest in their audience, a point to which we will return in the final chapter of this book, when we discuss foreign and domestic reporting in the newspaper press of nineteenth-century India.

***

This chapter has attempted to offer a panoramic view of the newspaper press in nineteenth-century India, using news reporting as a principle around which to organize the narrative. I began by reflecting on the many hierarchies that marked the colonial press world, in which English-language journalism was considered superior to vernacular journalism, 'Home' newspapers to the press published in India, and Anglo-Indian newspapers to their Indian counterparts. My interest in these hierarchies was motivated primarily by the desire to understand how colonial commentators used categories of reporting practice such as the style of writing, linguistic ability, news value, and so on, in order to construct a certain image of 'good' journalism. We have seen, for example, how Indian journals—and readers—were castigated for their 'hyperbolic' language and their alleged lack of interest in serious, independent, 'temperate' discussion of political and socio-economic issues.

The discussion then turned to the journalists themselves, in an attempt to sketch the portrait of an occupation—increasingly, profession—in nineteenth-century India. Who were the people who worked for newspapers as editors, subeditors (or assistant editors), correspondents, and sometimes as printers and compositors? How did they collect news and how did they transmit it with the help of steamers and telegraphs from Britain to India? How did they and other contemporary observers react to the incorporation of telegraphy into news-reporting practices?

The image that emerges is that of an interconnected press world, in which people, news, and newspapers circulated, in which the same person straddled the line between colonial administrator and 'journalist', between printer, proprietor, and editor, or, indeed, worked simultaneously for a number of newspapers. A world in which access to the latest news was important, but the convenience of a medium of communication like the electric telegraph did not preclude discussion about the disadvantages of this technology and questions about how to locate telegraphic intelligence within an already existing system of news reporting. For some, as we have seen, telegrams were merely a 'counterfeit' that lacked both the substance and the literary flair of a well-constructed news paragraph. In other cases—such as that of news announcing extreme weather conditions—the utility of a rapid means of communication like the telegraph was undeniable. But in all cases, the availability of the technology alone was only one piece in a puzzle in which it was the people who put technology to good or bad use, sending warning news about an approaching typhoon or perpetrating fraud by the telegraph.

The content of the newspaper was shaped by a number of actors: we have discussed, so far, the case of the journalists and other people associated with the production and circulation of the newspapers, but also the reading public who contributed, occasionally, items of intelligence to the press. In the next chapter, we turn our attention to the colonial government and Reuter's news agency, in an attempt to understand how colonial policy circumscribed processes of news reporting in the nineteenth century and how its visions of journalism were negotiated against those of other actors like Reuters.

Notes

1. Charles Bright, *Submarine Telegraphs: Their History, Construction, and Working* (London: Crosby Lockwood and Son, 1898), p. 174.
2. See 'Newspapers in India', *National Magazine*, 2 (1857), pp. 284–5, for an illustration of the widespread notion that early nineteenth century Anglo-Indian journals indulged in exaggerations, gossip, and scandal.
3. S. M. Mitra, *Anglo-Indian Studies* (New York, Bombay, and Calcutta: Longmans, Green & Co., 1913), p. 162.
4. Douglas Dewar, *Bygone Days in India* (London: John Lane the Bodley Head Ltd., 1922), p. 58; James Carey, 'The Problem of Journalism History', in *James Carey: A Critical Reader*, edited by Eve Stryker Munson and Catherine A. Warren (Minneapolis and London: University of Minnesota Press, 1997), p. 88. The notion that early journalists in India were mere 'adventurers' engaged in a questionable occupation was widespread among colonial administrators. In 1823, the chairman and deputy chairman of the East India Company described newspaper editors as 'a few European adventurers, who are found unfit to engage in any creditable method of subsistence'. See Letter from the Chairman and

Deputy Chairman of the East India Company to the Right Honourable Charles W. Williams Wynn, 17 January 1823, in United Kingdom, Parliament, House of Commons, *East India (Press): Papers Relating to the Public Press in India* (London, 4 May 1858), pp. 4–5.

5. In this connection, see Amelia Bonea, 'Telegraphy and Journalism in Colonial India, c. 1830s to 1900s', *History Compass* 12, no. 5 (2014): 387–97.
6. Victoria E. M. Gardner, 'Eighteenth-Century Newspapers and Public Opinion', in *The Routledge Companion to British Media History*, edited by Martin D. Conboy and John Steel (Abingdon: Routledge, 2015), p. 202. For an analysis of Hicky's practices and ideas of journalism in Calcutta, see Partha Chatterjee, *The Black Hole of Empire: History of a Global Practice of Power* (Princeton: Princeton University Press, 2012), pp. 109–20.
7. Alfred H. Watson, 'The Growth of the Press in English in India', *Journal of the Royal Society of Arts* 96, no. 4760 (1948): 121–30, at 122.
8. *Times of India*, 22 June 1876.
9. *Albina Carpaţilor*, 20 October 1877, p. 120.
10. Chatterjee, *The Black Hole of Empire*, pp. 109–20.
11. Martin D. Conboy, *Journalism: A Critical History* (London: Sage Publications, 2004), pp. 88–9; Gardner, 'Eighteenth-Century Newspapers and Public Opinion', pp. 195–205.
12. Aled Jones, *Powers of the Press: Newspapers, Power and the Public in Nineteenth-Century England* (Aldershot: Scolar Press, 1996), quoted in Conboy, *Journalism*, p. 89.
13. The sheer complexity of the press in colonial India frustrated Anglo-Indian commentators. J. D. Rees, for example, chose to distinguish between the Anglo-Indian press and the Indian press, by which he understood newspapers 'published by Indians for Indians'. A more elaborate classification was proposed by Arnold Wright, who identified four categories of newspapers: 'Anglo-Indian newspapers' or newspapers published in English by British residents in India; 'native papers' published in English; 'native papers' published partly in English and partly in the vernacular; and 'native papers' published entirely in the vernacular. See J. D. Rees, 'The Native Indian Press', *Nineteenth Century and After: A Monthly Review*, 49 (1901), p. 817; Arnold Wright, *Baboo English as 'Tis Writ: Being Curiosities of Indian Journalism* (London: T. Fisher Unwin, 1892), p. 9. Some contemporary scholars have advocated a similar interpretation of 'Indian newspapers' as being 'run by and for Indians', further distinguishing between English-language and vernacular newspapers, but also acknowledging that these journals were not ideologically monolithic. See Julie F. Codell, 'The Nineteenth-Century News from India', *Victorian Periodicals Review* 37, no. 2 (2004): 106–23, at 107.

14. William Knighton, *Tropical Sketches; Or, Reminiscences of an Indian Journalist*, vol. 1 (London: Hurst and Blackett, 1855), p. 228; Lucy Brown, 'The Treatment of News in Mid-Victorian Newspapers', *Transactions of the Royal Historical Society* 27 (1977): 23–39.
15. On paper production in India, see Ulrike Stark, *An Empire of Books: The Naval Kishore Press and the Diffusion of the Printed Word in Colonial India* (New Delhi: Permanent Black, 2009), p. 66. Chapter 1 of this book has also discussed the connection between postage and the choice of paper for the publication of newspapers in India. For an insight into such perceptions of 'Indian journals', understood here as English-language papers published by Anglo-Indians, see 'Indian Journals and Journalism', *Leeds Mercury*, 7 November 1865.
16. 'Journalism in India', *Reader* 6 (1865), p. 645, italics original. Also, 'Bombay: A Retrospect', *CR* 69 (1879), p. 277.
17. [William D. Arnold], 'Indian Light Literature', *CR* 51 (1856), p. 12.
18. In this connection, see also William Knighton's comment that 'No man can have been the editor of a newspaper anywhere, without making personal enemies. This is particularly the case in small communities, such as those of Colonial towns and the capitals of the Indian Presidencies.' Knighton, *Tropical Sketches*, p. vi.
19. Laurel Brake and Marysa Demoor (eds), *Dictionary of Nineteenth-Century Journalism in Great Britain and Ireland* (henceforth *DNCJ*) (Gent: Academia Press and the British Library, 2009), s.v. 'Anonymity and Signature', p. 18.
20. Arnold, 'Indian Light Literature', p. 12.
21. Notes on the subject of Government servants writing for the Press, Minute by Steuart Bayley, 4 June 1886, Foreign Department, Secret Branch I, August 1886, Nos 58–9, NAI.
22. W. M. Digby, 'The Native Newspapers of India and Ceylon', *CR* 65 (1877), pp. 360–1.
23. Wright, *Baboo English as 'Tis Writ*, p. 19.
24. Wright, *Baboo English as 'Tis Writ*, p. 16. Wright wrote, 'Between the Anglo-Indian papers and the native papers of the better class there is not such a wide gulf as those unacquainted with India are apt to suppose.' Note, however, that Wright emphasized the fact that this applied only to a few journals, '[t]he great majority [being] … poor specimens of journalistic enterprise. Badly printed, badly written, and dragging on a miserable existence with a handful of subscribers who are always in arrears with their subscriptions, they are contemptible as organs of public opinion. They are for the most part edited by aspiring native students, whose imperfect knowledge of English leads them to perpetrate most ridiculous blunders' (p. 17).
25. Roper Lethbridge, 'The Vernacular Press in India', *Contemporary Review* 37 (1880), p. 462.

26. On the emergence of Indian nationalism, see Sekhar Bandyopadhyay, *From Plassey to Partition: A History of Modern India* (New Delhi: Orient BlackSwan, 2009), pp. 184–226. On the reporting of the Ilbert Bill controversy in the British press, see Chandrika Kaul, 'England and India: The Ilbert Bill, 1883—A Case Study of the Metropolitan Press', *Indian Economic and Social History Review* 30, no. 4 (1993): 413–36.
27. S. Wheeler, 'The Indian Native Press', *Macmillan's Magazine* 58 (1888), p. 379.
28. G. M. Chesney, 'The Native Press in India', *Nineteenth Century: A Monthly Review* 43 (1898), pp. 269–71.
29. *DNCJ*, s. v. 'Journalism Schools', p. 326.
30. *DNCJ*, s. v. 'Journalism Schools', p. 326.
31. Knighton, *Tropical Sketches*, pp. 6–9. Knighton was not actually running the newspaper alone, but was helped by a Mr Fonseca, the clerk who 'received the advertisements, watched their insertion, computed their cost, and made out the bills', and by a Mr Perez, the head printer, who was in charge of a larger establishment of Portuguese and Sinhalese compositors.
32. Bipin Chandra Pal, *Memories of My Life and Times* (Calcutta: Bipin Chandra Pal Institute, 1973), pp. 301–2.
33. Pal, *Memories of My Life and Times*, p. 303.
34. J. K. Singh, *Media and Journalism* (New Delhi: A. P. H. Publishing Corporation, 2008), p. 2.
35. R. E. Wolseley (ed.), *Journalism in Modern India* (Bombay and Calcutta: Asia Publishing House, 1954), p. 236.
36. Robin Jeffrey, *India's Newspaper Revolution: Capitalism, Politics and the Indian-Language Press, 1977–1999* (London: Hurst & Co., 2000), pp. 140–1. Jeffrey's estimates are based on the Annual Report of the Registrar of Newspapers, which recorded 13,000 journalists in the 1990s. However, since the number of dailies recorded with the registrar was 700, of which only 320 submitted data regarding their employees, Jeffrey estimates that the real number of professional journalists was close to 25,000.
37. C. E. Buckland, *Dictionary of Indian Biography* (London: Swan Sonnenschein & Co., 1906).
38. Knight had many enemies in India due to his 'pro-native' opinions and he was also marginalized for 'not [being] part of that great fraternity of the covenanted service, a mere scribbler, with insignificant family and education, and a man of strange opinions'. See Edwin Hirschmann, *Robert Knight: Reforming Editor in Victorian India* (New Delhi: Oxford University Press, 2008), p. 131.
39. *Oxford English Dictionary*, s.v. 'journalist', available at: www.oed.com (accessed 25 June 2014).
40. The expression was familiar among journalists in colonial India. See Knighton, *Tropical Sketches*, p. 226; Dewar, *Bygone Days in India*, p. 85.

41. Sidney L. Blanchard, *Yesterday and To-day in India* (London: Wm. H. Allen & Co., 1867), p. 271.
42. J. H. Stocqueler, *The Memoirs of a Journalist* (Bombay: Times of India, 1873), pp. 62–3.
43. Pal, *Memories of My Life and Times*, pp. 359–60, 474. For comparison, his monthly expenses were Rs 20 for rent, Rs 8 for the cook, Rs 7 for a *chowkidar* (watchman) and a *punkha* (fan) puller, as well as a 'small sum' for a sweeper. Mutton and fish were sold for approximately 4 annas a seer in Lahore at the time, rice cost Rs 5 a maund, ghee 12 annas a seer, and milk was Re 1 per 8–10 seers.
44. Madan Gopal, *Life and Times of Dyal Singh Majithia* (New Delhi: Uppal Publishing House, 1999), p. 55.
45. Buckland, *Dictionary of Indian Biography*, pp. 306, 441; Dewar, *Bygone Days in India*, p. 63.
46. Buckland, *Dictionary of Indian Biography*, p. 50.
47. 'Dr. John Grant', *Parbury's Oriental Herald and Colonial Intelligencer* 2 (1838), p. 17. Dr Jameson of the same medical establishment also conducted the *Hurkaru and John Bull*. Dewar, *Bygone Days in India*, p. 65.
48. 'Government Advertisements', *Calcutta Gazette*, 18 May 1826, in A. C. Das Gupta (ed.), *The Days of John Company: Selections from the Calcutta Gazette, 1824–1832* (Calcutta: West Bengal Government Press, 1959), p. 116.
49. *Calcutta Monthly Journal and General Register of Occurrences, etc. for the Year 1837* (Calcutta: Samuel Smith & Co., 1838), p. 122.
50. Notes on the subject of government servants writing for the press, Note of Steuart Bayley, 4 June 1886, Foreign Department, Secret Branch I, August 1886, Nos 58–9, NAI.
51. A. F. S. Ahmed, *Social Ideas and Social Change in Bengal, 1818–1835* (Leiden: E. J. Brill, 1965), p. 61.
52. Buckland, *Dictionary of Indian Biography*, p. 441.
53. Knighton, *Tropical Sketches*, pp. 226–7.
54. The examples are numerous. George Roe Fenwick worked for the *Englishman*, the *Civil and Military Gazette*, and the *Broad Arrow*, while James Hutton wrote for the *Delhi Gazette, Bengal Hurkaru, Madras Times*, and the *Leader*. Similarly, James Mackenzie Maclean was associated with the *Newcastle Chronicle, Manchester Guardian*, and the *Bombay Gazette*, while Philip Stewart Robinson's name was connected with newspapers like the *Pioneer, Pall Mall Gazette*, and the *Daily Telegraph*. See Buckland, *Dictionary of Indian Biography*, pp. 144, 213, 265, 362. Also, James Mackenzie Maclean, *Recollections of Westminster and India* (Manchester: Sherratt & Hughes, 1901), pp. 14–19.
55. William Howard Russell, *My Indian Mutiny Diary* (London: Cassell, 1957).

56. Buckland, *Dictionary of Indian Biography*, p. 460. Another *Times* correspondent in India was Joseph Archer Crowe of the *Bombay Gazette* and *Bombay Standard*.
57. Surendranath Banerjea, *A Nation in the Making: Being the Reminiscences of Fifty Years of Public Life* (Calcutta: Oxford University Press, 1963 [1925]), p. 55.
58. Gopal, *Life and Times of Dyal Singh Majithia*, p. 82.
59. Knighton, *Tropical Sketches*, p. 3.
60. Mrs. Robert Moss King, *The Diary of a Civilian's Wife in India, 1877–1882*, vol. 1 (London: Bentley and Son, 1884), p. 117.
61. Dosabhai F. Karaka, *History of the Parsis: Including Their Manners, Customs, Religion, and Present Position*, vol. 1 (London: Macmillan and Co., 1884), p. 330.
62. Other famous Parsi journalists included Maneckji Minocher-Homji and Dinshaw Edulji Wacha.
63. *Times of India*, 13 June 1904. The *Indian Banner* was an English-language weekly established in Bombay in June 1860 for the purpose of 'supplying the want' of an English newspaper in Bombay 'under native proprietorship to advocate the rights and interests of the native community'.
64. Statement of English Newspapers and Periodicals published in the Bombay Presidency during the Year 1897, Foreign Department, Internal Branch B, December 1898, Nos 379/81, NAI.
65. Statement of English Newspapers and Periodicals published in the Bombay Presidency during the Year 1897, Foreign Department, Internal Branch B, December 1898, Nos 379/81, NAI.
66. *First Report on the Operations of the Electric Telegraph Department in India, from 1st February 1855 to 31st January 1856* (Calcutta: Thos. Jones, 1856), V/24/4282, p. 4, IOR.
67. *Delhi Gazette*, 13 January 1855; emphasis in original.
68. *Delhi Gazette*, 8 February 1855; emphasis added. Sixteen was the unit of length by which messages were charged at the time of the opening, that is, the cost of 16 words per 400 miles of telegraph line was Re 1.
69. Bright, *Submarine Telegraphs*, pp. 174–5.
70. Bright, *Submarine Telegraphs*, p. 169.
71. Bright, *Submarine Telegraphs*, p. 170. Even an enthusiastic commentator like Bright could not overlook the fact that the telegraph was a 'double-edged sword' whose use required a careful balancing act between national, international, and imperial interests. Nowhere was this more visible than in the discussion of Japan's rise to the status of an 'Oriental' power—which, Bright asserted, was inextricably connected with the consolidation of the cable system in East Asia—or the assertion that Germany was guilty of stealing and improving upon Britain's 'industrial thunder' (p. 169).

72. Ralph O'Connor (ed.), *Science as Romance*, vol. 7 of *Victorian Science and Literature*, edited by G. Dawson and B. Lightman (London: Pickering & Chatto, 2012), p. 327.
73. John Darwin, *The Empire Project: The Rise and Fall of the British World-System, 1830–1970* (Cambridge: Cambridge University Press, 2009), pp. 66–7; M. Elshakry and S. Sivasundaram (eds), *Science, Race and Imperialism*, vol. 6 of *Victorian Science and Literature*, edited by G. Dawson and B. Lightman (London: Pickering & Chatto, 2012), p. 299.
74. Knighton, *Tropical Sketches*, p. v.
75. Knighton, *Tropical Sketches*, pp. 19–20; emphasis added.
76. Terhi Rantanen, *When News Was New* (Chichester: Wiley-Blackwell, 2009), p. 14.
77. Sinclair refers here to the time difference between Germany and Britain. Alexander Sinclair, *Fifty Years of Newspaper Life, 1845–1895* (Glasgow: privately printed, c. 1898), p. 75.
78. Sinclair, *Fifty Years of Newspaper Life*, p. 578; Emily Dickinson, *The Complete Poems of Emily Dickinson*, edited by Thomas H. Johnson (Boston: Little, Brown, and Company, 1961), p. 1089; J. H. McCormack, 'Domesticating Delphi: Emily Dickinson and the Electro-Magnetic Telegraph', *American Quarterly* 55, no. 4 (2003): 569–601, at 570.
79. 'News', *Chambers's Journal of Popular Literature, Science and Arts*, p. 227.
80. For an overview of nineteenth-century approaches to literature and journalism in Britain, see *DNCJ*, s. v. 'Literature and Journalism', pp. 367–8.
81. 'News', *Chambers's Journal of Popular Literature, Science and Arts*, p. 227.
82. Rudyard Kipling, *The Man Who Would Be King & Other Stories* (Hertfordshire: Wordsworth Classics, 1994), p. 120.
83. Complaints about the tediousness of night shifts were common among the telegraphists themselves.
84. *DNCJ*, p. 81; *Bradshaw's Railway & c. through Route and Overland Guide to India* (London: W. J. Adam, 1858), p. 11.
85. *Bradshaw's Railway*, p. 132.
86. *Bradshaw's Railway*, p. 11.
87. William Acworth, 'The South-Eastern and the Chatham Railways', *Murray's Magazine* 4 (1888), p. 216.
88. Acworth, 'The South-Eastern and the Chatham Railways', p. 220.
89. Acworth, 'The South-Eastern and the Chatham Railways', p. 217.
90. Acworth, 'The South-Eastern and the Chatham Railways', p. 218.
91. Acworth, 'The South-Eastern and the Chatham Railways', p. 215. Letters for Belgium and south Germany were carried by Belgium, while Dutch and north German letters were carried by the Dutch.
92. Acworth, 'The South-Eastern and the Chatham Railways', pp. 220–1.

93. The Wheatstone automatic telegraph was patented in 1858, but was used in Britain only from 1867. Its main feature was that it separated the preparation of the message from its transmission through the use of a 'keying machine' that enabled operators to inscribe the message on paper tape as punch holes. The slip was then introduced into the transmitting instrument. See K. Beauchamp, *History of Telegraphy* (London: The Institution of Engineering and Technology, 2001), pp. 72–3.
94. 'The Signal Haulyards of the Empire', *Leisure Hour*, February 1901, pp. 271–2. The siphon recorder was a cable receiving device patented in 1867 by William Thomson and used by the British India Submarine Telegraph Company to facilitate the transmission of underwater signals. A description of the recorder can be found in Beauchamp, *History of Telegraphy*, p. 154: 'It resembled a modern moving-coil microammeter, having a coil suspended between the poles of a powerful magnet which moved when current flowed through it. This movement was conveyed to a capillary tube, one end of which moved across a paper ribbon, the other end dipping into a well of ink. The writing end of the tube did not touch the paper, so the device was virtually "friction free"; the ink was caused to emerge by maintaining an electric charge on the tube with the paper ribbon held at earth potential as it passed over a metal roller. The ink was ejected onto the paper as a series of closely spaced dots, giving a straight line in the absence of a signal, but moving to the left or right as the signal went positive or negative, to indicate a dot or a dash.'
95. 'The Signal Haulyards of the Empire', *History of Telegraphy*, p. 273.
96. *First Report on the Operations of the Electric Telegraph Department in India, from 1st February 1855 to 31st January 1856* (Calcutta: Thos. Jones, 1856), V/24/4282, p. 5, IOR.
97. *First Report on the Operations of the Electric Telegraph Department in India*, p. xxxviii.
98. *First Report on the Operations of the Electric Telegraph Department in India*, p. 282.
99. Joseph Archer Crowe, *Reminiscences of Thirty-Five Years of My Life* (London: John Murray, 1895), p. 259.
100. *First Report on the Operations of the Electric Telegraph Department in India*, pp. 20–1.
101. *First Report on the Operations of the Electric Telegraph Department in India*, p. 57.
102. C. Beadon to W. B. O'Shaughnessy, 22 October 1858, Foreign Department, Consultation No. 38, NAI; News brought by mail steamers arriving at Madras, Home Department, Public Branch, 5 February 1858, No. 76, NAI.
103. C. Beadon to W. B. O'Shaughnessy, 22 October 1858, Foreign Department, Consultation No. 38, NAI.

104. *Administration Report of the Indian Telegraph Department for 1860–1*, Appendix L, Government Telegraph Department, General Branch, Circular No. 37, V/24/4283, IOR.
105. *Administration Report of the Indian Telegraph Department for 1860–1*, Government Telegraph Department, General Branch, Circular No. 53, V/24/4283, IOR.
106. Minute of G. F. Edmonstone, 24 July 1857, Foreign Department, Consultation Nos 62–6, NAI.
107. *Administration Report of the Indian Telegraph Department for 1892–3*, V/24/4287, p. 16, IOR.
108. *Administration Report of the Indian Telegraph Department for 1880–1*, V/24/4286, p. 8, IOR.
109. *Administration Report of the Indian Telegraph Department for 1879–80*, V/24/4286, p. 7, IOR.
110. N. K. Sehgal and S. Mahanti (eds), *Memoirs of Ruchi Ram Sahni: Pioneer of Science Popularisation in Punjab* (New Delhi: Vigyan Prasar, 1997), pp. 6–7. For comparison, Dallas was paid a monthly salary of Rs 500.
111. Sehgal and Mahanti, *Memoirs of Ruchi Ram Sahni*, pp. 16–18.
112. *Times of India*, 26 June 1884; *Bharat Jiwan*, 7 July 1884.
113. Sehgal and Mahanti, *Memoirs of Ruchi Ram Sahni*, p. 25.
114. For a full description of the storm, see John Eliot, *Handbook of the Cyclonic Storms in the Bay of Bengal for the Use of Sailors* (Calcutta: Superintendent of Government Printing, 1890), pp. 172–82.
115. Sehgal and Mahanti, *Memoirs of Ruchi Ram Sahni*, pp. 25–7.
116. *Administration Report of the Indian Telegraph Department for 1885–6*, V/24/4286, p. 17, IOR.
117. 'The Cyclone on the Orissa Coast', *Times of India*, 2 October 1885; 'The Cyclone at False Point', *Times of India*, 5 October 1885, 12 October 1885; 'The Late Cyclone in Bengal', *Times of India*, 8 October 1885.
118. *Administration Report of the Indian Telegraph Department for 1871–2*, V/24/4284, p. 16, IOR.
119. *Administration Report of the Indian Telegraph Department for 1873–4*, V/24/4284, pp. 6–7, IOR.
120. *Administration Reports of the Indian Telegraph Department for 1876–7*, V/24/4285, p. 19, IOR.
121. *Administration Report of the Indian Telegraph Department for 1874–5*, V/24/4284, p. 9, IOR.
122. *Administration Report of the Indian Telegraph Department for 1880–1*, V/24/4286, p. 4, IOR.
123. *Administration Report of the Indian Telegraph Department for 1880–1*, V/24/4286, p. 8, IOR.
124. *Administration Report of the Indian Telegraph Department for 1879-80*, V/24/4286, p. 9, IOR.

125. *Times of India*, 2 July 1886.
126. *Bombay Quarterly Review*, 1 (1855), n.p.
127. Ahmed, *Social Ideas and Social Change in Bengal*, pp. 78–9; M. Barns, *The Indian Press* (London: George Allen & Unwin Ltd, 1940), pp. 181–2; J. Natarajan, *History of Indian Journalism* (New Delhi: Publications Division, 1954), pp. 33–5.
128. As Ahmed rightly points out, the *Calcutta Chronicle* had ceased to exist in 1827, which means that Stockwell was most probably referring to the *Bengal Chronicle*. Ahmed, *Social Ideas and Social Change in Bengal*, p. 79. During the same period, William Knighton reported 480 subscribers to the *Ceylon Herald*. Knighton, *Tropical Sketches*, p. 2.
129. Barns, *The Indian Press*, p. 182.
130. Barns, *The Indian Press*, pp. 182–3. According to Long ('Early Bengali Literature and Newspapers', p. 153), during 1820–35 there were six 'native' newspapers of which four were in Bengali and two in Persian.
131. Barns, *The Indian Press*, pp. 182–3.
132. Barns, *The Indian Press*, pp. 181–2.
133. 'Appeal of a Governor General to Public Opinion in India', *Oriental Herald*, 1 (1824), p. 9.
134. See, for example, the *Delhi Gazette* of 6 January 1855 and 31 March 1855.
135. Rev. James Long, 'Returns Relating to the Publications in the Bengali Language, in 1857, to which is added, a list of the Native Presses, with the Books Printed at Each, their Price and Character, with a Notice of the Past Condition and Future Prospects of the Vernacular Press of Bengal, and the Statistics of the Bombay and Madras Vernacular Presses', *Selections from the Records of the Bengal Government*, no. 32 (Calcutta: John Gray, 1859), p. 36. In comparison, the *Bharat Jiwan*, a popular newspaper in the North-West Provinces and Oudh, had a circulation of 1,500 at the end of the century. According to lists published in July 1884, its subscribers were based in Gazipur, Gaya, Benares, Patna, Danapur (Dinapur), Jaipur, Allahabad, Bijnor, Lahore, Shahjahanpur, and so on. See *Bharat Jiwan*, 7 July 1884, 21 July 1884; *Statement Exhibiting the Moral and Material Progress and Condition of India during the Year 1899–1900* (London: Eyre and Spottiswoode, 1901), p. 177.
136. *NNR*, Bengal, No. 36 of 1890, pp. 830–1.
137. *NNR*, Bengal, No. 36 of 1890, pp. 830–1.
138. *NNR*, Bengal, No. 36 of 1890, pp. 830–1.
139. Statement of English Newspapers and Periodicals Published in the Bombay Presidency during the Year 1897, Foreign Department, Internal Branch B, December 1898, Nos 379–81, NAI.
140. *Imperial Gazetteer of India*, vol. 4: *Administrative* (Oxford: Clarendon Press, 1909), p. 415.
141. Digby, 'The Native Newspapers of India and Ceylon', p. 363.

142. Shevantibai M. Nikambe, *Ratanbai: A Sketch of a Bombay High Caste Hindu Young Wife* (London: Marshall Brothers, 1895), p. 77, italics original. Ratanbai's story, although inspired by Nikambe's own experiences with upper-caste women's education in Bombay, is fictitious. For an example of such lists of successful candidates who passed the matriculation examination, see the *Times of India*, 23 December 1871.
143. A. R. Iyengar, *The Newspaper Press in India* (Bangalore: Bangalore Press, 1933), p. 5.
144. Digby, 'The Native Newspapers of India and Ceylon', p. 363.
145. Mark Hampton, *Visions of the Press in Britain, 1850–1950* (Urbana and Chicago: University of Illinois Press, 2004), p. 27.
146. G. F. Atkinson, *'Curry & Rice', On Forty Plates* (London: Day & Son, 1859?), n.p.
147. D. E. Wacha, *Shells from the Sands of Bombay, Being My Recollections and Reminiscences, 1860–1875* (Bombay: The Bombay Chronicle Press, 1920), p. 675. In Britain, the choice of newspapers from India was equally diverse, although in the early days there was a clear bias towards newspapers from Bengal. In 1845, among the newspapers available at the library of the East India Company in London were titles such as the *Calcutta Gazette*, the *Friend of India*, the *Maulmain Chronicle*, the *Murshidabad News*, the *Weekly Intelligencer*, and the *Bengal Catholic Herald*, all of them published in Bengal. See *East India Company Library: A Catalogue of the Library of the Hon. East-India Company* (London: J. & H. Cox, 1845), p. 123.
148. Sayagi Rao Gaekwar, 'My Ways and Days in Europe and India', *The Nineteenth Century and After* 49 (1901), p. 223.
149. Surendranath Banerjea, quoted in Somnath Roy, 'Repercussions of the Vernacular Press Act', *Journal of Indian History* 45, part 3 (1967): 735–48, at 738.
150. Digby, 'The Native Newspapers of India and Ceylon', p. 363.
151. N. J. Ratnagar, *Short Essays on Literary and Social Subjects for Matriculation Candidates and Others* (Bombay: Jehangir Karani, 1879), p. 84.
152. Stark, *An Empire of Books*, p. 360.
153. *Half-Yearly Report of the Committee of the Bengal Chamber of Commerce, Calcutta, November 1, 1855* (Calcutta: Military Orphan Press, 1855), pp. 3–4.
154. *Report of the Bombay Chamber of Commerce, 1864–5* (Bombay: Pearse and Sorabjee, 1866), pp. 49–50.
155. Banerjea, *A Nation in the Making*, pp. 64–5.
156. Margrit Pernau and Yunus Jaffery (eds), *Information and the Public Sphere: Persian Newsletters from Mughal Delhi* (New Delhi: Oxford University Press, 2009), pp. 2, 274.

157. M. Ranganathan, trans., *Govind Narayan's Mumbai: An Urban Biography from 1863* (London and New York: Anthem Press, 2008), p. 189.
158. [A. Fenton], *Memoirs of a Cadet* (London: Saunders and Otley, 1839), pp. 2–4, 33–4. The low-lying island of Saugor, situated at the mouth of the Hooghly, was three days' sailing distance away from Chandpal Ghat, the usual gateway to Calcutta and India.
159. Ralph Russell (ed.), *The Oxford India Ghalib: Life, Letters and Ghazals* (Oxford: Oxford University Press, 2003), p. 15; emphasis original.
160. King, *The Diary of a Civilian's Wife*, vol. 2, p. 230.

4 Making News and Views

Colonial Policy and the Role of Reuters

> As to the Press Commissionership and its work I have never been able to see why the Government of India should supply not merely gratis, but at a heavy cost to itself, newspaper owners with the raw material of their business. Butchers and bakers might just as reasonably ask us to provide them with meat and flour.
>
> —Whitley Stokes, *Foreign Department Proceedings* (1881)

The famous motto of the *New York Times*, 'All the news that's fit to print', was first used in 1896 by the American publisher Adolph Simon Ochs, but it would not have looked out of place on the masthead of many a newspaper published in colonial India. While Ochs's approach to reporting was shaped by his desire to distance himself from the yellow journalism of contemporaries like Joseph Pulitzer and William Randolph Hearst, in nineteenth-century India the notion of news that was 'fit to print' was inextricably linked to the imperatives of colonial rule and the colonial state's own vision of how journalism should be conducted. The mastheads of many an Anglo-Indian newspaper, with their titles, mottos, and accompanying visual ornamentation, document a history of political and technological transformation and testify to the intertwined nature of journalism and colonial politics.

Take, for example, the *Bombay Courier*, a newspaper established in 1790 by Luke Ashburner, senior member of the Mayor's Court of Bombay, whose front page displayed the coat of arms of the East India Company. In an environment where official patronage was crucial to the survival of a young journal, this public declaration of loyalty was also a strategic advertising ploy. The *Courier*, one of the earliest newspapers published in Bombay, proved successful in negotiating its relationship with the authorities, especially if we consider its lifespan and the fact that in the late eighteenth century it was regularly exchanged by post for 'Government newspapers' from Bengal.[1] By the mid-nineteenth century, however, both the political circumstances of British India and the technology itself had changed. The development of electric telegraphy prompted newspaper publishers around the world to incorporate the new technology not only in reporting practices but also in the very titles of their publications. In 1847, the *Courier* was merged with the *Bombay Telegraph* to form the *Bombay Telegraph and Courier*, which was itself incorporated into the *Times of India* in 1861. By this time, the days of the Company Raj were also over, as the coat of arms of the British Crown, now featured on the masthead of the *Times of India*, reminded its readers.[2]

Using the symbolism of the mastheads as an entry point, this chapter examines the relationship between the press and the colonial state in nineteenth-century India, aiming to understand how the latter formulated and attempted to impose its own vision of news that was 'fit to print', and how official designs coexisted or clashed with those of another central player in the process of news distribution between Britain and India, Reuter's news agency. The chapter begins with an overview of press regulations in the nineteenth century. This highlights the ways in which the evolving legislative framework of the colonial state circumscribed the publication of various types of intelligence in the newspaper press of British India. Early attempts to prohibit discussion of certain categories of information, especially of a military and commercial nature, were followed, in the second half of the nineteenth century, by more sustained efforts to control the dissemination of official intelligence through the implementation of a number of schemes of news distribution. The analysis focuses on the government's first major attempt to centralize the distribution of news through the institution of the press commissioner (1877–89). It maps the transformation of this institution from an office that was expected to 'manage' the government's relationship with the

English-language press to one that monitored and 'improved' the vernacular newspapers in the aftermath of the Vernacular Press Act (1878), and its eventual decline after the repeal of that Act in 1881. The chapter ends with an analysis of Reuter's position in the communication circuit of colonial South Asia. It traces the agency's ongoing negotiations with the colonial state and the press over the supply of foreign news to the subcontinent and identifies the priorities that shaped Reuter's approach to journalism.

Interrogating official rhetoric that often equated news reporting with the publication of 'objective facts', the discussion in this chapter shows that news in colonial South Asia was a field where power relations were constantly being played out. Attempts to regulate, control, and shape the circulation and content of intelligence were, in effect, exercises in defining news and advancing visions of journalism that were subservient to imperialist interests. The electric telegraph played an important role in debates about the meaning of journalism, as a technology that facilitated timely access to intelligence and was inextricably connected to the accumulation of political and economic capital.

But telegraphic communication remained costly during the nineteenth century. Differential access to telegraphy generated an ideological split between those who promoted an understanding of news as a public good and those, like Reuters and the *Pioneer*, who insisted that news was a commodity. The former view, enthusiastically espoused by many representatives of the vernacular press and Anglo-Indian newspapers who resented the *Pioneer*'s cosy relationship with the government, was also endorsed, albeit reluctantly and contextually, by some colonial administrators. Supplying a section of the press with official intelligence free of charge, they argued, would enable the colonial government to better manage its public image; the measure was also expected to 'improve' the 'tone' of the Anglo-Indian press and, by force of example, that of its vernacular counterpart. This view also became the basis on which the colonial authorities rejected Reuter's repeated requests that its telegrams be granted temporary copyright to prevent piracy by non-subscribing newspapers.

By contrast, advocates of the latter strand of opinion emphasized the work and financial effort involved in the collection and dissemination of information and argued that it was the duty of the newspapers to shoulder the costs. This position inevitably made the press dependent on Reuters for the supply of foreign news. It also created rifts between the *Pioneer* and the rest of the press, as well as between major newspapers published in urban centres and less financially viable journals that could not afford to hire special correspondents or pay Reuter's expensive subscription fees.

Regulating the News, 1780–1835

As Bernard Cohn has shown in his classic study of colonialism in India, law was one of the important 'instrumentalities' which helped the British colonizers to rule over various domains of Indian social life.[3] Like in other fields of activity, legal interventions in the press world were exercises in defining, ordering, and controlling. The regulating arm of the state extended not only to the content of intelligence, but also to the very media which transmitted it: the telegraph, the steamer, the railway, and so on. The official debates which surrounded the enactment of press laws at various times during the nineteenth century are particularly illuminating in this respect. The topics discussed, often subsumed under the generic title of 'liberty of the press', pertained to a wide range of issues such as the right of newspapers to publish and comment on official information, their access to postal and telegraphic services, the role of the press as an instrument of education and an organ of public opinion, colonial surveillance and censorship, and news copyright.

The colonial state attempted to control the activity of the press in the subcontinent in many ways, some more obvious, such as introducing a system of licensing for newspapers and prohibiting 'seditious' writing, and others more subtle, like withdrawing subscriptions and advertising, refusing to grant postal subsidies, and restricting access to sources of official information and to the technologies used to transmit it.[4] There was an increasing obsession with the 'seditious' activities of the vernacular press as the century advanced, an attitude which was inextricably linked with the creation and staging of difference between the press conducted by Indians and that conducted by their British rulers (see also Chapter 3).

The early history of the newspaper press in India, spanning the years between the publication, in 1780, of the 'first' Indian newspaper, Hicky's *Bengal Gazette*, and the passing, in 1835, of

Sir Charles Metcalfe's Act XI which 'liberated' the press by putting an end to the system of licensing then in force in Bengal and Bombay, can be described as a formative period. It was a time when the government was reluctantly coming to terms with the expansion and growing influence of the press and debating the advantages and disadvantages of having a 'free press' in India.[5] In what follows, I will trace these discussions with a focus on the right of newspapers to publish various types of intelligence, especially news about the affairs of the government.

At the end of the eighteenth century, two categories of information were particularly likely to attract the 'displeasure' of colonial officials: 'scandalous' items discussing the conduct of government officials, in the manner inaugurated by Hicky himself, and information about the military campaigns of the East India Company. In 1796, for example, the editor of the *Calcutta Gazette* was 'admonished' for inserting in his newspaper 'certain communications on the subject of peace, which had passed between the Court of London and the French Republic'. Two years later, Charles Maclean was deported to England for publishing a letter in the Calcutta newspaper, the *Telegraph*, in which he criticized the magistrate of Gazipur.[6] As J. Pattison and W. Wigram, chairman and deputy chairman respectively of the East India Company, observed, during the last two decades of the eighteenth century the government's position when dealing with such cases of insubordination oscillated between a more 'lenient' stance, usually censure, to the more drastic decision to deport the offender.[7]

In 1791, the Government of Bombay was the first to introduce formal regulations for the control of the press; eight years later, similar measures were enforced in Bengal and Madras.[8] According to the rules issued by Marquis Wellesley in May 1799, newspapers in Calcutta were required to publish the name of their printer at the bottom of the paper, while the identity and place of residence of the editors and proprietors had to be communicated to the secretary to the government. The content of the publication was also subjected to official scrutiny, no newspaper being allowed to go to the press without prior inspection by the same administrator. Wellesley's regulations restricted even more the range of news which could be published by the press: not only military intelligence, but also commercial information came under the purview of the new measure. Among the items prohibited was intelligence referring to the state of public credit and the finances of the East India Company; shipping news; military and naval information, such as that concerning the embarkation of troops, stores, or specie; personal information; and criticism of government officials and officers.[9]

These measures, however, were not easily implemented. Some editors refused to submit their publications to censorship or to disclose the names of their correspondents, many of whom were military officers. Others went on publishing intelligence of the kind prohibited by law. This included information about the British fleet in India, army lists, and military orders. On one occasion, 'an account of the route from Janickpoor to Catmandhoo' was published in the *Mirror* of Calcutta, despite the fact that the secretary to the government had prohibited the disclosure of this information.[10]

The regulations of 1799 were passed at a time when the liberty of the press was also a topic of heated debate 'at Home', not only in India; ironically, Wellesley was among those who had supported press freedom in Britain.[11] Once in India, however, he contrived to suppress 'the tribe of editors' in Calcutta and to make newspapers subservient to the expansionist designs of the East India Company. Apart from a general dislike towards the 'adventurers' who conducted the press, the government was also wary of the increasing importance of newspapers as a source of information about military and political affairs. This situation was not without its advantages for the government. On one occasion, Wellesley used newspapers to obtain intelligence about the movements of the French in the subcontinent and forwarded an article about Napoleon, originally published in a Frankfurt newspaper, to Ceylon, Goa, Mysore, and Malabar. In 1800, he also directed the British resident at Bussorah (Basra) to dispatch fortnightly, by boat or cruiser, 'all Continental journals and other public newspapers so highly important and interesting at the present conjuncture'.[12]

But the circulation of such sensitive information, especially via newspapers seemingly published 'under the authority of the Government', had the potential to undermine British interests in India. There was, of course, the danger that such information would fall into the hands of enemies. At the same time, public dissemination enlarged the sphere of those who could debate—and potentially question or criticize—the East India Company's motives and actions.[13] During a time of consolidation of British rule in the subcontinent, when fear of the French and the 'native' princes was taking a grip on the British imagination, suppressing the press became a convenient way of camouflaging the military campaigns of the East India Company and attempting to shroud its commercial affairs in a veil of secrecy.

Wellesley's legislation came under scrutiny during the governorship of Lord Hastings (1813–23), when an incident involving Jacob Heatley, the Eurasian editor of the Calcutta *Morning Post*, prompted the authorities to reconsider and eventually abolish the extant system of censorship. The limitations of expulsion as a means of punishing unflinching editors had become obvious when Heatley, who was born in Bengal, decided to go ahead and publish material deemed 'objectionable' by the chief secretary to the government.[14] Faced with the inefficiency of the existing system of censorship, the government decided to pass new regulations on 19 August 1818 which removed the obligation to obtain official sanction prior to publication, but prohibited certain types of intelligence from being discussed in the newspaper press. These included criticism of the East India Company and other relevant public authorities in England, information of a 'scandalous' nature, and 'discussions having a tendency to create alarm or suspicion among the native population, or any intended interference with their religious opinions or observances'.[15] Editors became responsible for the content of their newspapers, copies of which still had to be submitted to the authorities.

This relative relaxation in government control over the press did not bring the freedom of expression some editors had hoped for. In fact, responding to a correspondent's letter on 27 November 1822, the editor of the *Calcutta Journal*, James Silk Buckingham, exposed the ways in which censorship insinuated itself into editorial activity, shaping news values and the content of the newspaper:

> The Letter of 'A Griffin,' dated from Fort William, would, we fear, come also under one of the prohibited heads [that is, political transactions and personal remarks]. Some portions of it, complaining of the general and unmerited neglect shewn by the Society of India to King's Officers, as compared with the attentions they receive in foreign countries and at home, might perhaps be printed, as well as the complaints of the extravagant rates of admission to public places of amusement, as there [*sic*] are harmless subjects of discussion. But in the letter in question these parts are so mixed up with more inflammable matter, that we should dread a sudden combustion and explosion, if some one of the many who are always ready to ignite whatever we publish, were to fire the train.[16]

The period 1818–23 was marked by intense debate about the desirability and meaning of a free press in India. Much of this discussion was fuelled by Buckingham's radical journalism, which eventually led to his expulsion from India in 1823. His insistence on the benefits of a free press in India did not go down well with a colonial government which feared that public opinion could be easily swayed against it, especially, as Hastings had pointed out, since the empire itself was held through 'opinion'.[17] This was an early indication of the role of the press in mediating and shaping perceptions of British rule in India, not only for the public in India, but also, especially during the first decades of the nineteenth century, for readers 'at Home'. Hastings's temporary successor John Adam proved even less inclined to tolerate the insubordination of a clique of journalists who, as we have previously seen, were dismissed by many administrators as mere 'adventurers'. In March 1823, having resolved to revoke Buckingham's licence to reside in India, Adam changed the press legislation once again, introducing a cumbersome procedure for the licensing of newspapers and magazines published 'in any language or character whatsoever'.[18]

It was not only English-language opinion that the government feared. By this time, newspapers in Bengali, Urdu, and Persian were also beginning to proliferate in Bengal. As Lynn Zastoupil points out, Buckingham himself was deeply interested in Raja Rammohun Roy's journalism, frequently publishing the table of contents or translations of his articles from *Sambad Kaumudi* (1821, Bengali) and *Mirat-ul-Akhbar* (1822, Persian).[19] Like Buckingham, Roy was intensely preoccupied with the issue of press freedom. In a memorial submitted to the Supreme Court of Judicature at Fort William in March 1823, he and other representatives of the Bengali intelligentsia pointed out that the press was, along with colleges, schools, and courts of law, one of the 'beneficial institutions' introduced by the British to India, an instrument of social improvement which promoted free discussion and stimulated the appetite for knowledge among Indians.[20] Referring specifically to the newspapers he had established, Roy explained that they served this aim by publishing primarily two types of information: 'accounts of whatever occurs worthy of notice at the Presidency or in the country' and 'the interesting and valuable intelligence of what is passing in England and in other parts of the world, conveyed through the English Newspapers or other channels'. In addition, vernacular journals also published 'translations into the popular dialect of this country from the learned languages of the East' and 'literary intelligence drawn from foreign publications'.[21]

Thus, for Rammohun Roy the purpose of the newspaper was twofold: to inform and to educate. Regular access to foreign and domestic intelligence was central to this process of social and moral instruction. But the traffic of information mediated by the newspaper press was by no means unidirectional. As Roy and others after him insisted, newspapers facilitated conversation between the British rulers and their Indian subjects not only by informing the latter about official affairs, but also by enabling the former to familiarize themselves with the opinions of those they ruled.[22]

For the representatives of the East India Company, however, the idea of a free press was incompatible with India's form of government. A free press was an indispensable accessory to representative government, but, as Pattison and Wigram pointed out in 1823, '[I]n no sense of the terms can the Government of India be called a free, a representative, or a popular government. The people had no voice in its establishment, nor have they any control over its acts.'[23] The result was a paradoxical situation in which government and public opinion did not inhabit the same geographical space, for while the former was located in India, the latter, it was claimed, could only be located in England. India was denied the ability to nurture constructive debate and discussion. This idea proved enduring. As we will shortly see, it survived the expansion of the Indian press and saw colonial administrators like Owen T. Burne argue, well into the nineteenth century, that the only public opinion of any consequence was the one 'at Home', not in India.

Much to the dislike of the East India Company, on 3 August 1835, Governor General Charles Metcalfe decided to reverse Adam's decision, passing Act XI which repealed the previous press regulations in Bengal and Bombay. Despite this apparent 'liberation' of the press, the new measure still required newspaper managers to disclose the location of their offices and the names of those involved in the process of publication. In fact, as M. T. Boyce has pointed out, the Act was an exercise in legal standardization and a conciliatory measure towards the Indian press. Its ultimate aim, however, was to benefit the imperial enterprise through the promotion of 'useful' knowledge that was expected to 'remove prejudices, soften asperities, and substitute a rational conviction of the benefits of our government'.[24] Metcalfe's press was not 'free' in the sense that it could publish anything it wanted. The fact that the government recognized the right of the press to publish and engage with political and military intelligence was indeed a change from the late eighteenth century idea that the affairs of the East India Company should not form the object of reporting in the newspaper press. But few would have doubted that the government could still exercise its arbitrary power to close down or to censor the content of a newspaper.

Commenting on these developments and their ramifications into the second part of the nineteenth century, Partha Chatterjee has recently pointed out that during this period 'the idea of a free press would exist in India only to the extent that the language of opinion was English. Everything else was subject to the rule of colonial difference and liable to be declared as exceptions to the universal principle of liberty.'[25] Although correct, I believe this statement should be qualified by pointing out that despite colonial rhetoric, in practice the idea of a free press was rarely unproblematic, even in those cases when the language of opinion was English. In addition, the English-language press, as the following sections will also discuss, was beset by hierarchies. The principle of liberty was not universal in its application to the English-language press: what was tolerated of a British newspaper was not necessarily tolerated of an Anglo-Indian one. By the same token, what was acceptable in a major Anglo-Indian daily was not necessarily considered acceptable in a newspaper conducted by an Indian, and so on. Such differences, informed by race, class, and language, were especially visible in the government's highly discriminatory policy of distributing official intelligence to the press during the second half of the nineteenth century, which focused almost exclusively on the needs and news values of the major Anglo-Indian newspapers at the expense of other sections of the press, such as smaller English-language and vernacular publications.

Press Regulations in the Second Half of the Nineteenth Century

By the second half of the period, with the gradual change in government policy and the expansion of the newspaper press, both in the English language and the vernaculars, express prohibitions regarding the publication of certain items of intelligence in the press had become untenable. Far from suggesting that the authorities now welcomed such debates, what this meant in practice was that the government decided to refocus its energies from overt prohibition to devising more subtle ways of controlling and managing the dissemination of intelligence. Repressive practices by no means disappeared, as the Indian Mutiny and the Vernacular Press Act demonstrate, but there was a growing concern to 'educate' journalists to report 'correct information' and 'facts'. Another important development during this period was that the vernacular press became more clearly identified as a target of government intervention and control.

In 1856, the authorities acknowledged reluctantly that the publication of official documents 'of general interest [was] likely, under due regulation, to be attended with advantage both to the Government, and to the Community', as long as items were selected 'with the requisite caution' and the premature publication of issues under debate was avoided.[26] But the dramatic events of 1857 and the role of vernacular newspapers therein added a new impetus to the government's designs to monitor the press in order to identify and suppress potentially dangerous publications.[27] Prompted by the events of the Mutiny, Lord Canning reintroduced the system of licensing for newspapers with the passing of Act XV of 1857, also known as the Gagging Act. Although a short-lived measure that applied to both English-language and vernacular newspapers, the Act marked the beginning of an increasing obsession with the subversive activities of the vernacular press which was to continue well into the twentieth century. The Mutiny also represented an important catalyst for a final shift in government surveillance from the publication of official intelligence in general to a more specific type of material which was intended to question not only the motives of British rule in India, but also to promote 'hatred' against the colonial government or 'excite disaffection or unlawful resistance to its orders'.[28]

Over the following decades, one of the ways in which the government sought to contain the 'seditious' activities of the press was by criminalizing these activities under the Indian Penal Code. The code, first passed in 1860, allowed authorities to prosecute newspaper editors for defamation and obscenity; subsequent amendments made in 1870 and 1898 (Section 124A) added 'sedition' and 'promoting enmity between different classes of Her Majesty's subjects', respectively, to the extant list of offences.[29] Newspaper editors were allowed to criticize or to disapprove of the colonial government, as long as they did so 'by lawful means, without exciting or attempting to excite hatred, contempt or disaffection.[30] As Sukeshi Kamra has pointed out, 'Arguably, Section 124A was the most devastating of all the laws introduced between 1867 and 1910 for controlling public culture for the simple reason that it identified individual political subjectivity as a concern of criminal law.'[31]

The 1870s and 1880s also witnessed the passing of several other items of controversial legislation which were to have a profound impact on the activity of the press in the subcontinent. The most notorious example is that of the Vernacular Press Act of 1878, which operated in all provinces of British India except Madras, and specifically targeted publications in 'Oriental languages'. The Act forced editors of blacklisted newspapers to enter into a bond with their local governments and to submit to a year-long censorship which could result in the confiscation of their printing presses if they decided to publish 'matter likely to excite disaffection to the Government'.[32]

One of the main dilemmas that confronted the colonial government during the second half of the nineteenth century was how to control the access of the press to official intelligence without overtly appearing to censor or repress it. One way out of this conundrum was to argue that the government was under no obligation to supply the press with official intelligence at its own cost. Nevertheless, such a view undermined the colonial state's ability to maintain a certain degree of control over the content of official intelligence published in the newspaper press, while also exposing it to accusations of favouritism. As frustrated editors often alleged, official intelligence continued to find its way via the 'back door' to a very select circle of newspapers, of which the *Pioneer* was the most notorious. Although the government never managed to solve this dilemma, during the second half of the period examined, it became more actively engaged in the distribution of official news with the aim of correcting 'false' rumours and providing 'facts' to editors. This was the basis on which 'correct opinions' about the colonial administration and its actions were to be formed. In this way, the government not only promoted the idea that news was 'facts' and not 'opinions', but also that independent, 'objective' reporting was possible.[33] It followed from this that as far as the affairs of the government were concerned, only the colonial administration could be cognizant of the true 'facts'. A system of official news distribution became necessary in order to disseminate 'correct information' to the press.

Early Attempts to Distribute Official Intelligence

The issue of establishing a system of official news distribution was first raised in 1855, when the Government of India learned that officials in Madras and Bombay had decided to provide newspaper editors with select records that could be inspected in a special room set aside in the offices of the government.[34] Indeed, during the late 1850s, major Bombay newspapers regularly published news from this source in a special column titled 'Editor's Room'. Popular items of intelligence included reports about the state of telegraph and railway works in the subcontinent.[35] In Bengal, the procedure for obtaining official intelligence was more cumbersome and irregular, since editors had to apply for permission to inspect official documents, while the government itself sent news to the press only occasionally and 'when sufficiently interesting'. Similarly, in the North-West Provinces the exchange of news was unregulated, editors being allowed access to information only upon formal request.[36]

The debates which surrounded these early attempts to establish a system of news distribution betrayed the administrators' ambiguous attitude towards the press. In 1855, while pondering the advantages and disadvantages of establishing an 'Editor's Room', some members of the Governor General's Council argued against this measure, claiming that it would turn newspapers into objects of partisan opinion. The patronizing attitude towards editors as a professional group found expression in the words of J. P. Grant, who described them as men who 'rarely know what papers to ask for' and recommended the distribution of news via a government newspaper modelled after the French *Moniteur*. Others, like Sir B. Peacock, opposed the idea, advocating a system that did not discriminate between newspapers. The final decision was a compromise which reflected the limits of press freedom in India. As Lord Dalhousie put it, the supply of intelligence, while desirable, had to be made 'with caution and under proper regulations'.[37]

On 25 November 1855, the government passed a resolution which prohibited its officials from providing editors with political and military documents, as well as papers that were still under discussion and correspondence between the Government of India and the local administration. Communication was restricted to 'documents in which the public have a direct concern'; the government became the arbiter of public interest not only by deciding what to share with the press, but also by making the publication of such items dependent upon official sanction.[38] Under the new regulations, the administration resolved to set up an Editor's Room in each secretariat of the local governments and in the Home Department, but editors had to bear the cost of making copies of documents.[39] On 13 May 1856, the Court of Directors in London endorsed the resolution and requested that similar treatment be applied to 'questions specifically submitted for our orders … till our decision thereon shall have been received'.[40]

From its inception, this system of distributing official publications and papers was highly preferential. Documents were shared with a select number of institutions and newspapers across the subcontinent. In Bombay, official publications were supplied to the editors of the *Bombay Times* and the *Bombay Telegraph and Courier*; in Bengal, to the Director of Public Instruction, the Calcutta Public Library, the Asiatic Society, the Agricultural and Horticultural Society, the Civil Engineering College, and the editors of the *Englishman*, *Hurkaru*, *Phoenix*, and the *Friend of India*; in the North-West Provinces, to the editors of the *Delhi Gazette* and the *Mofussilite*; in Madras, to the Ootacamund Library and the editors of the *Athenaeum* and the *Spectator*, to Dr Edward Balfour, the Scottish surgeon and naturalist, and the Madras Reading Room. Other recipients included the editor of the *Lahore Chronicle*, the Anarkali Book Club in Lahore, and the Hyderabad Library.[41] Initially, the task of providing the intelligence was entrusted to the central authorities in Calcutta, but on 13 May 1859 it was decided to transfer it to the local governments.[42]

The practice of circulating official papers to select individuals and institutions in India and Britain was eventually discontinued on 16 December 1861 at the request of Secretary of State Charles Wood. Wood's decision was motivated by the *Nil Darpan* affair, which had seen Rev. James Long prosecuted for libel for publishing an English translation of Dinabandhu Mitra's popular Bengali play. But it wasn't only the 'mischief and embarrassment which have occurred from the circulation of Nil Durpan ostensibly, though not in reality, under the sanction of the Bengal Government' that outraged the secretary of state. There were other significant, albeit less publicized, incidents of 'premature' publication of official information which were similarly destined to 'embarrass' the authorities at this time of peasant unrest. One related example was a report on the Indigo Districts produced by Mr Morris, a copy of which 'was privately placed in my hands [in London], together with an elaborate paper upon it, by the "Landholders, and Commercial Association of British India" a considerable time before the report came to me from the Government of Bengal'.[43] Like in the earlier decades of the nineteenth century, the government found it difficult to balance the act of distancing itself from the activities of the press, in order to avoid accusations that 'premature' or 'inappropriate' information had been published with official sanction, and the need to be involved in the journalistic process in order to control what was published and when, and to avoid 'embarrassment' at the hands of the Home authorities and public opinion in England.

Another development which impacted the circulation of official intelligence was the decision, in 1860, to make such information available via a *Supplement to the Calcutta Gazette*. Published weekly or biweekly, the *Supplement* was envisaged as a platform for the publication of 'such official papers and information as the Government may deem to be of interest to the Public, and such as may usefully be made known'. As the specimen sheet for the first issue, dated 19 September 1860, shows, among the 'useful' items was meteorological intelligence about the failure of rains in the Upper Provinces. Papers of interest were to be forwarded to the Home Department, but publication was not guaranteed, except when ordered by the governor general in council. In the case of voluminous correspondence, only the most important letters were sent, the bulk of the correspondence being displayed for consultation on the Editor's Table.[44]

The tension between opinion which advocated the centralization of official news distribution and that which favoured a more decentralized system became visible in the debates that preceded the establishment of the *Gazette of India* on 1 January 1864. In the early 1860s, the government had decided, for reasons of economy, to discontinue the distribution of the *Calcutta Gazette* to other parts of India, requesting instead that local governments republish relevant information in their own gazettes. William Muir, member of the Sudder Board of Revenue of the North-West Provinces, in a letter to Colonel H. M. Durand, secretary to the Government of India, on 11 September 1863 criticized this move for its effect of 'diminishing' the government's 'own prestige and authority'. The central government, it was argued, was being deprived of a vehicle for the communication of official orders and intelligence 'immediately' and 'directly' to the rest of the country. The new measure also led to a confusion of informational hierarchies, with official orders and intelligence now left to compete with local matter for the attention of readers. As Muir knew all too well, timely and unobstructed access to means of communication was an important attribute of power. News itself was imperial performance, whose publication needed careful staging:

> Just got two or three of our Allahabad Gazettes and see the difference of the effect of an order received among the 'Republications from the Calcutta Gazette' inserted at the far-end of the orders and circulars of the North West, compared with the former system [of distribution via the *Calcutta Gazette*]. Take one of the announcements of a Durbar during the Viceroy's progress, and see how different it looks and reads in that position from the original.[45]

Muir was also critical of the practice of distributing the 'English Gazette' to 177 *tahsildars* (revenue officers), 44 honorary magistrates, and 75 *munsifs* (Indian civil judges), 'few of whom understand English, and who if they did are seldom affected directly by the orders of the Government of India'. Introduced after an earlier decision to discontinue the local vernacular gazette and to insert relevant notices in the *Calcutta Gazette*, the practice was considered costly, in addition to depriving the government of a means of reaching out to the Indian population in its own language. The limits of English-language communication were all too apparent to Muir, who pointed out that language circumscribed the efficiency of official news distribution to the Indian population and that news values were not necessarily universal:

> But apart from this, it seems to me a serious defect in the administration that we have no vernacular Gazette, as an exponent to the native officials and the people at large, of official orders and announcements. It is very true that the Hindi–Urdu Gazette had become lately very fry and barren. But the remedy lay, I would submit, in rendering it more ample and useful, not in abolishing it altogether. We cannot expect the bulky and expensive English Gazette to find its way into native circulation in virtue of the few vernacular entries interspersed here and there throughout its pages.
>
> If the Lieutenant Governor should see reason to reestablish [*sic*] the Vernacular Gazette I would recommend that it be no longer a diglossia of Urdu and Hindi, but an Urdu Gazette simply in the Persian type. There might also be a Hindi version in the Nagri type for places

> (as Kumaon, Jubbulpoor) where Hindi only is used, and for Hindi subscribers generally. To save space, orders of appointment, leave, etc. might be tabulated as was at one time done in the vernacular gazette by Mr. Thomason's orders.[46]

By 1864, it was reported that the Editor's Room in the Home Department had fallen into disuse due to the publication of the *Supplement*. Such reports notwithstanding, the government decided to make similar arrangements in the office of the financial secretary for the publicity of papers which could not be included in the *Supplement*. This proved to be a failure, as was the appointment, in 1868, of a clerk in the secretariat offices of each department, who was entrusted with the compilation of a précis of intelligence for the press. A year later, in yet another attempt to reorganize the system, the duty of preparing the précis was transferred to the under-secretaries of each department.[47]

Thus, apart from informal channels of communication, until the 1870s the Government of India distributed official information to the press via official gazettes, Editor's Rooms, and appointed clerks who compiled summaries of intelligence. The first option was arguably the most accessible to newspapers. It was certainly the most successful in terms of both lifespan and the breadth of the information supplied. While the latter experiments proved to be short-lived, the gazettes were published throughout the period examined. Their role was to publicize information about various matters which the authorities considered relevant to the public, for example in the field of legislation, economy, sanitation, and communications. Among the items most commonly featured were acts of the governors and legislative texts, notices of appointments, sales of land, insolvencies, development plans, and private advertisements.[48]

Owen T. Burne's Vision for the Reorganization of Official News Distribution

The viceroyalty of Lord Mayo (1869–72) witnessed a renewed interest in reorganizing the relationship between the Government of India and the press, both in the subcontinent and at 'Home'. One of the architects of this reorganization was Sir Owen Tudor Burne, Mayo's private secretary, who was asked to prepare a confidential memorandum on this topic soon after the new viceroy's arrival in India. Burne's survey betrayed the low esteem in which he held

'Indian editors'. He repeatedly described them as an 'underbred class of men' who must be kept at a distance and closely monitored.[49] The targets of his criticism were not, however, the Indian editors. By 'Indian press', Burne understood Anglo-Indian newspapers such as the *Friend of India*, the *Times of India*, the *Pioneer*, the *Englishman*, the *Indian Daily News*, the *Bombay Gazette*, the *Delhi Gazette*, and the *Mofussilite*.[50] Burne had clear ideas about the hierarchies of the press and believed that the interests of the colonial government were best served by cultivating its relationship with the press in Britain, not with its 'inferior' counterpart in India:

> There is no Public Opinion of any moment in India. The snobbish abuse of the 'Englishman', the vulgar snobbisms of the 'Indian Daily News', or the consequential vapor of the 'Pioneer', go but a little way with the official or non-official Public; and the Man who wastes his time in reading their Leading Articles is a fool. The only formidable Public Opinion, which is the more formidable for being distant from India, in the heart of the British Parliament, and liable to real or intended error—is that *at Home*.[51]

In order to 'improve' the government's relationship with the press, Burne proposed the establishment of a highly preferential system whereby information would be disseminated to a handful of newspapers either by correspondents in India or by 'trusted agents' in London. Correspondence was to be conducted with a number of journals that catered to various sections of the British public: *The Times* as 'the leading journal', the *Pall Mall Gazette* as 'a fashionable and extensively read newspaper', the *Daily Telegraph* as 'a paper much read by the masses', the *Asiatic* as 'an essentially Indian and well-written paper', and the *Illustrated London News*. This last was selected due to the fact that 'sketches of scenes in India are more valuable than writing', a statement which testifies to the growing importance of illustrated journalism during this period.[52] Great emphasis was also placed on establishing a relationship of mutual trust between the Indian correspondents of these newspapers and the Government of India. As Burne himself admitted, achieving this was problematic due to the entangled nature of British and Anglo-Indian journalism. Ironically, many of the correspondents he wished to pacify were the very same Anglo-Indian editors he dismissed as 'underbred' and unprofessional. For example, George Smith, the editor of *Friend of India* (1859–75), also acted as Indian correspondent of *The Times*.[53]

Turning to the newspapers in the subcontinent, Burne criticized the Government of India for having 'leaned' too much towards the press in the past and proposed a system of news distribution whose purpose was to weaken the press by playing one newspaper against the other.[54] The press was to be divided into 'imaginary classes', with the first class including newspapers such as the *Friend of India*, the *Times of India*, the *Pioneer*, and the *Englishman*, and the second class including newspapers like the *Indian Daily News*, the *Bombay Gazette*, the *Delhi Gazette*, and the *Mofussilite*. The rationale which informed this classification remains unclear, but it is obvious that Burne's intention was to supply information only to the major English-language dailies in a manner that was scrupulously prescribed:

> … communicate quickly and judiciously, to the 1st Class and less often to the 2nd Class newspapers such *facts*, and occasionally in a friendly way even the Government's view of questions, as may be valuable to the Press, and above all suitable to the *interests of Government*. They [Government clerks] may be instructed in general terms to use a wise discrimination in the matter; to send no one fact to more than one or at least two newspapers—one fact to one, another fact to another—playing in reality one off against another and making it all on the part of Government a matter of *pure* favor, without any appearance of control or favoritism, which must as a rule be strictly avoided.[55]

Burne's policy is a perfect illustration of the old principle of divide and rule as applied to the field of journalism, and stemmed partially from his firm belief in the unequal nature of journalistic enterprise in India and Britain. To begin with, the Indian press—understood here as newspapers published by Indians—did not even feature in his memoranda. Within the Anglo-Indian press, itself construed as inferior to its British counterpart, distinctions were established between the major dailies located in Calcutta, Madras, and Bombay, and the rest of the press. Only the former were entitled to receive news, as 'all other local Papers are not worth the snuff of a candle'.[56] Furthermore, Burne advised the government to provide selected newspapers with 'sharp, short, decisive, and plain fact'.[57] The notion of news he advocated was in tune with contemporary developments in Victorian journalism. As Mark Hampton has cogently argued, in the last decades of the nineteenth century, journalists became increasingly preoccupied with 'facts'.[58] This 'vision of the press', to use Hampton's inspired phrase, proved alluring to Burne, since it provided a seemingly rational, 'objective' yardstick by which to judge 'good' journalism, and benefited a colonial administration that had an entrenched fear of 'rumours' and 'opinions'.

There is no indication that Burne's recommendations were implemented in the form he proposed. Nevertheless, as we shall shortly see, he played a crucial role in future attempts to organize a system of official news distribution in his capacity as private secretary to another viceroy, Lord Lytton (1876–8). It was during this period that the institution of the press commissioner was established and the man appointed to this office was Burne's close friend, Roper Lethbridge, a former employee in the Education Department of Bengal and editor of the *Calcutta Quarterly Review* (1871–8).[59] Burne shaped the Indian government's policy towards the press not only through his influential position in the colonial administration, but also through his extensive connections with the press world, both in Britain and in India. Apart from acting as the private secretary to two viceroys, he also worked in the Foreign Department of the India Office for various periods during the 1870s, a situation which placed him in an ideal position to monitor the flow of information to the Indian and the British press. In 1879, Burne also began to contribute to *The Times*.[60] His correspondence with Lethbridge shows that the two men were in regular communication with the editors of Conservative papers like the *Saturday Review* and *The Times* and with the satirical weekly *Vanity Fair*.

In addition, both Burne and Lethbridge invested considerable effort in monitoring the intelligence provided to the press in Britain and India, especially on such sensitive topics as the Vernacular Press Act and the North-West Frontier.[61] In fact, as Burne remarked in his *Memories*, Queen Victoria's private secretary Henry Ponsonby frequently referred to him Her Majesty's questions about India and foreign policy. The difficulty of this position was brought home in a letter received around July 1875, in which Ponsonby briefed Burne about the Queen's news interest and advised vigilance in observing informational hierarchies. Since access to information was a way of legitimizing and preserving power, the Queen and her advisors were very clear about what intelligence they wanted to read and when:

> Serious questions with native princes; anything to do with the Afghans as regards Persia or Russia, and, perhaps, anything of interest from Kashgar.... She does not, in fact, like reading a sensational telegram in *The Times*, and not hearing anything on the subject from the India Office.[62]

In India, it was Lethbridge's duty as press commissioner to mediate the interaction between the colonial government and the press; the following section discusses the establishment and demise of this institution and highlights the ways in which the telegraph was used to provide official intelligence to newspapers.

The Press Commissionership: The Early Stage

In 1908, an account of the Indian press commissionership initially published in the *Calcutta Review* echoed what had already become a familiar narrative about this institution. The press commissionership, it was argued, had been an exercise in the centralization of news distribution, designed to provide the press in India with accurate information about the affairs of the government:

> 'Falsehood goes twice around the globe while Truth is putting on her boots. The object is to give the truth a day's start of the lie.' That was, in brief, the sufficient reason of the Commissionership. Lord Lytton aimed at furnishing the Press with constant, timely and accurate information in order to minimise their ignorant and uninstructed criticism of Government and its measures. Its general principle was simplicity itself. The Press Commissioner was the recognized intermediary between the Government and the Press, the editor being informed that he was authorised to address them on behalf of the Government, and also to receive and reply to all inquiries, complaints and interpellations.[63]

In reality, the arrangement was anything but simple. Burne himself hinted as much in a private letter to Roper Lethbridge, shortly after the latter's appointment: 'I hope you are well and really like your present position. It is really not an easy one! There is so much to say and yet to leave unsaid, and so many batteries turned on you in a time like the present that your difficulties must be very great.'[64] By contrast, in his *Memories* he chose to reiterate the familiar official narrative, betraying nothing of the difficulties to which he alluded in his private correspondence:

> Lord Lytton much appreciated the help given at this time [1877] by (Sir) Charles Lawson, then engaged in journalism in Madras. His clear and able views on famine and other State questions were of great value.... I may add that the untiring exertions of (Sir) Roper Lethbridge at headquarters among other duties at this and other periods, as Press Commissioner (charged with giving correct and frequent information on all

subjects to European and native newspapers throughout India) were productive of great advantage to all concerned. It was a pity, in my opinion, that this useful office was abolished later on.[65]

As Chandrika Kaul has pointed out, the press commissionership was the Government of India's first attempt to centralize the distribution of news to the press.[66] There were many considerations which led to the establishment of this institution, but the immediate impetus, according to official correspondence, was provided by a few letters addressed to the new viceroy, Lord Lytton, by a number of leading Anglo-Indian editors who asked the government to reconsider its relationship with the press.[67] A. P. Sinnett, editor of the *Pioneer*, claimed that the letters represented the apex of a longer press campaign led by the *Statesman* and the *Friend of India*. Its aim was to challenge the *Pioneer*'s privileged access to news as a semi-official organ of the government.[68] Predictably, Sinnett dismissed the complaints as unfounded, but his position did little to allay general resentment against his newspaper's 'backstairs' access to official intelligence.

It was against this background that the new experiment in providing the press with 'authentic news' and 'correct[ing] false reports and misrepresentations' began.[69] At Lytton's initiative, Burne invited the editors of the *Pioneer*, the *Civil and Military Gazette*, the *Indian Daily News*, the *Madras Times*, the *Statesman*, the *Indian Public Opinion*, the *Englishman*, the *Times of India*, and the *Bombay Gazette* to submit their suggestions about the best system of official news distribution.[70] No representative of the Indian press was consulted at this stage; however, Kristo Das Pal of the *Hindoo Patriot* and Babu Narendra Nath Sen of the *Indian Mirror*—the first English-language daily in Bengal conducted by an Indian—were later asked to evaluate the work of the press commissioner.[71]

The opinions of the editors were divided, despite their unanimous conviction that the Government of India needed to improve its relationship with the press. Some, like Edward V. S. Cullin of the *Indian Public Opinion*, emphasized the suitability of previous arrangements in the form of an 'Editor's Room' in each department of the colonial government.[72] Others, however, suggested that centralization was the only viable alternative. James Wilson of the *Indian Daily News* believed that what was needed was a reliable person who would examine, edit, and supply official documents simultaneously to a select number of newspapers, while

Malcolm McPherson of the *Bombay Gazette* and Robert Knight of the *Statesman* proposed the establishment of an Intelligence Department and Press Bureau respectively.[73] Unsurprisingly, Sinnett argued for the maintenance of the status quo, whereby carefully selected news would continue to be distributed to 'properly qualified representatives of the press'.[74]

Two trends emerged from these responses. Firstly, with the exception of Sinnett, who argued that the collection of official news was the duty of journalists and not of the colonial government, all the editors consulted welcomed Lytton's decision to actively supply news to the press. In other words, unlike Reuters, for whom news was a commodity to be sold in exchange for a price, the editors of the leading Anglo-Indian papers insisted that the government was responsible for supplying the press with official news at its own cost. Secondly, with the possible exception of Robert Knight, none of the editors consulted believed that access to official news should be provided indiscriminately to all newspapers in India. Only a limited number of publications were to benefit from the government's measure, and Indian newspapers did not even feature as a subject of discussion in this correspondence. Knight was the only editor who recommended that 'influential Native papers' published in the English language should be included in the scheme, although he conceded that it would be difficult to extend the same measure to the vernacular press.[75] The vision of the public that emerges from these debates confirms Partha Chatterjee's argument, discussed previously, that colonial prescriptions aimed to confine the language of opinion to English and to restrict debate to the Anglo-Indian public and, to a limited extent, Indian elites who were literate in English. The evidence also suggests some of the other hierarchies that shaped opinion expressed in the language of the colonizers, since it is clear that not all newspapers published in English enjoyed the same position in the eyes of the colonial government, or were regarded as equal exponents of public opinion.

At the beginning of 1877, the government initiated an experimental system of official news distribution and appointed Roper Lethbridge in charge of the scheme. In a confidential report submitted to Burne on 31 October 1877, Lethbridge pointed out that his work consisted of two main tasks: to supply the press with 'early and accurate information' regarding matters of public interest and handle inquiries and complaints from editors, as well as to correct misunderstandings and misrepresentations published by the press.[76] Ironically, most of the information which Lethbridge distributed to the press originated with Burne, now private secretary to the viceroy. The two men appear to have visited each other on a daily basis. The secretaries to the government in the various departments also supplied Lethbridge with occasional intelligence, as did other members of the government.[77] Information thus collected was distributed to the editors of eleven major newspapers, only two of which—the *Hindoo Patriot* and the *Indian Mirror*—were edited by Indians:

Calcutta:	*Englishman, Statesman, Indian Daily News, Hindoo Patriot, Indian Mirror*
Allahabad:	*Pioneer*
Lahore:	*Civil and Military Gazette*
Bombay:	*Bombay Gazette, Times of India*
Madras:	*Madras Times, Madras Mail*

Intelligence was transmitted to these newspapers by post or by telegraph, based on the cost and estimated degree of 'public' interest in the news. As Lethbridge confessed, he telegraphed 'all news-items with regard to which the interests of the State seemed to call for speedy distribution, as well as those which could be communicated in a few words, and those which would be likely to be exceedingly interesting to the public'.[78] Examples of distributed news included reports about the famine in southern India, especially daily weather reports, and information about the state of the grain market.

In addition to providing information to the press, Lethbridge also monitored its content and took steps to correct some of the alleged 'misstatements' published. The list of corrections proved long. Robert Knight's *Statesman* was a habitual offender, but a few inappropriate statements were also detected in the *Pioneer* and the *Englishman*. In one example, Lethbridge took objection to Knight's claim that the Indian government had rigged the market by making large purchases of stock and annexing the balances of various old famine relief funds.[79] Other 'misstatements' were also related to allegations of financial mismanagement and fraud perpetrated by the government, a topic which remained as sensitive in the late nineteenth century as it had been in the early decades of the period.

As Table 4.1 shows, the number of telegrams sent by Lethbridge between April and October 1877 fluctuated, peaking at 583 messages and a cost of Rs 1,977 in August that year. Most messages were sent

Table 4.1 Telegrams sent by Roper Lethbridge to the press, April–October 1877

Month	No. of telegrams	Cost (in Rs)
April	9	200
May	169	746
June	113	422
July	308	1,235
August	583	1,977
September	406	2,425
October (1–25)	531	1,544

Source: Lethbridge to Burne, 31 October 1877, Burne Papers, MSS.EUR D 951/27, IOR, British Library.

at the discounted press rate of Re 1 per 24 words, and were exempted from the rule of verbatim publication which applied to other press messages. The reason why Lethbridge was keen to eschew this rule was because the publication of identical telegrams in all newspapers would have attached official authority to his messages, thus making the government directly responsible for their content. Since the form of a telegram was easily recognizable to the reading public, Lethbridge asked editors to publish his telegraphic messages 'as Editorial paragraphs, and clothed by each Editor in his own language according to his own views'.[80] In addition, he requested that messages from editors, as well as communications between himself and *The Times* correspondent and Reuter's agents in Calcutta and Bombay, should be charged at press rates. In order to be able to transmit longer items of news, Lethbridge also proposed that the word limit of press telegrams should be raised from 200 to 500.[81]

Thus, during the early stage of its existence—roughly speaking, the period between April 1877 and February 1878—Lethbridge's office, not yet formally known as the press commissionership, was less preoccupied with monitoring the vernacular press than with pacifying the representatives of the Anglo-Indian press who protested against the *Pioneer*'s privileged access to official intelligence. To solve this conundrum, the government proposed a solution not entirely dissimilar to Burne's earlier proposal, namely to set up a centralized system of news distribution which would provide intelligence in a highly selective manner to a limited number of newspapers. The choice of technology for news transmission was informed by the dual principles of economy and the degree of 'public' relevance of the intelligence (as judged by the colonial state). The use of telegraphy was designed to benefit what I call the communication elite of colonial India, that is, the major Anglo-Indian newspapers, Reuters, and the correspondent of *The Times*. Indian newspapers did not feature prominently in the debate at this stage, but the situation was to change dramatically with the passing of the Vernacular Press Act in 1878.

The Press Commissionership Transformed

By the end of 1877, Lytton's administration was becoming increasingly preoccupied with the vernacular press. In his report to Burne dated 31 October 1877, Lethbridge turned his attention to this section of the press, asking the government to implement a series of measures that would help to 'improve' not only the vernacular newspapers but, as it turned out, his own personal situation. Lethbridge's main request was for the government to appoint him 'Reporter on the Vernacular Press', a position in which he would require four translators to supply him with extracts from relevant newspapers. He also proposed to publish and circulate among the English-language press a pamphlet containing translations from the vernacular press, and asked the government to continue supplying him with the weekly translations prepared by the reporters to the local governments.[82] The proposals were favourably received: four days after the passing of the Vernacular Press Act on 14 March 1878, Lethbridge's office was reorganized as the institution of the press commissioner.[83]

As many scholars have remarked, the Vernacular Press Act changed considerably the circumstances of the vernacular press. The *Amrita Bazar Patrika* turned from a bilingual newspaper into an English-language weekly; the *Som Prakash* was forced to cease publication, while the editors of other papers such as *Bharat Mihir*, *Dacca Prakash*, *Hindoo Hitoysini*, and *Sulav Samachar* were all called on to provide bonds to the government.[84] Although the Act was repealed in October 1881 by Lord Rippon, the blatant discrimination between the English and the vernacular press, which the government had formally and ostentatiously sanctioned, was to leave a deep impression on many a journalist's mind. If, before the passing of the Act, Lethbridge's position had resembled, at least on paper, that of a mediator between the Indian government and the press, while also performing monitoring duties on the side, in the aftermath of the Act this latter dimension of his office took centre stage.

Lethbridge took his duties seriously; in fact, evidence suggests that he did not confine himself to simply reading the press. Surendranath Banerjea, for example, claimed that he was also responsible for discouraging an anonymous Brahmo leader from joining him in the protest against the Vernacular Press Act.[85] The despatch of 18 March 1878, which had recommended Lethbridge's appointment as a press commissioner, left no doubt about the press commissioner's brief to police the vernacular press:

> … in order that the Government of India should be able to enforce the Act with judgment, and with a due regard for those rights of free thought and legitimate discussion which Her Majesty's Government have always jealously guarded, it is necessary for us to provide means whereby we may be kept fully and continuously informed of the tone and character of the utterances of the whole Vernacular Press of India, with a view to exercising the necessary control, not only over the journals which come under the operation of the present Act, but also over the action of the local authorities through whom its provisions will be carried out. To judge accurately of any particular case that may be brought before us, we must have means of learning with certainty the character, status, and general behavior of each vernacular newspaper.[86]

The task, however, was daunting. Writing to A. C. Lyall, secretary to the Government of India, on 17 June 1878, Lethbridge estimated that he would need to survey regularly at least 190 newspapers: approximately 37 publications in Bengali (including 5 dailies); 82 in Urdu, Hindi, and Persian; 72 in Marathi and Gujarati; and a smaller number in Tamil, Telugu, Canarese, and Malayalam. Since the government insisted on being supplied with 'full (instead of abstract) translations of important articles which may possibly appear to infringe Act IX of 1878', it soon became obvious that Lethbridge would require an expensive establishment to discharge his duties (Table 4.2).[87] This was to consist of two offices, one at Calcutta and one at Simla, whose estimated total cost was approximately Rs 1,675 per month, a sum eventually sanctioned by the Government of India on 7 February 1879.[88] In addition, the authorities approved three translators and two *munshis* (secretary, writer), instead of the five translators Lethbridge had asked for (a munshi was paid only half the salary of a translator). A further Rs 1,500 was also granted as subscription fees to various

Table 4.2 The press commissioner's establishment

Type of expenditure	Monthly cost (Rs)
1 Précis Writer	250
1 Translator	250
2 Translators on Rs 150 rising by annual increments of Rs 10 to Rs 250	450
2 Munshis on Rs 50 rising by Rs 5 a year to Rs 70	130
English Office and servants as above	445
Office rent Simla Rs 750, Calcutta Rs 100 per year	100
Office contingencies	50
Total	1,675

Source: Resolution, 7 February 1879, Foreign Department, General A, Nos 14–15, NAI.

newspapers. Driven by the logic of frugality, some members of the Viceroy's Council had opposed the last suggestion, claiming that many newspapers, especially vernacular ones, could be obtained for free in exchange for the *Gazette of India*.[89]

The ability to establish connections and generate social capital was central to Lethbridge's work as a press commissioner. As he divulged, his duties were of a 'personal nature' and involved the cultivation of social networks both in official and press circles.[90] He prided himself on being 'in constant confidential communication' with all the editors to whom he supplied information, including *The Times* correspondent, and was convinced that he exercised a positive influence on the press. According to him, this was visible in the 'improved tone' of newspapers like the *Madras Times*, the *Leader*, and the *Civil and Military Gazette*. He was less confident about his ability to influence the Bombay newspapers, as well as the *Statesman* and the *Indian Daily News* of Calcutta, but professed the loyalty of the *Englishman* and the *Pioneer*.[91]

Needless to say, not everyone appreciated Lethbridge's modus operandi. The press commissionership came under severe criticism both in Britain and India, with journalists complaining that the official intelligence distributed to the press was 'worthless'. An article in the *Examiner* of January 1879 pointed out that 'news of the more special order, which formerly found its way down the backstairs to certain folks, still reaches the same people by the same route', and suspected that the press commissionership was part of the Indian government's design to misinform public opinion in Britain. The press commissioner was called 'the official nobbler of the Press' and accused of having misinformed *The Times* about the state of public opinion in India and the events surrounding the Amir of Afghanistan, Sher Ali Khan.[92] Archibald Forbes, the famous nineteenth-century war correspondent, also referred to the press commissionership as a 'bewildering anachronism'.[93]

In India, arguably the most notorious criticism of the institution originated with William Riach of the *Statesman*, who ridiculed one of the official press releases as 'fatuous flapdoodle'.[94] C. E. Buckland, who was at the time replacing Lethbridge during his furlough in England, retaliated by removing the newspaper from his distribution list. As Edwin Hirschmann has pointed out, Buckland's drastic decision might have also been partly motivated by his personal rivalry with Robert Knight, owner of the *Statesman*.[95] But Riach's criticism touched a sensitive chord with the colonial administration. By accusing the *Pioneer* of retaining its old privileges, he effectively denied that there had been any change of consequence in the attitude of the government towards the press since the establishment of the press commissionership:

> I have already shown that information was communicated to the 'Pioneer' before the Press Commissioner sent it to the Press. It would have never occurred to me that the Press Commissioner himself was the Pioneer's early informant. Neither could I have supposed that the Foreign Secretary, or any other official having access to the Foreign Office, would have violated well-known rules by communicating the secrets of the office to the 'Pioneer'.[96]

The *Bharat Mihir*, a weekly newspaper from Mymensingh edited by Babu Anath Bandhu Guha, launched a similarly sharp critique.[97] Commenting on the unfavourable conditions under which the vernacular newspapers were forced to operate in the wake of the Vernacular Press Act, Guha pointed out that this section of the press was almost entirely dependent on its English counterpart for intelligence, 'with the exception of a few items of local news'. Vernacular newspapers had lower circulation figures and could not afford to hire as many correspondents or pay them the salaries offered by the Anglo-Indian press. The government, Guha alleged, was highly biased in its news-distribution practices. It ignored the news values of the vernacular press and insisted on patronizing the major English-language newspapers that already enjoyed privileged access to intelligence:

> Has the correspondence which took place between Shere Ali and the Government of India been all furnished to the press? The matter does not signify much to the English papers: they are able to get all the information for themselves. We, however, do not obtain the help which we once expected to obtain at the hands of the Press Commissioner. Of what use is it to us that we are informed of the appointments and transfers that are made and of deaths that take place of officers in the army, of those serving in the Punjab or in Southern India? What we want is complete information regarding important public topics which occupy the attention of the Governments of India and Bengal. True, the Press Commissioner has been favouring us with short *communiqués* regarding the events of the Afghan war; but as to the whereabouts of Shere Ali and his doings, whether the British army intend to advance or recede, what steps are being taken towards opening negotiations, what should be done in the event of the Amir not listening to terms, who will be made liable for the expenses of the war, and in case (which God forbid!) the charge is thrown upon our shoulders, by what means the Government of India propose to raise the money required—on all these important questions the Press Commissioner does not help us much.[98]

These were pertinent questions, but the government—and certainly the press commissioner—chose to ignore them. They were voiced by an increasingly inquisitive Indian public opinion that expected answers and proposed solutions. Thus, Guha suggested that the press commissioner should send different communiqués to English and vernacular newspapers. He argued that the news interests of Indian and Anglo-Indian readers usually converged in the sphere of the political, especially if the intelligence pertained to the affairs of their own presidencies or when it referred to measures of broader public interest. But in many other fields, news published in the Anglo-Indian press was 'too often out of place in a Native print'.[99]

Like other experiments in news distribution that preceded it, the press commissionership eventually succumbed to financial pressures. Indeed, it was not long before the government began to doubt the need to maintain what was increasingly regarded as a costly and inefficient institution. During Lethbridge's absence from India in 1880, his funds were cut, and it was decided that his duties could be satisfactorily discharged by an officer in the Foreign Department for a 'small allowance in addition to his salary'.[100] Critics also found reassurance in the fact that the duties of the press commissioner overlapped with already existing offices, such as the government translators who compiled the weekly *Native Newspaper Reports* and the officers appointed to collate extracts from the press as part of the secretariats of the Home and Foreign Departments. As A. C. Lyall pointed out in his minute of 10 July 1878, the colonial government was no longer willing to shoulder the costs associated with the establishment of a centralized system of news distribution.[101]

One significant cause for complaint was the high cost associated with the transmission of telegrams to the 'long list of newspapers' entitled to receive official intelligence from the press commissioner. As we have seen, before the formal establishment of the press commissionership, Lethbridge communicated information only to a handful of English-language newspapers. This policy changed after the reorganization of the institution, when the government agreed to add some of the vernacular newspapers to the list of journals that received these communiqués.[102]

Access to intelligence depended to a great extent on the whim of the press commissioner. For example, in February 1880, Acting Commissioner C. E. Buckland refused to provide intelligence to the *Bengal Times*, a newspaper published in Dacca by E. C. Kemp, on the grounds that it was a 'worthless paper' and that the short distance between Dacca and Calcutta did not justify 'the expense of telegraphing to new stations'. Kemp protested to the secretary to the Government of India, pointing out that his was a 'first-class bi-weekly provincial journal', unlike the *Darjeeling Times* which, although a 'small weekly paper … that cater[ed] for a district', was nevertheless on the press commissioner's list. The viceroy refused to overturn Buckland's decision.[103] In the same year, a similar judgment was passed with regard to the *Bombay Chronicle*, an Anglo-Gujarati weekly published by Cursetji Gandhi. In rejecting the application, Buckland made it clear that his policy was to avoid supplying 'every new upstart newspaper with Government papers and news until we have time to see how they are conducted'. Instead, he advised the editor to register his newspaper with the Telegraph Department in order to receive telegrams at the discounted press rates.[104]

Prior to June 1878, official regulations did not allow vernacular newspapers to make use of the press message privilege. According to the rules issued by the Public Works Department in 1874, a 'press message' was a telegram of 'manifestly public interest'—excluding, however, commercial information—which was addressed to a newspaper and written in the English language. The recipient had to be registered with the Indian Telegraph Department and was obliged to publish the telegram verbatim and its entirety.[105] In January 1876, vernacular newspapers were explicitly excluded from the press message privilege, although 'native editors' could apply to be admitted to the 'register of privileged journals'.[106] Their admission or rejection depended on the goodwill of the director general of telegraphs.

Among the vernacular newspapers that succeeded in securing the press message privilege was the *Bombay Samachar*, which appears to have received telegrams at the discounted press rates until the end of 1877. The circumstances that surrounded the withdrawal of this concession remain unclear, but in June 1878 we find the editor pleading with the press commissioner for the restoration of his former privilege.[107] Prompted by this case, the Home Department passed a resolution in the same month which granted vernacular newspapers the right to receive telegrams at the discounted press rates on condition that they should be published in English, verbatim, and accompanied by a vernacular translation if deemed necessary.[108] Official insistence on the observance of a specific format of reporting was likely connected to a desire to retain a certain degree of control over the circulation of such news. Telegrams were an easily identifiable form of reporting. Since they travelled at faster speeds than other types of news, there was a heightened danger that the information they conveyed was trafficked, stolen, or distorted. Rules that required newspapers to register themselves with the Telegraph Department and prescribed a format for the publication of press telegrams were thus an attempt on the part of the colonial state to impose order on a category of information whose sheer speed of movement made it notoriously difficult to control.

Scholars have usually connected the abolition of the press commissionership with the abolition of the Vernacular Press Act in 1881.[109] Indeed, the earliest proposal to put an end to this office dates to 3 August 1880 and was motivated by financial considerations. As some disgruntled officials were keen to point out, the high cost of telegrams and the press commissioner's expensive establishment, including his own salary, caused a serious strain on the budget.[110] The press commissionership had also been tainted through its association with the Vernacular Press Act, an aspect of its activity which became increasingly difficult to overlook in the aftermath of that act's abolition. As the editor of the *Times of India* wrote on 12 April 1881,

> The Press Commissioner was not intended to sit at Simla like a Delphic Oracle, answering with more or less uncertain phrases all manner of questions that might be addressed to him by curious publicists, but it was one of his most onerous functions to act as a censor of the Vernacular Press. He had a large staff of paid translators, and he was assisted by the various official translators in the different Presidencies. But, as the principle of censorship was fortunately repugnant to English feeling at home, these costly preparations to Russianize India were wasted, and it is not unnatural that a Liberal Government should be anxious to let the establishment follow the Vernacular Press Act as soon as possible.[111]

Lord Rippon might have been 'anxious' about this association, but it seems that he was not entirely prepared to discard the idea of a centralized system for the distribution of official news to the press. He abolished Roper Lethbridge's appointment as a 'separate office' upon the abolition of the Vernacular Press Act. But the arrangement itself was 'retained' and continued to function in the manner in force during Lethbridge's furlough in Britain. In other words, his former duties were passed onto the shoulders of an officer in the Foreign Department.

The decision to retain the press commissionership was most likely the outcome of pressure from representatives of the press. While the censorial dimension of the commissioner's work had come under severe attack, especially from Indian journalists, the idea of the government supplying regular official intelligence to the press remained popular with most representatives of the press. Animated by this impulse, and by circulating rumours that Reuter's agent in India was about to take over Lethbridge's job, becoming 'the official mouthpiece of the Government of India for the newspapers, not of India only, but of England and the world', a group of 124 editors and proprietors submitted a memorial to the government protesting against the proposed abolition of the institution. As the editor of the *Times of India* put it, the total cost of Rs 3,000–4,000 per month was 'insignificant … considering the importance of the experiment'.[112] A. C. Lyall responded by summarizing the objections of the government to the scheme:

> We cannot go on supplying news to the long list of newspapers which sign this memorial—the whole distribution has to be done by telegrams, in order that one journal may not anticipate the other, and because we

> cannot make endless copies for letters. The effect of this, and of other difficulties which I could mention, is that we must either supply news to a few leading papers, as in England, or the news which we distribute so largely to all papers must be scanty, and confined to a few important telegrams. In either case we do not need an expensive Press Commissioner to manage the business; and at the present moment I fancy Mr. Lethbridge has not much to do.[113]

On 21 June 1882, C. Grant remarked that the colonial government had simply decided 'to let matters remain as they are'.[114] As various options for the reorganization of the institution were discussed, it became increasingly clear that at the heart of the problem was the unsettled relationship between the press and a colonial government bent on financial economy and the autocratic control of news. For some government officials, like Whitley Stokes at the beginning of this chapter, news was a commodity, the raw material of a journalist's work which had to be purchased in the same way that a baker purchased his flour and the butcher his meat.[115] But others, like Lord Ripon, insisted that it was in the interest of the government to possess a channel for the dissemination of 'correct information' to the public, an institution that would turn the newspaper press in India from 'critics' into friends of the authorities.[116]

As Howard Hensman, *The Times*'s correspondent in India, pointed out, the office of the press commissioner 'lingered on' and was abolished only eight years later, in March 1889.[117] Indeed, throughout the 1880s, newspapers like the *Times of India* continued to publish occasional communications from the press commissioner on topics like financial statements and the knighting of the amir of Afghanistan, Abdur Rahman Khan.[118] As late as April 1888, the editor of *Dost-i-Hind*, a newly established vernacular newspaper from Bhera in Shahpur District (now in Pakistan) with a circulation of 700 copies per week, requested the press commissioner to supply him with the 'latest intelligence'. As the editor put it, 'Bhera being an out of the way station, we feel a great difficulty in gathering fresh news.' The application was rejected on the grounds that the list of newspapers supplied with intelligence was not revised at that time.[119] Nevertheless, the editor's application suggests some of the ways in which a central system of official news distribution might have made a difference in the lives of smaller and less viable newspapers in India.

Lethbridge himself seemed unable to leave his old job behind. On 4 December 1888, now a member of Parliament for Kensington

North, he asked the under-secretary of state for India to confirm the status of the press commissioner and pointed out that statements about the Sikkim affairs, which 'purport[ed] to issue from the Press Commissioner' and exposed the divergences between the Home and Indian governments, had been published in the *Indian Mirror* and other Indian newspapers. Sir John Gorst replied that the office itself had been abolished in 1880, but that its functions were now discharged jointly by the local and Foreign Departments.[120]

Following the final demise of the institution in 1889, newspapers were left to make their own arrangements for news distribution until the viceroyalty of Lord Curzon, who established press bureaus at Simla and Calcutta at the beginning of the twentieth century.[121] The final abolition of the press commissionership was followed, in typical bureaucratic fashion, by extensive debate, which spanned more than two years and once again saw administrators discuss alternative arrangements for the distribution of news to the press. Ironically, most of the schemes proposed were based on the same old ideas which had been deemed inefficient or unsuitable before, namely establishing an Editor's Room and distributing news through the *Official Gazette*.[122] The only relatively novel idea—relatively because less discussed, although it first cropped up in debates and circulated as rumour in the early 1880s—was the proposal to entrust Reuters with the distribution of news, a topic to which we turn in the next section.[123]

Reuters in India

Reuter's history and its role as the news agency of the British Empire have been discussed in a number of studies.[124] In this section I aim to contribute to that discussion by probing deeper into the relationship between this news agency, the colonial government, and the newspaper press in India, in an effort to understand the overlaps and disjunctures between the visions of news these various categories of actors promoted. As previous literature has shown, the introduction of telegraphy facilitated the exchange of intelligence on a global scale, concentrating news distribution in the hands of a few major news agencies such as Reuters, Havas, Wolff, and the Associated Press, and promoting the gradual commodification of news in the course of the second half of the nineteenth century. While the sphere of influence and activity of these agencies was inextricably circumscribed and shaped by geopolitical considerations, one important question, from the perspective of the present study, is to understand how Reuters negotiated its position in the colonial environment of nineteenth-century South Asia. In particular, how was its vision of news as a commodity reconciled with the competing idea, popular among the press and some colonial administrators, that news was a public good?

The agency's expansion into Asia was inextricably connected with the development of telegraphic communication, although its trade in Indian news pre-dated the establishment of a direct line of communication between India and Britain. An ad published on 8 March 1855 in the *North-China Herald*, a newspaper from Shanghai, shows that Julius Reuter, the founder of the agency, was already soliciting news from India and China to be sent 'by ELECTRIC TELEGRAPH from Trieste without any loss of time' to England, France, Germany, and other European countries.[125] In December 1857, Reuter asked Lord Clarendon, the foreign secretary, to supply him with telegraphic intelligence from India that could be forwarded to his subscribers on the continent. The request was granted; a few months later the agency counted among its subscribers *The Times* and other London dailies.[126] As the telegram books at the Reuters Archives demonstrate, the Indian intelligence sold by the agency at this time was predominantly of a political, shipping, and commercial nature, usually originating in Bombay and Calcutta, but also in Madras, Hong Kong, and Shanghai. One item dated simply 'Calcutta' and published in Reuter's 'Electric News' of 14 December 1858 announced that 'Splendid *fetes* [*sic*] took place here on the 9th November. The East India Company's stocks are rising, and trade is reviving, but communication with the Interior of India still difficult.' Since at the time there was as yet no direct telegraphic communication between Britain and India, this item of news was brought by mail to Marseilles and forwarded by telegraph to London.[127] The following year marked the beginning of a 'Special Indian Service' based on an agreement with the *Bombay Times*, reportedly the first newspaper in India to publish Reuter telegrams.[128]

Reuter's connection with the vibrant port city of Bombay, especially with its newspaper and shipping world, deserves some elaboration. Access to technologies of communication was undoubtedly a central ingredient in the agency's expansion into Asia—in fact, as one author has pointed out, Julius Reuter was well known for his motto of 'following the cable' and his own involvement in the telegraph business—but equally indispensable was the ability to tap into a network of human agents who could facilitate the collection and transmission of relevant items of intelligence.[129] In the early phase of Reuter's presence in the subcontinent—that is, prior to the establishment of the first Reuter's office in Bombay in 1866 by Henry Collins—this job was performed by local traders, Christian missionaries, and employees of the steamship companies. Robert Campbell and Co. acted as Calcutta agents for Reuter's Telegraphic Office as early as 1860, while Edwyn Dawes, who went on to become a 'leading figure' in the British shipping trade and was, at the time, employed with the P&O, worked as Reuter's agent in Bombay in 1862.[130]

Another important connection to which I have already alluded was that with the *Bombay Times* and its successor, the *Times of India*. This little-known aspect of Reuter's early history in the subcontinent demonstrates the existence of competing arrangements for the exchange of news between Britain and India, and the manner in which such attempts eventually succumbed to the agency's expansionist drive. Robert Knight, a journalist associated both with the *Bombay Times* and the *Times of India*, played an important role in this experiment.

Now hardly remembered—despite being credited with the establishment of two of India's most enduring newspapers, the *Times of India* and the *Statesman*—Knight went to Bombay in 1847 as a merchant, dabbling in several occupations before turning to journalism in 1857. An enterprising character, he demonstrated an early interest in exploring the lucrative potential of new means of communication and their importance for the emerging news trade: his four-year employment with Waghorn and Company (1852–6), the pioneer of the overland route to India, and his testimony before the Select Committee on East India Communications in 1866 provide a clear indication of this.[131]

In a recent biographic account of Knight, Edwin Hirschmann describes him as a man of liberal values and a staunch supporter of the principle of free trade, whose lower-middle-class background made him ill at ease with the society of covenanted civil servants in India. His criticism of the British Raj, which increased as the century advanced, made him unpopular with many of his Anglo-Indian contemporaries and a poor candidate for a prominent place in colonial narratives about journalism in India.[132] By contrast, on the occasion of Knight's death in 1890, Tilak paid homage to him as 'the Nestor of Indian journalists' and remembered him as a person thus: 'Whatever he said, he said fearlessly and honestly and was as severe in condemning the follies of the rulers as in censuring the absurdities of those who posed as the champions of the people.'[133] Similarly, Sisir Kumar Ghosh believed that he was 'hot-headed,' but 'thoroughly honest and [wrote] from deep conviction'.[134]

The evidence surrounding Knight's engagement with Reuters is somewhat contradictory. According to correspondence unearthed by Hirschmann, their collaboration began in 1860, when Reuters offered him 'his sole agency, not in the Western presidency only, but in all of India'. In the following year, Knight established the *Times of India*, also setting up an 'independent telegraphic agency with Europe' known as the *Times of India* Telegraphic Agency. This was used to sell intelligence, including Reuter telegrams, to 'all the leading Anglo-Indian newspapers' from the subcontinent, for a monthly subscription fee of Rs 500.[135] Later evidence suggests that Knight's partner in this venture was Manockji Pestonji Tuback, who appears to have worked as the local manager of the Bombay & Aden Steamship Company in the early 1850s.[136] Knight's biographer infers from archival records that Reuters took over Knight's venture either in 1862 or in 1864.[137]

A slightly different version of this story emerges from the pages of the *Times of India* and the *Englishman*. According to the former, in the course of 1865, a 'Press Telegraphic Service' came into being under the management of the *Times of India* office. The move had been suggested by the editor of the *Madras Times* and was widely referred to as an 'amalgamated service': in short, it was an attempt on the part of a section of the newspaper press in India to pool together resources in order to secure cheaper access to telegraphic intelligence from Europe. As Saunders noted, the *Times of India* 'got the majority of the Press of the three Presidencies to enter into a confederacy, whereby they would all receive the same telegrams at a rate considerably less than that which each journal was paying before the amalgamation.'[138]

The news was transmitted by the London agent of the *Times of India*, whose monthly salary, prior to the amalgamation, was £15; this increased to £20 after the amalgamation. Messages were sent from London to Bombay, from where they were distributed to the rest of India. The cost of transmission was shared between the subscribing newspapers. In addition to this service, the *Times of India* also provided its subscribers, free of charge, with 'local and other information of importance from whatever source it may reach us'.[139]

Before long, the arrangement came under criticism from the other newspapers. The *Madras Times* complained that the telegrams were 'infrequent' and 'stupid'. The *Englishman* argued that they were 'crammed' with cotton quotations and other commercial news which could only be of interest to the merchants and speculators of Bombay, and that the scarcity of political news was a 'serious drawback to the successful working of the joint system'.[140] Indeed, as the next chapter will discuss in more detail, the telegrams distributed by the *Times of India*—also known as 'subscription telegrams'—appeared to prioritize commercial news, which was usually reported ahead of other types of intelligence. The decision was hardly surprising, considering the socio-economic environment of Bombay and the fact that at this time selling news to the mercantile community was a much more lucrative venture than selling it to the newspaper press. But Reuter's strategy towards the newspaper press was different. It aimed its telegrams at a broader public, usually prioritizing political events. Its economic and political leverage was also different from that of the *Times of India*. In its defence, the newspaper reminded its critics that news values were not universal and that cost was a crucial factor that shaped access to telegraphic intelligence:

> … the editor [of *Madras Times*] holds us responsible for the frequent derangement of the telegraphic line during the past six months; and also, that because the Queen has not abdicated or the Emperor Napoleon been assassinated, or some equally sensational news flashed forward, we or our agent are very stupid people. The fact is, that beyond the general election and the cattle plague there has been little in the way of general news to communicate—what there has been of public interest, we assert has been furnished.
>
> Some 'notable East India firms', as the same journal states, do subscribe to the telegraphic service; but we instituted that service, and they subscribed long before the union telegraphic service was determined upon. We deny the charge, however, that 'the wants of Bombay merchants have been studied at the expense of other classes in the country.'
>
> With regard to obtaining more 'full and frequent telegraphic news from Europe', the *Times* talks as though it were to be had only for the asking. When has that journal ever given us to understand that it would like a 'full and frequent' supply regardless the cost?—because if that is not what it meant, the statement means nothing at all.[141]

Official correspondence shows that the viceroy of India was also on the list of individuals and organizations that subscribed to the *Times of India*'s service. The newspaper provided him with telegraphic summaries of mails.[142] But this arrangement was discontinued in July 1866, when it was decided that Henry Collins, Reuter's agent at Bombay, would supply the viceroy with a daily message in exchange for a monthly subscription fee of Rs 400.[143] Around the same period, quite possibly under mounting pressure from Reuters, Knight also decided to sell the whole 'confederate agreement' to the news agency: his letter to newspaper proprietors was followed by a circular from Reuters explaining the new terms under which they were to receive telegraphic intelligence from Europe.[144] There is little evidence to establish what prompted Knight to sell his news agency, but we know that the decision came at a time when he had already suffered significant financial losses, first in a coffee plantation in south India, and later when the Bank of Bombay crashed as a result of the drop in cotton prices which followed the American Civil War.[145]

The news of Reuter's takeover was not well received by the representatives of the press. Saunders accused Knight of being 'unscrupulous' and claimed that some of the editors had rejected the terms proposed by Reuters. The agency responded by temporarily depriving them of telegraphic intelligence. The final outcome was almost anticlimactic: the *Englishman*, which had initially refused 'to bind' itself to Mr Reuter before knowing the details of the new agreement, was soon forced to admit that it was 'willing to pay any charge which the agency chose to make for such messages as they may send to us'.[146]

As far as Knight was concerned, this was not his last attempt to establish a telegraphic agency. As his former partner at the *Times of India* and now embittered foe Matthias Mull wrote, in 1872, together with his old associate Manockji Tuback, Knight tried once again to 'enlist … the support of the Press of India as well as the public' for a similar cause.[147] The outcome is unknown, although Mull lost no time in reminding his readers about Knight's earlier unsuccessful attempt to establish a telegraphic agency, and about an old feud in which he had accused his former partner of selling 'the first look of the *Times of India*'s telegrams in 1862 … to Mr. [William] Sim', the editor of *Hurkaru*.[148] The quarrel remained unresolved, but the incident—and many other similar allegations encountered especially in Bombay—demonstrates that in nineteenth-century India, the 'first look' of telegrams was something many journalists, officials, and merchants considered worth fighting (and paying) for.[149]

In the following years, Reuter's business continued to prosper. After establishing the first office at Bombay in 1866, Henry Collins managed to expand the agency's reach all the way to Japan in only six years, following the expansion of telegraph cables to this part of the world.[150] As Kanji Ishii points out, the telegraphic connection between Japan and Europe was completed in 1871 when the Great Northern Telegraph Company, a Danish enterprise, connected the trans-Siberian cable which landed at Vladivostok with the port of Nagasaki. From this latter location, the cable had also been extended to Shanghai and Hong Kong, where it met the cables of the Eastern Telegraph Company, thus completing the telegraphic connection between South and East Asia.[151] In the early 1870s, the *Yokohama Mainichi Shimbun*, a Japanese-language newspaper published in the eponymous port city, featured telegrams from London—not attributed to Reuters—which reported on topics like the outbreak of cholera in Hamburg.[152] In fact, Reuter's reputation certainly travelled faster than the telegraph cables. In December 1867, a mock telegram from Paris published in the *Japan Punch* announced solemnly, 'The world bankrupt Louis Napoléon sent Mr. Fould to the moon to negotiate loan of £100,000,000,000,000,000.... Consols 10.2.13-. Ministerials at a discount. Paris and Orleans 52 to 1. The Globe lively.'[153]

By April 1866, Reuters had more than fifty subscribers in India, most of whom were merchants involved in the cotton trade and thus interested in the quotations of cotton prices from Liverpool and other English markets.[154] The list of subscribers continued to grow and came to include, in addition to the viceroy of India, various Indian newspapers and other officials such as the commissioner-in-chief, the governors of Bombay and Madras, and the lieutenant governor of Bengal.[155] The agency used the Indo-European telegraph system to dispatch telegrams each week alternatively to Bombay or Galle, from where they were telegraphed to the government at Simla 'under the Clear the Line Signal'.[156]

Throughout the period under discussion, access to Reuter's news service was drastically limited by price. The yearly subscription fee of Rs 4,800 was a sum which only the biggest newspapers in India could afford. According to the contracts signed in October–December 1879 by the *Englishman*, the *Bombay Gazette*, the *Civil and Military Gazette*, the *Pioneer*, and the *Madras Times*, the fee was paid in monthly instalments and news had to be acknowledged as 'Reuter's Telegrams' when published in the pages of the newspaper press.[157] Upon the renewal of the contracts in 1890–1, the subscription fee remained unchanged, but a new stipulation was introduced which entitled Reuters to increase the cost to Rs 6,000 'in times of war, civil or otherwise, in which England, or any great European power or America, may become involved, or during any prolonged political excitement affecting the international relations of any two of such Powers, and during a General election in the United Kingdom'.[158] The terms of the contracts effectively consecrated certain categories of events as newsworthy and relevant to the public in India, a situation which was reflected in newspaper coverage itself, as the next chapter will discuss. It was only in 1900 that the *Bengalee* became the first Indian-owned newspaper to subscribe to Reuter's service, an event which was advertised in the pages of the newspaper as a 'departure in native journalism'.[159]

Under these circumstances, it was often the case that newspapers that could not afford to subscribe to Reuter's services simply reproduced telegraphic news previously published in the big Anglo-Indian dailies. This was not simply a matter of 'stealing' news: rather, it was a practice which stemmed from a different understanding of journalism, one in which the clipping of news and other journalistic matter was acceptable, particularly if the source was acknowledged. This attitude towards the practice of clipping news and other journalistic matter is well illustrated by an editorial published in the pages of the *Hindoo Patriot* of 19 January 1863, in which Kristo Das Pal explained:

> The *Poona Observer* lately copied our review of Bap Deb Shastree's brochure on *Hindoo Astronomy*, but had put it to the credit of the *Indu Prakash*. In the next issue of his paper our contemporary corrects himself and quotes the *Indian Mirror* for his authority. As our contemporary took the trouble of correcting himself, we wish he had corrected himself correctly. Otherwise we would not have said a word on the subject.[160]

In the second half of the nineteenth century, this understanding of news as information that could be clipped from other newspapers came to be increasingly at odds with the idea, promoted by Reuters and some of the major Anglo-Indian newspapers that subscribed to its services, that news was a commodity for which the press had to pay and which even needed to be protected through copyright.

In their defence, Anglo-Indian and Indian journalists who clipped Reuter telegrams without actually subscribing to its services argued that such news was a 'public good'. One example comes from

Kandahar News, a handwritten newspaper established in the eponymous locality in 1879–80 for the perusal of the garrison stationed there. The newspaper was founded shortly after the completion of the telegraph line between Quetta and Kandahar in the spring of 1879, and was edited by Charles Edward Pitman. Eager to supply his readers with timely intelligence about current affairs, Pitman had arranged to receive the press commissioner's messages free of charge, as well as Reuter telegrams from the Pioneer Press at Allahabad. It wasn't long before Reuters came to know of the arrangement. The ensuing feud between the agency and the newspaper was a fairly typical example of the strategies adopted by Reuters in order to protect its telegrams and of the ways in which editors attempted to circumvent official rules regarding communication:

> Baron Reuter, or rather his Indian agent, has been guilty of a very questionable action. His terms for telegraphic news being beyond the means of an infant journal like the *Kandahar News*, the proprietors of the *Civil and Military Gazette* at Lahore, with a generosity for which they have the gratitude of the whole force up here, used to give us all their daily news of importance free of all charges except those actually incurred in transit. As soon as this reached the ears of Reuter's people, they informed the *Civil and Military Gazette* that if they did not stop it they would withhold all telegrams from them and also from the *Pioneer*. Under these circumstances the proprietors of the *Civil and Military Gazette* were of course obliged to stop giving us their news. However, Reuter cannot prevent private individuals reading the paper and then telegraphing us the news, which is what is now done, so they have gained nothing but ill-will by their ungenerous conduct.[161]

In a letter to the assistant resident at Hyderabad dated 6 November 1899, G. A. Fernandez, the press representative at Secunderabad (Sikanderabad), also pointed out that 'once Reuter's telegrams are published by the *Bombay Gazette* and *Times of India* each morning they become public property. As evidence of this I need only say that the Poona papers take Reuters telegrams from the morning papers and publish them the very evening.'[162] Indeed, if we judge by the pages of the newspapers themselves, it is doubtful that Reuters proved very successful in its attempts to police the circulation of its telegrams. In the 1870s and 1880s, the *Amrita Bazar Patrika* regularly published intelligence from this source, although there is no indication that the newspaper actually subscribed to Reuter's service.

What is clear, however, is that the telegrams were only occasionally credited to the agency—by being published under the headline 'Reuter's Telegrams'—while in other cases they were simply listed as part of a 'telegraphic summary'. Despite the lack of attribution, such foreign news most likely originated with Reuters. For example, on 16 July 1878 an unattributed telegram published in the *Amrita Bazar Patrika* reported, 'The German and Austrian semi-official Journals approve of the Convention. Doctor Nobiling has been sentenced to death.' The same telegram can be found, albeit in slightly modified form, in the *Times of India* of 12 July 1878, this time credited to Reuters: 'The German and Austrian semi-official journals approve of the Convention.... Dr. Nobiling, the Socialist who attempted to take the life of the Emperor William, has been sentenced to death.'

Protecting the News: Issues of Copyright

By the end of the nineteenth century, the issue of protecting news through copyright had become more and more pressing for Reuters. Although their telegrams were registered for copyright at Stationer's Hall in August 1870, this measure failed to offer the desired protection in Britain, let alone in India.[163] In 1881, in a famous decision in the case of *Walter vs Howe*, Sir George Jessel declared that newspapers were to be classed as books under the British Copyright Act of 1842. However, a decade later it was still unclear what categories of newspaper content were to be protected and how.[164]

A similar strategy was adopted in India. Between 1874 and 1878, Reuters made two unsuccessful attempts to persuade the colonial government to offer copyright protection to its telegrams for at least forty-eight hours after publication.[165] A new attempt initiated in 1878 met with a similar response. In a letter to S. C. Bayly dated 17 April 1878, F. J. Griffiths, secretary to Reuter's Company at Bombay, urged the government to grant copyright protection to telegrams published in India on the grounds that telegram piracy was a serious 'abuse':

> On the one hand, they [newspapers] are deprived in a measure of the value of the information which they receive from their own correspondents; on the other, as regards a subscription service like Reuter's telegrams, they are liable to pay a higher rate than might be necessary if all newspapers or individuals now publishing these telegrams had to purchase a license to do so.[166]

The practice was all the more objectionable, Griffiths argued, at a time when important political events took place in Europe and the 'extras' or news bulletins issued upon the receipt of telegrams were 'unscrupulously' reproduced by newspapers which did not subscribe to Reuters.[167] Griffiths's complaints suggest that the increasing commoditization of news during the last decades of the nineteenth century had led to a shift in perceptions regarding news reporting among certain sections of society. Clipping intelligence and articles from other newspapers, once a widely accepted journalistic practice, was now increasingly described as 'piracy'. In support of his argument, Griffiths cited a legislative act and two court cases from Victoria and Singapore which offered copyright protection to telegrams, conveniently forgetting to mention that both measures had been temporary.[168] Act no. 414, which offered copyright protection to telegrams for twenty-four hours, had been passed on 23 November 1871 by the Victorian legislature, but eventually expired on 31 December 1872.[169] The other example cited by Griffiths dated to 1873, when Justice Molesworth had granted an injunction to restrain the piracy of telegrams in Victoria. Molesworth's decision was a perfect illustration of the logic that informed the activity of news agencies like Reuters:

> This is an application for an injunction to restrain interference with a peculiar kind of property originating from the peculiar circumstances of this country. By means of telegraphs spread round the world we have the power of getting within a very short time intelligence from the greatest possible distance, and that intelligence is necessarily procured at very considerable expense, as telegraph charges must be imposed to compensate for the existence of the telegraph lines. Thus, there are now means by which from day to day intelligence can be received with the greatest possible celerity, and the obtaining of that information is attended with very considerable expense, and so far as a person who obtains the information can be said to have a property from the expenditure of money, that property is purchased here. On the other hand, persons of the class of newspaper proprietors, when they have received intelligence in this way, hope to make a profit to compensate them for the expense they have incurred, that profit arising from the increased circulation of the paper containing this peculiar kind of information which they are in a position to disseminate. That profit would be destroyed—at all events much impaired—if other newspaper proprietors who did not share in the expense had the same facilities to disseminate the information to the public. This is a kind of property which a peculiar state of society has brought in existence for the first time.[170]

The Government of India rejected Reuter's request, while nevertheless admitting that piracy of telegrams was proliferating.[171] In an ironic twist, especially for an administration that was notorious for its attempts to curb the right of newspapers to publish and comment freely on political and military information, when confronted with Reuter's request, most officials argued that the information contained in telegrams was public good, not private property. For example, C. Bernard pointed out that, unlike works of literature and art, where there was 'a distinct public advantage in granting protection', the dissemination of telegraphic information actually benefited public interest. Even more ironically, Whitley Stokes claimed that 'the benefit produced by the prompt dissemination of news outweighs the mischief (if any) done to Reuter's Company and the newspapers paying for telegrams.'[172] Since no public interest was harmed, government logic continued, the piracy of telegrams could not be declared a criminal offence. Furthermore, as Stokes pointed out, the piracy of telegrams did not constitute a criminal offence in any other country in the world. Since India 'should follow rather than lead more advanced countries in legislating on such matters as telegrams', Reuter's request was turned down.[173]

By the 1890s, the issue of news copyright had become an important topic of discussion in Britain, especially after the publication of Sidney Low's article 'Newspaper Copyright' in the *National Review* of July 1892. Low claimed that treating newspapers as books for purposes of copyright was inappropriate. He argued for a separate Newspaper Copyright Act which vested copyright in the registered proprietors or publishers of a paper, not in its 'authors', and allowed only owners of registered newspapers to sue for infringement of copyright. In addition, Low suggested that owners be allowed to have recourse to law only if they had expressly prohibited the reproduction of the whole newspaper or certain parts of its literary articles. He saw no rationale for granting copyright in news, although he believed that literary articles should be protected in the same way as those contributed to monthly magazines or periodicals.[174]

Opinions were divided regarding the possibility of news copyright. As Low explained, this was a battle between 'the austere vindicator of the sanctity of news, who would have every "pirate" promptly riddled below the water-line and sunk' and 'the bold "free-trader" who thinks that the newsmonger may cast his nets into every sea and land whatever fish he can draw into them'.[175] The issue at stake was whether it was indeed possible to protect the content and form of news. In a lawsuit against the *St. James Gazette* (*Walter vs Steinkopff*, 3 June 1892), *The Times* claimed that the *Gazette* had unlawfully reproduced three 'copyrighted' news paragraphs, as well as a descriptive article contributed by Rudyard Kipling. Justice North, while recognizing that copyright was infringed with regard to Kipling's article, ruled that there was no copyright in the three news paragraphs. Once published, he argued, news belonged to the public domain and was available to everyone. His decision was interpreted by legal practitioners to mean that there was no copyright in the content of news, only in the form in which it was expressed.[176] In response, the editor of *The Times* retaliated with an article which demonstrated how much the concept of news had changed by the end of the nineteenth century:

> News is not a spontaneous product; it does not make itself; it is not found ready made. It is a creation of man's industry, and bears the same relation to facts and events that a manufactured article does to raw material. Facts by themselves are not news. They have to be converted into news by the process of speaking or writing. For instance, suppose a great battle to have been fought in Central Africa on some day in last week—as there may have been, for all we know to the contrary. This is not news, because we have no news of it. Nor will it be news until we have. But now, suppose further that the *Times* has a Correspondent where that battle that took place [*sic*] He sends news of it to his paper—news which without him and his work would not, as far as this country is concerned, exist. That Correspondent has been sent to that quarter of the globe at great expense, and he has incurred great expense in sending home his news. He is the only man who does send it, and the *Times* has obtained it in the course of its operations as a Newspaper. This news is its property, and its own creation. The events out of which the news is made are a wholly different thing from the news, and the *Times* claims no property in them. But it claims the news as its own. If, then, there is to be any Copyright for Newspapers, what can be more unreasonable that to say that they cannot have it in respect of news?[177]

A survey undertaken in June–July 1895 by the Newspaper Society for the purpose of ascertaining the opinion of the press in Britain with regard to news copyright suggested that the press world was divided on this topic. Predictably, most provincial newspapers opposed news copyright. Of the newspapers that supported the measure most were weeklies, a group of publications that were less dependent on timely access to intelligence.[178] The responses of the editors suggest that three categories of factors were likely to influence their opinions as to the importance of copyright: the place of publication of a newspaper, its frequency, and its range of circulation. In this context, many editors argued that the practice of 'lifting' news, which was common among provincial papers, was not likely to harm the metropolitan press since their areas of circulation were distinct.[179] By contrast, as Lucy Brown has also shown, the major newspapers were more likely to oppose the clipping of telegrams. According to her, since the 1870s, 'London newspapers … complained bitterly of the fact that news which they had collected at great cost could so easily be copied by the provincial papers, but they were unprotected by copyright and could find no effective remedy.'[180]

Reuter's archival holdings—copies of copyright-related Indian legislation, such as Act XX of 1847 (the Copyright Act), Act XXV of 1867 (Press and Registration of Books Act), and Act X of 1890 (which amended Act XXV of 1867, especially the sections outlining the procedure for providing the government with free copies of printed books)—suggest that by the 1890s, the agency had reinforced its determination to protect its telegrams both in Britain and India.[181] To achieve this end, Reuters resolved to publish its telegrams in a daily news-sheet. Known as *Reuter's Journal*, this publication first appeared on 6 February 1890 and was thereafter sold for 6 pence at Reuter's head office in Old Jewry.[182] Before long, a similar paper was introduced in India under the name of *Reuter's Indian Journal*. On 30 August 1895, the agency's solicitors at Calcutta submitted the first copy of the journal for registration under Section 11 of Act XX of 1847, a move which enabled Reuters to gain official recognition as the owner of the journal's content. Published at Bombay, the journal featured, under the heading of 'Parliamentary News', a digest of Reuter telegrams on topics such as: 'Mr. Stanley on Uganda Railway', 'France and the Niger', 'Mr. Curzon on Egypt', 'The Siam Buffer State', and 'Lancashire Mill Owners and Cotton Duties'.[183] In addition, Reuters requested all agents and correspondents, regardless of location, to sign a form by which they 'invested [the Agency] with the copyright in telegrams and news communications supplied by them to us'. Edward J. Buck, Reuter's agent at Simla, relinquished his property rights in the news supplied to London on 23 February 1894.[184]

As individual requests for permission to republish Reuter telegrams continued to come in during the last decades of the century, the government's position towards this thorny issue proved inconsistent, its decisions usually shaped by 'reasons of a political character'. This was the case in 1898, when it turned down A. N. Templeton's application for permission to publish at Hyderabad or Secunderabad a paper called the *Hyderabad Chronicle's Summary of European and Indian Telegrams*. The main problem was that the government was adverse to the publication of newspapers in this region; it also regarded Templeton's continued residence in these towns as 'undesirable'.[185]

By contrast, a year later, G. A. Fernandez was allowed to republish London telegrams for the duration of the war in Transvaal and to distribute them among the garrison in Secunderabad and a number of other subscribers. The messages were received from A. J. Spalding, subeditor of the *Bombay Gazette*, and consisted of telegrams sent from London by James Mackenzie Maclean, member of Parliament, 'through the agency of the War Office', the *Pioneer* London telegrams, as well as occasional Reuter telegrams. In this latter case, Fernandez took great care not to infringe Reuter's 'copyright' by not reproducing its telegrams 'en bloc'. In recommending that permission be declined until Reuter's consent was obtained, H. Luson pointed out that the law in British India did not prohibit the republication of such telegrams, but that this might be different in Secunderabad. But Fernandez benefited from the support of Sir Trevor Chichele-Plowden, whose opinion prevailed in the end: 'It is a fact that Reuter's and other special telegrams after publication in the newspaper which receive them direct are republished by other newspapers throughout India, and it does not seem to me just that Mr. Fernandez should be prevented from doing at Secunderabad a thing which any person who chooses may do with impunity in British India.'[186]

The general confusion and lack of agreement on this issue were also demonstrated by the debates surrounding the Telegraphic Press Messages Bill, which the government proposed to introduce in 1899. The proposal was eventually withdrawn in the following year due to lack of agreement over the possibility of copyright in news and the actual period of protection. While some members of the Governor General's Council claimed that the measure would encourage newspaper enterprise in India by protecting those publications that paid for their telegrams, others rightly pointed out that what was needed, in fact, was a 'substantial diminution in the rates of telegraphic transmission from Europe'.[187] Representatives of the Indian press like Mahadeo Krishna Padhye, P. M. Mehta, Dinshaw E. Wacha, N. G. Chandavarkar, and Amiruddin Tyabji, backed also by Anglo-Indian newspapers like the *Capital*, *Indian Daily News*, *Statesman*, *Advocate of India*, and *Champion*, protested against the proposed measure. For Padhye, this was the latest in the string of 'illiberal measures' aimed at the newspaper press in India. But, as the government knew all too well, the attempt to control the circulation of news was bound to fail:

> It is impossible to check the smuggling of news. The composition or frame of public telegrams may, no doubt, be protected. But news having a hundred tongues would find expression everywhere unchecked and, very often, without the least *mala fides* on the part of the publisher. Bazar gossip may be the source of knowledge of the publisher, though the gossip may be born of a protected telegram. No amount of precautions would, also, enable an honest publisher to know whether the gossip he is going to give currency to has emanated from a telegram which is yet 'protected'. It would be very difficult to know when a particular news, not immediately traceable to a telegram, becomes punishable under the Act.[188]

***

This chapter has examined the relationship between the colonial state, Reuters, and the newspaper press in nineteenth-century India, aiming to understand how official visions of news and journalism circumscribed processes of reporting, and how they coexisted or clashed with alternative visions advocated by journalists and Reuters. The discussion has traced colonial attempts to centralize and standardize the distribution of news to the press, which ranged from official gazettes to Editors' Rooms to the notorious institution of the press commissionership and its association with the implementation of the Vernacular Press Act of 1878. It has been argued that attempts to standardize and centralize the distribution of official intelligence in the nineteenth century were intertwined with the aim of monitoring and controlling the press. Supplying the press with 'adequate' and 'correct' information about the affairs of the government was considered to have the dual advantage of educating the press and policing its content in order to detect and suppress potentially 'seditious' publications.

In essence, the government's attitude towards the reporting of political and military intelligence in the pages of the newspaper press changed but little in the course of the nineteenth century. Although the older view that such information should not form the object of debate in the press was no longer tenable, the authorities did not believe in the liberty of the press, be it Anglo-Indian or Indian, to publish and discuss freely subjects of their own choice. Rather, what we witness during this period is a consistent desire to devise and implement bureaucratic mechanisms that would enable the state to maintain a certain degree of control over the circulation and publication of intelligence, both for the preservation of empire and to avoid potential 'embarrassment' in the eyes of the India Office and the British public. The telegraph posed particular problems for the colonial administration, precisely because speed made the circulation of news more difficult to monitor.

In addition, the issue of cost complicated the process of transmission and featured prominently in debates about the centralization of official news distribution. It is here that the tension between different versions of news became particularly conspicuous: was official intelligence a public good that should be distributed to newspapers free of charge, or was it a commodity for which the newspapers themselves were expected to pay? Opinion was divided and highly contextual amongst colonial officials. What was a public good when faced with Reuter's demands for copyright protection of its telegrams appeared to be less so when the duty and the cost of delivering the telegrams fell on the shoulders of the colonial administration.

For Reuters, whose business was to sell news, the answer was clear. Its continuous attempts to limit the circulation of telegrams to non-subscribing newspapers, and its persistent demands that its telegrams be granted copyright protection, testify to its determination to push this agenda. But the representatives of the newspapers were themselves divided on the topic, their positions shaped by a host of factors, including their relationship with the colonial administration, location and frequency of publication, economic resources, and so forth. Thus, the *Pioneer* seemed happy with the status quo, its 'backstairs' access to official intelligence thoroughly resented by the journalistic community. Other major Anglo-Indian newspapers welcomed the idea of being supplied with official news, although they did not think that such a 'privilege' should be applied indiscriminately to all categories of newspapers. Smaller and less viable newspapers, many of which were published in the vernacular, also welcomed the idea of a centralized system of official intelligence, but they also pointed out that the news values promoted by the colonial government were not necessarily shared by their readers.

Notes

1. M. Barns, *The Indian Press* (London: George Allen & Unwin Ltd, 1940), pp. 59–61. Also, Veena Naregal, *Language Politics, Elites and the Public Sphere: Western India under Colonialism* (London: Anthem Press, 2002), p. 161.
2. For an account of early Madras newspapers and their use of mastheads, see C. J. Nirmal, 'The Press in Madras under the East India Company', *Journal of Indian History* 44, part 2 (1966): 483–515.
3. Bernard S. Cohn, *Colonialism and Its Forms of Knowledge: The British in India* (Princeton: Princeton University Press, 1996), p. 10.
4. As J. Silberstein-Loeb has pointed out, a similar situation existed in early nineteenth-century Britain: 'The method of regulation varied, but its effect was censorial. Government either censored directly, by prohibiting printers from publishing certain content, or indirectly, via taxation or controlling the number of printers.' See J. Silberstein-Loeb, 'The Structure of the News Market in Britain, 1870–1914', *Business History Review* 83, no. 4 (2009): 759–88, at 759. The Indian examples are numerous and span the nineteenth century. On 29 June 1824, Fardunji Dorabji Dastur asked the Bombay government to patronize his projected Persian-language newspaper by subscribing fifty copies of it. Faced with the initial refusal of the secretary to the government, Dastur insisted on being granted 'the indulgence of having your Excellency's name at the head of my subscribers for any number of copies your Excellency may deem proper, so as I may be able to say that my Press has the honor of your Excellency's Patronage, by which I may gain many subscribers, especially amongst the Natives, in whose eyes your Excellency is very much exalted'. The government eventually agreed to subscribe to four copies. See The Bombay Government subscribe to native newspapers in the Gujarati, Hindustani and Persian languages, 14 July 1824, F/4/816/21744, IOR. The Home Index at the NAI also provides useful insights into official patronage of the press via subscriptions. In 1874, the government subscribed, among others, to the *Pioneer*, *Delhi Gazette*, *Bombay Gazette*, *Madras Times*, *Indian Public Opinion*, *Jubbulpore Chronicle*, *Lucknow Times*, *Indian Statesman*, *Times of India*, *Madras Mail*, *Athenaeum and Daily News*, and *Indian Spectator*. In 1886, the list included the *Bengaleee*, *Reis and Rayyet*, *Amrita Bazar Patrika*, *Indian Nation*, the *Tribune*, the *Pioneer*, *Voice of India*, *Indian Mirror*, *Indian Daily News*, and *Indian Spectator*.

5. Muniruddin, *History of Journalism* (New Delhi: Anmol Publications, 2005), pp. 24–6.
6. Letter from the chairman and deputy chairman of the East India Company to the Right Honourable Charles W. Williams Wynn, 17 January 1823, in United Kingdom, Parliament, House of Commons, *East India (Press): Papers Relating to the Public Press in India* (London, 4 May 1858), p. 4. Among the most famous victims of this early system of press control was Hicky himself. After being prohibited from distributing his newspaper through the post office, he was twice imprisoned and fined and eventually had his press and types confiscated. See J. Natarajan, *History of Indian Journalism* (New Delhi: Publications Division, 1954), pp. 5–9; Hemendra P. Ghose, *The Newspaper in India* (Calcutta: University of Calcutta, 1952), pp. 5–11; Barns, *The Indian Press*, pp. 63–9.
7. Letter from the chairman and deputy chairman of the East India Company, p. 3.
8. Letter from the chairman and deputy chairman of the East India Company, pp. 17–18.
9. Barns, *The Indian Press*, pp. 74–5; Natarajan, *History of Indian Journalism*, pp. 13–14.
10. Letter from the chairman and deputy chairman of the East India Company, pp. 5–6.
11. R. R. Pearce, *Memoirs and Correspondence of the Most Noble Richard Marquess Wellesley*, vol. 1 (London: Richard Bentley, 1846), p. 283.
12. Pearce, *Memoirs and Correspondence*, pp. 278–9, 285.
13. Letter from the chairman and deputy chairman of the East India Company, p. 5.
14. A. F. Salahuddin Ahmed, *Social Ideas and Social Change in Bengal, 1818–1835* (Leiden: E. J. Brill, 1965), p. 63.
15. Barns, *The Indian Press*, p. 90.
16. 'To Correspondents', *Calcutta Journal of Politics and General Literature*, 27 November 1822, p. 368.
17. Letter from the chairman and deputy chairman of the East India Company, p. 8.
18. Barns, *The Indian Press*, p. 115.
19. Lynn Zastoupil, *Rammohun Roy and the Making of Victorian Britain* (New York: Palgrave Macmillan, 2010), p. 100.
20. Raja Rammohun Roy, 'Memorial to the Supreme Court', in *Britain in India*, 1765–1905, vol. 4: *Cultural and Social Interventions*, edited by J. Marriott and B. Mukhopadhyay (London: Pickering & Chatto, 2006), pp. 110–16.
21. R. R. Roy, 'Memorial to the Supreme Court', pp. 110–16.
22. R. R. Roy, 'Memorial to the Supreme Court', pp. 110–16.
23. Letter from the chairman and deputy chairman of the East India Company, p. 20.

24. M. T. Boyce, *British Policy and the Evolution of the Vernacular Press in India, 1835–1878* (Delhi: Chanakya Publications, 1988), p. 40.
25. Partha Chatterjee, *The Black Hole of Empire: History of a Global Practice of Power* (Princeton: Princeton University Press, 2012), p. 120.
26. Court's despatch regarding the communication of official documents to the newspapers, Foreign Department, Political Branch, 18 July 1856, No. 65, NAI.
27. In this connection, see Sukeshi Kamra, *The Indian Periodical Press and the Production of Nationalist Rhetoric* (New York: Palgrave Macmillan, 2011), pp. 67–98. Also see Kirti Narain's excellent *Press, Politics and Society: Uttar Pradesh, 1885–1914* (New Delhi: Manohar, 1998), pp. 21–4.
28. Barns, *The Indian Press*, p. 255.
29. Durga Das Basu, *Law of the Press in India* (New Delhi: Prentice-Hall of India Private Limited, 1980), pp. 249–50; G. K. Roy, *Law Relating to Press and Sedition* (Simla: Station Press, 1915), p. 18.
30. G. K. Roy, *Law Relating to Press and Sedition*, p. 18.
31. Kamra, *The Indian Periodical Press*, p. 89.
32. 'Document D: Act IX of 1878' and 'Document E: Annexure to Bill for the Better Control of Publications in Oriental Languages', in Boyce, *British Policy and the Vernacular Press in India*, pp. 158–69.
33. For a discussion of 'objectivity' as a specific American value and its contrast to 'independent reporting', the notion favoured in British journalism, see Mark Hampton, *Visions of the Press in Britain, 1850–1950* (Urbana and Chicago: University of Illinois Press, 2004); Mark Hampton, 'The "Objectivity" Ideal and Its Limitations in 20th-Century British Journalism', *Journalism Studies* 9, no. 4 (2008): 477–93.
34. The distribution of news to the press, Minute by E. W. Collin, 12 June 1881, Foreign Department, General A, August 1882, No. 43, p. 4, NAI.
35. See, for example, 'Report on Electric Telegraphs for 1855', *Bombay Times and Journal of Commerce*, 17 March 1857; 'Red Sea and India Telegraph Company', *Bombay Times and Journal of Commerce*, 12 October 1859; 'Transport Train', *Bombay Gazette*, 11 July 1860.
36. The distribution of news to the press, p. 4.
37. The distribution of news to the press, p. 4.
38. The distribution of news to the press, p. 4.
39. The distribution of news to the press, p. 5.
40. Court's despatch regarding the communication of official documents to the newspapers, Foreign Department, Political Branch, 18 July 1856, No. 65, NAI.
41. Decision that supply of official publication to institutions and newspapers should be left to local governments, and so on, Home Department, Public Branch, Consultation 13 May 1859, Nos 26–31, NAI.
42. Decision that supply of official publication to institutions and newspapers should be left to local governments.

43. The distribution of news to the press, p. 5; Regarding an Editor's Room to be established in the Financial Secretary's Office, Charles Wood to Governor General in Council, 16 December 1861, Home Department, Public Branch, 26 November 1864, No. 143, Part B, NAI. On the *Nil Darpan* affair, see *The History of the Nil Durpan, with the State Trial of the Reverend J. Long, etc.* (Calcutta, 30 July 1861). A twentieth-century example comes from Chandrika Kaul's work, which captures the diversity of opinions exhibited by Fleet Street journals in their coverage of Indian matters, and illuminates how the Indian government attempted to influence the British press by exploiting the communication gaps between Britain and India. Her analysis of the reporting of the Jallianwala Bagh massacre (1919), which became known to London papers through a *Times* telegram only nine days after it happened, is a revealing example of how the Indian government and the secretary of state attempted to control the circulation of news in the empire. Chandrika Kaul, *Reporting the Raj: The British Press and India, c. 1880–1922* (Manchester and New York: Manchester University Press, 2003), pp. 199–229.
44. Arrangements for the publication of a Supplement to the Calcutta Gazette, Home Office Circular, 18 September 1860, Home Department, Public Branch, 19 September 1860, Nos 41–43A, NAI.
45. Publication of an official gazette to be called the Gazette of India after 1st January 1864, W. Muir to Col. Durand, 11 September 1863, Home Department, Public Branch, 13 November 1863, Nos 29–31, Part A, NAI.
46. Publication of an official gazette to be called the Gazette of India.
47. The distribution of news to the press, pp. 5–6.
48. 'Government Gazettes of the British Empire and Commonwealth', available at: http://www.nationalarchives.gov.uk/records/research-guides/government-gazettes-empire-commonwealth.htm (accessed 17 June 2015).
49. Memoranda on improving relations between the Government of India and the press, 20 May 1870, Burne Collection, MSS.EUR D 951/27, IOR.
50. John Lang of the *Mofussilite* was Australian by birth.
51. Memoranda on improving relations between the Government of India and the press; emphasis original.
52. Memoranda on improving relations between the Government of India and the press.
53. C. E. Buckland, *Dictionary of Indian Biography* (London: Swan Sonnenschein & Co, 1906), p. 393.
54. Note that Burne's use of the term 'Indian press' refers to Anglo-Indian newspapers exclusively.
55. Memoranda on improving relations between the Government of India and the press; emphasis original.

56. Memoranda on improving relations between the Government of India and the press. Needless to say, confidentiality was essential to the success of Burne's proposed system: he even suggested the introduction of 'severe penalties' to ensure the secrecy of the scheme.
57. Memoranda on improving relations between the Government of India and the press.
58. See Hampton, *Visions of the Press in Britain*, pp. 75–82.
59. In fact, in 1878, Lethbridge wrote that he 'had the great advantage of a most careful training by Colonel O. T. Burne, the late Private Secretary, who personally looked into every detail of the working of the scheme during the first nine months of its existence, and worked with me on it for several hours nearly every day'. Lethbridge to A. C. Lyall, 17 June 1878, Foreign Department, General A, August 1879, Nos 14–15, NAI. See also Buckland, *Dictionary of Indian Biography*, p. 251; Appeal from Roper Lethbridge against the proposed abolition of the press commissioner, 18 August, 1880 L/PJ/6/20 File 1139, IOR.
60. T. R. Moreman, 'Burne, Sir Owen Tudor (1837–1909)', in *Oxford Dictionary of National Biography* (Oxford: Oxford University Press, 2004), available at: http://www.oxforddnb.com/index/101032184/Owen-Burne (accessed 13 April 2016).
61. Philip Harwood to Roper Lethbridge, 28 December 1874, Lethbridge Papers, MSS.EUR B 182, IOR; Narendra Nath Sen to Roper Lethbridge, 4 July 1877; Edward Lawson to Roper Lethbridge, 24 November 1878.
62. Owen T. Burne, *Memories* (London: Edward Arnold, 1907), pp. 198–9.
63. 'Government and Newspapers', *Review of Reviews for Australasia* 36 (1908), p. 249.
64. Burne to Lethbridge, 15 November 1878, Lethbridge Papers, MSS.EUR B 182, IOR.
65. Burne, *Memories*, p. 228. The reference is to the Madras famine of 1877.
66. Kaul, *Reporting the Raj*, p. 103.
67. Burne to the editors of Indian newspapers, 7 June 1876, Burne Papers, MSS.EUR D 951/27, IOR.
68. Sinnett to Burne, 10 June 1876, Burne Papers, MSS.EUR D 951/27, IOR.
69. Minute of A. C. Lyall, 14 June 1881, Foreign Department, General A, August 1882, No. 43, NAI.
70. Burne to the editors of Indian newspapers, 7 June 1876, Burne Papers, MSS.EUR D 951/27, IOR.
71. M. K. Chanda, *History of the English Press in Bengal, 1858–1880* (Kolkata: K. P. Bagchi, 2008), pp. 17–20, 50–3.
72. Cullin to Burne, 29 June 1876, Burne Papers, MSS.EUR D 951/27, IOR.
73. Wilson to Burne, 15 June 1876; McPherson to Burne, 30 June 1876; and Knight to Burne, 31 July 1876, all from Burne Papers, MSS.EUR D 951/27, IOR.

74. Sutherland to Burne, 8 July 1876; and Sinnett to Burne, 10 June 1876, both from Burne Papers, MSS.EUR D 951/27, IOR.
75. Knight to Burne, 31 July 1876, Burne Papers, MSS.EUR D 951/27, IOR.
76. Lethbridge to Burne, 31 October 1877, Burne Papers, MSS.EUR D 951/27, IOR.
77. Lethbridge to Burne, 31 October 1877.
78. Lethbridge to Burne, 31 October 1877.
79. Lethbridge to Burne, 31 October 1877.
80. Lethbridge to Burne, 31 October 1877. It is doubtful whether the editors actually observed this recommendation. At least after 1878, intelligence from the press commissioner was usually marked as such, either by being published with the byline 'From the Press Commissioner' in the case of telegrams, or by indicating the source of the news in the body of the text in the case of longer postal communications. The logic of publicity worked differently for the government and the journalists: while the former was keen to eschew responsibility for the content published, the latter wanted to emphasize the source of news as a means of legitimizing their work.
81. Lethbridge to Burne, 31 October 1877.
82. Lethbridge to Burne, 31 October 1877.
83. Government of India to Secretary of State for India, 3 August 1880, Foreign Department, General Branch A, August 1880, No. 3, NAI.
84. T. Banerjee, 'The Growth of the Press in Bengal vis-à-vis the Rise of Indian Nationalism (1858–1905)', in *The Indian Press*, edited by S. P. Sen (Calcutta: Institute of Historical Studies, 1967), p. 43; Sunit Ghosh, *Modern History of Indian Press* (New Delhi: Cosmo Publications, 1998), pp. 146–7.
85. S. Banerjea, *A Nation in the Making* (1925; reprint Calcutta: Oxford University Press, 1963), p. 56.
86. Resolution, 7 February 1879, Foreign Department, General Branch A, August 1879, Nos 14–15, NAI.
87. Roper Lethbridge to A. C. Lyall, 17 June 1878, Foreign Department, General Branch, August 1879, Nos 14–15, NAI.
88. Resolution, 7 February 1879.
89. Resolution, 7 February 1879. In his initial proposal Lethbridge had requested two translators for Urdu and one each for Bengali, Marathi, and Tamil.
90. Roper Lethbridge to A. C. Lyall, 17 June 1878, Foreign Department, General Branch, August 1879, Nos 14–15, NAI.
91. Roper Lethbridge to O. T. Burne, 31 October 1877, Burne Papers, MSS. EUR D 951/27, p. 6, IOR.
92. 'Lord Lytton', *Examiner* 3704 (1879), p. 104.
93. Archibald Forbes, 'War Correspondents and the Authorities', *Nineteenth Century: A Monthly Review*, 7 (1880), p. 185.

94. H. Hensman to the Private Secretary to the Viceroy, 28 June 1889, Home Department, Public Branch, December 1891, Nos 103–8, NAI.
95. Edwin Hirschmann, *Robert Knight: Reforming Editor in Victorian India* (New Delhi: Oxford University Press, 2008), pp. 193–4.
96. Stoppage of the supply of press telegrams to the *Statesman* newspaper, William Riach to Secretary to the Government of India, September 1879, Foreign Department, General Branch B, October 1879, No. 133, NAI.
97. The paper was transferred to Calcutta in the mid-1880s, and counted among its contributors the famous Indian nationalist Bipin Chandra Pal. See Bipin Chandra Pal, *Memories of My Life and Times* (Calcutta: Bipin Chandra Pal Institute, 1973), pp. 302, 359.
98. *Bharat Mihir*, 6 March 1879, *NNR*, Bengal, No. 11 of 1879, pp. 4–5, italics original.
99. *Bharat Mihir*, 6 March 1879, *NNR*, Bengal, No. 11 of 1879, p. 5.
100. Government of India to Secretary of State for India, 3 August 1880, Foreign Department, General Branch A, August 1880, No. 3, NAI.
101. Minute of A. C. Lyall, 10 July 1878, Foreign Department, General Branch A, August 1879, Nos 14–15, NAI.
102. Resolution, 7 February 1879, Foreign Department, General Branch A, August 1879, Nos 14–15, NAI.
103. Refusal of the press commissioner to supply the *Bengal Times* with news, Foreign Department, General Branch B, February 1880, Nos 217–18, NAI.
104. Application of the editor *Bombay Chronicle* to be supplied with news, in common with other newspapers, Foreign Department, General Branch B, February 1880, Nos 242–4, NAI.
105. Rules for 'Press' messages in India, Burmah and Ceylon sanctioned by the Governor General in Council with effect from the 1st of June 1874, Home Department, Public Branch A, June 1878, No. 114, NAI. The prescribed registration form for newspapers was as follows: 'I ___ (Proprietor or Editor) of the Newspaper published at ___ every ___, request that the concession respecting "Press" messages may be applied to the ___ Newspaper. I undertake to publish in its entirety the text of every telegram received by me at the reduced rate and to use it for no other purpose, or at once to pay into the nearest Government Telegraph Office the difference of the cost of the telegram at "Press" and ordinary rates. I also undertake to forward to the Telegraph Clerk Office, Calcutta, a copy of each issue of the ___ Newspaper.'
106. Minute of C. Bernard, 1 June 1878, Home Department, Public Branch A, June 1878, No. 114, NAI.
107. Minute of C. Bernard, 1 June 1878.

108. Press-Message privilege for Vernacular newspapers, Home Department, Public Branch A, June 1878, No. 114, NAI.
109. See for example Kaul, *Reporting the Raj*, p. 103; Ghosh, *Modern History of Indian Press*, p. 149; Natarajan, *History of Indian Journalism*, pp. 102–3.
110. According to the estimates of the Government of India, the establishment cost the government Rs 5,500 a month during the first year, a sum which was later reduced to Rs 3,800. See Government of India to Secretary of State for India, 3 August 1880, Foreign Department, General Branch A, August 1880, No. 3, NAI.
111. *Times of India*, 12 April 1881.
112. *Times of India*, 12 April 1881; Natarajan, *History of Indian Journalism*, p. 105.
113. Abolition of the appointment of the press commissionership as a separate office, Foreign Department, General Branch A, August 1882, No. 43, NAI.
114. Abolition of the appointment of the press commissioner as a separate office, C. Grant, 21 June 1882.
115. Abolition of the appointment of the press commissioner as a separate office, Minute of W. Stokes, 1 February 1881.
116. The distribution of news to the press, Minute of Lord Rippon, 22 June 1881, Foreign Department, General A, August 1882, No. 43, NAI.
117. H. Hensman to the private secretary to the viceroy, 28 June 1889, Home Department, Public Branch A, December 1891, Nos 103–8, NAI.
118. For example, *Times of India*, 15 March 1884, 8 June 1885, and so on.
119. Application from the proprietor of the *Dost-i-Hind* newspaper, Bhera (Shahpura) for press news, Foreign Department, Internal Branch B, May 1888, Nos 272–3, NAI.
120. United Kingdom, Parliament, House of Commons, Debate, 4 December 1888, vol. 331, cols 1011–12.
121. Kaul, *Reporting the Raj*, p. 103.
122. Arrangements consequent on the abolition of the press commissionership, Home Department, Public Branch A, December 1891, Nos 103–8, NAI.
123. Communication of official news to the press, Minute of J. C. Ardagh, 27 August 1889, Home Department, Public A, December 1891, Nos 103–8, NAI.
124. Donald Read, *The Power of News: The History of Reuters*, 2nd ed. (Oxford: Oxford University Press, 1999); Kaul, *Reporting the Raj*, among others.
125. *North-China Herald*, 8 March 1855; emphasis original.
126. Read, *The Power of News*, pp. 20–1.
127. For a collection of Reuter's Indian telegrams published in British newspapers between 1858 and 1881, see Reuters Telegram Books to 1881: Indian Telegrams, LN976, Reuters Archives (hereafter RA).

128. Reuters Telegram Books to 1881: Indian Telegrams, LN976, RA; see also S. Sapru, *The News Merchants: How They Sell News to the Third World* (New Delhi: Dialogue Publications, 1986), p. 9.
129. Terhi Rantanen, *When News Was New* (Chichester, West Sussex: Wiley-Blackwell, 2009), p. 51; Read, *The Power of News*, pp. 49–50.
130. Hirschmann, *Robert Knight*, pp. 3–5; *Half-Yearly Report of the Bengal Chamber of Commerce, November 1860–April 1861*, Appendix L, Robert Campbell and Co. to H. W. I. Wood, 27 November 1860. For an obituary of Dawes, see 'Sir Edwyn Dawes: A Remarkable Career', *Capricornian*, 13 February 1904.
131. Hirschmann, *Robert Knight*, pp. 18, 21.
132. Hirschmann, *Robert Knight*, pp. 18, 21.
133. 'The Death of Mr. Robert Knight', *Mahratta*, 2 February 1890.
134. *Amrita Bazar Patrika*, 21 April 1870.
135. Hirschmann, *Robert Knight*, p. 74.
136. *Times of India*, 5 January 1872; 'A Mission around the World without Purse or Scrip', *Juvenile Instructor* 35 (1900), p. 638.
137. Hirschmann, *Robert Knight*, p. 74.
138. *Englishman*, 13 July 1866. Saunders writes *Bombay Times* instead of the *Times of India*, but the newspaper had ceased to exist under that name in 1861, when it incorporated the *Bombay Standard* and became the *Times of India*. See also Alfred H. Watson, 'The Growth of the Press in English in India', *Journal of the Royal Society of Arts* 96, no. 4760 (1948): 121–30, at 124.
139. *Times of India*, 16 December 1865.
140. *Times of India*, 16 December 1865; *Englishman*, 13 July 1866.
141. *Times of India*, 16 December 1865.
142. Supply of daily message by Reuter's Company, Bombay, Home Department, Public Branch, July 1866, No. 192, NAI.
143. Supply of daily message by Reuter's Company, Bombay.
144. *Englishman*, 13 July 1866.
145. Hirschmann, *Robert Knight*, p. 99.
146. *Englishman*, 13 July 1866.
147. *Times of India*, 5 January 1872.
148. *Times of India*, 5 January 1872. On the feud between Knight and Mull, see Hirschmann, *Robert Knight*, pp. 101–4.
149. This was particularly the case with opium and exchange quotations. One famous example was the 'opium scandal' of 1861, which saw the falsification of opium advices from China and outraged the mercantile community of Bombay. See *Bombay Times and Standard*, 15 January 1861. Another example was reported in Calcutta in 1854. See *Half-Yearly Report of the Bengal Chamber of Commerce, Calcutta, November 1, 1854* (Calcutta: Military Orphan Press, 1854), p. xxi.

150. Graham Storey, *Reuters' Century, 1851–1951* (London: Max Parrish, 1951), p. 62. For an account of Reuter's expansion into South and East Asia, see Henry M. Collins's autobiography, *From Pigeon Post to Wireless* (London: Hodder and Stoughton, 1925).
151. Kanji Ishii, *Jōhō tsūshin no shakaishi: Kindai Nihon no jōhōka to shijōka* [The social history of information and telecommunications: Information society and marketization in modern Japan] (Tokyo: Yūhikaku, 1994), pp. 76–7.
152. *Yokohama Mainichi Shimbun*, 18 August 1871.
153. Achille Fould was the minister of finance in Louis Napoleon's cabinet, responsible for negotiating a loan of 300 million francs in 1863.
154. Storey, *Reuters' Century*, pp. 62–3.
155. Press Messages, Reuters, 23 September 1876, L/PWD/7/1056, File 368, IOR.
156. Read, *The Power of News*, p. 5.
157. Agreements between Reuters and the *Englishman, Bombay Gazette, Civil and Military Gazette, Pioneer*, and *Madras Times*, LN435, 1879, RA. The contract with the *Times of India* has not survived, but it is known that the paper was among the subscribers.
158. Agreements for supply of news between Reuters and the *Times of India, Civil and Military Gazette, Madras Mail, Rangoon Gazette, Pioneer, Bombay Gazette, Madras Times, Morning Post*, and *Englishman*, LN247, 1890–1, RA.
159. Banerjea, *A Nation in the Making*, p. 157.
160. *Hindoo Patriot*, 19 January 1863.
161. *Kandahar News*, October 1879, MSS.EUR E 193, IOR.
162. G. A. Fernandez to the 1st Assistant Resident, Hyderabad, 6 November 1899, Foreign Department, Internal B, December 1899, Nos 20–3, NAI.
163. Read, *The Power of News*, p. 59.
164. *DNCJ*, s.v. 'Copyright', p. 143; Sidney J. Low, 'Newspaper Copyright', *National Review*, 19 (1892): 648–66.
165. 'Copyright of Telegrams', Minute of C. Bernard, 11 May 1878, Home Department, Public Branch A, June 1878, Nos 36–9, NAI.
166. 'Copyright of Telegrams', Griffiths to Bayly, 17 April 1878, Home Department, Public Branch A, June 1878, Nos 36–8, NAI.
167. 'Copyright of Telegrams', Griffiths to Bayly, 17 April 1878.
168. 'Copyright of Telegrams', Griffiths to Bayly, 17 April 1878.
169. 'Copyright of Telegrams', Minute of W. Stokes, 27 May 1878, Home Department, Public Branch A, June 1878, Nos 36–9, NAI.
170. 'Copyright of Telegrams', letter from F. J. Griffiths to S. C. Bayley, 17 April 1878.
171. 'Copyright of Telegrams', Minute of C. Bernard, 11 May 1878.

172. 'Copyright of Telegrams', Minute of C. Bernard, 14 May 1878; Minute of W. Stokes, 27 May 1878.
173. 'Copyright of Telegrams', Minute of C. Bernard, 14 May 1878; Minute of W. Stokes, 27 May 1878.
174. This was in accordance with Article 7 of the Berne Convention for the Protection of Literary and Artistic Works (1886), which stated: 'Articles in newspapers or magazines published in any country of the Union may be reproduced, in original or in translation, in the other countries of the Union, unless the authors or publishers have expressly forbidden it. For magazines, it is sufficient if the prohibition is made in a general manner at the beginning of each number of the magazine. No prohibition can in any case apply to articles of political discussion or to the reproduction of news of the day or miscellaneous items (notes and jottings).' Berne Convention (1886), in L. Bently and M. Kretschmer (eds), *Primary Sources on Copyright (1450–1900)*, p. 675, available at: www.copyrighthistory.org (accessed 26 March 2011); Low, 'Newspaper Copyright', p. 666.
175. Low, 'Newspaper Copyright', p. 662.
176. Low, 'Newspaper Copyright', p. 658.
177. Low, 'Newspaper Copyright', p. 662.
178. Copy report from Newspaper Society monthly circular re: copyright in news, 1 August 1895, LN777, RA.
179. Copy report from Newspaper Society, 1 August 1895.
180. Lucy Brown, 'The Treatment of News in Mid-Victorian Newspapers', *Transactions of the Royal Historical Society*, 27 (1977), p. 39.
181. See, for example, Copyright Act (India) 1847—certified copy made in 1896, 12 June 1896, LN1036, RA, as applied to Reuters.
182. Read, *The Power of News*, p. 59.
183. Copyright registry of Reuter's Indian Journal, Home Department, Books and Publications, September 1895, Nos 114–18, NAI.
184. Copyright agreements of agents and correspondents, 26 January 1894, LN39, RA.
185. Foreign Department, Internal B, October 1898, Nos 514/516, NAI.
186. G. A. Fernandez to the 1st Assistant Resident, Hyderabad, 6 November 1899, and Minute by H. Luson, 4 November 1899; Trevor Chichele-Plowden to Secretary to the Government of India, 4 November 1899, Foreign Department, Internal B, Dec. 1899, Nos 20–3, NAI.
187. The Telegraphic Press Messages Act, 1899, L/PJ/6/516, File 1479, 20 July 1899, IOR; Withdrawal of the Telegraphic Press Messages Bill, 29 March 1900, L/PJ/6/537, File 708, IOR.
188. Letter by Mahadeo Krishna Padhye, 1 August 1899, L/PJ/6/519, File 1767, 31 August 1899, IOR, italics original.

5 Reporting Foreign and Domestic News

I keep six honest serving-men
(They taught me all I knew);
Their names are What and Why and When
And How and Where and Who.
I send them over land and sea,
I send them east and west;
But after they have worked for me
I give them all a rest.

—Rudyard Kipling, *Just So Stories* (1902)

The previous chapters have examined the infrastructure of news communication in nineteenth-century India, the ways in which various categories of social actors responded to the introduction of new technologies of communication, and how the colonial government and Reuters regulated and shaped the channels and content of news reporting during this period. In this final chapter, attention shifts to the newspapers themselves. I propose to examine the use of telegraphy in journalism from an additional angle that enables us to understand how newspapers negotiated the extant communication order and how news reporting developed in the nineteenth century.

The chapter examines the 'environment' of newspapers in colonial India with a focus on the content and the form of news. My aim is to understand what was reported and how, and how the form and content of reporting changed over time. For example, I pay attention to the elements of news discourse—the 'who', the 'what', the 'when', the 'where', the 'why', and the 'how' to which Kipling alludes in the poem quoted above—to the topics that became the subject of news, the ways in which people featured in news stories, how war and grief were reported, but also to changes in page size and the number of newspaper pages, to headlines, bylines, and inter-line spacing, the use of fonts, punctuation, illustrations, and so on. I borrow the concept of 'environment' from Kevin Barnhurst and John Nerone's seminal work on the history of news in the United States, in which they argue that

> the form of news creates an environment: it invites readers into a world molded and variegated to fit not only the conscious designs of journalists and the habits of readers, but also the reigning values in political and economic life.... Form structures and expresses that environment, a space that comfortably pretends to represent something larger: the world-at-large, its economics, politics, sociality, and emotion.[1]

There is, however, one aspect in which my analysis departs from that of Barnhurst and Nerone's, namely in its emphasis on the dialogical relationship between newspapers and their audiences in colonial India. Although I subscribe to their view that 'the form of news constructs the audience's field of vision', I am rather sceptical about the way in which Barnhurst and Nerone use this argument to 'question the notion of individual sovereign readers'.[2] While it is true that newspapers, through both their form and their content, mediate a particular understanding and view of the world, the readers in my story were rarely simple consumers of intelligence who lacked any awareness of the context in which news was made and reported. Arguably, understanding how audiences respond to the content of the newspaper is a difficult undertaking even for the contemporary scenario, let alone for that of the nineteenth century. Yet, in the case of colonial India such a task is not impossible, especially if we remember that journalists themselves were often a newspaper's most vocal and hence publicly visible audience. As the previous chapters have pointed out—for example in the discussion of the Indian editors' criticism of official reports about the amir of Afghanistan Sher Ali Khan—news often became the object of debate, discussion, comparison, refutation, or contestation.

Put differently, newspapers in colonial South Asia did not only shape their audiences, but were in turn shaped by them. Consider, for example, the organization of a newspaper like the *Englishman*, which during the 1840s–1860s resembled a collection of individual 'gazettes', each aimed at a specific audience, as demonstrated by the fact that the *Englishman* proper was followed by a 'Commercial Gazette' and a 'Military Chronicle'.[3] This approach to journalism suggests that the newspaper tried to meet the different news needs of its potential audiences. Furthermore, readers themselves often became suppliers of news, not only in the form of occasional correspondence—see Elizabeth Augusta Egerton's example in Chapter 3—but also in the form of occasional telegrams. This was particularly the case with members of the mercantile community, who shared their telegrams with the newspaper press, a practice which underscored the symbiotic relationship between commercial enterprise and newspapers. The examples are numerous: the *Phoenix* of 16 July 1861 published 'copies of telegrams received by a Calcutta house from Mauritius', while in July 1865, the *Bengal Hurkaru* published commercial telegrams from Hong Kong and Madras addressed to the Chamber of Commerce at Calcutta.[4]

The previous chapters have discussed some of the competing interests and visions of journalism which influenced the development of the newspaper press in nineteenth-century India. Here I examine the form and content of news from two additional, and at the same time complementary, angles: a long-term, comparative analysis of news reporting in the nineteenth century which revolves primarily around the *Englishman* of Calcutta and the *Bombay Gazette*; and a short-term, event-specific examination that focuses on the Austro-Prussian War (1866) and the murder at Poona (Pune) of two European officers associated with the plague-relief measures in 1897. In this latter case, the evidence used is derived primarily from the extant files of major English-language dailies like the *Times of India*, the *Englishman*, the *Madras Times*, the *Lahore Chronicle*, and the *Bombay Gazette*. Despite the emphasis on these publications, the discussion also makes frequent reference to other important newspapers, including the *Bengalee*, *Amrita Bazar Patrika*, *Hindoo Patriot*, *Bangalore Chronicle*, *Bharat Jiwan*, and so on. For a detailed discussion of the rationale which informed the choice of newspapers examined, the reader is invited to refer to the relevant sections in the introduction.

The Form of Newspapers

Both the *Bombay Gazette* and the *Englishman* were published as daily newspapers during most of the period examined in this book; the former also appeared as a weekly in the 1830s and later as a tri-weekly, eventually becoming a daily in 1843.[5] During its weekly phase, the *Bombay Gazette* was a six-page newspaper. As the frequency of publication increased, the number of pages decreased to four, which was the standard for most English-language dailies in India during the period 1840s–1880s.[6] This was to change in the last two decades of the nineteenth century, when the number of pages doubled as editors sought to accommodate an increasing amount of information and advertisements.

The move to eight pages was in tune with global trends in English-language journalism during this period. As Barnhurst and Nerone have pointed out for the United States, the late 1880s was a period which 'saw a definitive break with the four-page limit': most urban dailies increased their pages to eight, although they continued to be shorter than leading metropolitan newspapers such as the *New York Times* or *The Times*.[7] Thus, seen strictly from the point of view of their size, many of the English-language dailies published in India during the period examined resembled provincial urban dailies in Britain such as the *Birmingham Daily Post*, which followed a similar trend of increasing its pages from four to eight in the last decades of the century.

Prior to the 1890s, the English-language dailies examined here looked crammed and difficult to read, with the possible exception of the advertising and latest news sections. This aspect of the newspaper layout was a direct result of limited access to an important resource: paper. As Ulrike Stark points out, until the 1870s, when the Government of India decided to encourage local production, most of the paper used in the subcontinent was either imported from Europe at a high cost or produced locally on a scale which could hardly meet the growing demand for this material.[8] Since increasing the number of pages would have been expensive during this period, editors usually increased the number of columns within a page in order to accommodate more material. The layouts of the *Bombay Gazette* and the *Englishman* clearly illustrate this trend. Although the number of pages remained constant during the 1840s–1880s, the number of columns within a page expanded continuously, from four in the 1850s to six in the 1860s and seven in the 1870s in the case of the *Gazette*, and from six in the early years of the *Englishman*'s publication to seven in the 1860s. The number of columns within a page was also connected to the frequency of publication: the *Bharat Jiwan*, a Hindi-language weekly from Benares, had only three columns per page in the 1880s, the same as Tilak's *Mahratta* a decade later. Similarly, the *Amrita Bazar Patrika*, published as a weekly in the 1870s and 1880s, increased the number of its columns from three to four, eventually increasing it to five upon its transformation into a daily in 1895. By the turn of the century, the standard number of pages for an English-language daily in India was between eight and ten, while the number of columns per page was usually six or seven.[9]

The amount of typographic attention dedicated to advertisements and news matter suggests that these two categories of newspaper content played an important role in the economic survival of a newspaper. Indeed, if we are to believe Stocqueler, who edited the *Englishman* in 1835, the exclusive publication of a piece of news about the attempted assassination of King Louis Philippe in the course of that year was responsible for adding no less than '£1,200 per annum to the permanent receipts of the paper'.[10] As far as advertising was concerned, medical advertisements, especially those for patented medicines, represented an important source of revenue. The *Phoenix*, a daily newspaper published in Calcutta until September 1861, featured an impressive number of medical advertisements, among which were cures for 'spasmodic asthma', 'Dinneford's Pure Fluid Magnesia'—believed to be efficient in disorders of the digestive system—and 'Holloway's Pills', which promised to cure a wide range of illnesses like 'chest complaints, windy or watery dropsy, disorders peculiar to women, children's complaints, indigestion, bile, and sick headaches'. One particular advertisement even offered potential patients residing in India the option of being treated 'by correspondence'.[11]

The *Bangalore Herald*, a biweekly newspaper published on Tuesdays and Fridays in 1861, also featured medical advertisements on a regular basis, especially remedies for impotency, nervousness, and the purification of the blood.[12] The rates of advertising were publicized in the newspaper itself, usually on the front or last page.

In the case of a weekly newspaper like the *Indian Spectator* from Bombay, the advertising fee was Rs 15 per column per month in 1882 (or Rs 8 per half column and Rs 5 per quarter column). Special advertisements were charged Re 1 per four lines or less, with each additional line being charged 4 annas.[13] For comparison, advertisements in the weekly *Amrita Bazar Patrika* cost 4 annas per line in 1882.[14]

Another type of content likely to attract the attention of the reading public and thus benefit the 'fortunes' of the newspaper press were government advertisements. In a letter dated 20 February 1822, the well-known printer and editor Fardunji Marzban petitioned the Bombay authorities to allow him 'to give for insertion' in his projected Gujarati weekly, the *Bombay Samachar*, 'such Government advertisements in Guzerattee which may be requisite to notify the Natives'. Despite Marzban's promise to 'charge no more than one half of the rate of that which is generally charged by the other Printing offices to your Honorable Government', the authorities refused to allow the insertion of government ads, deciding instead to patronize the young newspaper by subscribing fifty copies of it.[15]

Needless to say, not all newspapers were equally successful in enlisting the patronage of the government and attracting advertisers, nor indeed did they share the same approach to advertising. In fact, there were significant differences even between major urban dailies like the *Bombay Gazette* and the *Englishman*. Within the crammed columns of a four-page newspaper, the usual way to emphasize items of interest was by increasing the leading and the amount of white space which surrounded a particular item, using headlines, and setting text in different sizes and designs. Both newspapers employed these techniques. Overall, however, advertising in the *Bombay Gazette* was much more conspicuous and vibrant than in the *Englishman*. This difference can be ascribed, partly at least, to what C. A. Bayly describes as Bombay's 'culture of cosmopolitan commercial sociability', characterized, among other things, by the interconnected development of commercial enterprise, means of communication, and the newspaper press. As we have already seen in Chapter 3, members of the Parsi community played an important role in 'promot[ing] a local commercial knowledge economy through bulletins of intelligence, which later became newspapers'.[16]

The evolution of advertising in the course of the nineteenth century was shaped by economic circumstances, available technology, and the journalistic vision of those involved in the production of newspapers. In the beginning of the 1830s, the advertising sections of the *Gazette* featured notices in English, Gujarati, and Marathi. Some of these ads were enclosed in their own compartments, separated from each other by double rules. A great variety of fonts—italics, bolds, and upper case—as well as different leadings were used to emphasize the products and their retailers.[17] This was followed by a less innovative phase which lasted until about the 1880s, when the layout of the newspaper was transformed under the leadership of two well-known figures of Anglo-Indian journalism, Grattan Geary and Thomas Jewell Bennett.

During Geary's editorship, the staff of the *Bombay Gazette* consisted of three other Anglo-Indians—an assistant editor, a subeditor, and a chief reporter—and four Indians who were employed as local reporters.[18] Between 1884 and 1892, the post of assistant editor was occupied by Bennett, whose name is usually remembered in connection with his activity at the *Times of India*.[19] Bennett was an enterprising and, by all accounts, well-connected man who was keen to make a name for himself in the newspaper business in India. After acquiring the proprietorship of the *Times of India*, he founded, together with the London master printer F. M. Coleman, a publishing company which went on to become the precursor of the Times Group, India's largest contemporary media group. Writing in the mid-twentieth century, A. H. Watson, former editor of the *Statesman*, credited Bennett, Coleman, & Co., as it was then known, with showing 'outstanding enterprise in developing' the *Times of India* and 'furthering illustrated journalism' in the subcontinent (see Illustration 5.1).[20]

In the pages of the *Bombay Gazette*, the outcome of Geary and Bennett's collaboration was visible in the considerable increase of white space, in the expansion of advertisements, which broke free of the confines of single columns, and the continuous diversification of the use of types. In addition, the increase in the number of newspaper pages during this period also translated into an increase in the amount of space dedicated to advertising matter. If, before the 1890s, advertisements usually occupied two pages of the *Bombay Gazette*—initially the first two and, later, the front page and the last—by the last decade of the nineteenth century they could be found inside the newspaper as well, interspersed with news, official reports, and other journalistic matter.[21]

Illustration 5.1 News composing room, *Times of India*, November 1898
Source: © The British Library Board, Shelfmark: Photo 643/ (14).

For the *Bombay Gazette*, the last decade of the nineteenth century was also marked by the proliferation of illustrations in advertising.[22] An elaborate ad for Harlene's Shampoo published in the issue of 19 July 1900 featured an illustration of a mother and her daughter which spread over half of the newspaper page. The advertisement invited readers into the confines of a middle-class boudoir: standing in front of a mirror and brushing her luxurious long hair, the mother reassured her doting daughter that she would grow up to have the same beautiful hair if only she used 'Edwards' Harlene'. Apart from the innovative use of illustrations to reinforce the textual message, such advertisements also reflected changes at other levels, for example the move from generic to specific ads and the gradual exposure of private aspects of (middle-class) everyday life to the public eye.[23] Such an image would have been out of place in the pages of *Amrita Bazar Patrika*: a similar advertisement for 'Harlene for the Hair', published in the issue of 19 July 1901, consisted only of text, without the accompanying illustration. The advertisement was enclosed in a square and vied for the attention of the readers by promising to 'restore the hair, promote the growth, arrest the fall, strengthen the roots, remove the dandruff [and] allay irritation'. The same issue, however, made use of illustrations to advertise a wide range of other products, among which were 'Freeman's Original Chlorodyne', 'Kishori Lall Khettry's Tambul-Bihar', and 'Rigaud's Kenanga of Japan toilet water'.

Compared to the *Bombay Gazette*, the *Englishman* strikes the reader as a newspaper which devoted considerably less attention to advertising and, generally speaking, to design and ornamentation. Undoubtedly, advertisements generated an important part of the newspaper's profits, but the typographic investment in advertising techniques did not match that of the *Bombay Gazette*. For a good part of the nineteenth century, advertisements in the *Englishman* looked more like a succession of notices rather than printed matter whose design aimed to capture the attention of readers. Although the amount of space dedicated to advertisements had practically doubled by the 1890s—from the front and last page to the first two and last two pages—the most conspicuous development, as in other sections of the newspaper, was the increase in inter-line spacing and white space, not necessarily the innovative use of types. During the last decade of the nineteenth century, individual items were sometimes enclosed in a square—a practice already present in the *Bombay Gazette* in the 1830s—but illustrations remained largely absent.[24] The only illustrations we can identify were occasional weather charts and generic engravings of vessels, which had been a regular feature of shipping advertisements since the beginning of the century.[25]

This brief incursion into the form of the *Bombay Gazette* and the *Englishman*, with a focus on their overall layout and advertising strategies, suggests that the development of the newspaper form in the nineteenth century was shaped both by global trends in English-language journalism and the specific environment of British India. Access to cheaper sources of paper led to an increase in the number of pages of many newspapers towards the end of the period examined. This allowed editors to publish more information and advertisements, but also to make the layout of the newspaper easier to read, by increasing the leading and the amount of white space used for advertisements and news. Newspapers responded differently to these developments, a fact which testifies to their differential access to resources as well as to the existence of different visions of journalism.

Patterns of News Reporting in the Nineteenth Century

During the nineteenth century, news discourse in the *Bombay Gazette* and the *Englishman* was heterogeneous in presentation, content, linguistic features, and function. Indeed, the concept of 'news' itself was fluid: newspapers published a variety of more or less timely intelligence pertaining to political, economic, social, and cultural events, but the degree of interest and public relevance of such items was varied and often contested. Like today's online journalism, nineteenth-century editors and readers actively questioned the news value of particular items of intelligence. For example, on 21 August 1874, E. A. Reeves, Reuter's agent in India, was forced to react to accusations published in the *Madras Times* that the agency's telegrams were 'ridiculous', 'exasperating', 'stuff', and 'rubbish'. Outraged by the tone of the criticism, Reeves admitted that 'the telegrams are occasionally obscure, and that more care in their compilation is desirable', particularly with regard to European affairs. As he pointed out, '… the sender sometimes apparently forgets that a message respecting Continental politics and events which may appear perfectly clear to *him*, may be at the same time almost incomprehensible to *us*, who are not at the time in possession of the newspapers giving details, and this point I shall bring to the notice of the Head Office in London.'[26] His comment underscored the shortcomings of telegrams as a means of reporting and the ways in which readers were forced to recreate events far removed from their physical location based on the limited information supplied. Price, Reeves went on to argue, prevented Reuters from sending longer account of events; since news values were likely to differ from one person to the other, he exculpated the agency by pointing out that it was 'difficult to please all'.

One important category of intelligence regularly featured in the pages of the newspaper press in the nineteenth century was shipping information pertaining to the arrival and departure of vessels and ships. This information was usually published under easily recognizable headlines like 'Shipping' and 'Shipping Intelligence'. Prior to the development of the newspaper press, it was the duty of town criers to publicize the schedule of departures and arrivals, as Dinshaw E. Wacha reminisced in his account of mid-nineteenth-century Bombay:

> In those days the medium of advertisement for vessels to ply backwards and forwards was not the 'Times of India' and the 'Bombay Chronicle'

> or the 'Bombay Samachar' and the 'Jame Jamshed'. A Parsi-crier or two went round the native town, halting at centres were business men and women congregated.... There were a couple of criers with lungs of brass and stentorian voices. Each took his turn. The crier would stand at one of the recognised business centres in the native part of the Fort while all and sundry gathered round him. He then proclaimed the date on which the vessel would start, the name of the bunder from which the start would be made, the names of the ports at which it would anchor to embark and disembark passengers.... Perhaps it would not be uninteresting to give a sample of the Gujarathi [*sic*] programme in English of the departure of the coasting steamers.
>
> 'Be it known as a public notice to the passengers going to Surat, that the steamer "Flox" will positively sail at ... o'clock on ... the ... instant. From Surat she will sail to Gogo [Ghogha], and from Gogo to Bhavnagar. Tickets may be had at the office of Messrs.... in the Bazar Gate Street till the evening of....'[27]

The contrast between items of shipping intelligence and shipping advertisements during the early decades of the nineteenth century is worth exploring at some length. Unlike the contemporary practice of publishing the latest or most important news stories on the front page, in the nineteenth century this section of the newspaper was usually filled with advertisements. Thus, to the extent to which we accept the proposition that the location of an item in the pages of the newspaper was an index of its importance, the conclusion we can derive from this practice is that many editors of English-language newspapers were more concerned to emphasize advertisements rather than news.[28] In 1840, for example, some items of shipping intelligence published in the *Englishman* were printed on the front page, that is, in the advertising section, while others appeared in a section titled 'Commercial Gazette', which published a medley of news of potential interest to the mercantile public and was usually printed on the second page of the newspaper. In those early days of journalism, when the choice of advertising techniques was relatively limited, the difference between shipping advertisements and shipping intelligence was much less conspicuous than it would become in later decades. Advertisements were usually generic, not individualized, as demonstrated by the engravings of vessels which preceded them and the relatively uniform vocabulary of advertising, with ships being invariably described as 'fine', 'good', or 'fast', and the accommodation they provided as 'excellent' or 'splendid'.[29] Details of the shipping agent and the destination—for example, London, Liverpool, or Rangoon—were also provided.

By contrast, the shipping items published in the 'Commercial Gazette' section were listed in an orderly sequence without any effort at special emphasis. More importantly, such items were stripped of any additional wording besides that which was necessary in order to convey essential information. Compare, for example, the following two items which appeared in the *Englishman* of 23 July 1840, the former in the 'Commercial Gazette' section and the latter in the advertising section on the front page (the original formatting in terms of capitalization, punctuation, italics, and so on has been retained):

> (1) July 22. Bark *Christopher Rawson*, Smellie, for the Mauritius, in a day or two; bark *Santon*, Huxtable, for Liverpool, in a day or two, and the schooner *Margaret*, Thaddeus, for Rangoon, in a day or two.
>
> (2) For Liverpool,
> *With immediate despatch.*
> The new fast sailing ship *Warlock*, of 350 Tons, Capt. George Seymour. —For Freight or Passage, having splendid accommodations, apply to the Capt. Fergusson, Brothers and Co.

Both items are characterized by brevity. Beyond this similarity, however, the layout and the content of news and advertisements were shaped by the different functions they were expected to fulfil. One crucial difference between the two types of journalistic content was the absence or presence of temporal markers: news, as we can see from the above example, usually contained references to the date and/or the exact time of dispatch of intelligence (the latter in the case of telegrams). The concern with temporality in nineteenth-century reporting cannot be overemphasized. As the discussion in the previous chapters has shown in regard to telegrams, colonial administrators often pointed out that without temporal markers, such items of intelligence would have been of little use to the reading public. In addition, they were also more difficult to monitor for 'errors' in transmission and for potential 'abuses', such as the falsification of intelligence. Thus, while shipping advertisements emphasized the qualities of the vessel and informed potential passengers about the schedule of departure, shipping news conveyed information about specific events by focusing particularly on dates, places, and the actors involved.

Another point worth emphasizing here is that shipping news familiarized the reading public with a brief and concise style of reporting—two qualities with which telegraphic news would later come to be associated—before the actual introduction of electric telegraphy into India. Needless to say, this phenomenon was not restricted to the Indian subcontinent. As Matthew Rubery has suggested, this concise style of reporting was not a product of the nineteenth century: the market and shipping intelligence published in news-sheets such as that of Lloyd's in eighteenth-century London was reported in a similarly lapidary manner.[30] A typical item of shipping intelligence, which Rubery calls anachronistically a 'telegram', included the name of the ship, the place of departure and destination, the type of event (safe arrival, shipwreck, and so on), the place of the incident in the case of shipwrecks and other accidents, and, if known, the date of occurrence and information regarding casualties. For example, *Lloyd's List* of 19 January 1753 announced that 'The Thomas and Rebecca, Ellery, from London for Dublin, is lost off Wexford.' A more detailed piece of news occasionally ran over five to ten lines of a column and used a similar style of reporting:

> The New Spain Man of War, from Cadiz for Vera Cruz, put into the Canaries the latter End of Novemb, leaky, with two other Ships from Cadiz in Company with her, one from Buenos Ayres, who fail'd thence the 28th of November, the other for Carthagena: The latter of which meeting with some squa'ls off this Island, was oblig'd to cut away her Mizen Masts, and throw her Guns and Provisions overboard, no farther Damage [*sic*].[31]

According to Michael Harris, the roots of this style of news reporting can be traced to the seventeenth century, when serial publications began to appear in London. Commercial intelligence such as exchange rates, the prices of goods and stocks, and shipping reports occupied an important place in these early newspapers; their prosaic style resulted from a combination of factors such as limited newspaper space, the scarcity and unreliability of news, and attempts to systematize shipping reports.[32]

In the twentieth century, brevity and concision in news reporting have often been identified as markers of 'objective', factual reporting; as discussed in the introduction, some scholars and historians of journalism have associated the rise of this style of reporting with the use of telegraphy. Yet, as Mark Hampton points out, the history of British journalism in the eighteenth and nineteenth centuries was far from 'unambiguously linear'. In fact, in the eighteenth century, newspapers were also concerned with the publication of 'facts', as opposed to opinion and commentary, which were usually relegated to the domain of other printed genres like pamphlets. During the last decades of the nineteenth century, this preoccupation with 'facts' became increasingly conspicuous in Britain, but Hampton argues that the trend was far from novel. As he puts it, 'The late-Victorian shift from "views" to "news" was thus not a brand-new development but in some ways a return to older emphases.'[33]

Seen in this light, the style of reporting in nineteenth-century telegrams appears more like a continuation of earlier modes of reporting commercial news, especially shipping intelligence, rather than a 'revolutionary' break with previous journalistic practice. Due to their relatively high cost, telegrams were indeed shorter and conveyed only the gist of events, without the elaboration characteristic of letter writing. However, the news stories examined in the *Englishman* and the *Bombay Gazette* suggest that 'dry', factual news devoid of any type of elaboration was not the ideal towards which newspaper editors aspired. After the tariff for inland press telegrams was reduced in 1880, domestic telegrams from various places within India increased in number and length as more detail and even commentary began to find their way into reporting by telegraph. Compare, for example, foreign and domestic telegrams in the 1860s, which hardly occupied more than five lines of a column—and were more often than not confined to one or two—to telegrams at the turn of the century, when it was not unusual to see messages from London spread over fifteen lines, and news from Rangoon and other parts of South Asia cover even more newspaper space.[34]

It is hardly surprising, therefore, that the earliest type of telegraphic intelligence published by the newspaper press was shipping information about the arrival and departure of vessels. Prior to the introduction of electric telegraphy, such intelligence was transmitted via the semaphore towers that linked Calcutta with Diamond Harbour (see Chapter 1), which enabled newspapers like the *Calcutta Courier* and the *Englishman* to publish reports about the movement of vessels in the late 1830s and early 1840s. For example, the *Calcutta Courier* of 15 June 1839 published semaphoric intelligence 'from 4 P. M.' announcing the arrival of two ships from Boston and Sydney as well as the sighting of vessels at Kedgeree, Cowcolly Light House, Diamond Harbour, Hooghly Point, and Moyapore.[35] Semaphoric news also travelled to other parts of India such as Bombay, although the extent of its circulation was by no means as wide or as regular as that of its electric successors. One example comes from the issue of 30 December 1841 of the *Bombay Gazette*, which informed its readers that 'Yesterday's semaphore announced the arrivals of the Wanderer, Smith, from Hull, 2nd July.'[36] Early 'electric news' thus followed a format which was highly similar to that of semaphoric telegrams, as the following examples suggest (the original punctuation and formatting has been retained):

> Semaphoric Intelligence, - July 22.
> AT KEDGEREE. – *Charles Dumergue* and *Oriental* passed up at 10 A.M.
>
> —*Englishman*, 23 July 1840

> LATEST INTELLIGENCE.
> (*By Electric Telegraph.*)
> MADRAS.
> WEDNESDAY, 18*th July*.
> The steamer *Jeddo*, from Bombay, was signalled at Galle on Wednesday last at 7 A.M.
>
> —*Bombay Gazette*, 20 July 1860

Telegrams such as these indicate that, as far as journalism was concerned, the semaphore was used almost exclusively for the transmission of shipping intelligence. By contrast, the electric telegraph was used for the transmission of more diverse news content. In the 1860 issues of the *Bombay Gazette* and the *Englishman*, shipping intelligence was published alongside commercial information, such as the price of opium and cotton, bank shares, and exchange rates. By the 1870s, foreign—mostly political and military—events reported by Reuters had become a regular feature of telegraphic news, while a decade later we witness an 'explosion' of domestic telegrams in the pages of these publications. The most common topics covered were political events, murders and other criminal offences, the activity of important public figures, the outbreak and evolution of epidemics, natural calamities, the state of the troops, and so on. Other more mundane topics were also featured, as the following report published in the *Bengalee* of 13 January 1883 suggests: 'Mr Gladstone is suffering from insomnia.'

Telegraphic intelligence was published in a separate section of the newspaper, usually located on page two, under suggestive headlines such as 'Latest Intelligence' (*Bombay Gazette*, 4 July 1860), 'Latest Telegrams' (*Englishman*, 7 July 1890), 'Telegrams' (*Amrita Bazar Patrika*, 13 January 1893; *Bangalore Spectator*, 6 May 1890), 'Telegraphic Summary' (*Indian Spectator*, 8 January 1882), and so on. The importance of certain items of intelligence was further emphasized by the occasional use of multi-decked headlines, as in the case of *Amrita Bazar Patrika*'s reporting of the Transvaal War, which highlighted sub-topics such as 'Women Traitors' and 'Boer Refugees' (5 November 1900), or the *Bombay Gazette*'s account of 'The Crisis in China', when the main headline was followed by two other headlines announcing the 'Chinese Military Operations at Canton' and 'The Black Flags on the Move' (9 July 1900).

Telegraphic intelligence did not enjoy the same degree of prominence in all the newspapers examined for the purposes of this book. To begin with, in the case of weekly publications, news timeliness was less important than in the case of dailies, which thrived on the publication of timely intelligence. More importantly, a regular and comprehensive supply of telegrams remained a luxury not all newspapers were able to afford during the nineteenth century. Unlike the *Bombay Gazette* and the *Englishman*, a weekly like the *Hindoo Patriot* had no regular column of telegrams in the 1860s, with telegrams usually published once a month. The same was true of the *Mahratta*, which in the 1890s relied predominantly on 'local notes', letters from correspondents, 'reliable sources', and selections from other newspapers like the *Times of India* for its supply of news matter. There was no attempt to emphasize journalistic content besides the usual bold subheads which announced 'Serious News from Baroda' or the 'Brutal Murder' of two children in Somwar Peth.[37] References to telegrams, when published, were often indirect, suggesting reliance on major Anglo-Indian newspapers, especially in the case of foreign news:

> The *Bombay Gazette*'s Central News telegram says that several prominent members of the Liberal-Unionist party at a recent private meeting severely criticized the Government, denouncing the Ministers as guilty of blundering. However, a Reuter's telegram says that they are still resolved to support the Government.[38]

A similar format can be encountered in the *Bharat Jiwan*, which featured editorials, items of intelligence of local and foreign interest, book reviews, correspondence, and advertisements (*vigyāpan*) published on the last two pages of the newspaper. The format of the telegram, with its characteristic temporal indicators, was not identifiable in the issues of July 1884 examined. This was in contrast to another Hindi-language weekly, the *Shree Venkateshwar Samachar*, published in Bombay by Khemraj Shrikrishnadas, which two decades later featured a 'Gist of Telegrams' (*tārsār*) dedicated to the reporting of foreign news, including Reuter telegrams.[39] One notable feature of the *Bharat Jiwan* was its practice of publishing domestic and foreign snippets of intelligence in the same section (*samāchārāvalī*, or miscellany of news), unlike most of the other English-language dailies examined. The issue of 7 July 1884, for example, included news about Bombay, Dacca, Meerut, Lahore, Allahabad, Vienna, Java, and Sumatra, and then again about the maharajas of Burdwan and Cooch Behar. Political news was also mixed up with news about anonymous individuals, such as one item which reported that 'In the city of Vienna a man set himself on fire after pouring kerosene over his cloths.' Onlookers, the report continued, witnessed this dramatic event and called for a doctor, but the unfortunate man was 'unrecognizable' by the time he arrived.[40] For comparison, in the *Times of India* of the same date, foreign and domestic intelligence was relegated to different sections of the newspaper, namely 'Reuter's Telegrams' and 'Arrival of the Overland Mail-Heads of Intelligence', and 'Local' respectively. Among the telegraphic topics featured were 'The relations between France and China' and 'Increase of cholera in the South of France', while the overland mail reported on the Prince and Princess of Wales, 'Mr. Gladstone', the Duke of Argyll, the match between Cambridge and the Australians, and the 'Health Exhibition' in South Kensington.[41]

In the second half of the nineteenth century, telegraphic news coexisted with intelligence sent by post from other parts of South Asia, Britain, and Europe. It is true, however, that as the price of telegrams became less prohibitive towards the end of the period examined, the number and length of telegrams also increased. This was particularly the case with domestic news. In fact, the analysis of news reporting practices suggests that prior to the 1880s, when the reduction in the rates for the transmission of domestic press telegrams was sanctioned, the telegraph was a technology associated primarily with the reporting of foreign news and, in the case of domestic news, with shipping and commercial intelligence. The most obvious indication of this state of affairs comes from the fact that the headline 'Latest Intelligence' was usually reserved for Reuter's telegrams or, when sent by the 'Indian Telegraph', for steamer reports and commercial information. It is only in the 1880s that domestic political news, on topics such as 'The Viceroy on the Afghan War' (*Times of India*, 3 January 1880), came to be regularly included in the 'Latest Telegrams' section.

In the absence of anecdotal evidence we can only speculate about the reasons for this state of affairs, especially if we consider that for a short period in the mid-1850s, during the initial phase of the introduction of telegraphy into the Indian subcontinent, a newspaper like the *Bombay Times and Journal of Commerce* did publish longer items of domestic intelligence sent by 'special telegraph' from Calcutta. For example, the issue of 14 April 1855 contained a medley of news that originated in Calcutta on 5 and 6 April 1855 and reported, among other things, that 'Lord Dalhousie's health has much improved', 'The *Friend of India* confirms the warlike rumours from Ava', 'Some one in the Mofussil has offered Government the secret of an infernal machine', and 'Demonstrations have been made at Madras against the telegraphic messages'. Over the following two decades, however, such domestic telegrams almost disappeared from the 'Latest Intelligence' section, perhaps as a result of the combined influence of increased government regulation, standardization of telegraphic communication, and prohibitive prices of communication. Thus, during this earlier phase in the history of electric telegraphy in the subcontinent, the new technology seems to have been used predominantly to transmit the heads of intelligence of overland news (see Illustration 5.2), shipping, and commercial intelligence. The situation changed visibly in the 1880s, when domestic telegrams featuring general news, mostly of a political nature, were regularly published as part of the 'Telegrams' or 'Latest Telegrams' section. Indeed, not only did the number and average length of such items increase, but their place of origin also diversified considerably.

In fact, examining the place of origin of telegrams provides important clues about the most important nodes in the communications system of colonial South Asia, as well as the type of events whose news value was considered particularly high. In the case of the *Englishman*, Simla, the summer capital of British India, was an important source of news in the last decades of the nineteenth century: the issue of

THE HINDOO PATRIOT.

PUBLISHED EVERY WEDNESDAY EVENING.

VOLUME VIII. NUMBER 28. | BHOWANIPORE IN THE SUBURBS OF CALCUTTA:—WEDNESDAY, JULY 11, 1860. | *Subscription—1 Ru in advance monthly 10 Rupees per year.*

ENGLISH MAIL NEWS.

FIRST BULLETIN.

From Galle, 5th July, 4-25 afternoon. To Calcutta.

FROM MR. FLEMING TO SECRETARY TO GOVT.

STEAMER "Nemesis" arrived from Suez 12th, and Aden 27th, June.

The following is taken from the *Home News* of the 10th June:—

The capitulation was not concluded till June 6th between Garibaldi and the Neapolitan Government.

Numerous desertions have taken place from the Royal Army.

Garibaldi has organized measures for taking the votes of the Sicilians on the question of annexation to Piedmont. He has already formed a provisional Government.

The King of Naples has besought the interposition of the five Powers to preserve Sicily. They have declined to inferfere.

A Meeting is to take place at Baden between the Prince Regent of Prussia and the Emperor Napoleon.

A Commercial Treaty is about to be concluded between France and Belgium.

The Lord Justices this morning confirmed Sir Page Wood's decision in the case of the Westminster Hotel Company; and the removal of the India Office is expected to take place shortly.

The general letter-carriers of the Post Office have threatened the authorities with a strike if the proposed plan for amalgamating them with, the district carriers be put into operation.

SECOND BULLETIN.

PUBLIC Meetings have been held in different places at which resolutions have been adopted condemning the proceedings of the Lords on the Paper Duty; and Meetings have also been held on the subject of Reform.

A Committee of the House of Commons is now taking evidence on a project for embanking the Thames.

A Meeting has taken place between the Prince Regent of Prussia and the King of Bavaria, and a General Meeting of German Princes concerning German interests is expected shortly to take place.

The question of slavery is undergoing an ordeal of public discussion in all parts of the United States.

Mr. McGernick (?) and Mr. Calcott have been declared by Election Committees of the House of Commons duly elected for Londonderry and Clare.

The debate of the motion for the Reform Bills going into Committee has been twice adjourned.

The Volunteer movement continues to advance steadily.

The Cup at Ascot has been won by Mr. Hamilton's "Rupee."

Recruiting for the Pope is going forward openly in Ireland.

Subscriptions in aid of Garibaldi are proceeding in all parts of the kingdom.

The brother of the Count Montemolien has formally declared his intention of asserting the rights of his family to the Throne of Spain.

The Emperor of the French has adjourned the ratification of the recent Treaty with Abyssinia.

The Reports of Committee of the Military Organization and national defences are ready.

Between three and four hundred vessels were wrecked in the recent stormy weather.

The half yearly examination of Cadets at Addiscombe College was held on the 8th of June.

The Half-yearly Meeting of the Peninsular and Oriental Steam Company was held on the 6th of June.

A trial trip has been made successfully by the "Great Eastern."

A Parliamentary Committee had been appointed to enquire into the organization of the transport service.

The Irish and Scotch Reform Bills have been withdrawn by the Government.

The evacuation of Lombardy by the French troops is completed.

Obituary.—In H. M.'s Indian Service:—Col. F. S. Hawkins, Bengal Infantry; J. S. Torrens, Esq., late Bengal Civil Service. Miscellaneous.—General Sir William Chalmers.

From Bombay, 10th July, 8-20 morning. To Calcutta.

To Secretary to Government of India.

Arrived Steamer "Colombian" with Mail of the 18th June.

The following is taken from the "Home News:

FIRST BULLETIN.

The embarkation of Royal Troops has been carried out at Palermo.

The defences of the City have been increased: popular Government is re-organized all over the country, and the local Councils are restored.

Austria and France have refused to guarantee Sicily to the King of Naples.

Ministers have withdrawn the Reform Bill.

The Secretary of State for India has introduced his measure for the re-organization of the Army in India. The debate was adjourned till the 21st June.

Lord Clyde succeeds to the command of the Coldstream Guards. Major Generals Maunsell and Onnis (?) obtain the two other vacant Coloneleies.

SECOND BULLETIN.

A Meeting has taken place at Baden between the Emperor Louis Napoleon and the Kings and Princes of Germany, as a measure of conciliation between France and Germany.

A Neapolitan Ambassador has been sent to Paris, but has abandoned his original design of going to London, in consequence of declarations made by Lord Palmerston in condemnation of the barbarities of Neapolitan rule.

The Neapolitans are said to have captured some of the insurgent's Vessels, with 800 Volunteers, 82 Guns, and 50,000 Muskets.

The "Great Eastern" left the Southampton waters

THE WEEK.

THURSDAY, THE 5TH JULY.

THE "FRIEND OF INDIA" says, that the success of t
Income Tax scheme will entirely depend upon t
personal character of the Collectors and Assesso
He recommends that the Sub-Deputy Opium agen
and men of their class should alone be employed
the task. Any how fearful oppression will be pra
tised, and the class which will be most oppressed
that unaccustomed to the courts,—women, priest
Lakhirajdars, &ca.

THE CASE of libel brought by Assistant Comm
sioner Ramdyal against the proprietors of the *Ou*
Gazette appears to be taken in some quarters as a
attempt on the part of the authorities to "gag" th
press. We hope none of our contemporaries will pe
sist in this view of the matter. Had it been th
Supreme Court where the case was to be tried, a
acquittal would have not been an honor nor conden
nation a cause of shame. We are sure the defendan
will meet with fair play. The paper itself will im
mensely gain if the proprietors come off victorious.

LIQUOR AMMONIA has been tested and reported o
on the Bombay side as a sovereign remedy for snak
bites. Men have been treated with it under the mo
desperate circumstances. It is worth while to kee
the thannahs in supply with this inexpensive articl
The experiment won't cost much.

THE "ENGLISHMAN" hears from Mynpoorie, that th
rails have been laid down from Cawnpore to withi
fourteen miles of Etawah, and that the engines
are proceeding with the work at the rate of a mile
week. Fiftytwo miles a year, and even that is con
dered too good to be practicable.

THE SAME JOURNAL says, that the Bank of Beng
will now realize the interest of Government Securiti
entrusted to its charge at the same rate of commissio
that is charged by other banks and agents.

THE "HURKARU" says, that the Government of Be
gal has refused permission to Rajah Konduppessu
Singh of Seebsagur in Assam to return to his nativ
country. For the present the Rajah remains at Bu
dwan under surveillance.

FRIDAY, THE 6TH JULY.

A CORRESPONDENT of the *Hurkaru*, who calls him
self "a poor ex-student," complains of the resolutio
of the Government, that only those who have attaine
the degree of B. L., or that of Licentiate of Law i
the Calcutta University, shall be deemed to be elig
ble to practise at the bar of the Sudder and Mufuss
Courts. It is simply impossible to impose this res
triction, and to keep out of the most popular of pro
fessions, the mass of educated men.

A CORRESPONDENT of the *Englishman* says, that th
Nawab of Moorshedabad will proceed to England in
five or six months, and that he will be attended ther
by 195 members of his family.

THE "ENGLISHMAN," reviewing the local marke
comes to the conclusion that the consumption of coun
try produce in the country itself is increasing, which is
a sign of increasing prosperity. There is a great deal

Illustration 5.2 Bulletins of overland news, *Hindoo Patriot*, 11 July 1860

Source: © The British Library Board, Shelfmark: MFM.MC1108, 11/07/1860.

19 July 1900 has no less than eleven telegrams originating in this place, with Bombay and Bangalore also occupying a prominent position. A similar scenario was observed in the case of the *Bombay Gazette* where, apart from Simla, Poona and Allahabad also emerged as important places where news originated. The items of domestic telegraphic intelligence most frequently published in the pages of the newspapers examined here pertained to the affairs of the central government, and events taking place in towns with political, economic, and administrative relevance, such as Bombay, Calcutta, Bangalore, Poona, or Allahabad, as well as in regions of notorious military interest such as the North-West Frontier. Out of fifteen telegrams published by the *Bombay Gazette* on 7 July 1880, no less than nine reported on the military operations on the North-West Frontier. Smaller towns such as Dwarka and Mehsana (both in present-day Gujarat) only received attention if they became the theatre of important events.

Several principles guided the organization of news content in the nineteenth-century newspapers examined. The first level of distinction was that between 'Home' and 'India' news. London was an important centre of news by virtue of its status as the metropole of the empire and its central position in the system of telecommunications.[42] Within this broad geographical organization, there were further subdivisions, based either on geography or on topic. Interestingly, topical division predominated in European news and geographical division in Indian news. Thus, while the headlines in the 'Home News' section announced topics such as 'The Corn Laws' and 'Revival of Pugilism', in the 'Indian Intelligence' section items were frequently listed under geographical headings such as 'Madras', 'North-West Provinces', and so on.[43]

Second, as the century advanced, there was a visible move from geographic to topical organization with regard to both categories of news, overland and telegraphic. In other words, news headlines began to place more emphasis on events rather than the place of origin of intelligence. In the case of telegrams, the transition from geographical to topical organization was visible even earlier. For example, in 1860, both the *Bombay Gazette* and the *Englishman* organized telegraphic news according to their place of origin, but by the 1870s topical organization was already predominant. Headlines in the 'Latest Telegrams' section no longer announced 'News from China', but caught the attention of readers with information on such topics as 'The Nawab Nazim', 'The War in South Africa', or the 'Mohol Station Dacoity'.[44]

Joshua Meyrowitz has argued in a different context that electronic media such as the telegraph, television, radio, and computers have eroded informational distances between places and changed the 'situational geography of social behaviour', promoting the erosion of the sense of place.[45] While it is true that the electric telegraph facilitated the circulation of news between various parts of the world, enabling readers to engage with and position themselves vis-à-vis events in other geographical locales which might have been inaccessible to them in pre-telegraph days, it is important, in my opinion, not to lose sight of how communication mediated by such technologies also inscribed certain places with visibility and significance at the expense of others. In colonial India, for example, the regular publication of telegraphic news, most of which originated in London, was a constant reminder not only of Reuter's privileged position as the 'news agency of the British Empire', but also of Britain's imperial supremacy and London's central place as the centre of imperial communications. In addition, news about Britain, especially parliamentary debates or cabinet changes, were almost invariably placed at the top of the telegrams list, sometimes even at the expense of war news from Europe, in another reminder of how politics structured geography and news reporting. More importantly, Anglo-Indian newspapers catered predominantly to an Anglo-Indian audience, paying little attention to the news needs of their Indian readers, as demonstrated not only by the topics reported, but also by typographic techniques which aimed to emphasize the importance of news about Britain and the British Empire more generally. In this respect, it can be argued that the newspaper was not simply a vehicle for the communication of news, but that news itself became an imperial performance.

Predictably, the use of the telegraph diminished the temporal gap between the occurrence of an event and its publication in the newspaper press. In 1840, it took three weeks for a correspondent's report of a murder in Trichinopoly to be published in the *Bombay Gazette*. The news 'travelled' the 800 miles between Trichinopoly and Bombay via Madras, where it was published in the *United Service Gazette* and later clipped by the editor of the *Bombay Gazette*. By the end of the century, the time lag between the moment of dispatch of telegraphic news and its publication in the *Bombay Gazette* and the *Englishman*, in the case of both domestic and foreign news, had been reduced to one day.

The examination of news received from correspondents by post shows that all the elements we associate with contemporary news stories—the 'who', the 'when', the 'where', the 'what', the 'why', and the 'how'—can be identified during this period as well. The same elements were also present in the case of telegraphic news, with certain variations which appeared to depend on the perceived degree of importance of the subject matter. Generally speaking, telegraphic news about wars and other disturbances, as well as decisions of the British Parliament which were relevant to Indian affairs, tended to be longer and usually addressed the standard questions of the news story. In the case of less important events, telegrams were shorter and contained only basic information about the persons involved, the location, and the time of the event.

In their letters, correspondents reported events chronologically, in a manner similar to a personal narrative. The issue of chronology was irrelevant for short, concise telegrams, but it is worth mentioning that, as telegraphic news became longer towards the end of the nineteenth century, there was a similar tendency towards reporting events chronologically. The correspondents' news was datelined according to the date of publication of the newspaper from which it was clipped or the date of the correspondent's letter. Temporal adverbials like 'yesterday', which lend a sense of immediacy to news reporting and have been usually associated with telegraphic news, were also present. Their use seemed to depend less on the technology employed for the transmission of news and more on the distance between the source of news and the newspaper. In the *Bombay Gazette*, for example, during the 1840s–1860s such temporal markers could be found in the 'Local News' section, where intelligence from Bombay was published. This means that reading such news required the public to make a distinction between the correspondent's 'yesterday' and their own 'yesterday'. Telegraphic news occasionally made use of the temporal adverb 'today', but the immediacy they implied was misleading, since the telegraph's 'today' coincided in fact with the reader's 'yesterday'. In some cases, it was even older.

Put differently, the act of reading necessitated an effort on the part of the reader to establish the chronology of events, especially when telegrams and overland news were published side by side in the same issue of the newspaper. To facilitate reading, some newspapers like the *Phoenix* published a 'Latest News' section listing the dates of the most recent intelligence received in town from a number of locations such as London, Adelaide, Cape, Ceylon, China, California, Mauritius, Moulmein, Penang, and so on.[46]

As Isabel Hofmeyr cogently points out in her discussion of reading practices in relation to Gandhi's periodical publications, imperial modernity relied on the 'condensation of a condensation'; in other words, on summaries, telegrams, clippings, and extracts.[47] Making sense of this information and establishing its accuracy was not a straightforward task, as the journalists themselves testified. Writing an editorial, for example, required a 'very careful study' of other newspapers, which, in turn, led to comparisons, predictions, and speculations; in other cases, it required the reconciliation of mail news and telegrams and the illustration of one type of intelligence by the other.[48] The following passage from the *Delhi Gazette*, discussing the Crimean War, illustrates well these practices of reading, which represented an integral part of a journalist's work:

> The overland telegraphic message is now fairly due. We shall be agreeably disappointed if it brings any decisive tidings. The Siege of Sebastopol had fairly set in for the winter, and a very careful study of the newspapers does not incline us to revise the opinion which we have already expressed, that the place will not be taken until after a long Campaign in the open country. Such a Campaign may be now taking place, during these winter months. But it is more likely that both the Russians and the allies will be unwilling to leave such quarters as they have been able to provide for themselves.
>
> We hazard this opinion with our eyes open to the possibility that all our predictions may be falsified to-morrow. But the chances against speedy success are so overwhelming that we make the venture.

Wars were one type of event likely to generate significant commentary and speculation, on account of their increased news value. Reporting about wars was also the one field of journalism with which the electric telegraph has most often been associated. The telegraph helped to transform media reports of battles: in addition to the usual letter, war correspondents could now 'flash' out more or less regular updates from the field of operations. The Crimean War to which I have alluded above was the first instance of the reporting of a war by the telegraph. In what follows, I will focus on another example, the Austro-Prussian War of 1866, in an attempt to understand how the telegraph mediated the coverage of this event in nineteenth-century India.

(Mis-)Reporting the Austro-Prussian War (1866)

Although at first glance the Austro-Prussian War of 1866 might appear as an event of little relevance to India, especially since Britain was not directly involved in the conflict, the coverage of the war offers important insights into the news reporting practices of English-language newspapers and the ways in which the telegraph was used in this process. A brief outline of the event provides some of the necessary context for the ensuing discussion of reporting practices. As is widely known, the conflict pitted Prussia and Italy against Austria and its allies in the German Confederation—namely Saxony, Bavaria, Hanover, Württemberg, Hesse-Kassel, and Hesse-Darmstadt—eventually leading to Prussia's victory and ensuring its hegemonic position among the German-speaking states.[49] The pretext for war was provided by Prussia's annexation, in the early months of 1866, of the Duchies of Holstein and Schleswig, a former Danish possession which had been jointly administered by Prussia and Austria since 1864.[50] For the purpose of our discussion, a timeline of the unfolding of the war is useful. The hostilities began on 15 June 1866, with Prussia's invasion of Saxony, Hanover, and Hesse-Kassel, and were followed by a series of battles at Nachod (27 June), Trautenau (27 June), and Skalitz (28 June). The decisive encounter, in which some 240,000 Austrian soldiers fought against a combined Prussian force of approximately 250,000 men, took place on 3 July at a village called Sadowa, near Königgrätz, and resulted in a Prussian victory.[51] The war was officially concluded on 23 August 1866 with the Treaty of Prague, which led to the establishment of a new Northern German Confederation under the influence of Prussia, and saw Austria losing Venice to Italy as a result of the war.

In colonial India, the event received significant attention, as coverage in the *Times of India*, the *Madras Times*, the *Englishman*, and the *Lahore Chronicle* suggests. The war occurred about a year after the establishment of direct telegraphic communication with Britain via Teheran and Karachi, and coincided with Reuter's opening of its first office at Bombay. It was during this time that Reuters established itself as the sole supplier of foreign news to the Anglo-Indian press, pushing aside, as we have seen in the previous chapter, the *Times of*

India's Telegraphic Agency. It was also during this period that the first Reuter credits appeared in the newspapers examined here. Thus, the Austro-Prussian War was an event with significance not only in the early history of foreign news reporting by the telegraph, but also in Reuter's Indian history.

For Reuters and the other newspaper correspondents, war was an ideal topic to report on both because of its socio-economic and political significance and because of the element of sensationalism it entailed. Conflicts among European powers had a direct bearing on Britain's own security and position in the international geopolitical order. They represented, therefore, a subject of great interest to the British public both at 'Home' and in the colonies.[52] For the readers of Anglo-Indian newspapers, especially the merchants operating in the subcontinent, the value of war news was inextricably connected to their commercial significance, since wars in Europe and other parts of the world could have dramatic consequences for their trading activities.[53] As Graham Storey has also pointed out, the Bombay cotton market was in a 'state of great agitation' during this period as the cotton boom caused by the American Civil War was slowly coming to an end: the drop in cotton prices eventually drove many merchants to bankruptcy.[54] The disruption was also reflected in the content of telegrams as well as the declining number of private telegrams sent to and from India during this period: the statistics of the Indian Telegraph Department show that there was a steady decrease in Indo-European messages from May to August 1866, a situation which led officials to conclude that there was economic stagnation as a result of the American Civil War, further compounded by the conflict in Europe.[55]

As a medium of communication, the telegraph was particularly well suited for the transmission of war news, enabling the military and political authorities and, to a more limited extent, the general public to access timely intelligence on a relatively regular basis. In situations of crisis, access to intelligence was crucial: indeed, it could even make the difference between victory and defeat. The use of the telegraph shaped the conduct of war not only by allowing combatants to make strategic decisions based on the information available, but also by enabling them to manipulate news for the purpose of propaganda. One well-known example comes from the Crimean War, famously covered for *The Times* by the pioneer war correspondent William Howard Russell, when both 'the military and the state also made use of it [the telegraph] to generate news'.[56]

Indeed, rumours were an important part of nineteenth-century news reporting.[57] They infiltrated news transmitted by post as well as by telegraph, despite occasional intimations from contemporary journalists that the telegraph was a technology which delivered 'facts'.[58] 'It is rumoured', 'It is darkly rumoured', and 'We hear, but can scarcely credit, a rumour that the Government …' were not uncommon phrases in the news columns of the newspapers examined.[59] A telegram published in the *Times of India* during the Austro-Prussian War announced, for example, the 'rumoured … engagements between the Austrians and the Prussians in which the Austrians were successful'.[60] When information was not 'stated', it was either 'heard', 'understood', or 'suggested'. Its sources were many and their credibility depended not only on the physical distance from the actual place of the event, but also on the socio-political and economic standing of the suppliers of news. Rumours circulated alongside 'acknowledged facts', statements made 'on good authority' and even 'on Native authority', but ultimately it was the responsibility of the readers to make sense of the information offered through the mediating channels of correspondents, Reuters, the Indian government, foreign governments, or the Chambers of Commerce of Calcutta and Bombay.[61]

Rumours about a possible war in Europe had been circulating for some time in the European and Indian press before the actual outbreak of hostilities in June 1866. Since March 1866, when the London correspondent of the *Times of India* first reported on Bismarck's moves towards 'the destruction of the constitutional liberties of his country', the newspaper had been anticipating the conflict by informing its readers about 'the threatened war in Germany', 'the quarrel between Austria and Prussia', and 'the crisis in Germany'.[62] There was much debate and discussion of European affairs in editorials and letters from continental correspondents, while telegrams flashed out regular updates about the changing fortunes of the parties involved. The declaration of war itself became the subject of speculation, with the *Englishman* reporting in a lapidary telegram dated London, 14 June 1866, that '[There are] adverse rumours that Austria has declared war against Prussia.'[63] Notwithstanding the occasional confusion, the fact that such reports could reach the reading public on a regular basis and thus prepare them for the possibility of a war was in itself proof of the improved system of communication between Britain and India. Unlike the Australian press which, half a decade later, still found itself startled by the outbreak of the Franco-Prussian War (1870–1) that came, as Peter Putnis has shown, with 'no note of warning', the editors of the newspapers examined here were well aware of the impending war and expressed no surprise when news about its outbreak finally reached them at the end of June 1866.[64]

Based on the means of communication which was used to transmit information to India, news about the Austro-Prussian War can be divided into two categories: postal news sent via the overland mail that consisted of regular digests of 'Home News', letters from correspondents, and articles clipped from various European newspapers; and telegraphic news received via the telegraph route recently opened between Britain and India. As far as the former category of news was concerned, the principles of publication were relatively similar for all the newspapers examined. Based on the rules of the Indian Telegraph Department outlined in Chapter 4, a telegraphic summary of the mail news was delivered free of charge to the major newspapers published at the principal telegraphic stations, a condition fulfilled by all four papers. The headlines of intelligence were usually published in advance of the 'General Summary' sent by post which elaborated on each item of news, providing a more detailed account of the events. Since the same overland mail that brought the 'Home News' also brought letters from European correspondents and articles clipped from the main continental and British papers, all these sources were used complementarily to report the Austro-Prussian War.

Telegraphic news was published in a special section of the newspaper usually located on the second or third page in the case of the *Times of India*, the *Englishman*, and the *Madras Times*, and on the fourth in the case of the *Lahore Chronicle*. The former three journals were all daily publications at the time of the war, while the *Chronicle* was published biweekly. The telegrams section was identified either by the type of news it contained—'Telegrams' in the case of the *Chronicle* and the *Englishman* and 'Latest Intelligence' in the case of the *Madras Times*—or by the means of communication used to transmit it, that is, 'By Indo-European Telegraph' in the case of the *Times of India*. With regard to layout, it is worth highlighting the elaborate use of headlines and even double headlines in the *Times of India*, whose reporting vied for the attention of the readers. Such devices were only rarely used in the other newspapers examined.

The war telegrams published in the *Times of India* and the *Englishman* were divided into two categories, namely 'subscription telegrams' and 'Reuter's telegrams'. As the previous chapter has shown, 'subscription telegrams' originated with the *Times of India* Telegraphic Agency, a short-lived venture established by Robert Knight and his associate Manockji Tuback for the purpose of delivering European intelligence to the major newspapers in the Indian subcontinent. Indeed, the reporting of the Austro-Prussian War mirrored the fate of the agency, as it succumbed to Reuter's expansionist drive in Asia. The first Reuter credit appeared in the *Times of India* on 12 June 1866, with the *Englishman*, the *Madras Times*, and the *Lahore Chronicle* soon following suit. Within a month of the publication of the first 'Reuter's telegrams', 'subscription telegrams' disappeared completely from the pages of the *Times of India* and the *Englishman*. The latter continued to publish occasional telegrams from Bombay datelined 'London', but these were likely sent by individual correspondents rather than as part of an organized system of news distribution. 'Subscription telegrams' could not be identified in the *Madras Times* and the *Lahore Chronicle*. A look at the war telegrams published by these two newspapers prior to the appearance of the first Reuter telegrams in their pages shows that some telegraphic news was not credited, while other news was credited to newspapers such as the *Times of India* (*Madras Times* of 13 July 1866), the *Pioneer*, and the *Delhi Gazette* (*Lahore Chronicle*, 4 August 1866 and 15 August 1866).

The different approaches to news reporting of the *Times of India* and Reuters were reflected not only in the content of telegrams, but also in the organization of intelligence. As a rule, all telegrams were published in batches, in the chronological order of their dispatch; however, the order in which individual telegrams within a batch were arranged was different in the case of 'subscription' and Reuter telegrams. The former were invariably shorter and resembled more a paragraph of unconnected sentences, rather than a coherent account of events. Furthermore, commercial information such as market quotations was prioritized and almost invariably transmitted before news about the war and other political events. Compare, for example, the following telegrams, published in the

Englishman and the *Times of India* (original formatting in terms of capitalization, punctuation, italics, and so on, has been retained for reference):

> (1) *Englishman*, 27 June 1866
> FROM LONDON.
> *To Englishman Office, Calcutta.*
> [Subscription Telegram.]
> *London, 16th June.*—Cotton not quotably lower. War in Germany commenced. Prussians entered Saxony and Hanover. Saxony and Hanover Treasury and valuables sent to Bohemia.
>
> REUTER'S MESSAGES.
> *To Englishman's Office, Calcutta.*
> *London, 19th June.*—Government has been defeated on an amendment to Clauses of the Reform Bill by majority of 315 to 304.
> Prussia and Italy have declared war against Austria. Prussians occupied Hanover, Dresden Hesse Cassel. Hostilities have commenced.
>
> (2) *Times of India*, 26 June 1866
> BY INDO-EUROPEAN TELEGRAPH.
> [SUBSCRIPTION TELEGRAMS.]
>
> LONDON, June 16, 5.15 P.M.
>
> Cotton not quotably lower.
> War has commenced in Germany, and the Prussians have entered Saxony and Hanover. All movable articles of value have been sent from Saxony into Bohemia.
>
> [REUTER'S TELEGRAMS.]
> DECLARATION OF WAR BY PRUSSIA AND ITALY AGAINST AUSTRIA
>
> LONDON, JUNE 19.
>
> The Governments of Prussia and Italy have declared war against Austria.
> Hanover has also announced her intention of going to war.
> The Prussian troops occupy Hanover, Dresden and Hesse-Cassel.
> Hostilities have commenced.
> The Government have been defeated on the amendment to Clause S of the Reform Bill by 315 to 304 votes.

> The Liverpool Cotton market to-day closed depressed.
> Fair Dhollera 8 ¼ d.
> At Manchester to-day the market was quiet and prices drooping.

Comparing the above telegrams, one can begin to contemplate what prompted J. O'B. Saunders to complain that 'subscription telegrams' were crammed with commercial information, and to dismiss the telegrams supplied by the *Times of India* as 'useless'. While Knight and Tuback might have regarded the members of the mercantile community as the main target audience for their telegraphic intelligence, Reuter's approach was to appeal to a wider audience by emphasizing that part of its news which was likely to interest a broader reading public, not only the 'merchants and speculators of Bombay', as Saunders alleged. At the very least, it is obvious from the telegrams reproduced here that the order in which news was transmitted in the case of 'subscription telegrams' was the reverse of that employed by Reuters: while the former usually began with commercial information and market quotations, the latter focused on the transmission of political and military intelligence. Reuter's news did not only prioritize 'sensational' events such as wars over commercial information, but it was also longer and more regular than that transmitted by Knight and his agents. At a more general level, this suggests a gradual expansion in the customer base of news agencies and 'news merchants', to use S. Sapru's inspired formulation, from a target audience which revolved around commercial and mercantile groups to one that also included newspapers. In this respect, the episode presented here illustrates well the differences between these two visions of news, that is, one which was predominantly commercial and another which was more journalistic in outlook.

As I have shown elsewhere, the area of circulation of 'subscription telegrams' was not limited to the Indian subcontinent, but also extended to newspapers published in other parts of Asia, for example Japan.[65] Tracing the circulation of such items of intelligence affords fascinating insights into the interconnected development of journalism in various parts of the world, as well as the ways in which the expansion of networks of communication in the nineteenth century enabled newspapers to draw on a variety of sources of information for the supply of their news. As the issue of 26 January 1866 of the *Japan Times* suggests, 'subscription telegrams' originally published in Indian newspapers travelled to Yokohama by steamer via Hong Kong, eventually ending up in the pages of this well-known English-language newspaper from Japan.[66] At the same time, however, the publication of telegrams from India and about the British Empire more generally in the pages of Japan-based newspapers, both English-language and Japanese, also demonstrates the extent to which interest in news was shaped by broader political and socio-economic developments. Although a newspaper like the *Japan Gazette* continued to publish telegrams from India in the 1880s, by the 1890s there was a visible shift of interest towards the publication of intelligence from China and Korea, a clear reflection of Japan's changing geopolitical ambitions. Some topics like famines and epidemics continued to attract the attention of journalists, with the same newspaper reporting on 11 July 1900, in an article clipped from the *China Gazette*, that 'local Chinese officials have distinguished themselves by raising a subscription of magnificent dimensions for the Indian Famine Fund'.[67]

To return to the reporting of the Austro-Prussian War, the quantitative and qualitative examination of the war news published in the four newspapers allows us to rank them according to the timeliness of their intelligence. Predictably, the *Times of India* was 'the first with the news', followed closely by the *Madras Times*, the *Englishman*, and the *Lahore Chronicle*. As a newspaper published in Bombay, the *Times of India* received the fullest and most timely coverage: not only was Bombay the point of arrival of overland news, but also the headquarters of Reuter's operations in the subcontinent. The *Madras Times* followed closely, usually publishing the same telegrams on the same day or a day later, although its news was not as frequent as that published in the *Times of India* and it was also visibly shorter. The *Englishman* was rarely able to keep up with the *Times of India* and usually lagged behind one or two days, its news also visibly shorter, while the *Lahore Chronicle* published telegrams which were, on average, five days behind those of the Bombay newspaper, due to the biweekly nature of its publication.

Furthermore, the publication of war telegrams was irregular: if some items appeared on consecutive days, at other times gaps of as many as four to six days were recorded. The temporal gap between the event and its reporting in the newspaper usually amounted to a week in the *Times of India* and increased accordingly in the case of the *Englishman* and the *Lahore Chronicle*. The latter, in particular, published telegrams which were, on average, eighteen to nineteen days old: on such occasions, telegrams sent over three or more days were usually published simultaneously.[68] For example, in the issue of 29 August 1866, the *Chronicle* published, in this order, telegrams dated London, 22 August, 7 August, 10 August, 11 August, 13 August, 14 August, 15 August, and 16 August, some of which were clipped from the *Pioneer*. The practice of clipping telegraphic news from other newspapers was also occasionally encountered in the *Madras Times* (13 July 1866, from the *Times of India*), but not in the *Englishman* and the *Times of India*.

These findings illustrate well the structure of the telegraph network during this period, with messages taking at least five days to travel from Karachi to London via the Turkish or the Persian routes, and even longer via the Russian route.[69] They also reflect the complex nature of telegraphic communication between India's main cities. In terms of physical distance, Bombay was indeed closer to Madras, but the two towns were also linked by a direct telegraph line which enabled the relatively swift transmission of intelligence. On the other hand, messages between Bombay and Calcutta had to pass via Agra, Allahabad, and even Madras, and took an average of nine hours to reach their destination.[70] By comparison, steamers also enabled only an irregular coverage of the war, but the temporal gaps were visibly longer in the case of overland news than in the case of telegrams. Although mail news was published fortnightly upon the arrival of the P&O steamer, it usually reported events which were a month old by the time they reached India. The complementary use of telegraphs and steamers thus ensured a fairly regular and comprehensive coverage of the event by visibly shortening the temporal gaps between events in Europe and their publication in the newspaper press in India.

The wording of telegrams changed in the process of transmission. Generally speaking, the war telegrams published by the *Times of India* were longer than those published by the *Madras Times* and the *Englishman*. Compare, for example, the following Reuter telegram announcing the progress of the Italian troops, which had been dispatched from London on the morning of 26 June 1866:

> *Times of India*, 2 July 1866:
> London, June 26, morning. After the battle at Verona on Sunday last, in which the Italians were defeated, they recrossed the river Mincio and have since crossed the To (Po?).

> *Madras Times*, 2 July 1866:
> London, 26th A.M. The Italians have recrossed the Mincio after a battle at Verona.
> London, 26th P.M. The Italians have recrossed the Po.
>
> *Englishman*, 3 July 1866:
> London, 26th June, morning. Italians recrossed the Mincio after the Battle at Verona. In the afternoon Italians recrossed the Po.

The 'compression' of telegraphic news by almost 30 per cent by the time it reached Calcutta and Madras is somewhat puzzling. For its part, Reuters claimed to pursue a policy of equal treatment towards all subscribing newspapers by supplying them with 'like copies' of news items and requested newspapers to publish its telegrams verbatim.[71] In the absence of anecdotal evidence, we can assume that the actual wording of messages changed during the process of transmission, as telegrams were encoded and decoded. We can also suspect a certain degree of editing on the part of the newspaper staff, as well as the fact that telegrams might have been intentionally shortened for domestic transmission for reasons of economy.

The telegrams reproduced above illustrate another problem of telegraphic transmission, one that was particularly vexing during the early years of telegraphy, as the annual reports of the Indian Telegraph Department also testify. This regarded the issue of decoding correctly certain words such as numerals and proper names. The latter, in particular, turned out to be a real challenge for telegraph operators during the Austro-Prussian War: the new technology offered speedy access to news, but it also challenged the geographical imaginary of readers and tested the telegraph operators' knowledge of geography. In some respects, decoding a telegram was like solving a puzzle. In the case of Morse instruments, a misplaced dot or dash could alter the meaning of a message. As one commentator observed, telegraph operators were required to 'read [their] message correctly as from the signals, but also with intelligence, so as to avoid sense being converted into nonsense'.[72]

The numerous question marks which appear in telegrams during this period betray the weakness of the signals received in India and the operators' lack of geographical knowledge. In the above telegrams, the name of the river Po was garbled as 'To' in the *Times of India*, but it was corrected by the time the news reached the *Madras*

Times and the *Englishman*. Other examples of misreporting included 'Tianernau' (*Englishman*) or 'Tranernau' (*Madras Times*) instead of Trautenau, and 'Weurtzburg' instead of Wuerzburg; the Italian village Rovigo completely eluded correct decoding and was instead misspelled as 'Rovindo', 'Rovoredo', and 'Ruindo'.[73] In another example, Prince Amadeus of Saxony was baptized as 'Amodeus' and mistaken for General Cerale by the *Times of India*.[74]

It wasn't only proper nouns that caused confusion. On 22 August 1866, readers of the *Lahore Chronicle* were left wondering whether the King of Prussia had 'made no statement concerning future measures with, or the appointing (*apportioning*?) of Germany' (emphasis in original). Arguably the most amusing incident was the publication of a telegram which announced the unlikely news that 'Austria has ceded Venetia to Force (?)' (*Times of India*), which was eventually corrected to 'Austria has ceded Venetia to France' by the time it reached Calcutta, Madras, and Lahore. Incidents like these drove editors to exasperation:

> No one ever expected to keep the wires up in the cyclone, and all reasonable men will suffer the inconveniences which result from similar accidents in silence; but it passes endurance when, without any cause whatever, letters from Bombay come quicker than telegrams, or when a telegraph office clerk at Allahabad states that he never heard of such a place as Bankipore.[75]

The telegraph intensified the flow of news towards the newspapers examined, enabling them to receive more frequent reports and to become part of an increasing community of readers who shared the same or highly similar information. But it did not invariably make communication easier for the reading public. On the contrary, not only the occasional blunders, but also the irregular times of delivery forced readers to go back and forth in time in order to understand how the war was unfolding. Events were not delivered in an orderly chronological sequence; since the means of communication were diverse, it took some effort to make sense of the unstructured information offered. For example, after having been provided with various telegrams, correspondence reports, and articles from the European press which occasionally made contradictory predictions about the possibility of a war, readers of the *Times of India* were finally informed about the outbreak of the war through a Reuter telegram on 26 June 1866, more than ten days after the actual commencement of hostilities.[76] Then, on 10 July, the newspaper again informed its readers about the outbreak of the war by publishing news from two overland mails (of 11 June and 18 June), but by this time Reuter telegrams were already announcing in big capitalized headlines the 'Cession of Venetia by Austria' and the 'Acceptance of Mediation' for the conclusion of peace.[77]

Interruptions frequently interfered with telegraphic communication, a situation which was reflected in news reporting itself. As Henry Collins reminisced in his memoirs of work in Bombay and a number of other Asian cities, such incidents were particularly common in the 1850s and 1860s, during the early days of telegraphic communication. In fact, one such incident occurred at the height of the Austro-Prussian War:

> … the Indian markets were greatly perturbed by the course of events in Europe … a sudden and complete interruption of the overland line via Persia and Russia took place, lasting for no less than seventeen days. Consequently, there was an entire absence of news from the outer world, and this at a moment of political and financial crisis.[78]

Incidents like this plunged communication into pre-telegraphic modes of transmission and reminded observers of how fragile their newly found technological emancipation could turn out to be. *Allen's Indian News*, a monthly précis of intelligence from all parts of India published in Poona, captured the mood cogently when it reported on 19 July 1854 that 'Lord Elphinstone, at Poona, finds the Electric Telegraph for all India out of order. Obliged to trust to horse expresses, like his predecessor.' Any assessment of the way in which telegraphy was used in the field of journalism during the nineteenth century must take into account such instances of communication failure. Collins himself, while not having to resort to horses, was able to overcome the situation by making use of the little-known Turkish line via Fao: in this way, and jealously guarding his secret from possible competitors, he was able to provide his subscribers in India with the latest information from the seat of war, as well as market quotations from Liverpool.[79]

As suggested above, another vexing problem of telegraphic communication was that the telegraph could be used both to inform and to misinform. For journalists and readers in India, there seemed to be little option to check the accuracy of a particular piece of news but to wait patiently for the next telegram or overland mail which would confirm or deny the already available information. Despite the fact that European correspondents were dispatched to the seat of war, it was difficult to receive reliable accounts of battles, especially when the combatants themselves used the telegraph to disseminate 'false' news about the fate of the war. In his report of the battle of Königgrätz, the *Times of India*'s correspondent recounted how London penny journals reported the battle both as 'Great Defeat of the Prussians' and 'Great Defeat of the Austrians', and how even Reuter's agents were misled by 'official' declarations about the outcome of the war. The correspondent's report illustrates well the ways in which journalists and readers tried to make sense of the conflicting news about the battle which reached them:

> What comes from Berlin as a victory comes from Vienna as a defeat—and the reverse. Holding the balance with all fairness, we were therefore, for some time destined to believe that neither party had gained much advantage over the other. The 'official' accounts contradict each other even more than the reports in the German newspapers. Mr. Reuter's telegrams gave us yesterday the following as 'official' from Vienna—'The Prussians were yesterday (Thursday, the 28th) completely defeated by the Austrian forces under General Von Gablenz....' In the same column, we have an 'official' from Berlin which tells us that 'the Austrian corps under General Von Gablenz was completely broken up....' Our own journals, one and all, comment upon the extreme difficulty of getting at the truth. But the difficulty somewhat disappears when people look more closely into the matter with an especial reference to dates. It seemed that up to the close of the 28th of June, the fighting was in favour of the Austrians, but that on the 29th and 30th the tide of victory was turned in favour of the Prussians. But even this now appears to be doubtful.[80]

For his part, the editor of the *Lahore Chronicle* was under no illusions that it was possible to establish the truth, when this seemed to elude even the higher circles in London:

> When even English journals are so mystified by the false telegrams daily issued from Berlin and Vienna, that no certainty can be arrived at as to which side has suffered, and which been victorious: it will be clear that to attempt to offer any comments *here* in India must simply be absurd. The latest telegrams specially are in utter confusion. The same victory

> is claimed for both parties, and the same defeat cast on both. At one time, it is stated that Prussia grants the truce to Austria; at another, that Austria accepts Prussia's proposal for a truce. Finally, we have the words that 'Austria is excluded from the Confederation.' The strength of Austria has not been broken either in the South or in the North, and as it was for the sole purpose of maintaining the Confederation that Austria took up arms, we do not see clearly how she can be excluded.[81]

Under these circumstances, the best course of action was to treat telegraphic news with the requisite caution. Or, as the London correspondent of the *Times of India* put it, '... the continental telegraph flashes its intelligence with lightning speed, [but] telegrams are not always to be relied on.'[82] The 'facts' transmitted by the electric telegraph had to be confirmed and pondered against news from other sources, most commonly against the detailed reporting of mail news, in order to become 'acknowledged facts'. As the editor of *Lahore Chronicle* wrote on 18 August 1866, in a follow-up to his earlier lamentations about the untrustworthy nature of telegraphic news,

> The latest news from Home enables us to see our clear [*sic*] through the late conflicting reports of the War. The Prussians stand undeniably the victors, and the Austrians are thoroughly beaten. The 'needle-gun' has done all the mischief. The finest army in Europe evidently cannot stand before this deadly weapon. 'It mowed down the Austrians as a swift scythe mows down the grass.'[83]

Poetic language and detail were out of place in telegraphic correspondence, a situation which often led commentators to lament the declining quality of journalism and to question whether telegrams were 'real' news. It was left to correspondents to fill in the sketchy accounts of telegraphic communication with more complete and, it was believed, more accurate information about the remarkable deeds that had unfolded before their eyes. This was quite literally the case with William Russell, the famous correspondent who represented *The Times* at the Austrian headquarters. Unable to leave the headquarters of the Austrian army because he lacked the required pass, Russell observed the battle of Sadowa from a 'lofty tower commanding the Prague gateway, whence Josephstadt on the north and the whole of the position of the Army were displayed as if on a raised map.'[84] His report of the encounter was seasoned with political comment, but it was also dense in information and included detailed accounts of the movement of troops, the names of military combatants, the exact time and place of each military encounter. Moreover, his account testifies to the strong connections between literature and journalism during this period:

> The sun that rose this morning on a gallant army full of hope and confidence in itself and its chief has just set amid masses of scarlet clouds behind the same army, baffled and dissemfitted, flying before an enemy they had despised, and leaving behind them flames of burning villages that will redden the sky long after the last hue of twilight has faded.[85]

Russell's report was a far cry from the Reuter telegram, published in the *Times of India* of 16 July 1866, which announced laconically that '[a]nother great battle [was] fought yesterday near the Fortress of Königgrätz in Bohemia, between the combined armies of Prussia and the Austrian troops, resulting in a complete victory for the former, who captured twenty guns after a battle of eight hours' duration. Latest advices announce that the Austrian army was retreating, and that the Prussians were in pursuit. The King of Prussia has joined the army.'[86] For comparison, the same telegram appeared in the following form in the other newspapers examined:

> *Madras Times*, 16 July 1866
> The combined Prussian Armies gained another complete victory near Konnigratz yesterday after eight hours fighting, capturing 20 guns. Austrians retreating. Prussians pursuing.
> The King of Prussia is with the Army.
>
> *Englishman*, 17 July 1866
> The combined Prussian armies have gained another complete victory near Konnigratz yesterday, after eight hours' fighting, capturing 20 guns. The Austrians were retreating; Prussians pursuing.
> The King of Prussia was with the Army.
>
> *Lahore Chronicle*, 21 July 1866
> The combined Prussian armies gained another complete victory near Konnigratz yesterday, after eight hours fighting, capturing twenty guns. The Austrians were retreating, the Prussians pursuing.

These telegrams demonstrate that the four newspapers published, with the slight alterations of language discussed previously, similar accounts of the event. The same was true, to a certain extent, of mail news. For example, Russell's earlier mentioned account of the battle of Sadowa was also published by the *Madras Times* on 15 August 1866. This suggests that one of the most important aspects of the use of telegraphy in the nineteenth century was that it facilitated the syndication of news, a fact which resulted in newspapers frequently sharing similar, and often identical, information about specific events. This was the case not only with newspapers in India, but also in other parts of the world. Whether this led to a community of thinking and opinion, as technology enthusiasts, both past and present, would have us believe, is a matter of debate. At the very least, however, we can argue that these technologies mediated the exposure of an increasingly global public to highly similar information content. What the telegraph offered was unprecedentedly timely, but not necessarily accurate news. Like any other technology, it was not immune to technical failures and human manipulation and tampering.

'The Poona Tragedy': Reporting Domestic News in the Late Nineteenth Century

The assassination at Poona on 22 June 1897 of two European officers associated with the plague relief measures was widely reported in the newspapers of India and Britain, but also around the world in the United States, Singapore, Australia, and New Zealand.[87] The incident took place at a time when Queen Victoria's Jubilee celebrations were in full swing. The readers of the *Madras Times*, the *Bombay Gazette*, and the *Englishman* were treated to detailed accounts of the events, from the moment the attack was first reported in the issues of 24 June 1897 to the death of Special Plague Commissioner W. C. Rand in hospital on 3 July 1897, and the ensuing arrest of Bal Gangadhar Tilak for sedition. In Britain, the event brought back memories of 1857, and while there was unanimous condemnation of the crime, opinions were divided regarding the role of the government in fuelling the crisis, most conspicuously through what was perceived by some observers as inadequate plague relief measures.[88]

The outbreak of the plague in Bombay was first acknowledged by the colonial administration in September 1896; during the following months, the municipal authorities were invested with special powers which allowed them to enforce a wide range of sanitary measures such as house-to-house visitations, forced hospitalizations, destruction of insanitary housing, and cleansing of infected houses.[89] As Prashant Kidambi has argued, the plague policies of the colonial administration had, from the very beginning, a 'class-specific' character: plague was seen as a 'disease of locality' whose outbreak was traced to the poor quarters of the town and explained as a direct result of the insanitary conditions in which the inhabitants of the 'slums' lived.[90]

As the government's weekly reports on the vernacular press suggest, the outbreak of the plague and the official attempts to contain it attracted a considerable amount of attention from Indian journalists, especially since the crisis overlapped with another, of even bigger proportions: the Indian famine of 1896–7. The plague was thus only the latest in a series of misfortunes whose combined action wreaked havoc among the Indian population. A correspondent for the *Aina-i-Alam*, a bimonthly publication from Jhansi, reported that contemporary India was 'haunted by various kinds of devils', in the form of the famine, the 'bubonic fever', and discord, whose direct outcome had been the rise of British rule in the subcontinent.[91] Pundit Banwari Lal Misra's *Colonel*, a weekly from Moradabad, published cartoons in which the plague and the famine were depicted as Kali or as demons who shared the same body and threatened to devour the Indian people; similar representations of the plague appeared in the *Oudh Punch*.[92] The growing influence of these nefarious forces was not always traced exclusively to British presence in India, but was also described as the inevitable outcome of moral failure on the part of Indian society. For example, the *Prayag Samachar* of Allahabad ascribed the recent famine to 'the increase of sin and crime and the wickedness of all classes of people'.[93]

Reactions to the official measures were equally diverse. As R. Chandavarkar has pointed out in his authoritative account of the plague in Bombay, the Indian population's responses to the epidemic were shaped less by cultural conceptions of medicine and medical care; rather, they 'arose from the political conjuncture in which the plague was constructed'.[94] While some newspapers admitted that intervention was necessary and took the government to task for failing to prevent the spread of the plague, others focused on the intrusive nature of official measures and the discontent they had generated among the local population. The *Azad*, a weekly from Lucknow, drew attention to the nexus between disease transmission and lines of communication, urging the local governments and municipal boards to stop 'all communication with the infected towns', including the delivery of letters and newspapers.[95]

By contrast, other press reports spoke vividly about local opposition to forced removals from homes and the feelings of alienation which overcame many plague patients when separated from their relatives. Measures like these were resented just as much as intrusions upon the body which took the form of 'medical examination[s] in a very objectionable manner'.[96] The solution, according to Munshi Ganga Prasad Varma of Lucknow, editor of the Urdu weekly *Hindustani*, was for the government to improve the living conditions of the poor by providing them with enough food and money, rather than imposing restrictive measures after the outbreak of the epidemic. Food, he went on to argue, was 'more necessary to life than cleanliness', especially if poverty was so rampant that people could ill afford to repair their houses. By contrast, *Ar-Rashid* of Allahabad, a weekly newspaper published by Munshi Nazir Ahmad, questioned the efficiency of official measures and urged the government to seek the assistance of 'native physicians who practice on the *yunani* (Greek) system and are thought so little of by the authorities'.[97]

It was against this background that the murder of the two European officers took place. The incident brought the men to the attention of the newspaper-reading public for various periods of time between 1897 and 1899, when the alleged perpetrators of the crime, the Damodar brothers, were eventually hanged. Lieutenant Ayerst had not been a member of the Plague Committee and appears to have been mistakenly killed, a fact which led the *Englishman* to liken his murder to Lord Frederick Cavendish's assassination by Irish nationalists in 1882. Walter Charles Rand, on the other hand, was by no means unknown to the public in India.[98] As Myron Echenberg points out, Rand had a reputation for being a ruthless and 'stern disciplinarian', who completely disregarded local approaches to disaster management; his appointment as special plague commissioner had been severely criticized by the local elites of Poona, especially by Tilak in the pages of his *Kesari* and *Mahratta*.[99]

The coverage of the Poona murders shows how much reporting had changed by the end of the nineteenth century. Gone were the days when the telegrams section was exclusively occupied with news of foreign events, most of which pertained to Britain and Europe. For example, the *Madras Times* of 24 June 1897 published intelligence about events in London, Italy, Austria, Thailand, Greece, Turkey,

Japan, America, along with lengthy reports of the plague in Bombay and the murders in Poona. The increase in the number and length of messages, as well as the diversification of topics they reported on, was obvious. As the earlier examination of the *Bombay Gazette* and the *Englishman* has also shown, this diversification was impressive especially as far as domestic news was concerned. Indeed, to the extent to which layout can be regarded as an accurate indicator of the importance of news, one could argue that this was the period when Anglo-Indian newspapers appropriated domestic news. It was no longer only events such as the Austro-Prussian War or the Franco-Prussian War that attracted headlines. Telegraphic reports of the Poona murders now ran over half-columns, while headlines such as 'The Poona Tragedy' (*Bombay Gazette*), 'The Tragedy at Poona' (*Madras Gazette* and the *Englishman*), 'The Poona Outrages', or 'The Poona Murders' competed for the attention of the reader.

The visual layout of the news was calculated to attract the attention of the reading public. The *Madras Times* (Illustration 5.3) was the most conspicuous in this regard, although, ironically, the content of the coverage did not match that of the *Bombay Gazette* and the *Englishman* in detail and extent. The latter newspaper, in particular, was a far cry from the double and triple headlines, the amount of white space, and the great variety of fonts employed by the *Madras Times*. The *Bombay Gazette*'s decision not to make greater use of such visual devices is puzzling, considering that they were frequently used in other contexts, such as the reporting of foreign events.

The attacks on Lieutenant Ayerst and Walter C. Rand were first reported on 24 June 1897, two days after the event took place. The *Bombay Gazette* and the *Madras Times* reported at length about the circumstances of the murder, about Mrs Ayerst's ordeal as she witnessed her husband's instantaneous death, and Rand's struggle for survival in the Sassoon Hospital in Poona. The *Englishman*'s account at this stage consisted only of a short telegram which reproduced, almost verbatim, the longer telegram published on the same day by the *Bombay Gazette*. All three newspapers were unanimous in their condemnation of the crimes and rallied behind the government in support of its anti-plague measures: as the editor of the *Bombay Gazette* wrote, Rand had done 'splendid service to humanity by delivering Poona from an outbreak of plague, which if allowed to develop unchecked would have depopulated the Native Town'.[100]

2 THE MADRAS TIMES, MONDAY, JULY 5, 1897.

TELEGRAMS.

[REUTER'S.]

THE COLONIAL AND INDIAN TROOPS.

LONDON, JULY 2.*

An army order issued states that the Queen is specially gratified at the presence of the Colonial and Indian troops at Aldershot, rendering the review memorable in the annals of the empire.

THE KING OF SIAM.

Off to Russia.

The King of Siam has gone to St. Petersburg.

LONDON, JULY 4.

The King of Siam has arrived at St. Petersburg, where he was received by the Tsar, and drove to the Palace.

IN THE HOUSE OF COMMONS.

LIGHTS OFF AFRICA.

Lord George on the Indian Press.

Mr. Ritchie, replying to a question in the House of Commons, said that the Board of Trade would spare no pains to overcome the difficulties hitherto attending the lighting of Guardafui and Socotra.

Sir W. Harcourt asked Lord George Hamilton whether he would undertake to previously submit to the House of Commons any alteration proposed in the Indian Press Laws. Lord George declined to pledge himself, and said that there was no ground for departing from established principle.

[Lord George here is somewhat Delphic in his ambiguous phraseology.]

SUGAR IN AMERICA.

WASHINGTON, JULY 2.*

The Senate has adopted a clause surtaxing bountified sugars.

TURKEY.

RESOLVES TO STICK TO THESSALY.

The Powers Insist!!

LONDON, JULY 3.*

The Turkish Ministers in Council have unanimously resolved to maintain Turkey's right to Thessaly.

[What will the Powers say—by their word of honour!]

LONDON, JULY 4.

In consequence of the Porte's perpetual delays, the foreign ambassadors yesterday presented a collective note, insisting on Turkey's deciding concerning the Greek Frontier Question.

FRANCE AND RUSSIA.

President Faure's Visit.

The visit of President Faure to the Czar is fixed to take place on the 23rd of August.

THE SOUTH AFRICAN INQUIRY.

MR. CHAMBERLAIN'S NAME DRAGGED IN.

"Hushing up the Affair."

The series of telegrams which were exchanged, between Miss Flora Shaw and Mr. Cecil Rhodes just prior to the Jameson raid were produced at a committee meeting of the Chartered Company yesterday. In them Miss Shaw assured Mr. Rhodes that Mr. Chamberlain was sound, and wished him to act immediately. Miss Shaw, on being examined regarding this statement said that it was merely her own view, and not obtained from Mr. Chamberlain. The Chairman then announced that it was intended to examine Dr. Harris, but that he had gone abroad.

Several papers criticise the tendency that there is to hush up the affair.

[Miss Shaw seems to have telegraphed "Chamberlain is sound and wishes you to act immediately," and this Miss Shaw now declares was merely "her own view." A false note somewhere!]

LONDON, JULY 4.

It is believed that Dr. Harris sailed quietly for the Cape with Dr. Jameson, a week ago.

JUBILEE MEDALS.

A PRESENTATION.

LONDON, JULY 3.*

The Prince of Wales, on behalf of the Queen, this afternoon, presented Jubilee medals to the Colonial troops and to Indian Officers and Princes, at Buckingham Palace, in the presence of the Princess of Wales, the Duke and Duchess of York, the Colonial Premiers, Lord

of Hawaii which is related closely by ties of blood to the American people. The message further stated that the United States would not allow any country to interfere with the internal administration of Hawaii. It was expected that the Senate would ratify the treaty. The Marquis Ito, the distinguished Japanese statesman, who had been consulted about the matter, expressed the opinion that the new treaty would certainly not create any international difficulty between America and Japan.]

THE WASHINGTON SENATE.

LONDON, JULY 4

The Washington Senate have finished their sittings on the Tariff Bill.

"THE ADEN."

SURVIVORS IN ENGLAND.

The *India* has arrived at Suez, with the survivors from the *Aden* who are doing well.

(FROM OUR OWN CORRESPONDENTS.)

THE POONA TRAGEDY.

Death of Mr. Rand.

THE INQUEST.

Inquiries in Camera.

BOMBAY, JULY 3.*

Mr. Rand's temperature rose to 106° at 1 A.M., and increased to 107° by three. It remained at this high point for eighteen minutes, when the patient breathed his last. Medical officers were in attendance early in the night, and when the pulse began to beat weak Dr. McConaghy was summoned, but he pronounced the case hopeless. At the *post mortem* examination held this morning, at the inquest, Lieut. Owen Lewis, first examined, repeated his statement regarding the order of carriages returning from the Ganeshkind banquet; he related how he and his companion had their attention attracted by the cries of Mrs. Ayerst, and spoke to finding Mr. Rand lying insensible in his carriage. Mrs. Ayerst was the next witness examined. She was overwhelmed with grief, and broke down. The Press were asked to retire during her examination and that of Dr. McConaghy.

[The news of Mr. Rand's death comes especially sadly after such long delay, during which there seemed hopes that he would recover. Mr. Walter Charles Rand joined the Bombay Civil Service on the 6th of September, 1883, and had thus served for nearly fourteen years.]

THE TOCHI EXPEDITION.

THE MALIKS WANT TO TREAT.

DETAILS OF THE DISASTER.

SIMLA, JULY 3.*

In the matter of the Tochi disaster, the Maliks are anxious to treat, but no communication will be held with them until the troops are concentrated at Maizar.

SIMLA, JULY 4.

Mr. Gee's report of the Tochi disaster adds a few particulars not hitherto known. At first the villagers appeared quite friendly, talking freely with the Pathan sepoys. Supplies were readily brought, the British officers being pressed to partake of the prepared food. Mr. Gee was told that the local *Jirga* had come to an amicable agreement, Malik Sadda Khan's statement to this effect being a deliberate lie. His concealment of the true state of the case led directly to a catastrophe.

The attack began at 2 P.M. Lieut. Seton-Browne was hit by the second shot, and Surg.-Capt. Cassidy bound up the wound. Then Col. Bunny was mortally wounded. At the same moment Lieut. Higginson was hit on the left arm. The guns were at once opened with case shot, but in five minutes the ammunition was expended, and Col. Bunny ordered a retirement. The retreat was continued slowly, across six ridges, positions being taken up on each of the successive ridges.

The tribesmen began to come on in large numbers, but the force took up a strong position, at 5-30 P.M., awaiting reinforcements from Datta Khel, which arrived at 6-15, covering nine miles in ninety minutes.

Evidence points to Sadda Khan as having been pre-eminent in the treachery. The Wazira loss was about 100, some 35 being killed by case-shot in one place.

Maizar, where the troops will concentrate, is a group of villages above the junction of Shawal Algad, and the Tochi. It lies two miles beyond Sheranna, and is occupied by Drepalari, Khoji Khel, Alikhan Khel, and Machia sections of the Ger position of the Madda Khel tribe. The main road to Ghazni runs through it.

THE CALCUTTA RIOTS.

A MAHOMEDAN LEAFLET.

A POSSIBILITY OF MORE TROUBLE.

CALCUTTA, JULY 3.*

The Mahomedan riot has for the present subsided. The firing of ball-cartridge by the troops and police on Thursday had a salutary effect. The heads of the organisation took a very astute step yesterday by issuing a leaflet, saying that, Maharajah Sir Jotendro Mohun Tagore, having granted to the Mahomedans the land on which the disputed mosque stood, there was no further necessity for violence. As a matter of fact, the Maharajah has done nothing of the kind, having only a life interest in the land in question, which belongs to a syndicate at home. The object of the leaflet was to show that the rioters had won all along the line. A very disagreeable impression has been created by the leaflet, and intense indignation prevails among the European and Hindu community at the halting policy of the authorities in this matter. Two of the three Anglo-Indian and the three Anglo-Bengali dailies are unanimous in condemning the weak and halting policy of the authorities in dealing with the rioters, the exception being the *Statesman*, which makes a feeble defence of the Mahomedans. That the Capital of India should practically have been in the hands of Mahomedan mobs for 48 hours is exactly what has happened. Yesterday the news reached headquarters that a large gathering of Mahomedans, including many itenerant Kabulis, were making their way from Garden-reach to Calcutta, that they had cut the telephone wires and had assumed a very defiant attitude. A large police force was immediately sent to the scene, and the rioters were prevented from crossing the bridge into Calcutta. On seeing the police, the rioters dispersed. To-day all is quiet, but it is generally believed that when ignorant Mahomedans realise that there is no truth in the compromise published in the leaflet, there will probably be more trouble.

SIMLA, JULY 4.*

The report current in some of the papers that the authorities at Calcutta telegraphed to the Viceroy for leave to fire on the rioters is absolutely without foundation.

THE OVERLAND MAILS.

Due To-day.

BOMBAY, JULY 3.*

The mail steamer was signalled at a quarter past eight this morning. The mails leave by mail train this evening.

DISTRESS IN HYDERABAD.

SECUNDERABAD, JULY 4.

The gravest anxiety is felt here owing to the complete absence of rain, and affairs in the districts are alarming. Food-stuffs have risen to famine prices, and the poor, in consequence, resort to anything for sustenance. This has brought about cholera in its worst possible form.

MRS. TUCKER.

General Tucker's wife has almost completely recovered from the attack which caused endless anxiety till yesterday.

CRICKET AT OOTY.

GYMKHANA v. THE LIARDET LEAGUE.

OOTACAMUND, JULY 4.

A cricket-match was played yesterday between the Gymkhana and the Liardet League, in very fine weather. The ground was in good condition, and the play was undisturbed by rain. Capt. Carrich 1, Capt. Reay 3, Lord Herbert Scott 4, Mr. Geddes 12, Major Callough 3, Mr. Buriton 4, Mr. Somerseve 13, Mr. Clarke 5, Mr. Lissenburg 3, Mr. Fisher 10, Surg.-Capt. Gibbard 3, Extras 15, total 76. In the second innings, Capt. Carrich 37, Mr. Geddes 12, Mr. Gibbard 20, Extras 12, whole team out for 112. In the first innings the barrister, Mr. Sidney, took 8 wickets for 13 runs, while the other bowlers gave more runs for wickets. The Liardet League entered first venture, Mr. Burby scoring 23, Mr. Rowlands 20, Mr. Sewell 32, Extras 20, the team being out for 115. Mr. Fisher, of the Gymkhana team, took 6 wickets for 45 runs. The match resulted in a draw.

THE District Magistrate of the Kinta district in Perak reported that a remarkable find of tin has taken place in Kinta. Two or three Chinamen had a sub-lease of the land from a Malay, and had been working with very little success till they suddenly came on a very rich

Illustration 5.3 Foreign and domestic telegrams at the end of the century, *Madras Times*, 5 July 1897

Source: © The British Library Board, Shelfmark: MFM.MC1158D, 05/07/1897.

Table 5.1 Telegrams reporting the Poona murders, 24 June–5 July 1897

Date of newspaper issue in which published	Place of origin of telegrams and date when sent		
	Bombay Gazette	*Englishman*	*Madras Times*
24 June 1897	Poona, 23 June	Poona, 23 June	Bombay, 23 June
25 June 1897	Poona, 24 June	Poona, 23 June	Bombay, 24 June
26 June 1897	Poona, 25 June	Poona, 24 June Poona, 25 June	Bombay, 25 June
27 June 1897	N/A	N/A	N/A
28 June 1897	Poona, 27 June London, 26 June	Poona, 27 June	N/A
29 June 1897	Poona 28 June	Poona, 28 June	N/A
30 June 1897	Poona, 29 June	N/A	Bombay, 29 June
1 July 1897	Poona, 30 June	Poona, 30 June	Bombay, 30 June
2 July 1897	Poona, 1 July	N/A	Bombay, 1 July Simla, 1 July
3 July 1897	Poona, 2 July London, 2 July	London, 2 July Poona, 2 July	London, 2 July Bombay, 2 July
4 July 1897	N/A	N/A	N/A
5 July 1897	N/A	Poona, 3 July Poona, July 4	Bombay, 3 July

Source: Compiled from *Bombay Gazette*, *Englishman*, *Madras Times*, June–July 1897.

Table 5.1 shows the place of origin and the date of all relevant telegrams published by the three newspapers in connection with the murders, from the moment of the attack until the death of Walter C. Rand in hospital on 3 July 1897, which was communicated to the public two days later. The almost daily frequency of coverage suggests that the news value of the event was high. There was a visible increase in news timeliness, as compared to previous decades, which was indicated by the shorter temporal gap between the occurrence of the event and its reporting in the newspaper press examined. The news published in all newspapers was one or two days old. The situation was identical in the case of foreign news sent from London, which could now be published by all newspapers one day after their dispatch by Reuters. Furthermore, the supply of news had acquired a certain degree of regularity and routine which was less pronounced in the earlier decades, when interruptions to the lines had been a much more common occurrence.

As regards the place of origin of news, all domestic telegrams were sent from Poona in the case of the *Bombay Gazette* and the *Englishman*, and from Bombay in the case of the *Madras Times*. The news was sent by the newspapers' own correspondents. There was much overlapping of news matter between the three newspapers and in particular between the *Bombay Gazette* and the *Englishman*, a fact which suggests that the two journals might have shared the same correspondent or that their news delivery arrangements were connected. For example, the telegrams published by the *Englishman* on 25 June reproduced almost verbatim telegrams published in the *Bombay Gazette* of 24 and 25 June. The same was true of the *Englishman* issues of 26, 28, and 29 June, whose telegrams were almost identical to those published by the *Bombay Gazette* of 25, 28, and 29 June respectively. A similar trend can be noticed for the *Madras Times*, although the overlap in this case was less visible and frequent. One aspect of news reporting which was peculiar to the *Madras Times*, however, was its practice of republishing telegrams. For example, the issue of 25 June reprinted the telegrams from the previous day announcing the incident at Poona, possibly out of a desire to emphasize the importance of the event and to complement the lack of longer telegrams such as those published by the *Bombay Gazette*.

Another important development, clearly visible in all the newspapers examined, was the fact that readers could follow closely and in significant detail the unfolding of events. Furthermore, the coverage, whether it took the form of telegraphic news, letters from members of the public, or editorial comment, was infused with personal detail and populated with men and women with whose plight the public was expected to identify.

Much of the reporting was centred on the figure of the two victims and their respective families. For example, a short obituary published by the *Bombay Gazette* informed readers that Lieutenant Ayerst had arrived in India in 1893 and had been attached to the chief commissariat officer in Poona after successfully passing his examinations in Hindustani and Marathi.[101] His death, at the early age of 27, was all the more dramatic since he left behind a widow and an infant child. In addition, Ayerst had not been associated with the plague relief operations, a fact which led the press and the colonial administrators to speculate that his death was due to a case of mistaken identity.

The real target, it was believed, had been Lieutenant Owen Lewis, in whose horse carriage Ayerst and his wife had been travelling at the time of the incident.

Rand's struggle for survival at the Sassoon Hospital was another aspect of this drama which fed the news media of the day. The three papers reported almost daily on the state of his health; the coverage was impressive in its detailed monitoring of the patient's condition. Readers were thus treated to news about the evolution of Rand's fever (which, we find out, increased from 101 on 29 June to 102.6 on 1 July), his general condition (he was 'restless' or 'passed a quiet night'), the onset of pneumonia, the arrival of a certain Dr Collis Barry, 'chemical analyzer' from Bombay, with a Röntgen ray apparatus and, finally, Rand's demise on the morning of 3 July at 3.18 a.m.[102] That telegrams, which had been formerly filled almost exclusively with 'important' political, military, and commercial intelligence—such as news about disturbances and wars, decisions of the Government of India or of the British Parliament, market quotations, and so on—should now contain reports about the health of people other than the Queen or prominent political figures, was in itself a significant development. Perhaps even more intriguing was the inclusion of information which clearly went beyond the domain of the 'bare facts' with which telegraphic reporting has been usually associated. For example, a reference to the crime scene published in the *Englishman* contained a description of the surroundings as a 'place … full of trees'.[103]

The figure of the widow also occupied a central place in newspaper coverage of the event. Mrs Ayerst's plight attracted particular attention on account of her having witnessed her husband's death. The first telegrams contained graphic reports of the 'unfortunate lady [being] covered in blood'.[104] In Rand's case, on the other hand, physical distance compounded grief and amplified the dramatic tenor of the event. As the press pointed out, Mrs Rand was unable to nurse her husband in the last hours of his life, since news of his death reached her at Aden, on her return from England to India. Upon arrival in Bombay, she was greeted by the brother-in-law and hosted 'at the house of a Hon. Mr. Crowe'.[105]

In their discussion of the assassination of American presidents Garfield, McKinley, Harding, Roosevelt, and Kennedy, Barnhurst and Nerone point out that the 'grieving widow' received constant and 'unwholesome' attention in the coverage of their husbands' deaths: 'They anatomized her grief for the edification of the nation, applying the same values over time. She underwent scrutiny for the proper balance of emotion and self-control. Expected to grieve, even to make a display of grief, she also had to maintain her composure and conduct the complicated funeral arrangements with skill and grace.'[106]

A similar conduct was expected of Rand's widow. Newspaper reports described her as 'most painfully affected' and 'in very deep mourning', yet dignified and composed. Solidarity from other women and members of the public more generally became an important form of moral support for the bereaved widow, but was also regarded as an opportunity for the colonized Indians to show their allegiance to their imperial rulers by condemning such acts. Pundit Narayan Baba Gurjar, Ayerst's former teacher of Marathi, wrote a letter to the *Bombay Gazette* praising the character of the deceased.[107] The *Englishman* also reported on 24 July that '[t]he Brahmin ladies have sent a letter of condolence to Mrs. Rand. Replying from Surat, she expressed her gratitude for their kind letter and sympathy. It was some consolation to her to know that the native ladies of Poona felt for her in her deep grief and irreparable loss.'

The report about the Brahmin ladies had clear political connotations. For days after the incident, speculation was rife about the possible perpetrators and many were convinced that the murders were the result of a conspiracy by a section of the Poona Brahmins.[108] The confidential report prepared by the Government of Bombay on 29 July 1897 remarked that opinion was divided over the cause of the attack: some argued that it was a case of personal spite, while others maintained that it was related to the plague operations and instigated by 'the peculiarly violent writing of the Poona papers regarding plague administration'. Yet others claimed that it was a 'political plot' of some Poona Brahmins whose aim was 'to embarrass the Government'.[109]

Like in the case of the Austro-Prussian War, a good part of the information published by newspapers was nothing more than speculation and rumour. For example, a headline in the *Bombay Gazette* of 24 June 1897 announced in big letters that there had been 'YET ANOTHER ATTEMPT AT MURDER'. This time, the alleged victim was none other than Lieutenant Owen Lewis. The news was also published in the *Madras Times* of the same date. A day later, both newspapers were forced to dismiss the story as untrue: 'A Poona telegram contradicts the statement that Owen Lewis was shot last evening. The story concerning him seems wholly unfounded.'[110] According to other newspaper reports, a schoolmaster and a lecturer—both Brahmins—were apprehended on 19 August in Bombay, although 'no direct clue to the murder [was] discovered'.[111]

Tilak was eventually arrested and put on trial for sedition under the accusation that he had instigated the murder through his writings in the *Kesari* and the *Mahratta*. As the official records show, the Government of India once again failed to inform the India Office in due course about the unfolding events. Despite the existence of fast and reliable media of communication, the secretary of state came to know from a Reuter telegram about the arrest of Damodar Chapekar and his alleged confession to murdering the two officers. This development was followed shortly by the government's announcement that it was willing to reward anyone who could provide clues regarding the murder with Rs 20,000.[112] The secretary dismissed the Reuter report as 'doctored' and asked for an inquiry to be conducted. Much to the dismay of the secretary and the Government of India, Reuters confirmed that Chapekar had indeed taken all the guilt upon himself, exonerating in this way the 'natives' of Poona.[113] A further telegram from the Governor of Bombay reached London on 10 October 1897 and announced to the secretary of state that 'Rand's murderer made full confession before Chief Presidency Magistrate. Case will proceed.'[114] Eventually, Damodar and his two brothers, Balkrishna and Vasudeo, were put on trial and convicted for the two murders. They were hanged in 1899.

***

The face of the newspaper press examined here changed significantly in the course of the nineteenth century: from four-page publications which depended for intelligence on the more-or-less regular arrival of mails, to eight or more pages in which telegrams flashed the latest news from various corners of the world and vied for the attention of readers through their use of elaborate fonts and spacing techniques. Advertising itself was transformed, as newspapers became increasingly commercialized, a situation that prompted nostalgic observers to comment that journalism was not what it used to be.[115] Advertisements gradually changed from simple and generic—one formula which could be applied to multiple products, as was the case of shipping ads—to visually appealing and individualized, aiming to lure the reader-cum-customer through increasingly ingenious combinations of text and illustration.

Within these broader developments, I have also tried to capture the hierarchies of communication and the individuality of each newspaper, in effect arguing that the final product—the newspaper—was shaped not only by the politics of the colonial government and by economic considerations, but also by the editors', proprietors', and printers' own visions of journalism and news reporting. The journalism practised by the *Bombay Gazette*, as we have seen, emerged out of the specific environment of the town in which it was published, but was also shaped to a considerable extent by the personal vision of people like T. J. Bennett. By contrast, a newspaper like the *Englishman* appeared almost conservative in its approach to reporting and advertising.

The two case studies examined, that of the Austro-Prussian War of 1866 and of the assassination at Poona, in 1897, of the two European officers associated with plague relief measures, have provided further insights into the mechanisms of foreign and domestic news reporting in nineteenth-century India. The discussion has highlighted the advantages of telegraphic communication—most prominently the possibility of accessing intelligence on a timelier basis—but has also pointed out its pitfalls, in the form of mistakes in reporting, manipulation of telegraphic communication by the authorities, the absence of detail, and so on. In this respect, the chapter has argued that the telegraph was a technology which not only facilitated communication, but also led to numerous instances of miscommunication.

Overall, the image that emerges is that of an increasingly interconnected press world, interconnected both in its reporting and its misreporting. Since newspapers in India were largely dependent on Reuters for their foreign intelligence, the telegrams they published were often strikingly similar not only in their content, but also in the language they used. The period was thus marked by a growing integration and standardization of reporting practices in the English-language press.

Notes

1. Kevin G. Barnhurst and John Nerone, *The Form of News: A History* (New York and London: Guilford Press, 2001), p. 6.
2. Barnhurst and Nerone, *The Form of News*, p. 7.

3. See, for example, *Englishman*, 25 July 1850.
4. *Bengal Hurkaru*, 7 July 1865, 8 July 1865, 10 July 1865.
5. Hirschmann, *Robert Knight*, p. 20.
6. The *Times of India* and the *Madras Times* also shared this format, but the *Delhi Gazette* had eight pages in the mid-1850s, which increased to twelve two decades later.
7. Barnhurst and Nerone, *The Form of News*, p. 82.
8. Ulrike Stark, *An Empire of Books: The Naval Kishore Press and the Diffusion of the Printed Word in Colonial India* (New Delhi: Permanent Black, 2009), pp. 187–92.
9. See also the *Bangalore Spectator*, which had seven columns per page in the 1900s.
10. J. H. Stocqueler, *The Memoirs of a Journalist* (Bombay: Times of India, 1873), p. 97.
11. *Phoenix*, 16 July 1861. For a short history of this newspaper, see M. K. Chanda, *History of the English Press in Bengal, 1858–1880* (Kolkata: K. P. Bagchi & Company, 2008), pp. 21–2.
12. *Bangalore Herald*, 20 August 1861.
13. *Indian Spectator*, 8 January 1882.
14. *Amrita Bazar Patrika*, 6 April 1882. Considerations of space do not allow us to examine medical advertising in more detail, but Projit Bihari Mukharji's *Nationalizing the Body: The Medical Market, Print and Daktari Medicine* (London: Anthem Press, 2009), especially pp. 100–5, contains valuable insights into the different approaches to the form and content of English-language and Bengali advertisements (*vigyāpan*), particularly in books and almanacs. See also Madhuri Sharma, 'Creating a Consumer: Exploring Medical Advertisements in Colonial India', in *The Social History of Health and Medicine in Colonial India*, edited by Mark Harrison and Biswamoy Pati (Abingdon: Routledge, 2009).
15. The Bombay Government subscribe to a weekly newspaper in Gujarati published by Fardonji Marzbanji, 20 February 1822 and 12 April 1822, F/4/709/19247, IOR.
16. C. A. Bayly, 'Afterword: Bombay's Intertwined Modernities, 1780–1880', in *Trans-Colonial Modernities in South Asia*, edited by M. S. Dodson and B. A. Hatcher (Abingdon: Routledge, 2012), pp. 234–5.
17. *Bombay Gazette*, 21 July 1830.
18. Pat Lovett, *Journalism in India* (Calcutta: Banna Publishing Company, [1929]), p. 16.
19. 'Thomas Jewell Bennett', *Journal of the Royal Society of Arts* 73, no. 3766 (1925): 243–4. For a biography of Bennett, see Chandrika Kaul, 'Bennett, Sir Thomas Jewell (1852–1925)', in *Oxford Dictionary of National Biography* (Oxford: Oxford University Press, 2004), available at: www.oxforddnb.com/view/article/58684 (accessed 25 March 2011).

20. A. H. Watson, 'The Growth of the Press in English In India', *Journal of the Royal Society of Arts* 96, no. 4760 (1948): 121–30, at 124.
21. *Bombay Gazette*, 2 July 1890.
22. But note Ulrike Stark's observation that Munshi Naval Kishore's *Avadh Akhbar* was making use of illustrations in news reporting as early as the 1870s. According to Stark, Kishore took inspiration from the *Illustrated London News*. Stark, *An Empire of Books*, pp. 354–62.
23. For a parallel with American newspapers, see Barnhurst and Nerone, *The Form of News*, pp. 84–95.
24. See, for example, *Englishman*, 5 July 1900.
25. *Englishman*, 2 July 1890.
26. *Times of India*, 26 August 1874; emphasis original.
27. D. E. Wacha, *Shells from the Sands of Bombay, Being My Recollections and Reminiscences, 1860–1875* (Bombay: The Bombay Chronicle Press, 1920), pp. 15–17.
28. There were exceptions to this rule. The *Scotsman in the East*, a short-lived newspaper published in Calcutta in 1824, planned to run advertisements on the last sheet, the first three pages being dedicated to European and foreign politics, literature, science, miscellaneous matter, and Asiatic intelligence, in this particular order. Munshi Naval Kishore's *Avadh Akhbar* also published news on the front page. See Anil Chandra Das Gupta (ed.), *The Days of John Company: Selections from Calcutta Gazette, 1824–1832* (Calcutta: West Bengal Government Press, 1959), p. 36; Stark, *An Empire of Books*, p. 365.
29. *Englishman*, 23 July 1840.
30. Matthew Rubery, *The Novelty of Newspapers: Victorian Fiction after the Invention of the News* (Oxford: Oxford University Press, 2009), pp. 26–7.
31. *Lloyd's List*, 19 January 1753, in *Lloyd's List, 1753 & 1755* (Westmead, UK: Gregg International Publishers, 1969), n.p.
32. See Michael Harris, 'Shipwrecks in Print: Representations of Maritime Disaster in the Late Seventeenth Century', in *Journeys through the Market: Travel, Travellers and the Book Trade*, edited by R. Myers and M. Harris (New Castle, DE: Oak Knoll Press, 1999).
33. Mark Hampton, *Visions of the Press in Britain, 1850–1950* (Urbana and Chicago: University of Illinois Press, 2004), pp. 37–8.
34. *Englishman*, 28 July 1860; 11 July 1900.
35. *Calcutta Courier*, 15 June 1839; *Englishman*, 23 July 1840.
36. The first name indicates the name of the ship, the second the name of the captain, followed by the place of origin and the date when it had sailed off.
37. *Mahratta*, 20 July 1890.
38. *Mahratta*, 29 June 1890.
39. For example, *Shree Venkateshwar Samachar*, 8 October 1909.

40. *Bharat Jiwan*, 7 July 1884. All translations from Hindi are my own.
41. *Times of India*, 7 July 1884.
42. In this connection, see also R. Wenzlhuemer, 'London in the Global Telecommunication Network of the Nineteenth Century', *New Global Studies* 3, no. 1 (2009): Art. 2.
43. For example, *Bombay Gazette*, 15 July 1840, 4 July 1860, and 22 July 1880.
44. See *Bombay Gazette*, 6 July 1870; *Englishman*, 19 July 1900; *Bombay Gazette*, 19 July 1900.
45. Joshua Meyrowitz, *The Impact of Electronic Media on Social Behavior* (New York and Oxford: Oxford University Press, 1985), p. 6.
46. *Phoenix*, 29 August 1861.
47. Isabel Hofmeyr, *Gandhi's Printing Press: Experiments in Slow Reading* (Cambridge, MA, and London: Harvard University Press, 2013), p. 17.
48. *Delhi Gazette*, 6 February 1855; *Times of India*, 22 August 1878.
49. Brian Bond, 'The Austro-Prussian War 1866', *History Today* 16, no. 8 (1966): 538–546, at 538.
50. See the *Times of India*, 5 February 1866, 20 February 1866, and 3 March 1866.
51. Arden Bucholz, *Moltke and the German Wars, 1864–1871* (New York: Palgrave, 2001), pp. 113–38.
52. For an analysis of the Austro-Prussian War and its reporting by the British press, see E. W. Ellsworth, 'The Austro-Prussian War and the British Press', *Historian* 20, no. 2 (1958): 179–200.
53. Graham Storey, *Reuters' Century, 1851–1951* (London: Max Parrish, 1951), p. 63.
54. Storey, *Reuters' Century*, p. 63.
55. Administration Report of the Indian Telegraph Department for 1866–67, Appendix D, p. v, V/24/4284, IOR.
56. *DNCJ*, s.v. 'War and Journalism', p. 661.
57. For an interesting anthropological perspective on rumours and their role in predicting political and military events, see Matt Tomlinson, 'Speaking of Coups before They Happen: Kadavu, May–June 1999', *Pacific Studies* 25, no. 4 (2002): 9–28.
58. See the editorial comment in the *Lahore Chronicle* of 28 July 1866.
59. See, for example, *Lahore Chronicle*, 4 August 1866 and 29 August 1866.
60. *Times of India*, 4 July 1866.
61. *Englishman*, 18 July 1866; *Lahore Chronicle*, 25 August 1866.
62. *Times of India*, 15 March 1866, 27 April 1866, and 7 May 1866.
63. *Englishman*, 25 June 1866.
64. Peter Putnis, 'Overseas News in the Australian Press in 1870 and the Colonial Experience of the Franco-Prussian War', *History Australia* 4, no. 1 (2007): 6.1–6.19, at 6.1.

65. Amelia Bonea, 'Telegraphy and Journalism in Colonial India, c. 1830s–1900s', *History Compass* 12, no. 5 (2014): 387–97, at 394.
66. Bonea, 'Telegraphy and Journalism in Colonial India', p. 394.
67. *Japan Gazette*, various issues from 1880, 1891, 1892, and 1900.
68. See, for example, the *Lahore Chronicle* of 21 July 1866 and 25 July 1866.
69. Dwayne R. Winseck and Robert M. Pike, *Communication and Empire: Media, Markets, and Globalization, 1860–1930* (Durham and London: Duke University Press, 2007), p. 4.
70. Administration Report of the Indian Telegraph Department 1866–67, p. 10, V/24/4284, IOR; Administration Report of the Indian Telegraph Department 1867–68, Appendix I, V/24/4284, IOR.
71. Agreement between Reuters and the *Englishman*, 3 October 1879, LN435, 1879, RA.
72. 'How They Telegraph', *Chambers's Journal of Popular Literature, Science and Arts* 10 (1893), p. 201.
73. *Times of India*, 7 July 1866; *Englishman*, 7 July 1866; *Madras Times*, 13 July 1866; *Madras Times*, 13 August 1866; *Lahore Chronicle*, 15 August 1866.
74. *Times of India*, 30 June 1866.
75. *Englishman*, quoted in Charles C. Adley, *The Story of the Telegraph in India* (London: E. & F. N. Spon, 1866), p. 32.
76. *Times of India*, 25 June 1866.
77. *Times of India*, 9 July 1866 and 10 July 1866.
78. Henry Collins, *From Pigeon Post to Wireless* (London: Hodder and Stoughton Limited, 1925), p. 69.
79. Collins, *From Pigeon Post to Wireless*, p. 69.
80. *Times of India*, 24 July 1866.
81. *Lahore Chronicle*, 4 August 1866; emphasis original.
82. *Times of India*, 25 July 1866.
83. *Lahore Chronicle*, 18 August 1866. The Austro-Prussian War has often been described as a landmark in modern European warfare and military communications, due to the use of the needle-gun by the Prussian army. Railroads and the telegraph were also used for transport, communication, and strategic purposes. See Bond, 'The Austro-Prussian War 1866', p. 546; Bucholz, *Moltke and the German Wars*, pp. 104–11.
84. J. B. Atkins, *The Life of Sir William Howard Russell, the First Special Correspondent*, vol. 2 (London: John Murray, 1911), p. 139.
85. *Times of India*, 9 August 1866.
86. *Times of India*, 16 July 1866.
87. See *New York Times*, 5 October 1897; *Straits Times*, 14 October 1897, 17 March 1899; *Singapore Free Press and Mercantile Advertiser*, 14 October 1897; *Advertiser* (Adelaide), 6 October 1897; *Brisbane*

Courier, 5 February 1898; *West Australian* (Perth), 5 February 1898; *Auckland Star*, 4 February 1898.

88. See, for example, an article published in the *Speaker* which suggested that the sanitary measures taken by the Indian government in connection with the plague might have been difficult to enforce even in Europe a century ago, and that the measures 'had been so carelessly carried out as to provoke acute native resentment and lead to the assassinations' ('Poona and Chitpur', *Speaker*, 16 [1897], p. 34). On the other hand, the *Saturday Review*, in a review of Arthur Crawford's book *Our Troubles in Poona and the Deccan* (1897), traced these disturbances to the 'seditious propaganda' of a handful of Poona-based Mahratta Brahmins, 'the genesis and development of a typical native newspaper, hostile to constituted authority, and subsisting on blackmail and bought support of unworthy objects and intriguers [Tilak's *Kesari*]' and 'the sham revival of the nationalistic cult of Shiwajee'. 'Our Troubles in Poona and the Deccan', *Saturday Review of Politics, Literature, Science and Art* 85 (1898), pp. 49–50.
89. P. L. Malhotra, *Administration of Lord Elgin in India, 1894–99* (New Delhi: Vikas, 1979), p. 145; Prashant Kidambi, '"An Infection of Locality": Plague, Pythogenesis and the Poor in Bombay, c. 1896–1905', *Urban History* 31, no. 2 (2004): 249–67, at 250.
90. Kidambi, 'An Infection of Locality', 250, 257.
91. *Aina-i-Alam*, 1 January 1897, *NNR*, North-Western Provinces & Oudh, No. 2 of 1897, p. 28.
92. *Colonel*, 1 January 1897, *NNR*, North-Western Provinces & Oudh, No. 5 of 1897, p. 79; *Colonel*, 8 February 1897, *NNR*, North-Western Provinces & Oudh, No. 7 of 1897, p. 112; *Oudh Punch*, 18 February 1897, *NNR*, North-Western Provinces & Oudh, No. 11 of 1897, p. 184.
93. *Prayag Samachar*, 4 February 1897, *NNR*, North-Western Provinces & Oudh, No. 6 of 1897, p. 98.
94. R. Chandavarkar, *Imperial Power and Popular Politics: Class, Resistance and the State in India, c. 1850–1950* (Cambridge: Cambridge University Press, 1998), pp. 236–7.
95. *Azad*, 5 February 1897, *NNR*, North-Western Provinces & Oudh, No. 6 of 1897, p. 96. See also an article from Munshi Muhammad Agha Jan's Urdu weekly *Mashir-i-Saltanat*, 'The Recrudescence of the Plague in Poona', in which he praises the government for the measures adopted and argues that 'the *parda* cannot be dearer than life'. He also claimed that, unlike Emperor Jahangir who did nothing to contain the bubonic plague that erupted in his time, the British administration 'at once framed strict sanitary rules as soon as the disease asserted itself' (*Mashir-i-Saltanat*, 28 September 1897, *NNR*, North-Western Provinces & Oudh, No. 40 of 1897, p. 623).

96. *Rahbar*, 8 March 1897, *NNR*, North-Western Provinces & Oudh, No. 11 of 1897, p. 183. Also *Nasir-i-Hind*, 20 March 1897, *NNR*, North-Western Provinces & Oudh, No. 12 of 1897, p. 204.
97. *Hindustani*, 12 March 1897, *NNR*, North-Western Provinces & Oudh, No. 11 of 1897, p. 183; *Hindustani*, 12 March 1897, *NNR*, North-Western Provinces & Oudh, No. 11 of 1897, p. 183; *Ar-Rashid*, 11 January 1897, *NNR*, North-Western Provinces & Oudh, No. 3 of 1897, p. 47.
98. Cavendish, an English politician, was mistakenly murdered in Dublin in an attack which targeted his companion, the permanent under-secretary T. H. Burke (*Englishman*, 7 July 1897).
99. M. Echenberg, *Plague Ports: The Global Urban Impact of Bubonic Plague, 1894–1901* (New York and London: New York University Press, 2007), pp. 66–7.
100. *Bombay Gazette*, 24 June 1897.
101. *Bombay Gazette*, 24 June 1897. In 1897, the newspaper also published a letter from his former Marathi language teacher.
102. *Englishman*, 5 July 1897.
103. *Englishman*, 24 June 1897.
104. *Bombay Gazette*, 24 June 1897; *Englishman*, 25 June 1897.
105. *Englishman*, 12 July 1897.
106. Barnhurst and Nerone, *The Form of News*, p. 152.
107. *Bombay Gazette*, 29 June 1897.
108. 'Were the Brahmins in It?', *Bombay Gazette*, 29 July 1897.
109. The murder of two British officers at Poona, 28 July 1897, L/PJ/6/454, File 1657, IOR.
110. *Madras Times*, 25 June 1897.
111. *Englishman*, 20 August 1897.
112. Murder at Poona of two informers in the case against Damodar Chapekar, 9 February 1899, L/PJ/6/501, File 258, IOR. This reward was mentioned in the three newspapers examined and it was increased from an initial Rs 10,000 to Rs 20,000.
113. Poona murders: Alleged confession of Damodar Chapekar to the murder of Rand, 6 October 1897, L/PJ/6/457, File 1999, IOR.
114. Copy of telegram from Governor, Bombay, 10 October 1897, L/PJ/6/458, File 2010, IOR.
115. A similar complaint can be encountered in the early decades of the twentieth century, for example, in Pat Lovett's Adhar Chandra Mukherjee Lectures delivered at the University of Calcutta in 1926, discussed in the introduction.

Conclusion

In this book I have examined, from a historical perspective, the news reporting practices of English-language newspapers in nineteenth-century India, with a particular focus on the ways in which electric telegraphy intersected with the development of the newspaper press and journalism. Despite this professed primary focus on electric telegraphy, I have tried to avoid examining this technology in isolation, aiming instead to understand how it was incorporated into and used as part of a broader system of communications in colonial India. The analysis has shown how the production and dissemination of foreign and domestic news was a complex process which involved multiple layers of participants and drew on a variety of technologies of communication, both old and new. These media of communication were used complementarily in order to facilitate the circulation of intelligence within the Indian subcontinent as well as between Britain, India, and other parts of the world such as Japan. The study has been informed by the conviction that we cannot understand the ways in which technology shaped journalism—and vice versa—without the simultaneous evaluation of the political, socio-economic, and technological circumstances that surrounded their interaction during this period and without drawing on the insights of multiple categories of historical actors.

The book has tried to weave together two distinct fields of investigation, namely the history of journalism and the history of technology, in an attempt to illuminate their interconnected development in colonial South Asia. Over the years, the newspaper press has morphed into an important source of research for historians of the Indian subcontinent, providing insights into a variety of fields and topics of inquiry, ranging from the history of the press to economic and agrarian history to political biographies, and, to a lesser extent, the history of medicine. By contrast, in this study I have attempted to look at newspapers both as vehicles of opinion and information about particular topics of interest—for example, the history of telegraphy, the murder in Poona of the two European officers associated with the plague relief measures, and so on—and as media which deserve to be studied in their own right. In other words, I conceptualized newspapers not only as media which reflect and illustrate social change, but also as media which were not immune to change themselves.

The main research questions that have guided this study have been: How did news reporting and newspapers more generally change in the nineteenth century? What role, if any, did technologies of communication like the electric telegraph play in the development of journalism during this period? I have attempted to provide answers to these and other related questions by drawing on a wide range of documents which span not only different genres of historical sources, but also linguistic and geographical barriers. Much of the material discussed in this book comes from the newspapers themselves, which have been examined with an eye to both the form and the content of reporting. Put differently, I have focused both on the type of news that was reported—political, military, commercial, shipping, and so on—and on the use of typographic techniques, the development of advertisements, and the relationship between paper production in colonial India and the number of pages of a newspaper.

The study was motivated by a simple rationale, namely the lack of a systematic study of news reporting practices in nineteenth-century India that paid attention to the development of newspapers and journalism and the ways in which the electric telegraph was incorporated into practices of reporting and journalism more generally. The electric telegraph was undoubtedly essential in facilitating rapid and regular communication between Britain and India, as a number of studies discussed in this book have also demonstrated. By shifting the focus to journalism, my own concern was not to draw superficial distinctions between various sites of use of telegraphy (see Chapter 3), but to recover some of the other practices associated with its use and to consider how they intersected with the fields of colonial administration and military and commercial affairs, which had been documented to a certain extent in previous literature.

With this in mind, the book has examined engagements with telegraphy across a variety of geographical and social contexts, reminding readers that technology-in-discourse and technology-in-practice are not necessarily overlapping domains, and attempting to bridge the gap between the discourses and practices of telegraphy in the nineteenth century. Chapter 2, for example, aimed to capture the wide range of responses to and experiences of telegraphy in colonial South Asia, showing how the telegraph was represented as an instrument of social and moral improvement, as one in a long list of 'modern' technologies which the British colonizers introduced to India in their attempts to 'civilize' the inhabitants of the subcontinent. Such accounts celebrated the triumphs of Western science, portraying the telegraph as a neutral technology which was divorced from its socio-economic and political context, and often depicting Indians as little inclined towards the study and the use of technology. Accounts like these stood in stark contrast to evidence which suggested not only an early interest in the study of subjects connected to electricity and electro-magnetism, but also the existence of relevant publications in vernacular languages, of attempts to build telegraphic instruments and, indeed, evidence of its use for the transaction of commercial activities, the communication of personal news, appeals against death sentences, and even blessings.

Other commentators discussed in the book focused on the impact of technology on journalism and voiced criticism of the ways in which it allegedly promoted the rise of a 'sensational' style of reporting, a development which, they claimed, saw journalistic writing increasingly divorced from its literary roots. 'Good journalism', as the editor of the *Bombay Gazette* reminded its readers on 20 December 1841, required time to think, read, and write, all activities which allegedly suffered as a result of the increased traffic of news and the rapid speed at which it travelled. Speed—or 'hurry', as the editor put it—was the hallmark of modern life and of daily journalism. Some of the consequences of this 'evil of no small magnitude' were errors and the poor quality of editorial writing. This complaint is certainly not unfamiliar to twenty-first-century commentators, who grapple themselves with the transformations in life and work routines which have resulted from the use of the internet.

Accounts like these reflect the wide range of experiences and opinions relating to telegraphy in the nineteenth century. The telegraph was an imperial tool, but it was also a convenient mode of communication for merchants, traders, speculators, as well as the general public, journalists, and nationalist leaders. This included a 'techno-scepticist' leader like Gandhi, whose writings are peppered with references to this medium of communication. Reactions to and practices of technology were highly contextual, shaped by the socio-economic and political circumstances of various categories of actors. Think, for example, of Govind Narayan, whose account of mid-nineteenth-century Bombay described the telegraph as a 'truly remarkable method [of transmission]', emphasizing its importance for the commercial undertakings of Parsi businessmen. But Narayan was no naive commentator on the benefits of technology, as his remark about the inextricable connection between telegraphy and imperial rule soon reminds us: 'How can one not be stunned by the manner of the English people in running their Empire!'[1]

Similarly, Gandhi was well aware of how Reuter telegrams could be used to manipulate public opinion, especially after he was himself 'almost lynched' in Durban in 1896 as a result of a contentious Reuter telegram which brought his *Green Pamphlet* to the attention of the public in Natal. As Gandhi put it, 'This [Reuter] cable was not longer than three lines in print. It was a miniature, but exaggerated, edition of the picture I had drawn of the treatment accorded to the Indians in Natal, and *it was not in my words*.'[2] The topic of reporting and misreporting by telegraph is one which has also received attention in this study, most conspicuously in the analysis of war news undertaken in Chapter 5.

Throughout the book, I have also tried not to lose sight of the materiality of technology and the role of human actors in processes of technology use. While it was beyond the scope of this study to revisit what is a familiar and by now worn-out debate about the relationship between signs or 'signifiers' and material reality, I nevertheless would like to reiterate my conviction that the call for a return to 'things' and the 'material stuff of life', often voiced in the aftermath of the linguistic turn, has been particularly relevant for how we study the history of technology.[3]

In the specific context of the history of telegraphy, this approach has translated, in the course of the last decade, into a growing interest in cables, instruments, and engineering equipment such as grapnels and jointing boxes.[4] It is indeed possible to *see* samples of the Red Sea Cable, not only to *read* about it. Among the items displayed at the Porthcurno Telegraph Museum, a well-known telegraph station in Cornwall where the line from Bombay was landed in 1870, is a presentation case containing samples of the cable. Thus, while I agree with Roland Wenzlhuemer and other writers that the telegraph 'dematerialized' communication by separating the message from its material substratum during the process of transmission, in this book I have also aimed to emphasize the human and material dimensions of telegraphy which were inscribed in various media such as cables, telegraphic instruments, and telegrams.[5]

Indeed, one such substratum was represented by the telegrams published in nineteenth-century newspapers which, as Chapter 5 has discussed in more detail, offered a unique opportunity to investigate not only the practices of telegraphy, but also the development of journalism more generally. This chapter reconstructed the patterns of use of telegraphy from a different and previously little-explored angle, examining actual instances of telegraphic and overland news reporting in a selection of English-language newspapers published in nineteenth-century India. The discussion identified certain trends in the evolution of journalism during this period—for example, the gradual move from a four-page format to an eight-page format in the 1880s—highlighting the complementarity of technologies of communication, the types of communications they facilitated and how their content was shaped by imperial and commercial imperatives, as well as the practices of reading engendered by these methods of communication. Telegrams and letters, as some scholars aptly suggest, occupied different 'niches' in the communication system: while the former provided short, concise accounts of events, it was the latter which filled the news narrative with detail, occasionally dissipating the confusion created by hastily sent telegraphic reports.[6] Journalists and readers often complained about the 'unsatisfactory' state of communication, but they also proved extremely adept at navigating communication gaps and reading across sources and genres of news.

There are, of course, obvious differences between a cable displayed in a museum and one submerged in the Indian Ocean and regularly used for the transmission of messages. It is here that context and relations become particularly important. In this study I have tried to pay attention to some of the engineering minutiae of telegraphy, and to show how the technical characteristics of the medium shaped processes of communication and, to a certain extent, the form and content of the message. But I also follow Samer Faraj and Bijan Azad in arguing that the materiality of technology needs to be understood relationally.[7] In other words, materiality is not, in and by itself, sufficient to understand the complexity of telegraphic practices and discourses in colonial South Asia (or anywhere in the world, for that matter). We also need to pay attention to individual experiences and the social conditions which shaped the use of technology.

The emphasis on the materiality and practices of technology as well as the human actors involved therein is important for an additional reason. As Greg Downey has pertinently observed with regard to the internet, 'Paradoxically, the more the Internet grows in scale and scope, the more its virtual attractions obscure its physical foundation.'[8] In making this argument, Downey's particular agenda was to draw attention to the invisibility of human actors in information networks. His own study of telegraph messenger boys in the United States is an excellent example of how scholars can render such actors more 'visible' by writing a history of telegraphy which brings the issue of 'labour' to the forefront of the investigation.[9] Undoubtedly, this is one line of research which deserves more attention in the case of colonial South Asia. D. K. Lahiri Choudhury has set a valuable precedent with his study of the Indian telegraph strike of 1908, but there were many other actors—engineers, artificers, and so on—without whose work neither the construction nor the functioning of the telegraph network would have been possible.[10]

The book has also emphasized the ways in which access to information in nineteenth-century India was shaped by the imperatives of colonial rule, especially as far as political, military, and commercial intelligence was concerned (see Chapter 4). Here, the analysis was organized around the colonial government's attempts to centralize and control the flow of official intelligence to the newspaper press, and the tension between two equally powerful visions of news: one which regarded political and military intelligence as a 'public good' which should be supplied for free to the newspaper press, and the other which argued that news was a commodity for which the press had to pay by subscribing to Reuters or hiring its own correspondents.

Access to intelligence was marked by a number of colonial hierarchies, for example, the selective grant of postal privileges, the withdrawal of patronage in the form of subscriptions and advertising, the decision to deny newspapers access to information at discounted press rates, the non-recognition of vernacular languages as valid languages of communication, or indeed, the colonial state's conscious policy of supporting Reuters in its attempts to become the 'news agency of the British Empire' at the expense of other initiatives for distributing news. For the newspapers that could not afford Reuter's costly services and were overwhelmed by competition even on the domestic news market, dominated by journals such as the *Pioneer*, the *Englishman*, and the *Statesman*, the only solution available was to organize an independent news agency. One such example comes from Ceylon, where in 1887 the *Colombo Observer* and the *Ceylon Times* discontinued their subscription to Reuters and formed the Ceylon Associated Press. The plan was to appoint an agent in Madras who would provide them with Reuter telegrams published in the *Madras Mail* and the *Madras Times*. The editor of the former newspaper professed his relief that the example had not been followed in India, describing this method of obtaining news as 'undignified' and 'unjust to Reuter's Telegram Company, and to the subscribers to the Eastern Press service'.[11] But only a decade later, in 1899, K. C. Roy made a similar attempt to establish an alternative news agency. This was modelled after the Associated Press of New York and was known as the Associated Press of India. Replicating a familiar scenario, it too succumbed to Reuter's expansionist designs in the aftermath of World War I, after undergoing a merger with Everard Cotes's Indian News Agency in 1914.[12]

As analysis of the coverage of the Austro-Prussian War and of the Poona murders has shown, one important aspect of telegraphy was that it made it easier for newspapers, especially those which could afford to subscribe to Reuter's services, to share identical or highly similar content. It can be said, therefore, that the use of telegraphy promoted the standardization of news content for the English-language newspapers examined in this context. In the interest of academic transparency, it must be mentioned that the findings in this book are circumscribed by the lack of an extensive reading of vernacular newspapers. It is true that the rise of daily journalism in Indian languages is a phenomenon associated with the first decades of the twentieth century, but as a future line of inquiry, it would certainly be beneficial to weigh these findings against an analysis of the news reporting practices of vernacular newspapers. Ulrike

Stark's discussion of the *Avadh Akhbar* has already provided fascinating insights into the particular vision of journalism of Munshi Naval Kishore, highlighting his interest in the publication of news and his different approach to advertising, which led to the publication of news on the front page of his newspaper and of advertisements on the inside pages, as opposed to the practice of most of the English-language newspapers examined here.[13] My own reading of selected issues of *Bharat Jiwan* also suggests some of the ways in which reporting in this vernacular newspaper overlapped with or departed from the conventions of English-language journalism, for example in the absence of a telegraphic format in news reporting, and the practice of mixing domestic and international news rather than relegating them to distinct sections of the newspaper.

Many of the asymmetries in communication described in this book have persisted long after the demise of colonialism. For example, in 1986, Somnath Sapru drew attention to the one-sided nature of international news flows and their inherent bias in reporting about developing countries: 'The complaint of most of the former colonies, now loosely grouped together as the Third World, is that though they represent two-thirds of the world's population and area, events concerning the West get the major news coverage, and whatever they see of themselves in the First World media is mainly as part of disasters, coups, epidemics and the like.'[14] As far as international news coverage is concerned, the story does not appear to be very different three decades later. In a recent study of English-language newspapers in India which focused on the *Times of India*, the *Hindu*, and the *Hindustan Times*, Kapil Arya concluded that although there were differences between the newspapers examined, they were still highly dependent on Reuters and the Associated Press for their supply of foreign news matter. Even more intriguing, in light of the present study, is his conclusion that, 'The results of the analysis demonstrate that a large number of world stories published in the three newspapers are near complete replications of the agency wire copy.'[15]

This is not to say, however, that journalism in India has not undergone significant changes in the post-independence period. Indeed, as Robin Jeffrey has pointed out in his pioneering work on the Indian-language press, increasing literacy, improved technologies of printing and communication, and gradual commercialization through advertising, especially in the aftermath of the economic liberalization of the 1990s, has significantly enlarged participation in the public sphere.[16] This has been reflected, among other things, in a visible proliferation of vernacular newspapers, community media, and the emergence of numerous online media platforms which provide an outlet for a variety of alternative voices and types of journalism.[17]

Against this background, one question that has driven the writing of this book is how to write an account of the use of telegraphy in journalism in colonial India which captures the complexity of human interactions with technology and balances 'big' and 'small' history, avoiding the uncritical repetition of more or less familiar 'grand narratives' of communication and its media. The task was all the more intriguing since the few references to this subject I was able to identify in previous literature seemed to reproduce exactly the tropes I was trying to question about the ability of technologies of communication—in this case, the electric telegraph—to generate not only media 'revolutions', but also, more problematically in my opinion, to act as instruments of democracy or nation-building, for example by facilitating participation in public debates and helping to create a 'consensus of opinion' among various sections of the public. From this perspective, the importance of this study also stems from the historical insights it offers into a debate which continues to be relevant in the contemporary context. I was recently reminded of this when, in the process of writing the concluding paragraphs of this book, my attention was drawn to Nissim Mannathukkaren's ominously titled piece 'The Grand Delusion of Digital India', which takes issue with how we think about technology and the role it has played in imaginations of modernity:

> A glib modernity has perpetrated the belief that technology can bring about the liberation of human beings. Therefore, it is not surprising that the post-colonial history of colonised nations is also largely a history of this unrealisable fantasy. Digital India is the latest enchantment. The irony is that what goes missing in the search of a 'technological fix' is human beings themselves. What should worry us is not the digital divide, but the fundamental divide between a rapidly growing technological capability and a snail-like growth in eliminating human deprivation.[18]

Nobody would deny, I think, that technology changes the way we live and interact with each other. In the field of contemporary journalism, such developments have long been the subject of popular and scholarly debate. Focusing on the scenario in nineteenth-century India, this book has argued that the introduction and use of the telegraph in the Indian subcontinent during this period was piece-meal and gradual, shaped by the political and economic imperatives of the colonial state, market trends, personal interests, the gradual development of scientific knowledge, and even by the vagaries of the natural environment. In this respect, I can but reiterate Biswajit Das's observation that subscribing to the 'ideological euphoria' of media revolutions and other such grand narratives is 'essentially a mirage, if not a complete denial, of the political'.[19] It might be that some of the messages disseminated by contemporary media outlets are (or remain) as similar across geographical divides as they used to be in the nineteenth century, but our responses to them also continue to be shaped by the specific socio-economic and political environments in which our lives unfold.

Notes

1. M. Ranganathan (trans.), *Govind Narayan's Mumbai: An Urban Biography from 1863* (London and New York: Anthem Press, 2008), pp. 189, 205.
2. M. K. Gandhi, *An Autobiography, or the Story of My Experiments with Truth* (1927; reprint, Ahmedabad: Navajivan Trust, 1998), p. 8; emphasis added.
3. For example, Frank Trentmann, 'Materiality in the Future of History: Things, Practices, and Politics', *Journal of British Studies* 48 no. 2 (2009): 283–307. See also Daniel Miller's anthropological study of material culture in Daniel Miller, *Stuff* (Cambridge: Polity Press, 2010).
4. A jointing box contained the tools necessary to join cables together, and was used in the process of laying the cable.
5. Roland Wenzlhuemer, *Connecting the Nineteenth-Century World: The Telegraph and Globalization* (Cambridge: Cambridge University Press 2012), pp. 30–6.
6. For example, see Richard B. Kielbowicz, 'News Gathering by Mail in the Age of the Telegraph: Adapting to a New Technology', *Technology and Culture* 28, no. 1 (1987): 26–41.
7. Samer Faraj and Bijan Azad, 'The Materiality of Technology: An Affordance Perspective', in *Materiality and Organizing: Social Interaction in a Technological World*, edited by P. M. Leonardi, B. A. Nardi, and J. Kallinikos (Oxford: Oxford University Press, 2012).
8. Gregory J. Downey, 'Virtual Webs, Physical Technologies and Hidden Workers: The Spaces of Labor in Information Networks', *Technology and Culture* 42, no. 2 (2001): 209–35, at 211.

9. Gregory J. Downey, *Telegraph Messenger Boys: Labor, Communication, and Technology, 1850–1950* (London and New York: Routledge, 2002).
10. D. K. Lahiri Choudhury, *Telegraphic Imperialism: Crisis and Panic in the Indian Empire, c.1830* (Basingstoke: Palgrave Macmillan, 2010), pp. 157–78.
11. *Times of India*, 5 January 1888.
12. G. N. S. Raghavan, *PTI Story: Origin and Growth of the Indian Press and the News Agency* (Bombay: Press Trust of India, 1987), pp. 54–5.
13. Ulrike Stark, *An Empire of Books: The Naval Kishore Press and the Diffusion of the Printed Word in Colonial India* (New Delhi: Permanent Black, 2009).
14. Somnath Sapru, *The News Merchants: How They Sell News to the Third World* (New Delhi: Dialogue Publications, 1986), p. 2.
15. Kapil Arya, 'The Over-Dependence of Indian English Language Newspapers on Global News Agencies for International News', MA Dissertation, University of Leeds, 2011, p. 2.
16. Robin Jeffrey, *India's Newspaper Revolution: Capitalism, Politics and the Indian-Language Press, 1977–99* (London: C. Hurst & Co., 2000).
17. On community radio, see V. Pavarala and Kanchan K. Malik, *Other Voices: The Struggle for Community Radio in India* (London and New Delhi: Sage Publications, 2007).
18. Nissim Mannathukkaren, 'The Grand Delusion of Digital India', *Hindu*, 10 October 2015.
19. Biswajit Das, 'The Quest for Theory: Mapping Communication Studies in India', in *Media and Mediation*, vol. 1, edited by Bernard Bel, Jan Brouwer, Biswajit Das, Vibodh Parthasarathi, and Guy Poitevin (New Delhi: Sage Publications India, 2005), p. 23.

GLOSSARY

akhbarat	Mughal newsletters
banghy	parcel post
bania	merchant
bunder	Persian for port
chowkidar	watchman
cossid	courier, runner
dak	post
dewan	financial administrator
durbar	imperial assembly
harkara	runner
jagir	here, lands granted to the British in present-day Tamil Nadu; a grant of land which conferred upon the grantee the right to collect revenue
jemadar	chief peon
jiv	soul, life
kabūtar bāzī	pigeon rearing and racing
khansama	butler, steward, cook
lascar	here, common soldier
mahajan	merchant
maund	unit of weight measurement, usually equivalent to 40 *seer*
munshi	secretary, writer
munsif	Indian civil judge
Pindari	here, marauder
punkha	fan

seer	unit of weight, usually equivalent to 80 *tola*s
shikaree	hunter, sportsman
sircar	here, house steward
sowar	here, line rider
tahsildar	revenue officer
tārsār	gist of telegrams
tindal	petty officer
tola	unit of weight equivalent to approximately 0.4 ounces
vigyāpan	advertisement
zamindar	landlord

SELECT BIBLIOGRAPHY

Official and Institutional Records

National Archives of India (NAI), New Delhi

Foreign Department External Branch Files.
Foreign Department General Branch Files.
Foreign Department Internal Branch Files.
Foreign Department Political Branch Files.
Foreign Department Secret Branch Files.
Home Department Public Branch Proceedings.

Nehru Memorial Museum and Library, New Delhi

Native Newspaper Reports, 1896–7, for the North-Western Provinces and Oudh.

Oriental and India Office Collections, British Library (IOR), London

Board of Control Records (F).
East India Company: General Correspondence (Bombay and Madras Despatches E/4).
Indian States Residencies Records (R/2).
Native Newspaper Reports, various years 1879–90, for Bengal (L/R/5/5–16).

Proceedings and Consultations (India Telegraph Consultations P/189).
Public and Judicial Department Records (L/P&J).
Public Works Department Files (L/PWD).

Reuters Archives (RA), London

Administration Files.
Editorial Files.
History Files.
Legal Files.
Staff Files.

British Postal Museum and Archive (BPMA), London

Packet Minute Series (POST/29).

Private Papers

Oriental and India Office Collections, British Library, London

Papers of Sir Owen Tudor Burne (1870–7). Mss Eur D951.
Papers of Sir Roper Lethbridge (1874–1914). Mss Eur B182.
Papers of William Digby (1889–1904). Mss Eur D767.

Official Publications

Abstract of the Proceedings of the Council of the Governor-General of India, Assembled for the Purpose of Making Laws and Regulations, 1865, vol. 4. Calcutta: Military Orphan Press, 1866.

Administration Report of the Indo-European Telegraph Department, 1897–8. London: Eyre and Spottiswoode, 1898.

Administration Reports of the Indian Telegraph Department, 1855–1905, V/24/4282–4288, IOR.

Annual Report of the Post Office of India for the Year 1900–1901. Calcutta: Superintendent of Government Printing, 1901.

The Gazetteer of Bombay City and Island, 3 vols. Bombay: Times Press, 1909–10.

Government Indo-European Telegraph Department. *The Tariff of Rates for Messages between Any Telegraph Station, etc.* Bombay: Times of India, 1865.

Grant, A. *Catalogue of Native Publications in the Bombay Presidency up to 31st December 1864.* Bombay: Education Society's Press, 1867.

The Imperial Gazetteer of India, vol. 3: *Economic.* Oxford: Clarendon Press, 1908.

The Imperial Gazetteer of India, vol. 4: *Administrative*. Oxford: Clarendon Press, 1909.

Indian Postal Guide, August 1897. Calcutta: Office of the Superintendent of Government Printing, 1897.

Indian Postal Guide, July 1900. Calcutta: Superintendent of Government Printing, 1900.

Long, Rev. James. 'Returns Relating to Native Printing Presses and Publications in Bengal; and A Return of the Names and Writings of 515 Persons Connected with Bengali Literature, Either as Authors or Translators of Printed Works. Chiefly during the Last Fifty Years; And a Catalogue of Bengali Newspapers and Periodicals Which Have Issued from the Press from the Year 1818 to 1855'. In *Selections from the Records of the Bengal Government*, no. 22. Calcutta: 'Calcutta Gazette' Office, 1855.

———. 'Returns Relating to the Publications in the Bengali Language, in 1857, to which is added, a list of the Native Presses, with the Books Printed at Each, their Price and Character, with a Notice of the Past Condition and Future Prospects of the Vernacular Press of Bengal, and the Statistics of the Bombay and Madras Vernacular Presses'. In *Selections from the Records of the Bengal Government*, no. 32. Calcutta: General Printing Department, 1859.

The New Postage Act (XVII of 1854-Rules, etc.). 1855.

O'Shaughnessy, William B. *Report on the Electric Telegraph between Calcutta and Kedgeree*. Calcutta: Military Orphan Press, 1852.

Report of the Commissioners for Post Office Enquiry, with Appendixes. Calcutta: Military Orphan Press, 1851.

Statement Exhibiting the Moral and Material Progress and Condition of India during the Year 1860–61, Part I. London: George Edward Eyre and William Spottiswoode, 1862.

Statement Exhibiting the Moral and Material Progress and Condition of India during the Year 1898–1899. London: Eyre and Spottiswoode, 1900.

Statement Exhibiting the Moral and Material Progress and Condition of India during the Year 1899–1900. London: Eyre and Spottiswoode, 1901.

Telegraphic Phrase-Code for Indian Field Post Offices, 3rd edn. Lahore: Tribune Press, 1904.

United Kingdom, Parliament, House of Commons. *Copy of Two Memorials to the Governor General from the Commercial Communities of Calcutta and Bombay, on the Subject of Telegraphic Communication, together with Other Despatches and Papers on the Same Subject*. London, 1868.

———. *East India (Native Press). Copy of Opinions, and Reasons for the Same, Entered in the Minutes of Proceedings of the Council of India, Relating to the Vernacular Press Act, 1878*. London, 1878.

———. *East India (Press): Papers Relating to the Public Press in India*. London, 1858.

———. *Report by the Commission Appointed to Inquire into Postal Communication in India*. London, 1852.
———. *Report from the Select Committee on Steam Navigation to India*. London, 1834.
———. *Report from the Select Committee on East India Communications*. London, 1866.

Publications of Other Organizations

Blumhardt, J. F. *Catalogue of Hindustani Printed Books in the Library of the British Museum*. London: Longmans and Co., 1889.
Half-Yearly Reports of the Committee of the Bengal Chamber of Commerce, 1854–69.
Reports of the Bombay Chamber of Commerce, 1864–95.

Newspapers and Periodical Publications

Allen's Indian News, Poona. British Library.
Amrita Bazar Patrika, Calcutta. British Library.
Asiatic Journal and Monthly Register, London. Hathi Trust Digital Library.
Asiatic Mirror and Commercial Advertiser, Calcutta. British Library.
Bangalore Herald. British Library.
Bengalee, Calcutta. British Library.
Bengal Hurkaru, Calcutta. British Library.
Bharat Jiwan, Benares. Nehru Memorial Museum and Library.
Bombay Builder. British Library.
Bombay Gazette. British Library.
Bombay Telegraph and Courier. British Library.
Bombay Times and Journal of Commerce. British Library.
Calcutta Courier. British Library.
Calcutta Friday Morning Post and Advertiser. British Library.
Calcutta Journal of Politics and General Literature. British Periodicals Database.
Calcutta Review. British Periodicals Database.
Ceylon Herald. British Library.
Chambers's Journal of Popular Literature, Science and Arts, London. *British Periodicals* Database.
Dacca News. British Library.
Delhi Gazette. British Library; Nehru Memorial Museum and Library.
Denshin kyōkai kaishi, Tokyo. Meiji Shinbun Zasshi Bunko (Meiji Newspaper and Periodical Archives), University of Tokyo.
Englishman, Calcutta. British Library; Nehru Memorial Museum and Library.

Government Gazette Extraordinary. British Library.
The Hills, Mussoorie. British Library.
Hindoo Patriot, Calcutta. British Library.
Illustrated London News. Illustrated London News Historical Archive (1842–2003).
Indian Engineer, Calcutta. British Library.
Japan Gazette, Yokohama. Hitotsubashi University Library.
Japan Punch, Yokohama. Hitotsubashi University Library.
Japan Times, Yokohama. Meiji Shinbun Zasshi Bunko, University of Tokyo.
Kandahar News. British Library.
Lahore Chronicle. British Library.
Leisure Hour, London. *British Periodicals* Database.
Madras Government Gazette. British Library.
Madras Times. British Library; Nehru Memorial Museum and Library.
Manufacturer and Builder, New York. Hathi Trust Digital Library.
National Budget and Vernacular Reporter, Calcutta. British Library.
Oriental Herald and Journal of General Literature, Calcutta. *British Periodicals* Database.
Oriental Star, Calcutta. British Library.
The Phoenix, Calcutta. British Library.
Pioneer, Allahabad. British Library.
Reis and Rayyet, Calcutta. British Library.
Shree Venkateshwar Samachar, Bombay. British Library.
Times of India, Bombay. British Library.
Yokohama Mainichi Shimbun. Meiji Shinbun Zasshi Bunko, University of Tokyo.

Books and Articles up to 1900

Acworth, William. 'The South-Eastern and the Chatham Railways'. *Murray's Magazine* 4 (1888): 209–25.
Adams, M., comp. *Memoir of Surgeon-Major Sir W. O'Shaughnessy Brooke, in Connection with the Early History of the Telegraph in India.* Simla: Government Central Printing Office, 1889.
Adley, Charles C. *The Story of the Telegraph in India.* London: E. & F. N. Spon, 1866.
Anderson, James. 'Statistics of Telegraphy'. *Journal of the Statistical Society of London* 35 (1872): 272–326.
Anon. *Lightning Flashes and Electric Dashes: A Volume of Choice Telegraphic Literature, Humor, Fun, Wit & Wisdom.* New York: W. J. Johnston, 1877.
———. 'Sixty Years of the *Times of India*'. *Calcutta Review* 108 (1899): 86–104.
———. 'Speculation Mania'. *Examiner* 907 (1825): 383–4.

———. 'The Romance of the Electric Telegraph'. *New Monthly Magazine and Humorist* 89 (1850): 296–307.
———. 'The Three Great Indian Physicians; Or, Railways, Canals, and Telegraphs'. *Leisure Hour* 147 (1854): 663–6.
Atkinson, G. F. *'Curry & Rice', on Forty Plates*. London: Day & Son, 1859(?).
Babbage, Charles. *On the Economy of Machinery and Manufactures*. London: Charles Knight, 1832.
Barber, James. *The Overland Guide-Book: A Complete Vade-Mecum for the Overland Traveller*. London: Wm. H. Allen and Co., 1845.
Bilgrami, S. H. *A Memoir of Sir Salar Jung*. Bombay: Times of India Steam Press, 1883.
Blanchard, Sidney L. *Yesterday and To-day in India*. London: Wm. H. Allen & Co., 1867.
Bradshaw's Railway & c. through Route and Overland Guide to India. London: W. J. Adam, 1858.
Bright, Charles. *Submarine Telegraphs: Their History, Construction, and Working*. London: Crosby Lockwood and Son, 1898.
Calendar of Mail Steamer Departures from Bombay, etc. Calcutta, 1873.
Chatterjee, Bankim Chandra. *The Poison Tree: A Tale of Hindu Life in Bengal*, translated by Miriam S. Knight. London: T. Fisher Unwin, 1884.
Chesney, G. M. 'The Native Press in India'. *Nineteenth Century: A Monthly Review* 43 (1898): 266–76.
Cooper, F. H. *The Handbook for Delhi*. Lahore: Lahore Chronicle Press, 1865.
Cotton, A. *Public Works in India: Their Importance*. London: W. H. Allen, 1854.
Crowe, Joseph Archer. *Reminiscences of Thirty-Five Years of My Life*. London: John Murray, 1895.
De Pontevès-Sabran, Jean. *L'Inde à fond de train*. Paris: Alphonse Lemerre, 1887.
Digby, W. M. 'The Native Newspapers of India and Ceylon'. *Calcutta Review* 65 (1877): 356–94.
Dodd, George. *Railways, Steamers and Telegraphs*. London and Edinburgh: W. & R. Chambers, 1867.
East India Company Library: A Catalogue of the Library of the Hon. East-India Company. London: J. & H. Cox, 1845.
Eliot, John. *Handbook of the Cyclonic Storms in the Bay of Bengal for the Use of Sailors*. Calcutta: Superintendent of Government Printing, 1890.
[Fenton, A.]. *Memoirs of a Cadet*. London: Saunders and Otley, 1839.
FitzGerald, William G. 'The Romance of Our News Supply'. *Strand Magazine* 10 (1895): 69–79.

Forbes, Archibald. 'War Correspondents and the Authorities'. *Nineteenth Century: A Monthly Review* 7 (1880): 185–96.

Goldsmith, F. J. *Telegraph and Travel: A Narrative of the Formation and Development of Telegraphic Communication between England and India, etc.* London: Macmillan, 1874.

Harlow, A. F. *Old Wires and New Waves: The History of the Telegraph, Telephone and Wireless*. New York and London: D. Appleton-Century Company, 1936.

Harris, Mrs James P. *A Lady's Diary of the Siege of Lucknow, Written for the Perusal of Friends at Home*. London: John Murray, 1858.

Highton, E. *The Electric Telegraph: Its History and Progress*. London, 1852.

The History of the Nil Durpan, with the State Trial of the Reverend J. Long, etc. Calcutta, 30 July 1861.

Karaka, Dosabhai F. *History of the Parsis: Including Their Manners, Customs, Religion, and Present Position*, vol. 1. London: Macmillan and Co., 1884.

Karkaria, R. P. *India, Forty Years of Progress and Reform: Being A Sketch of the Life and Times of Behramji M. Malabari*. London: Henry Frowde, 1896.

———. 'The Oldest Paper in India: The *Bombay Samachar*'. *Calcutta Review* 106 (1898): 218–36.

———. 'The Revival of the Native Press of Western India: The *Rast Goftar*'. *Calcutta Review* 107 (1898): 226–43.

King, Mrs Robert Moss. *The Diary of a Civilian's Wife in India, 1877–1882*, vol. 1. London: Bentley and Son, 1884.

Knies, Karl. *Der Telegraph als Verkehrsmittel* [The telegraph as a means of communication]. Tübingen: Laupp & Siebeck, 1857 (in German).

Knighton, William. *Tropical Sketches; Or, Reminiscences of an Indian Journalist*, vol. 1. London: Hurst and Blackett, 1855.

Lardner, Dionysius. *The Electric Telegraph Popularized*. London: Walton and Maberly, 1855.

La Beaume, Michael. *On Galvanism, with Observations on Its Chymical Properties and Medical Effi cacy in Chronic Diseases*. London: Highley, 1826.

Lethbridge, Roper. 'The Vernacular Press in India'. *Contemporary Review* 37 (1880): 459–73.

Lloyd's List, 1753 & 1755. Westmead, UK: Gregg International Publishers, 1969.

Long, J. *A Descriptive Catalogue of Bengali Works, Containing a Classified List of Fourteen Hundred Bengali Books and Pamphlets, etc.* Calcutta: Sanders, Cones, and Co., 1855.

[Long, J.]. 'Early Bengali Literature and Newspapers'. *Calcutta Review* 13 (1850): 124–61.

Low, Sidney J. 'Newspaper Copyright'. *National Review* 19 (1892): 648–66.

Luke, P. V. 'How the Electric Telegraph Saved India'. *Macmillan's Magazine* 76 (1897): 401–6.

Lynn, Thomas. *An Improved System of Telegraphic Communication*. London: Cox and Baylis, 1814.

Macdonald, John. *A Treatise Explanatory of a New System of Naval, Military and Political Telegraphic Communication*. 1808. Reprint, London: T. Egerton's Military Library, 1817.

Macintosh, Charles A. *Popular Outlines of the Press, Ancient and Modern*. London: Wertheim, Macintosh, and Hunt, 1859.

Mackenzie, A. R. D. *Mutiny Memoirs: Being Personal Reminiscences of the Great Sepoy Revolt of 1857*. Allahabad: Pioneer Press, 1892.

Maitra, Kalidas. *The Electric Telegraph or The Telegraph Office Assistant's Manual*. Serampore: Tomohur Press, 1855.

Malcolm, John. *The Government of India*. London: John Murray, 1833.

M'Gregor, W. L. *The History of the Sikhs*, vol. 1. London: James Meaden, 1846.

Mountain, Mrs Armine S. H., ed. *Memoirs and Letters of the Late Colonel Armine S. H. Mountain, C.B., Aide-de-Camp to the Queen and Adjutant-General of Her Majesty's Forces in India*. London: Longman, Brown, Green, Longmans & Roberts, 1858.

Nikambe, Shevantibai M. *Ratanbai: A Sketch of a Bombay High Caste Hindu Young Wife*. London: Marshall Brothers, 1895.

Nowrojee, Jehangir, and Hirjibhoy Merwanjee. *Journal of a Residence of Two Years and a Half in Great Britain*. London: Wm. H. Allen & Co., 1841.

O'Shaughnessy, William B. *The Electric Telegraph in British India: A Manual of Instructions for the Subordinate Officers, Artificers, and Signallers Employed in the Department*. London, 1853.

Osman, A. H. 'Pigeons as Messengers of War'. *Strand Magazine* 19 (1900): 160–4.

Pasley, C. W. *Description of the Universal Telegraph for Day and Night Signals*. London: T. Egerton, 1823.

Pearce, R. R. *Memoirs and Correspondence of the Most Noble Richard Marquess of Wellesley*, vol. 1. London: Richard Bentley, 1846.

Pebody, Charles. *English Journalism and the Men Who Have Made It*. London: Cassell, Petter, Galpin & Co., 1882.

Plomer, Henry R. *A Short History of English Printing, 1476–1898*. London: Kegan Paul, Trench, Truebner & Co., 1900.

Porter, H. W. 'On the Influence of Railway Travelling on Public Health'. *Assurance Magazine, and Journal of the Institute of Actuaries* 11 (1863): 152–71.

Possmann, Julius. *Official History of the Persian Gulf Telegraph Cables Compiled under Instructions from the Director General of Telegraphs*. Karachi: Mercantile Press, 1889.

Quekett, W. 'The History and Progress of a Post-Letter from a Rag to India'. In *Warrington Church Institute Lectures*. Warrington: Guardian Office, 1854.

Ratnagar, N. J. *Short Essays on Literary and Social Subjects for Matriculation Candidates and Others*. Bombay: Jehangir Karani, 1879.

Russell, William Howard. *My Diary in India, in the Year 1858–9*. London: Routledge, Warne & Routledge, 1860.

Sanyal, Ram Gopal. *The Life of the Hon'ble Rai Kristo Das Pal Bahadur, C.I.E.* Calcutta: Bengalee Press, 1886.

Schwendler, Louis. 'On the General Theory of Duplex Telegraphy'. *Journal of the Asiatic Society of Bengal* 43 (1874): 1–21.

Shearman, R. M. *Copy of a Plan for a Day and Night Telegraph, and Proposed for General Communication of Intelligence throughout India*. London: T. Jones, 1807(?).

Sinclair, Alexander. *Fifty Years of Newspaper Life, 1845–1895*. Glasgow: privately printed, c. 1898.

Skrine, F. H. *An Indian Journalist: Being the Life, Letters and Correspondence of Dr. Sambhu C. Mookerjee*. Calcutta: Thacker, Spink & Co., 1895.

Souvenir of the Inaugural Fete [Held at the House of Mr. John Pender] in Commemoration of the Opening of Direct Submarine Telegraph with India, June 23rd 1870. London, 1870.

Steel, Flora Annie. *On the Face of the Waters*. London: William Heinemann, 1897.

Steele, Thomas. *An Eastern Love-Story: Kusa Jātakaya, a Buddhistic Legend.* London: Truebner & Co., 1871.

Stocqueler, J. H. *The Memoirs of a Journalist*. Bombay: Times of India, 1873.

Street's Indian and Colonial Mercantile Directory for 1869. London: G. Street, 1869.

Thom, Charles, and W. H. Jones. *Telegraphic Connections: Embracing Recent Methods in Quadruplex Telegraphy*. New York: D. van Nostrand Company, 1892.

Tyler, H. W. 'Routes of Communication with India'. *Journal of the Royal United Service Institution* 10 (1867): 276–88.

Waghorn, T. Comyns. 'The Pioneer of the Overland Route to India and Australasia'. *Once a Month: An Illustrated Australasian Magazine*, 3 (1885): 204–8.

Wheeler, S. 'The Indian Native Press'. *Macmillan's Magazine* 58 (1888): 377–84.

Wright, Arnold. *Baboo English as 'Tis Writ: Being Curiosities of Indian Journalism*. London: T. Fisher Unwin, 1892.

Books and Articles since 1900

Adas, Michael. *Machines as the Measure of Men: Science, Technology, and Ideologies of Western Dominance*. Ithaca and London: Cornell University Press, 1989.

———. 'Twentieth-Century Approaches to the Indian Mutiny of 1857–58'. *Journal of Asian History* 5, no. 1 (1971): 1–19.

Agarwal, Sushila. *Press, Public Opinion and Government in India*. Jaipur: Asha Publishing House, 1970.

Aguiar, Marian. *Tracking Modernity: India's Railway and the Culture of Mobility*. Minneapolis: University of Minnesota Press, 2011.

Ahmed, A. F. Salahuddin. *Social Ideas and Social Change in Bengal, 1818–1835*. Leiden: E. J. Brill, 1965.

Ahuja, Ravi. *Pathways of Empire: Circulation, 'Public Works' and Social Space in Colonial Orissa, c. 1780–1914*. Hyderabad: Orient BlackSwan, 2009.

Anderson, Benedict. *Imagined Communities: Reflections on the Origins and Spread of Nationalism*, 12th edn. London and New York: Verso, 2003.

Anon. 'The Signal Haulyards of the Empire'. *Leisure Hour* (1901): 267–77.

Arnold, David. *Science, Technology and Medicine in Colonial India*. Cambridge: Cambridge University Press, 2004.

Atkins, J. B. *The Life of Sir William Howard Russell, the First Special Correspondent*, 2 vols. London: John Murray, 1911.

Bagchi, A. K., Dipankar Sinha, and Barnita Bagchi, eds. *Webs of History: Information, Communication and Technology from Early to Post-Colonial India*. New Delhi: Institute of Development Studies Kolkata and Manohar, 2005.

Bakshi, S. R., and O. P. Ralhan. *Madhya Pradesh through the Ages*, vol. 2: *Pindaris and Marathas*. New Delhi: Sarup and Sons, 2007.

Bandyopadhyay, Sekhar. *From Plassey to Partition: A History of Modern India*. New Delhi: Orient BlackSwan, 2009.

Banerjea, Surendranath. *A Nation in the Making: Being the Reminiscences of Fifty Years of Public Life*. 1925. Reprint, Calcutta: Oxford University Press, 1963.

Banerjee, Indrajit, ed. *The Internet and Governance in Asia: A Critical Reader*. Singapore: Asian Media Information and Communication Centre, 2007.

Banerjee, T. 'The Growth of the Press in Bengal vis-à-vis the Rise of Indian Nationalism (1858–1905)'. In *The Indian Press*, edited by S. P. Sen, pp. 38–52. Calcutta: Institute of Historical Studies, 1967.

Barnhurst, Kevin G., and John Nerone. *The Form of News: A History*. New York and London: Guilford Press, 2001.

———. 'Journalism History'. In *The Handbook of Journalism Studies*, edited by Karin Wahl-Jorgensen and Thomas Hanitzsch, 17–28. New York and London: Routledge, 2009.

Barns, Margarita. *The Indian Press: A History of the Growth of Public Opinion in India*. London: George Allen & Unwin Ltd, 1940.

Barrier, N. G. 'Punjab Politics and the Press, 1880–1910'. In *Aspects of India: Essays in Honor of Cameron Dimock, Jr.*, edited by M. Case and N. G. Barrier, pp. 118–33. New Delhi: Manohar and American Institute of Indian Studies, 1986.

Barton, Roger N. 'The Birth of Telegraphic News in Britain, 1847–68'. *Media History* 16, no. 4 (2010): 379–406.

Basu, Durga Das. *Law of the Press in India*. New Delhi: Prentice-Hall of India, 1980.

Bayly, C. A. 'Afterword: Bombay's Intertwined Modernities, 1780–1880'. In *Trans-Colonial Modernities in South Asia*, edited by M. S. Dodson and B. A. Hatcher, pp. 231–48. Abingdon: Routledge, 2012.

———. *Empire and Information: Intelligence Gathering and Social Communication in India, 1780–1870*. Cambridge: Cambridge University Press, 1996.

———. 'Knowing the Country: Empire and Information in India'. *Modern Asian Studies* 27, no. 1 (1993): 3–43.

Beauchamp, K. G. *History of Telegraphy: Its Technology and Application*, History of Technology Series, no. 26. London: Institution of Engineering and Technology, 2001.

Bel, Bernard, Jan Brouwer, Biswajit Das, Vibodh Parthasarathi, and Guy Poitevin, eds. *Media and Mediation*, vol. 1. New Delhi: Sage Publications, 2005.

Bell, Allan. 'Text, Time and Technology in News English'. In *Redesigning English*, edited by S. Goodman, D. Graddol, and T. Lillis, pp. 79–112. New York: Routledge, 2007.

Bently, L., and M. Kretschmer, eds. *Primary Sources on Copyright (1450–1900)*. Available at: www.copyrighthistory.org (accessed 26 March 2011).

Bhargava, G. S. *The Press in India: An Overview*. New Delhi: National Book Trust, 2007.

Bhatnagar, R. *The Rise and Growth of Hindi Journalism*. Varanasi: Vishwavidyalaya Prakashan, 2003.

Bhattacharya, D., R. Chakravarty, and R. D. Roy. 'A Survey of Bengali Writing on Science and Technology, 1800–1950'. *Indian Journal of History of Science* 24, no. 1 (1989): 8–66.

Blondheim, Menahem. *News over the Wires: The Telegraph and the Flow of Public Information in America, 1844–1897*. Cambridge, MA: Harvard University Press, 1994.

———. '"Slender Bridges" of Misunderstanding: The Social Legacy of Transatlantic Cable Communications'. In *Atlantic Communications: The Media in American and German History from the Seventeenth to the Twentieth Century*, edited by N. Finzsch and U. Lehmkuhl, pp. 153–69. Oxford and New York: Berg, 2004.

Bond, Brian 'The Austro-Prussian War 1866'. *History Today* 16, no. 6 (1966): 538–546.

Bonea, Amelia. '"All the News That's Fit to Print?" Reuter's Telegraphic News Service in Colonial India'. In *Global Communication Electric: Business, News and Politics in the World of Telegraphy*, edited by M. Michaela

Hampf and Simone Mueller-Pohl, pp. 223–45. Frankfurt: Campus Verlag, 2013.

———. 'The Medium and Its Message: Reporting the Austro-Prussian War in the *Times of India*'. *Historical Social Research* 35, no. 1 (2010): 167–87.

———. 'Telegraphy and Journalism in Colonial India, c. 1830s to 1900s'. *History Compass* 12, no. 5 (2014): 387–97.

Boyce, M. T. *British Policy and the Evolution of the Vernacular Press in India, 1835–1878*. Delhi: Chanakya Publications, 1988.

Brake, Laurel, and Marysa Demoor, eds. *Dictionary of Nineteenth-Century Journalism in Great Britain and Ireland*. Gent and London: Academia Press and the British Library, 2009.

Brooker-Gross, S. R. 'The Changing Concept of Place in the News'. In *Geography, the Media and Popular Culture*, edited by J. Burgess and J. R. Gold, pp. 63–85. New York: St Martin's Press, 1985.

Brown, Lucy. 'The Treatment of News in Mid-Victorian Newspapers'. *Transactions of the Royal Historical Society* 27 (1977): 23–39.

Bucholz, Arden. *Moltke and the German Wars, 1864–1871*. New York: Palgrave, 2001.

Buckland, C. E. *Dictionary of Indian Biography*. London: Swan Sonnenschein & Co., 1906.

Bulley, Anne. *The Bombay Country Ships, 1790–1833*. Richmond, Surrey: Curzon Press, 2000.

Burne, Owen T. *Memories*. London: Edward Arnold, 1907.

Carey, James. *Communication as Culture: Essays on Media and Society*, rev. edn. New York and London: Routledge, 2009.

———. 'The Problem of Journalism History'. In *James Carey: A Critical Reader*, edited by Eve Stryker Munson and Catherine A. Warren, pp. 86–94. Minneapolis and London: University of Minnesota Press, 1997.

Carey, W. H. *The Good Old Days of Honorable John Company: Being Curious Reminiscences Illustrating Manners and Customs of the British in India*, vol. 2. Calcutta: R. Cambray & Co., 1907.

Case, Margaret, and N. Gerald Barrier, eds. *Aspects of India: Essays in Honor of Edward Cameron Dimock, Jr*. New Delhi: Manohar, and American Institute of Indian Studies, 1986.

Castells, Manuel. *Communication Power*. Oxford: Oxford University Press, 2009.

Chakravarty, Sumita S. 'Cultural Studies Legacies: Visiting James Carey's Border Country'. *Cultural Studies—Critical Methodologies* 9, no. 3 (2009): 412–24.

Chanda, M. K. *History of the English Press in Bengal, 1858–1880*. Kolkata: K. P. Bagchi, 2008.

Chandavarkar, R. *Imperial Power and Popular Politics: Class, Resistance and the State in India, c. 1850–1950*. Cambridge: Cambridge University Press, 1998.

Chatterjee, Partha. *The Black Hole of Empire: History of a Global Practice of Power*. Princeton: Princeton University Press, 2012.

———. 'Our Modernity'. SEPHIS/CODESRIA Lecture, 1997. Available at: http://ccs.ukzn.ac.za/files/partha1.pdf (accessed 14 March 2016).

Chaudhuri, Arun. *Indian Advertising, 1780 to 1950 A.D.* New Delhi: Tata McGraw-Hill, 2007.

Clarke, Geoffrey. *The Post Office of India and Its Story.* London: John Lane the Bodley Head, 1921.

Codell, Julie F. 'The Nineteenth-Century News from India'. *Victorian Periodicals Review* 37, no. 2 (2004): 106–23.

Cohn, Bernard S. *Colonialism and Its Forms of Knowledge: The British in India*. Princeton: Princeton University Press, 1996.

Collins, Henry. *From Pigeon Post to Wireless.* London: Hodder and Stoughton, 1925.

Conboy, Martin. *Journalism: A Critical History*. London: Sage Publications, 2004.

Conboy, Martin, and John Steel, eds. *The Routledge Companion to British Media History*. Abingdon: Routledge, 2015.

Darwin, John. *The Empire Project: The Rise and Fall of the British World-System, 1830–1970*. Cambridge: Cambridge University Press, 2009.

Das, Biswajit. 'The Quest for Theory: Mapping Communication Studies in India'. In *Media and Mediation*, vol. 1, edited by Bernard Bel, Jan Brouwer, Biswajit Das, Vibodh Parthasarathi, and Guy Poitevin, pp. 35–65. New Delhi: Sage Publications India, 2005.

Das Gupta, A. C. *The Days of John Company: Selections from Calcutta Gazette, 1824–1832*. Calcutta: West Bengal Government Press, 1959.

Das Gupta, J. B., ed. *Science, Technology, Imperialism and War*, vol. 15, part 1, of D. P. Chattopadhyaya (gen. ed.), *Science, Philosophy and Culture in Indian Civilization*. New Delhi: Pearson Longman, 2007.

Das Gupta, Uma. 'The Indian Press, 1870–1880: A Small World of Journalism'. *Modern Asian Studies* 11, no. 2 (1977): 213–35.

Datta, Utpal. *Girish Chandra Ghosh: Makers of Indian Literature*. New Delhi: Sahitya Akademi, 1992.

Deloche, J. *Transport and Communications in India prior to Steam Locomotion*, vol. 1: *Land Transport*. New Delhi: Oxford University Press, 1993.

Derbyshire, I. D. 'Economic Change and the Railways in North India, 1860–1914'. *Modern Asian Studies* 21, no. 3 (1987): 521–45.

Dewar, Douglas. *Bygone Days in India*. London: John Lane the Bodley Head, 1922.

Dickinson, Emily. *The Complete Poems of Emily Dickinson*, edited by Thomas H. Johnson. Boston: Little, Brown, and Company, 1961.

Dodson, M. S., and B. A. Hatcher (eds). *Trans-Colonial Modernities in South Asia*. Abingdon: Routledge, 2012.

Downey, Gregory J. *Telegraph Messenger Boys: Labor, Communication, and Technology, 1850–1950*. London and New York: Routledge, 2002.

———. 'Virtual Webs, Physical Technologies and Hidden Workers: The Spaces of Labor in Information Networks'. *Technology and Culture* 42, no. 2 (2001): 209–5.

Echenberg, M. *Plague Ports: The Global Urban Impact of Bubonic Plague, 1894–1901*. New York and London: New York University Press, 2007.

Ellsworth, E. W. 'The Austro-Prussian War and the British Press'. *Historian* 20, no. 2 (1958): 179–200.

Elshakry, M., and S. Sivasundaram, eds. *Science, Race and Imperialism*, vol. 6 of *Victorian Science and Literature*, edited by G. Dawson and B. Lightman. London: Pickering & Chatto, 2012.

Elwin, Verrier. *The Agaria*. London: Oxford University Press, 1942.

Evans, Richard B. *In Defence of History*. London: Granta Books, 1997.

Fanshawe, H. C. *Delhi Past and Present*. London: John Murray, 1902.

Faraj, Samer, and Bijan Azad. 'The Materiality of Technology: An Affordance Perspective'. In *Materiality and Organizing: Social Interaction in a Technological World*, edited by P. M. Leonardi, B. A. Nardi, and J. Kallinikos, pp. 237–58. Oxford: Oxford University Press, 2012.

Finzsch, N., and U. Lehmkuhl, eds. *Atlantic Communications: The Media in American and German History from the Seventeenth to the Twentieth Century*. Oxford and New York: Berg Publishers, 2004.

Fisher, Michael H. 'The East India Company's "Suppression of the Native *Dak*"'. *Indian Economic and Social History Review* 31, no. 1 (1994): 311–8.

———. 'The Office of Akhbār Nawīs: The Transition from Mughal to British Forms'. *Modern Asian Studies* 27, no. 1 (1993): 45–2.

Fletcher, Paul. 'The Uses and Limitations of Telegrams in Official Correspondence between Ceylon's Governor General and the Secretary of State for the Colonies, circa 1870–1900'. *Historical Social Research* 35, no. 1 (2010): 90–107.

Frost, Mark R. 'Asia's Maritime Networks and the Colonial Public Sphere, 1840–1920'. *New Zealand Journal of Asian Studies* 6, no. 2 (2004): 63–94.

Frykenberg, R. E., ed. *Christians and Missionaries in India: Cross-cultural Communication since 1500*. Grand Rapids, Michigan: Wm. B. Eerdmans, 2003.

Fuchs, Margot. 'The Indo-European Telegraph System 1868–1931: Politics and Technical Change'. *Berichte zur Wissenschaftsgeschichte* 13, no. 3 (1990): 157–66.

Gaekwar, Sayagi Rao. 'My Ways and Days in Europe and India'. *Nineteenth Century and After* 49, no. 288 (1901): 215–25.

Gandhi, M. K. *An Autobiography, or the Story of My Experiments with Truth*. Ahmedabad: Navajivan Trust, 1998 [1927].

Gardner, Victoria E. M. 'Eighteenth-Century Newspapers and Public Opinion'. In *The Routledge Companion to British Media History*, edited by Martin D. Conboy and John Steel, pp. 195–205. Abingdon: Routledge, 2015.

Ghose, H. P. *The Newspaper in India*. Calcutta: University of Calcutta, 1952.

Ghose, Saroj. 'Commercial Needs and Military Necessities: The Telegraph in India'. In *Technology and the Raj: Western Technology and Technical Transfers to India 1700–1947*, edited by Roy MacLeod and Deepak Kumar, pp. 153–76. New Delhi: Sage Publications, 1995.

Ghosh, Amitabha. 'Some Eminent Indian Pioneers in the Field of Technology'. *Indian Journal of History of Science* 29, no. 1 (1994): 63–75.

Ghosh, Anindita. *Power in Print: Popular Publishing and the Politics of Language and Culture in a Colonial Society, 1778–1905*. New Delhi: Oxford University Press, 2006.

Ghosh, Sunit. *Modern History of Indian Press*. New Delhi: Cosmo, 1998.

Gilmore, P. 'The Telegraph in Black and White'. *English Literary History* 69, no. 3 (2002): 805–33.

Gooday, Graeme. *Domesticating Electricity: Technology, Uncertainty and Gender, 1880–1914*. London: Pickering & Chatto, 2008.

Goodman, Bryna. 'Semi-Colonialism, Transnational Networks, and News Flows in Early Republican Shanghai'. *China Review* 4, no. 1 (2004): 55–88.

Gopal, Madan. *Life and Times of Dyal Singh Majithia*. New Delhi: Uppal Publishing House, 1999.

Gorman, Mel. 'Sir William O'Shaughnessy, Lord Dalhousie and the Establishment of the Telegraph System in India'. *Technology and Culture* 12, no. 4 (1971): 581–601.

Goswami, Manu. *Producing India: From Colonial Economy to National Space*. Chicago: University of Chicago Press, 2004.

Gotō, Shin. 'Indo e no kisen kōtsū no kakuritsu: Igirisu kaiun kigyō P&O no seiritsu ni yosete' [Establishment of steam communication with India: On the formation of the P&O Steam Navigation Company], *Kagawa Daigaku Keizai-Ronsō* 57, no. 3 (1984): 151–73 (in Japanese).

Habib, Irfan. 'Postal Communications in Mughal India'. In *Proceedings of the Indian History Congress, 46th Session*, pp. 236–52. Amritsar: Guru Nanak Dev University, 1985.

Hackett, Edward J. et al. eds. *The Handbook of Science and Technology Studies*. Cambridge, MA: MIT Press, 2008.

Hampf, M. Michaela, and Simone Mueller-Pohl, eds. *Global Communication Electric: Business, News and Politics in the World of Telegraphy*. Frankfurt: Campus Verlag, 2013.

Hampton, Mark. 'The "Objectivity" Ideal and Its Limitations in 20th-Century British Journalism'. *Journalism Studies* 9, no. 4 (2008): 477–93.

———. *Visions of the Press in Britain, 1850–1950*. Urbana and Chicago: University of Illinois Press, 2004.

Harcourt, Freda. *Flagships of Imperialism: The P&O Company and the Politics of Empire from Its Origins to 1867*. Manchester and New York: Manchester University Press, 2006.

Hardt, Hanno. *Social Theories of the Press: Early German & American Perspectives*. Beverley Hills and London: Sage Publications, 1979.

Harrington, R. 'The Railway Accident: Trains, Trauma, and Technological Crises in Nineteenth-Century Britain'. In *Traumatic Pasts: History, Psychiatry and Trauma in the Modern Age, 1870–1930*, edited by M. Micale and P. Lerner, pp. 31–56. Cambridge: Cambridge University Press, 2001.

Harris, Michael. 'Shipwrecks in Print: Representations of Maritime Disaster in the Late Seventeenth Century'. In *Journeys through the Market: Travel, Travellers and the Book Trade*, edited by R. Myers and M. Harris, pp. 39–63. New Castle, DE: Oak Knoll Press, 1999.

Harrison, Mark. *Public Health in British India: Anglo-Indian Preventive Medicine, 1859–1914*. Cambridge: Cambridge University Press, 1994.

Haynes, Douglas E. 'Selling Masculinity: Advertisements for Sex Tonics and the Making of Modern Conjugality in Western India, 1900–1945'. *South Asia: Journal of South Asian Studies* 35, no. 4 (2012): 787–831.

Headrick, Daniel R. *The Invisible Weapon: Telecommunications and International Politics, 1851–1945*. Oxford: Oxford University Press, 1991.

———. *The Tentacles of Progress: Technology Transfer in the Age of Imperialism, 1850–1940*. Oxford: Oxford University Press, 1988.

———. *The Tools of Empire: Technology and European Imperialism in the Nineteenth Century*. Oxford: Oxford University Press, 1981.

Hirschmann, Edwin. *Robert Knight: Reforming Editor in Victorian India*. New Delhi: Oxford University Press, 2008.

———. 'Using South Asian Newspapers for Historical Research'. *Journal of Asian Studies* 31, no. 1 (1971): 143–50.

Hofmeyr, Isabel. *Gandhi's Printing Press: Experiments in Slow Reading*. Cambridge, MA, and London: Harvard University Press, 2013.

Hoskins, H. L. *British Routes to India*. London: Frank Cass & Co., 1966.

Hunt, Bruce J. 'The Ohm Is Where the Art Is: British Telegraph Engineers and the Development of Electrical Standards', *Osiris* 9 (1994): 48–63.

Husain, Iqbal. 'Primitive Newspapers: The Eighteenth Century *Akhbarat*'. In *Webs of History: Information, Communication and Technology from Early to Post-colonial India*, edited by A. K. Bagchi, Dipankar Sinha, and Barnita Bagchi, pp. 131–44. New Delhi: Institute of Development Studies Kolkata and Manohar, 2005.

Inamdar, M. M. *Bombay G.P.O.* Mysore: Mysore Philatelics, 1983.

Innis, Harold A. *The Bias of Communication*. Toronto: University of Toronto Press, 1951.

Ishii, Kanji. *Jōhō tsūshin no shakaishi: Kindai Nihon no jōhōka to shijōka* [The social history of information and telecommunications: Information society and marketization in modern Japan]. Tokyo: Yūhikaku, 1994 (in Japanese).

Israel, Milton. *Communications and Power: Propaganda and the Press in the Indian Nationalist Struggle, 1920–1945*. Cambridge: Cambridge University Press, 1994.

Iyengar, A. R. *The Newspaper Press in India*. Bangalore: Bangalore Press, 1933.

Jasanoff, Sheila, 'Future Imperfect: Science, Technology, and the Imaginations of Modernity'. In *Dreamscapes of Modernity: Sociotechnical Imaginaries and the Fabrication of Power*, edited by Sheila Jasanoff and Sang-Hyun Kim, pp. 1–33. Chicago: University of Chicago Press, 2015.

Jeffrey, Robin. *India's Newspaper Revolution: Capitalism, Politics and the Indian-Language Press, 1977–99*. London: C. Hurst & Co., 2000.

Johnston, Anna. *Missionary Writing and Empire, 1800–1860*. Cambridge: Cambridge University Press, 2003.

Jones, Aled. *Powers of the Press: Newspapers, Power and the Public in Nineteenth-Century England*. Aldershot: Scolar Press, 1996.

Josephi, Beate, 'Journalism Education'. In *The Handbook of Journalism Studies*, edited by Karin Wahl-Jorgensen and Thomas Hanitzsch, pp. 42–56. New York and London: Routledge, 2009.

Joshi, Chitra. 'Dak Roads, Dak Runners, and the Reordering of Communication Networks'. *International Review of Social History* 57, no. 3 (2012): 169–89.

Joshi, Priya. *In Another Country: Colonialism, Culture, and the English Novel in India*. New York: Columbia University Press, 2002.

Kamra, Sukeshi. *The Indian Periodical Press and the Production of Nationalist Rhetoric*. New York: Palgrave Macmillan, 2011.

Kaul, Chandrika. 'Bennett, Sir Thomas Jewell (1852–1925)'. In *Oxford Dictionary of National Biography*. Oxford: Oxford University Press, 2004. Available at: www.oxforddnb.com/view/article/58684 (accessed 25 March 2011).

———. 'England and India: The Ilbert Bill, 1883—A Case Study of the Metropolitan Press'. *Indian Economic and Social History Review* 30, no. 4 (1993): 413–36.

———. *Reporting the Raj: The British Press and India, c. 1880–1922*. Manchester: Manchester University Press, 2003.

Kerr, Ian J. *Building the Railways of the Raj, 1850–1900*. New Delhi: Oxford University Press, 1997.

Kesavan, B. S. *History of Printing and Publishing in India: A Story of Cultural Re-awakening*, 3 vols. New Delhi: National Book Trust India, 1997.

Khare, G. H. 'News-Letters of the Medieval Period'. In *The Indian Press*, edited by S. P. Sen, pp. 146–50. Calcutta: Calcutta Press, 1967.

Khare, P. S. *The Growth of Press and Public Opinion in India, 1857 to 1918*. Allahabad: Piyush Prakashan, 1964.

Kidambi, Prashant. '"An Infection of Locality": Plague, Pythogenesis and the Poor in Bombay, c. 1896–1905'. *Urban History* 31, no. 2 (2004): 249–67.

Kielbowicz, Richard B. 'News Gathering by Mail in the Age of the Telegraph: Adapting to a New Technology'. *Technology and Culture* 28, no. 1 (1987): 26–41.

Kieve, J. L. *Electric Telegraph: A Social and Economic History*. Newton Abbot: David and Charles, 1973.

Kipling, Rudyard. *The Man Who Would Be King and Other Stories*. Hertfordshire: Wordsworth Classics, 1994.

Kirk, R. *British Maritime Postal History*, vol. 1: *The P&O Bombay and Australian Lines, 1852–1914*. Norfolk: Studio Print, n.d.

———. *British Maritime Postal History*, vol. 2: *The P&O Lines to the Far East*. Heathfield, Sussex: Proud-Bailey, n.d.

Knuesel, A. 'British Diplomacy and the Telegraph in Nineteenth-Century China'. *Diplomacy and Statecraft* 18, no. 3 (2007): 517–37.

Krishnamurthi, N. *Indian Journalism: Origin, Growth and Development of Indian Journalism from Asoka to Nehru*. Mysore: University of Mysore, 1966.

Kulkarni, G. T. 'M/s Khemkaran Mansaram: The World's First Ever News Selling Agency during the Eighteenth Century Maratha Rule'. In *Webs of History: Information, Communication and Technology from Early to Post-colonial India*, edited by A. K. Bagchi, Dipankar Sinha, and Barnita Bagchi, pp. 145–64. New Delhi: Institute of Development Studies Kolkata and Manohar, 2005.

Kumar, Arun. 'Thomason College of Engineering, Roorkee, 1847–1947'. In *History of Science, Philosophy, and Culture in Indian Civilisation*, vol. 15, part 4: *Science and Modern India: An Institutional History, c. 1784–1947*, edited by D. P. Chattopadhyaya, pp. 453–76. New Delhi: Centre for Studies in Civilizations, 2011.

Kumar, Deepak. *Science and the Raj, 1857–1905*. New Delhi: Oxford University Press, 1995.

Lahiri Choudhury, D. K. '"Beyond the Reach of Monkeys and Men?" O'Shaughnessy and the Telegraph in India c. 1836–56'. *Indian Economic and Social History Review* 37, no. 3 (2000): 331–59.

———. 'Sinews of Panic and the Nerves of Empire: The Imagined State's Entanglement with Information Panic, India c. 1880–1912'. *Modern Asian Studies* 38, no. 4 (2004): 965–1002.

———. *Telegraphic Imperialism: Crisis and Panic in the Indian Empire, c. 1830*. Basingstoke: Palgrave Macmillan, 2010.

Lak, Daniel. 'South Asia Keeping the Police Pigeons Flying', BBC News, 11 February 1999. Available at: http://news.bbc.co.uk/2/hi/south_asia/277047.stm (accessed 15 March 2012).

Lal, K. Sajan. 'The Omdat-ul-Akhbar of Bareilly'. *Indian Historical Records Commission: Proceedings and Meetings*, 24th Session, pp. 100–5. Jaipur, 1948.

Lew, B., and B. Cater. 'The Telegraph, Co-ordination of Tramp Shipping, and Growth in World Trade, 1870–1910'. *European Review of Economic History* 10, no. 2 (2006): 147–73.

Llewellyn-Jones, Rosie. *The Great Uprisings in India, 1857–58: Untold Stories, Indian and British*. Woodbridge: Boydell Press, 2007.

Lovett, Pat. *Journalism in India*. Calcutta: Banna Publishing Company [1929].

Maclean, James Mackenzie. *Recollections of Westminster and India*. Manchester: Sherratt & Hughes, 1901.

MacLeod, Roy, and Deepak Kumar, eds. *Technology and the Raj: Western Technology and Technical Transfers to India, 1700–1947*. New Delhi: Sage Publications, 1995.

Malhotra, P. L. *Administration of Lord Elgin in India, 1894–99*. New Delhi: Vikas, 1979.

Mann, Michael. 'Telegraphy and the Emergence of an All-India Public Sphere'. In *Global Communication Electric: Business, News and Politics in the World of Telegraphy*, edited by M. Michaela Hampf and Simone Mueller-Pohl, pp. 197–222. Frankfurt: Campus Verlag, 2013.

Mannathukkaren, Nissim. 'The Grand Delusion of Digital India'. *Hindu*, 10 October 2015.

Marriott, J., and B. Mukhopadhyay, eds. *Britain in India, 1765–1905*, vol. 4: *Cultural and Social Interventions*. London: Pickering & Chatto, 2006.

Marx, Karl. *Grundrisse: Foundations of the Critique of Political Economy*. London: Penguin Books, 1973.

McCormack, J. H. 'Domesticating Delphi: Emily Dickinson and the Electro-Magnetic Telegraph'. *American Quarterly* 55, no. 4 (2003): 569–601.

McReynolds, Louise. 'Autocratic Journalism: The Case of the St. Petersburg Telegraph Agency'. *Slavic Review* 49, no. 1 (1990): 48–57.

Mehta, Gita. *Snakes and Ladders: A View of Modern India*. London: Minerva, 1997.

Menke, Richard. *Telegraphic Realism: Victorian Fiction and Other Information Systems*. Stanford: Stanford University Press, 2008.

Menon, E. P. *Journalism as a Profession*. Tellicherry: Vidya Vilasam Press, 1930.

Menon, K. B. *The Press Laws of India*. Bombay: Tutorial Press, 1937.

Metcalf, Thomas R. *Ideologies of the Raj*. Cambridge: Cambridge University Press, 1995.

Meyrowitz, Joshua. *The Impact of Electronic Media on Social Behaviour*. New York and Oxford: Oxford University Press, 1985.

Mill, John Stuart. *Essays on Politics and Society*, vol. 18, edited by J. M. Robson. Toronto: Routledge & Kegan Paul/University of Toronto Press, 1977.

Miller, Daniel. *Stuff*. Cambridge: Polity Press, 2010.

Mitra, S. M. *Anglo-Indian Studies*. New York, Bombay, and Calcutta: Longmans, Green & Co., 1913.

Mohanrajan, P. A. *Glimpses of Early Printing and Publishing in India: Their Contribution towards Democratisation of Knowledge*. Madras: Mohanavalli, 1990.

Mohapatra, Prabhu P. '"Following Custom"? Representations of Community among Indian Immigrant Labour in the West Indies, 1880–1920'. *International Review of Social History* 51, supplement S14 (2006): 173–202.

Moitra, M. *A History of Indian Journalism*. Calcutta: National Book Agency, 1969.

Morus, Iwan Rhys. 'The Electric Ariel: Telegraphy and Commercial Culture in Early Victorian England'. *Victorian Studies* 39, no. 3 (1996): 339–8.

———. '"The Nervous System of Britain": Space, Time, and the Electric Telegraph in the Victorian Age'. *British Journal for the History of Science* 33, no. 4 (2000): 455–5.

Mukharji, Projit Bihari. 'Jessie's Dream at Lucknow: Popular Memorializations of Dissent, Ambiguity and Class in the Heart of Empire'. *Studies in History* 24, no. 1 (2008): 77–113.

———. *Nationalizing the Body: The Medical Market, Print and Daktari Medicine*. London: Anthem Press, 2009.

Mukherjee, Rudrangshu. *Awadh in Revolt, 1857–1858*. New Delhi: Permanent Black, 2001.

Muley, Gunakar 'The Introduction of Semaphore Telegraphy in Colonial India'. In *Webs of History: Information, Communication and Technology from Early to Post-colonial India*, edited by A. K. Bagchi, Dipankar Sinha, and Barnita Bagchi, pp. 165–72. New Delhi: Institute of Development Studies Kolkata and Manohar, 2005.

Muniruddin. *History of Journalism*. New Delhi: Anmol Publications, 2005.

Munro, J. Forbes. *Maritime Enterprise and Empire: Sir William Mackinnon and His Business Network, 1823–93*. Rochester, NY: Boydell Press, 2003.

Munson, Eve Stryker, and C. A. Warren. 'Introduction'. In *James Carey: A Critical Reader*, edited by Eve Stryker Munson and Catherine A. Warren, pp. ix–xix. Minneapolis and London: University of Minnesota Press, 1997.

———. eds. *James Carey: A Critical Reader*. Minneapolis and London: University of Minnesota Press, 1997.

Nair, Savithri Preetha. '"Bungallee House Set on Fire by Galvanism": Natural and Experimental Philosophy as Public Science in a Colonial Metropolis (1794–1806)'. In *The Circulation of Knowledge between Britain, India and China: The Early-Modern World to the Twentieth Century*, edited by B. Lightman, G. McOuat, and L. Stewart, pp. 45–74. Leiden: Brill, 2013.

Nakazato, Nariaki. 'Harish Chandra Mukherjee: Profile of a "Patriotic" Journalist in an Age of Social Transition'. *South Asia: Journal of South Asian Studies* 31, no. 2 (2008): 241–70.

Narain, Kirti. *Press, Politics and Society: Uttar Pradesh, 1885–1914*. New Delhi: Manohar and The Book Review Literary Trust, 1998.

Narain, Prem. *Press and Politics in India, 1885–1905*. Delhi: Munshiram Manoharlal, 1970.

Naregal, Veena. *Language Politics, Elites and the Public Sphere: Western India under Colonialism*. London: Anthem Press, 2002.

———. 'Vernacular Culture and Political Formation in Western India'. In *Print Areas: Book History in India*, edited by A. Gupta and S. Chakravorty, pp. 139–68. New Delhi: Permanent Black, 2004.

Natarajan, J. *History of Indian Journalism*. New Delhi: Publications Division, 1954.

Natarajan, S. *A History of the Press in India*. Bombay: Asia Publishing House, 1962.

Nickles, D. P. *Under the Wire: How the Telegraph Changed Diplomacy*. Cambridge, MA: Harvard University Press, 2003.

Nirmal, C. J. 'The Press in Madras under the East India Company'. *Journal of Indian History* 44, part 2 (1966): 483–515.

Noakes, Richard. 'Industrial Research at the Eastern Telegraph Company, 1872–1929'. *British Journal for the History of Science* 47, no. 1 (2013): 119–46.

Norman, Henry W., and Mrs Keith Young, eds. *Delhi 1857: The Siege, Assault, and Capture as Given in the Diary and Correspondence of the Late Colonel Keith Young*. London and Edinburgh: W. & R. Chambers, 1902.

Nye, David E. *American Technological Sublime*. Cambridge, MA: MIT Press, 1994.

O'Connor, Peter. *The English-Language Press Networks of East Asia, 1918–1945*. Folkstone, Kent: Global Oriental, 2010.

O'Connor, Ralph, ed. *Science as Romance*, vol. 7 of *Victorian Science and Literature*, edited by G. Dawson and B. Lightman. London: Pickering & Chatto, 2012.

O'Malley, Tom. 'History, Historians and the Writing of Print and Newspaper History in the UK, c. 1945–1962'. *Media History* 18, nos 3–4 (2012): 289–310.

Örnebring, Henrik. 'Technology and Journalism-as-Labour: Historical Perspectives'. *Journalism* 11, no. 1 (2010): 57–74.

Orsini, Francesca. *Print and Pleasure: Popular Literature and Entertaining Fictions in Colonial North India*. Ranikhet: Permanent Black, 2009.

The P.&O. Pocket Book. London: Adam and Charles Black, 1908.

Pal, Bipin Chandra. *Memories of My Life and Times*, 2 vols. Calcutta: Bipinchandra Institute, 1973.

Palit, Chittabrata. *Scientific Bengal: Science Education, Technology, Medicine and Environment*. Delhi: Kalpaz Publications, 2006.

Paranjape, M. R. *Making India: Colonialism, National Culture, and the After-life of Indian English Authority*. Dordrecht: Springer, 2013.

Pauly, John. 'Introduction: On the Origins of Media Studies (and Media Scholars)'. In *James Carey: A Critical Reader*, edited by Eve Stryker Munson and Catherine A. Warren, pp. 3–13. Minneapolis and London: University of Minnesota Press, 1997.

Pavarala, V., and Kanchan K. Malik. *Other Voices: The Struggle for Community Radio in India*. London and New Delhi: Sage Publications, 2007.

Pernau, Margrit, and Yunus Jaffery, eds. *Information and the Public Sphere: Persian Newsletters from Mughal Delhi*. New Delhi: Oxford University Press, 2009.

Perry, C. R. 'The Rise and Fall of Government Telegraphy in Britain'. *Business and Economic History* 26, no. 2 (1997): 416–25.

Peterson, Indira Viswanathan. 'The Schools of Serfoji II of Tanjore: Education and Princely Modernity in Early Nineteenth-Century India'. In *Trans-colonial Modernities in South Asia*, edited by M. S. Dodson and B. A. Hatcher, pp. 15–44. Abingdon: Routledge, 2012.

Phillimore, R. H., ed. *Historical Records of the Survey of India*, vol. 1. Dehra Dun: Surveyor General of India, 1946–58.

Potter, Simon. *News and the British World: The Emergence of an Imperial Press System*. Oxford: Oxford University Press, 2003.

———, ed. *Imperial Communication: Australia, Britain, and the British Empire c. 1830–50*. London: Menzies Centre for Australian Studies and University of London, 2005.

Pöttker, Horst. 'News and Its Communicative Quality: The Inverted Pyramid—When and Why Did It Appear?' *Journalism Studies*, 4, no. 4 (2003): 501–11.

Putnis, Peter. 'Overseas News in the Australian Press in 1870 and the Colonial Experience of the Franco-Prussian War'. *History Australia* 4, no. 1 (2007): 6.1–6.19.

———. 'Reuters in Australia: The Supply and Exchange of News, 1859–1877'. *Media History* 10, no. 2 (2004): 67–88.

Putnis, Peter, Chandrika Kaul, and Juergen Wilke, eds. *International Communication and Global News Networks: Historical Perspectives*. New York: Hampton Press, 2011.

Raghavan, G. N. S. *The Press in India: A New History*. New Delhi: Gyan Publishing House, 1994.

———. *PTI Story: Origin and Growth of the Indian Press and the News Agency*. Bombay: Press Trust of India, 1987.

Raina, Dhruv. *Images and Contexts: The Historiography of Science and Modernity in India*. New Delhi: Oxford University Press, 2003.

Raleigh, T. *Lord Curzon in India: Being a Selection from His Speeches as Viceroy and Governor-General of India, 1898–1905*. London: Macmillan, 1906.

Ranganathan, M., ed. and trans. *Govind Narayan's Mumbai: An Urban Biography from 1863*. London: Anthem Press, 2009.

Rantanen, Terhi. *When News Was New*. Chichester, West Sussex: Wiley-Blackwell, 2009.

Rau, M. Chalapathi. *The Press in India*. Bombay: Allied Publishers, 1968.

Read, Donald. *The Power of News: The History of Reuters*. Oxford: Oxford University Press, 1999.

Rees, J. D. 'The Native Indian Press'. *Nineteenth Century and After: A Monthly Review*, 49 (May 1901): 817–28.

Roy, G. K. *Law Relating to Press and Sedition*. Simla: Station Press, 1915.

Roy, Somnath. 'Repercussions of the Vernacular Press Act, 1878'. *Journal of Indian History* 45, part 3 (1967): 735–48.

Roy, Tapti. 'Disciplining the Printed Text: Colonial and Nationalist Surveillance of Bengali Literature'. In *Texts of Power: Emerging Disciplines in Colonial Bengal*, edited by Partha Chatterjee, pp. 30–62. Minneapolis: University of Minnesota Press, 1995.

Rubery, Matthew. *The Novelty of Newspapers: Victorian Fiction after the Invention of the News*. Oxford: Oxford University Press, 2009.

Russell, Ralph, ed. *The Oxford India Ghalib: Life, Letters and Ghazals*. Oxford: Oxford University Press, 2003.

Russell, William Howard. *My Indian Mutiny Diary*. London: Cassell, 1957.

Sapru, Somnath. *The News Merchants: How They Sell News to the Third World*. New Delhi: Dialogue Publications, 1986.

Sarkar, Smritikumar. *Technology and Rural Change in Eastern India, 1830–1980*. Oxford: Oxford University Press, 2014.

Sastri, K. N. V. 'History of Mysore in the XIX Century Illustrated from Contemporary Newspapers'. In *Indian Historical Records Commission: Proceedings and Meetings*, vol. 22, Peshawar, October 1945, pp. 74–5. Calcutta: Superintendent Government of India, 1945.

Schivelbusch, Wolfgang. *The Railway Journey: Trains and Travel in the 19th Century*. New York: Urizen Books, 1979.

Schudson, Michael. *Discovering the News: A Social History of American Newspapers*. New York: Basic Books, 1978.

Schwarzlose, R. A. 'Early Telegraphic News Dispatches: Forerunner of the AP'. *Journalism Quarterly* 51, no. 4 (1974): 595–601.

Secord, James A. *Victorian Sensation: The Extraordinary Publication, Reception, and Secret Authorship of Vestiges of the Natural History of Creation*. Chicago: University of Chicago Press, 2000.

Sehgal, N. K., and S. Mahanti, eds. *Memoirs of Ruchi Ram Sahni, Pioneer of Science Popularisation in Punjab*. New Delhi: Vigyan Prasar, 1994.

Sen, B. K. *Growth of Scientific Periodicals in India (1788–1900)*. New Delhi: Indian National Science Academy, 2002.

Sen, S. P., ed. *The Indian Press*. Calcutta: Calcutta Press, 1967.

Shahvar, Soli. 'Concession Hunting in the Age of Reform: British Companies and the Search for Government Guarantees—Telegraph Concessions through Ottoman Territories, 1855–58'. *Middle Eastern Studies* 38, no. 4 (2002): 169–93.

———. 'Iron Poles, Wooden Poles: The Electric Telegraph and the Ottoman-Iranian Boundary Conflict, 1863–1865'. *British Journal of Middle Eastern Studies* 34, no. 1 (2007): 23–42.

Sharma, Madhuri. 'Creating a Consumer: Exploring Medical Advertisements in Colonial India'. In *The Social History of Health and Medicine in Colonial India*, edited by Biswamoy Pati and Mark Harrison, pp. 213–28. London: Routledge, 2009.

Shelangoskie, Susan. 'Anthony Trollope and the Social Discourse of Telegraphy after Nationalisation'. *Journal of Victorian Culture* 14, no. 1 (2009): 72–93.

Shridharani, K. *Story of the Indian Telegraphs: A Century of Progress*. New Delhi: Government of India Press, 1953.

Sidebottom, John K. *The Overland Mail: A Postal Historical Study of the Mail Route to India*. London: George Allen and Unwin, 1948.

Silberstein-Loeb, J. 'The Structure of the News Market in Britain, 1870–1914'. *Business History Review* 83, no. 4 (2009): 759–88.

Simonson, Peter, Janice Peck, Robert T. Craig, and John P. Jackson, Jr. 'The History of Communication History'. In *The Handbook of Communication History*, edited by Peter Simonson, Janice Peck, Robert T. Craig, and John P. Jackson, Jr., pp. 13–57. New York: Routledge, 2013.

———, eds. *The Handbook of Communication History*. New York: Routledge, 2013.

Simpson, Maurice G. 'The Indo-European Telegraph Department'. *Journal of the Royal Society of Arts* 76, no. 3928 (1928): 382–94.

Singh, J. K. *Media and Journalism*. New Delhi: A. P. H. Publishing Corporation, 2008.

Singh, S. K. *Press, Politics and Public Opinion in Bihar, 1912–1947*. New Delhi: Manak Publications, 2010.

Sinha, Nitin. *Communication and Colonialism in Eastern India: Bihar, 1760s–1880s*. London: Anthem Press, 2014.

Smethers, J. S., and Lee Jolliffe. 'The Partnership of Telegraphy and Radio in "Re-creating" Events for Broadcast'. *Journal of Radio Studies* 1, no. 1 (1992): 83–96.

Smith, Max, and Robert Johnson. *Express Mail, After Packets and Late Fees in India before 1870*. Stuart Rossiter Trust, 2007.

Srinivas, M. D., T. G. Paramasivam, and T. Pushkala. *Thirupporur and Vadakkuppattu: Eighteenth Century Locality Accounts*. Chennai: Centre for Policy Studies, 2001.

Stark, James. '"Recharge My Exhausted Batteries": Overbeck's Rejuvenator, Patenting, and Public Medical Consumers'. *Medical History* 58, no. 4 (2014): 498–518.

Stark, Ulrike. *An Empire of Books: The Naval Kishore Press and the Diffusion of the Printed Word in Colonial India*. New Delhi: Permanent Black, 2009.

———. 'Knowledge in Context: Raja Shivaprasad as Hybrid Intellectual and People's Educator'. In *Trans-colonial Modernities in South Asia*, edited by M. S. Dodson and B. A. Hatcher, pp. 68–91. Abingdon: Routledge, 2012.

Storey, Graham. *Reuter's Century*. London: Max Parrish, 1951.

Taylor, James. 'Business in Pictures: Representations of Railway Enterprise in the Satirical Press in Britain, 1845–1870'. *Past & Present* 189, no. 1 (2005): 111–45.

Thiaga Rajan, S. P. *History of Indian Journalism*. Thanjavur: Columbia House, 1966.

———. *Introduction to Journalism*. Madras: Educational Publishing Company, 1938.

Thompson, H. T., and J. Sinclair. 'Telegraphists' Cramp'. *Lancet* 179 (1912): 888–90.

Thompson, John B. *The Media and Modernity: A Social Theory of the Media*. Cambridge: Polity Press, 1995.

Thompson, R. L. *Wiring a Continent: The History of the Telegraph Industry in the United States, 1832–1866*. Princeton: Princeton University Press, 1947.

Tomlinson, John. *The Culture of Speed: The Coming of Immediacy*. London: Sage Publications, 2007.

Tomlinson, Matt. 'Speaking of Coups before They Happen: Kadavu, May–June 1999'. *Pacific Studies* 25, no. 4 (2002): 9–28.

Tracy, Louis. *The Red Year: A Story of the Indian Mutiny*. New York: Edward J. Clode, 1907.

Trentmann, Frank. 'Materiality in the Future of History: Things, Practices, and Politics'. *Journal of British Studies* 48, no. 2 (2009): 283–307.

Tully, John. 'A Victorian Ecological Disaster: Imperialism, the Telegraph, and Gutta Percha'. *Journal of World History* 20, no. 4 (2009): 559–79.

Varughese, Shiju Sam. 'Media and Science in Disaster Contexts: Deliberations on Earthquakes and in the Regional Press in Kerala'. *Spontaneous Generations: A Journal for the History and Philosophy of Science* 5, no. 1 (2011): 36–43.

Venkatachalapathy, A. R. *The Province of the Book: Scholars, Scribes, and Scribblers in Colonial Tamilnadu*. New Delhi: Permanent Black, 2012.

Wacha, D. E. *Shells from the Sands of Bombay: Being My Recollections and Reminiscences, 1860–1875*. Bombay: Bombay Chronicle Press, 1920.

Wagle, N. K., ed. *Writers, Editors and Reformers: Social and Political Transformations of Maharashtra, 1830–1930*. New Delhi: Manohar, 1999.

Wahl-Jorgensen, K., and T. Hanitzsch, eds. *The Handbook of Journalism Studies*. New York and London: Routledge, 2009.

Waits, Robert K. 'Gustave Flaubert, Charles Dickens, and Isaac Pulvermacher's "Magic Band"'. In *Literature, Neurology, and Neuroscience: Historical and Literary Connections*, edited by A. Stiles, S. Finger, and F. Boller, pp. 219–40. Amsterdam: Elsevier, 2013.

Ward, Stephen J. A. *Invention of Journalism Ethics: The Path to Objectivity and Beyond*. Montreal: McGill-Queen's University Press, 2004.

Watson, Alfred H. 'The Growth of the Press in English in India'. *Journal of the Royal Society of Arts* 96, no. 4760 (1948): 121–0.

———. 'Origin and Growth of Journalism among Europeans'. *Annals of the American Academy of Political and Social Science* 145, part 2 (1929): 169–4.

Wenzlhuemer, Roland. *Connecting the Nineteenth-Century World: The Telegraph and Globalization*. Cambridge: Cambridge University Press, 2012.

———. 'London in the Global Telecommunication Network of the Nineteenth Century'. *New Global Studies* 3, no. 1 (2009): Art. 2.

———, ed. 'Global Communication: Telecommunication and Global Flows of Information in the Late 19th and Early 20th Century'. *Historical Social Research* 35, special issue (2010).

Williams, Raymond. *Keywords: A Vocabulary of Culture and Society*. London: Fontana Paperbacks, 1983.

Winseck, Dwayne R., and Robert M. Pike. *Communication and Empire: Media, Markets, and Globalization, 1860–1930*. Durham and London: Duke University Press, 2007.

Wolseley, Roland E. *Journalism in Modern India*. Bombay and Calcutta: Asia Publishing House, 1953.

Wouters, Paul et al. 'Messy Shapes of Knowledge: STS Explores Informatization, New Media and Academic Work'. In *The Handbook of Science and Technology Studies*, edited by Edward J. Hackett, Olga Amsterdamska, Michael Lynch, and Judy Wajcman, pp. 319–52. Cambridge, MA: MIT Press, 2008.

Zastoupil, Lynn. *Rammohun Roy and the Making of Victorian Britain*. New York: Palgrave Macmillan, 2010.

Unpublished Dissertations and Conference Papers

Arya, Kapil. 'The Over-Dependence of Indian English Language Newspapers on Global News Agencies for International News'. MA dissertation, University of Leeds, 2011.

Headrick, Daniel. 'British Imperial Postal Networks'. Paper presented at the International Economic Congress, Helsinki, August 2006. Available at: http://www.helsinki.fi/iehc2006/papers3/Headrick.pdf (accessed 15 March 2016).

Joshi, Sanjay. 'Historicizing the Archive: Making of the Native Newspaper Reports in Colonial India'. Paper presented at the Western Conference of the Association for Asian Studies, Provo, Utah, 27 September 2002.

INDEX

accelerators 45, 79
Act XX of 1847 (Copyright Act) 251
Act XXV of 1867 (Press and Registration of Books Act) 251
Acworth, William 170–1
Adam, John 211–12
Aden 54–5, 172, 311
Adley, Charles C. 50, 56, 73, 80, 113–14, 116, 119
advertising 20, 103, 115, 157, 184, 205, 207, 269–74, 276–7, 313–14, 327–8;
  for Harlene's Shampoo 273
Advocate of India 185, 253
Afghan campaigns 163
Afghan war 233
Ahmad, Munshi Nazir 306
Ahmed, Maulvi 58
Aina-i-Alam 305
Akbar Shah II, King 10, 189
akhbarat (Mughal newsletters) 10–11, 44, 189
Albina Carpaţilor (The Carpathian Bee) 151
Albion, Robert 9
Alexandria 53, 56, 62–3, 172
Ali, Haidar 65
Ali, Munshi Anwar 103
Ali-ul-Hashmi, Ram 156
Allahabad 73, 106, 246, 282, 285, 297, 299
Allen's Indian Mail 169
Allen's Indian News 300
American journalism 10, 18
Amrita Bazar Patrika 112, 119, 151, 229, 246–7, 268, 270–1, 273, 281;
  on medical advertising 315*n*14
Anand, Babu Ram 49, 58
Anderson, David 155
Anglo-Indian: dailies 245;
  editors 221, 225;
  journalism 221, 272;
  journals 153;
  merchants 3;

newspapers 31, 191, 204, 206, 213, 221, 229, 241, 245, 253–4, 281;
press 28, 152, 206, 222, 228, 232–3, 289
Anglo-Indians 31–2*n*5, 157, 185, 213, 226, 254, 272
Arnold, William D. 23, 153
Ar-Rashid 306
Ashburner, Luke 205
Asiatic Journal and Monthly Register 85*n*47
assassinations, reporting of 311
Associated Press (of New York) 18, 238, 327–8
Associated Press of Ceylon 327
Associated Press of India 327
Atkinson, G. F. 187
audio-visual media 19
Aurangzeb, Emperor 45
Austro-Prussian War 28, 31, 55, 173, 268, 288–340, 307, 312, 318*n*83, *see also* war reporting
Avadh Akhbar 188, 328
Ayerst, Lieutenant 28, 306–7, 310–12
Azim, Syed Muhammad 158

Babbage, Charles 126
Baksh, Pir 106
Balfour, Edward 217
bamboo whistles 48
Banerjea, Surendranath 12, 160, 187, 189, 230
Bangabasi 158
Bangalore Chronicle 268
Bangalore Herald 270
banghy (parcel post) 59
Bank of Bombay 243
Barnard, Thomas 65
Barnhurst, Kevin G. 7, 267, 269, 311
Barns, Margarita 14
Baroda 100, 160, 187, 281
Barrow, Sir John 66
Battle of Königgrätz 289, 301, 303
Battle of Sadowa 302, 304
Battle of Verona 298
battles at Nachod 289
Bavaria 289
Bayley, Steuart Sir 153, 159
Bayly, C. A. 4, 22, 44, 271
Behar Landholders' Association 107
Bengal 13, 26, 48, 66;
telegraph system in 68, 154, 189, 208, 211–12, 216–17
Bengal Gazette 150, 207
Bengal Hurkaru 169, 183, 268
Bengalee 12, 56–7, 189, 245, 268, 281;
as Indian-owned newspaper 245
Bengali intelligentsia 211
Bengali journalism 11
Bennett, Coleman, & Co. 272
Bennett, T. J. 272, 314
Bentinck, William 183
Bernard, C. 249
Berne Convention 265*n*174
Besant, Annie 156
Bhagvat Tatwa Bodhika 154
Bharat Jiwan 26, 178, 268, 270, 282, 328
Bharat Mihir 158, 229, 232
Bhatavadekar, Krishna Sastri 120
bicycles 79
bimonthly 305
Biswa Duta 154
biweekly 168, 183, 185, 234, 270, 292, 296
Blackwood's Magazine 123
Blanford, Henry Francis 176, 178–9
blind men, employing of 87*n*78
Bombay & Aden Steamship Company 241

Bombay 13, 27, 51, 60, 62, 97, 100, 105, 108, 120, 162, 174–5, 178, 185, 212, 228, 239, 244, 285, 282;
newspapers published in 26
Bombay and Bengal Steamship Company 55
Bombay Chronicle 275
Bombay Courier 157, 205
Bombay Gazette 27–8, 169, 185, 221–2, 225–7, 268–9, 271–5, 279–81, 285–7, 307, 309–10, 312
Bombay Guardian 169
Bombay Herald 169
Bombay Quarterly Review 183
Bombay Samachar 13, 161, 235, 271, 276
Bombay Telegraph 169, 205
Bombay Telegraph and Courier 205, 217
Bombay Times 60, 112, 114, 158, 162, 217, 239–40, 283
Bombay Times and Journal of Commerce 60, 112, 283
Bombay Times and Standard 158
Bombay–Suez line 55, 62
Boyce, William 66
Boyd, Hugh 158
Boydell, Captain 151
Brake, Laurel 155, 167
Brendish, William 130–4
Bright, Charles Tilston 149, 163–4
Brindisi 62–3, 170–1
British colonizers 4, 21, 108, 124, 207, 323
British India Steam Navigation Company 55
British-Indian Submarine Telegraph Company 78
Brooke, W. R. 102
Brooker-Gross, S. R. 27
Brooks, Charles William Shirley 169
Brown, Lucy 251
Buck, Edward J. 251
Buckingham, James Silk 158, 183–4, 210–11
Buckland, C. E. 157, 232, 234
Burne, Owen Tudor 102, 212, 220–9

Calcutta 27, 46–5–8, 60–2, 66–9, 71, 100–1, 173–6, 183–5, 208–10, 217–19;
newspapers of 64, 208;
underwater telegraphy in 71
Calcutta and Burmah Steam Navigation Company 55
Calcutta Chronicle 183
Calcutta Courier 64, 279
Calcutta Gazette 169, 208, 218–19
Calcutta Journal 67, 69, 183, 210
Calcutta Journal of Politics and General Literature 48, 110
Calcutta Quarterly Review 223
Calcutta Review 12, 153, 159, 224
Canning, Lord 103, 214
Cape of Good Hope 51–2, 54
Capital 253
Carey, James 8, 16–17;
on telegraph 17
carrier pigeons 24, 47–8, 110;
see also runners
Castells, Manuel 22
Cavallo, Tiberius 110
Cavendish, Lord Frederick, assassination of 306
censorship 13–14, 207, 209–10, 215, 236
Ceylon 13, 55, 110, 170, 187, 209, 288
Ceylon Herald 12, 155, 159–60
Ceylon Observer 169

Chalapathi Rau, M. 10
Chamber of Commerce 100, 158, 162, 166–7, 173, 189, 268, 291;
of Bombay 189, 100, 291;
of Calcutta 100, 291
Champion 253
Chandavarkar, N. G. 252
Chandavarkar, R. 305
Chapekar, Damodar 313
Chappe, Claude 67
Chappe brothers 65
Chatterjee, Bankim Chandra 123
Chatterjee, Partha 99, 213
Chaudhury, Radhanath 161
Chaudhury, Raj Chandra 161
Chesney, G. M. 155
Chichele-Plowden, Sir Trevor 252
China 10, 63, 71, 169, 181, 239, 281–2, 288, 296
China Gazette 296
Chronicle 292, 297
circulation figures 183, 186
Civil and Military Gazette 225, 231, 244, 246
Civil Service Gazette 169
Clarendon, Lord 239
Clarke, Geoffrey 45
clerks 99, 165, 172, 176, 220, 299
Cobbet, William 188
Cohn, Bernard 207
Coleman, F. M. 272
Collins, Henry M. 50, 240, 243–4, 300
Colombo Observer 169, 327
colonial modernity 10, 98
colonialism 153
Colvile, Sir James 106–7
Commercial Gazette 268, 276–7
commercial intelligence 47, 96, 161, 174, 189, 278, 283, 311, 326
communication 8, 15, 22, 43–4, 51, 56, 66, 71, 216;
auxiliary means of 47;
boarded telegraphs for land 66;
modes of 25, 43, 45, 49, 69, 79;
modes of distance 44–50;
personal 45;
state and non-state actors in 22–5;
theories of 15–21;
Thompson on 23
contributors 12, 50, 157–8, 160, 166, 173
conveyance of mails 45, 62–3
Cooper, F. H. 129
copyright 30, 245, 247–53
correspondents 2–3, 157, 160, 162–3, 173, 221, 231–2, 250–1, 286–7, 290–3, 301–2
Cotes, Everard on Indian News Agency 327
Courier 205
Crimean War 160, 173, 288, 290
Crowe, Joseph Archer 173, 311
Curzon, Lord (viceroy) 133, 251

Dacca 58, 234, 282
Dacca Prakash 229
Daftar Ashkara Press 161
Daily Commercial Sale Report 162
Daily News 173, 246
daily newspapers 59, 157, 159, 167, 178, 185, 188, 269–70;
see also government newspapers; Indian newspapers; vernacular newspapers
Daily Telegraph 116, 155, 162, 185, 221
Daily Trade Return 162
dak: *dâk*-bearer 45;
'Dawk Walas of Bengal' 46;
native *dawk* 45;
Nizamut *dawk* 44;
private 45 *see also* messenger pigeons; runners

Dalhousie, Lord 64, 71, 127, 162, 216, 283
Dallas, W. H. 176, 178
Das, Biswajit 19, 330
Dass, Jumnath 58
Dawes, Edwyn 240
De Pontevès-Sabran, Jean 95
De, Bani Madhub 49
De, Sushil Kumar 11
Deccan Herald 162
Deccan Post 150
Delhi 60, 131
Delhi Durbar 160
Delhi Gazette 27, 61, 131, 158, 162, 169, 184, 217, 221–2, 288, 293
Delhi Telegraph Memorial 133
delivery times 60, 62
dematerialization 144*n*116
Demoor, Marysa 155, 167
Denshin kyōkai kaishi 96
Derby Mercury 159
Dewar, Douglas 150
Dhunjibhoy, Pestonji 45
Diamond Harbour 58, 66, 69, 71, 178, 279–80
Dickinson, Emily 166–7
Digby, William M. 13, 154, 186–8
Digital India 329
domestic telegrams 279–80, 283, 308, 310
donkeys 54
Dost-i-Hind 237
Douglas, Major C. 175
Duane, William 159
duplex telegraphy 114
Durand, H. M. 218
Dutta, Harihar 110

East India Company 44–5, 49, 51–4, 113, 159, 184, 205, 208–10, 212–13, 239;
military campaigns of 208
Eastern Star 169
Eastern Telegraph Company 78, 171, 244
Edinburgh, The 187
editing 156, 162, 185, 298
editors 1–2, 12, 112–14, 157–62, 186–9, 208–10, 215–17, 225–9, 236–7, 241–3, 250–1
Editor's Room 30, 216–17, 220, 225, 238
education and professionalization 117–19, 258*n*43
effect research 18–19
Egerton, Elizabeth Augusta 105–6, 108, 124, 160–1, 190, 268
electric news 280;
of Reuter 239
electric telegraph/telegraphy 1–2, 5, 16–17, 29, 43, 49, 64–5, 69–71, 79, 98, 103–4, 109, 119–20, 128–9, 135, 278–80
electrical science 119–20
electricity 29, 70, 95–7, 110–12, 117–21, 123, 127–8, 164, 323
electromagnetism 5, 114
electrotherapy 111
Elwin, Verrier 122–3
Empire Press Union 64
English language 12, 26, 213, 226, 235;
dailies 185, 222, 268–9, 282;
journalism 30, 191, 269, 274, 328;
newspapers 31, 42, 64, 154, 158, 162, 233–4, 276, 289, 296, 325, 327–8;
newspapers in British India 26;
press 206, 213, 229, 314
English people in India 21–2*n*5;
see also Anglo-Indian

English-educated Indians 3
Englishman 27–8, 113–14, 151–2, 241–4, 268–71, 274–7, 279–81, 291–3, 296–7, 306–7, 310–11
Enlightenment 19, 126
entrepreneurs 19, 51, 164
European intelligence 169, 175, 293
Evening Mail 187
Everest, George 67
express mail 60

False Point Cyclone 178
famine 4, 74, 101, 125, 181, 190, 224, 227, 296, 305;
  Irish 167;
  in southern India 101
Fenton, Albert 55, 190
Ferguson, James 110
Fernandez, G. A. 246, 252
Forbes, Archibald 232
foreign intelligence 43, 314
foreign news 55, 206–7, 247, 281–3, 286, 289–90, 309 (*see also* Reuter's Telegrams);
  reporting 28
Framjee, Dossabhoy 45
Franco-Prussian War 47, 62, 292, 307
Fraser, William 189
free press 183, 211–13;
  in India 208
Frere, Henry Bartle Sir 1
Friend of India 60, 217, 221–2, 225, 283

Gaekwar, Sayajirao (Maharaja) 187
Gagging Act (Act XV of 1857) 214
Galle 62, 74
galvanism 110–12, 114–15
Gandhi (Mahatma) 288, 324
Gandhi, Cursetji 234
Gazette of India. See *India Gazette*
Geary, Grattan 272
geographical reporting 3, 15, 25, 67, 73, 121, 286
Ghalib 42
Ghosh, Moti Lal 118
Ghosh, Sisir Kumar 241
Ghosh, Sitanath 112, 122
Gisborne, F. 76
Glasgow Herald 165
global telecommunications 20
global village 18
Gorst, Sir John 238
Goswami, Manu 7, 135
Government Gazette 30, 158, 183–4; see also *Gazette of India*
government newspapers 205, 216; *see also* daily newspapers; Indian newspapers; vernacular newspapers
Grant, C. 237
Grant, J. P. 216
Grant, John 158
Grant, Ulysses S. 116–17
Great Northern Telegraph Company 244
Green Pamphlet 324
Griffiths, F. J. 247–8
Grindlay & Co. 169
Guha, Anath Bandhu 232–3
Gurjar, Narayan Baba 312
gutta-percha 71, 97, 124

Haldar, Nilratan 44–5
Hampton, Mark 222, 279
Harris, Georgina 106
Harris, Rev. James P. 106–7
Hastings, Lord 152, 210–11
Havas 47, 173, 238
Headrick, Daniel 23
Hearst, William Randolph 204
Heatley, Jacob 210

Heaton, John Henniker 64, 164
Hensman, Howard 237
Hesse-Darmstadt 289
Hesse-Kassel 289
Hicky, James Augustus 11, 150, 152, 207--8
Hills, The 27
Hindoo Hitoysini 229
Hindoo Patriot 12, 154, 160, 227, 245, 268, 281, 284
Hindostan 54
Hindu Reformer 188
Hindu, The 154, 328
Hindustan Times 328
Hindustani (Urdu) 120, 306, 310
Hircarrah 158
Hirschmann, Edwin 12, 157, 232, 240–1
Hofmeyr, Isabel 288
Home News 169, 173, 292
Hong Kong 54, 170, 239, 244, 268, 295
horses 43–4, 58, 81*n*4, 300
Hosein, Khadim 57
Hull Advertiser 159
Hurkaru 152, 217, 243
Hyderabad 67–8, 178, 217, 247, 252
Hyderabad Chronicle 252

Illustrated London News 46, 173, 221
'Impact talk' 18, 39*n*64
imperial penny postage 63
Imperial Postal Conference 64
Impey, Elijah 152
India Gazette 158, 183, 218, 231
India Sporting Review 159
Indian Daily News 221–2, 225, 227, 253
Indian Engineers' Association 119
Indian Famine Fund 296
Indian journalists 10, 154, 157, 236, 305
Indian mails 51, 63, 170–1
Indian Mirror 225, 227, 238, 245
Indian Navy steamers 53
Indian News 169, 174
Indian News Agency 176
Indian newspapers 59, 154, 226, 229, 238, 244, 295
Indian Observer 158
Indian press 9, 13, 152, 154, 180, 212, 221–2, 225, 252, 291
Indian Press Commissioner 224
Indian Public Opinion 225
Indian Spectator 154, 162, 271, 281
Indian Telegraph Department 56, 72, 99–100, 130, 176, 182, 235, 290, 292, 298
Indian telegraph system 124;
  for public 29
Indian Telegraphic Journal 119
Indian Telegraphist of Allahabad 119
Indo-European telegraph system 244;
  Telegraph Company 78;
  Telegraph Department 76, 78, 102
Industrial Revolution 152
information panic 22–3
information, transmission of 5, 30, 69;
  telegraphy as means of 74
Innis, Harold 9, 16, 18
insulation 5, 76, 97
Intelligence, distribution of official 216–20;
  items of 3, 192, 213, 277, 281–2, 295
International News Service 156
Ishii, Kanji 244
Iyengar, A. R. 186

Jaghire lands 89*n*110
Jallianwala Bagh massacre, reporting of 258*n*43;
  see also war reporting

Jam-i-Jahan Numa 110
Jamshed, Jam-e 276
Janardhunjee, Dhondoo 119
Japan 3, 71, 111, 150, 244, 295–6, 307
Japan Journal 150
Japan Punch 244
Japan Times 151, 295
Japanese Telegraph Association 96
Jasanoff, Sheila 24
Jeffrey, Robin 328
Jessel, Sir George 247
John, C. S. 118
Joshi, Chitra 46, 104
journalism 3–12, 14–23, 25, 149–57, 159–64, 166–7, 206, 222–4, 313–14, 328–9;
in colonial India 149–56;
education 4, 9–10, 156, 187, 207;
history of 6–9, 12, 14–15, 17, 19, 26, 149, 156;
in India 14, 156–62, 240, 328;
Indians in 10;
and literature 10, 17;
and medicine 115;
models of 10;
and science 119, 151;
sources for history of 7–9;
in South Asia 9–15, 26

Kandahar News 27, 246;
as handwritten newspaper 246
Karachi 55, 74, 77–9, 178, 289, 298
Karkaria, R. P. 12–13
Kaul, Chandrika 20, 22, 225
Kedgeree 58, 69, 280
Kemp, E. C. 234
Kesari 313
Kesavan, B. S. 11
Khan, Abdur Rahman 237
Khan, Khan Bahadur 129
Khan, Sher Ali (Shere Ali) 232–3, 268
Khare, G. H. 48
Khemkaran Mansaram 48
Kidambi, Prashant, on plague policies 305
Kipling, Rudyard 167, 250, 266
Kishore, Munshi Naval 316*n*22, 316*n*38, 328
Knies, Karl 126
Knight, Robert 12, 157, 159, 161–2, 226–7, 232, 240, 293
Knighton, William 12, 152, 155, 159–60, 165, 194*n*18
knowledge production 5
Kooka Revolt 101
Korea 71, 296
Krishnaji, Ganpat 120
Kulkarni, G. T. 48
Kurrachee Advertiser 169

La Beaume, Michael 111
Ladysmith pigeons 47
Lahiri Choudhury, D. K. 23, 49, 71–2, 96, 119, 130, 326
Lahore 60, 119, 156, 168, 173, 246, 282, 299
Lahore Chronicle 27–8, 158, 217, 268, 289, 292–3, 296, 299, 301–3
Lahore Tribune 40*n*70, 158
Lancaster Guardian 160
Landholders, and Commercial Association of British India 218
Lardner, Dionysius 95
'Latest Intelligence' 43, 175, 189, 237, 280–1, 283, 292
'Latest Telegrams' 43, 281, 301
Lawson, Charles 224
Leader 231
Lethbridge, Roper 102, 154, 223–4, 226–34, 236–7, 259*n*59

letters 42–3, 49–50, 56–8, 63–4, 79–80, 100–7, 134, 169–70, 190, 291–2, 312;
delivering 56;
delivery of 58
Lévi-Strauss, Claude 15
Lewis, Lieutenant Owen 311–12
Lindsay, Hugh 52, 190
Lloyd's (Austrian) 55
Lloyd's List 278
London telegrams 252
Long, Rev. James 11–12, 184, 201*n*135, 217
Lovett, Pat 9
Low, Sidney, 'Newspaper Copyright' by 249
Luke, P. V. 130–2
Luson, H. 252
Lyall, A. C. 230, 234, 236
Lytton, Lord 223–5

M'Gregor, W. L. 111–12
Macdonald, Lieutenant Colonel John 66, 71, 110
Macintosh, Charles A. 7
Mack, John 120
Mackenzie, Colin 67
Mackinder, Halford 164
Mackinnon, William 55
Maclean, Charles 208
Maclean, James Mackenzie 252
Madras 13, 26–7, 44, 51–2, 54, 60–2, 64, 68, 71, 74, 98, 100, 168, 173–5, 209, 216, 222, 239, 244, 285, 297–9
Madras Government Gazette 169
Madras Mail 227, 327
Madras Morning Chronicle 169
Madras Reading Room 217
Madras Times 27–8, 154, 186, 225, 231, 241–2, 292–3, 296–9, 303–4, 306–8, 310;
'By Indo-European Telegraph' in 43, 292
mail carts 45–6, 58, 79
mail dacoities 46
mail news 43, 174, 288, 292, 297, 302, 304
mail on horseback 46, 54;
mail horses 47
mail steamer departures 55
Maitra, Kalidas 119–20
Malabari, Behramji Merwanji 12–13, 162
Malcolm, Governor John 68
Malta 53, 172
manias 52–3
Manufacturer and Builder 47, 50, 71
Marseilles 53–6, 58, 62–3, 169, 239
Marzban, Fardunji 161, 271
Mashir-i-Saltanat 319*n*95
materiality 121, 324, 326;
material substratum 25, 325
Mayo, Lord 116–17, 220
McLuhan, Marshall 9, 18
McPherson, Malcolm 226
mechanical telegraphs 64–70
media: of communication 15, 25–6, 43, 79, 126, 149, 313;
revolutions 25, 330;
see also print, explosion of
medical journalism 20;
see also journalism
Mediterranean Electric Telegraph Company 76
Mediterranean Extension Telegraph Company 76
Meerut 282
Mehta, P. M. 252
Menon, E. P. 9
Merwanji, Hirjibhoy 62
Messageries Impériales 55
messenger pigeons 47;
bred in Bengal 48

messengers 47, 99;
  see also runners; mail on horseback; messenger pigeons
Metcalfe, Charles 68, 208, 212
Metcalfe, Thomas R. 117
meteorology 117
Meyrowitz, Joshua 286
Military Chronicle 268
Mirat-ul-Akhbar 211
Mist, Nathaniel 150
Mitra, Siddha Mohana 150
modernity, technologies of 121–8
Mofusilite 169
Mohapatra, Prabhu 108
Molesworth, Justice 248
Mookerjee, Sambhu C. 12
Morse telegraph 72, 137*n*19, 174, 298
Mountain, S. H. 45;
  on runners 45
Muir, William 218–19
Mukherjee, Harish Chandra 9, 12
Mukherjee, Rudrangshu 129
Mulji, Karsondas 120
Mull, Matthias 158, 243
Muniruddin, delivery peon 57;
  see also messengers; runners
Murray, Lord George 65, 67
Murray, R. 181
mutiny 23, 72, 76, 96, 103, 106, 108, 129–30, 132–4, 160, 214
Mutiny Telegraph Memorial 132–3
Mymensingh 156, 232
Mysore 68, 209

Nair, Savithri Preetha 110
Nakazato, Nariaki 12
Naoroji, Jamsetji 52, 161
Naoroji, Jehangir 62
Napoleonic Wars 65
Narayan, Govind 190, 324
Naregal, Veena 120
national consciousness 21
Native Newspaper Reports 28, 234
native press 152, 154, 184
Naval and Military Gazette 169
Naval Kishore Press 188
Nerone, John 7, 267, 269, 311
New York Herald 18, 116
New York Times 18, 204, 269
Newall, R. S. 76
news agencies 2, 5, 8, 18–20, 23, 47–8, 176, 238, 243, 248, 327
news communication 10–11, 266;
  see also communication; journalism; government newspapers; Indian newspapers; newspaper press; vernacular newspapers
news distribution 20, 30, 205, 215–16, 218–19, 222–6, 228, 233–4, 237–8, 254, 293
news reporting 2–5, 10–11, 17–18, 20–3, 25, 27–31, 43, 64, 149, 191–2, 266–8, 275–93, 314;
  see also journalism; war reporting
news transmission 5, 42–3, 45, 47, 49, 51, 53, 55, 57, 59, 61, 168–82
news-free messages 176–7
newspaper press 28–30, 114–17, 161–2, 184, 190–1, 212–13, 237–8, 241–2, 253, 268, 271;
  see also journalism; print, explosion of
Newspaper Society 250
newspaper: circulation 182–5;
  forms of 269–74;
  reading 185–92;
  readers 19;
  traffic of 169;
  to Yokohama 295;
  see also communication; journalism; government newspapers; Indian newspapers; newspaper press; vernacular newspapers

news-writing 44
Nikambe, Shevantibai M. 105, 186
Nil Darpan affair 217
North-China Herald 239
Northern German Confederation 289

objectivity: in American journalism 18, 257*n*33
Ochs, Adolph Simon 204
online journalism 275;
see also journalism, news reporting; newspapers
opium 44–5, 49, 75;
merchants 87–8*n*87
O'Shaughnessy, William Brooke 64, 71–3, 101, 119, 128, 162, 174
Osman, A. H. 47
Overbeck, Otto 115
overland: mail 43, 58, 62, 77, 79, 173, 282, 292, 300–1;
mail steamer 175;
telegraphic message 288

Padhye, Mahadeo Krishna 253
Paine, Thomas 152
Pakshi, Rupchand 123
Pal, Bipin Chandra 106, 156, 158, 161
Pal, Rai Kristo Das 12, 225, 245
Pall Mall Gazette 221
Pan-Anglican Federation 164
Pan-Britannic Zollverein 164
Pande, Jemadar Ishwari 103
Pande, Mangal 103
paper production 71
Paridarshak 156, 161
Parsi community 107, 162, 271
Pasha, Midhat Raschid 151
Paton, G. 46
Pattison, J. 208, 212
Peacock, Sir Barnes 103, 216
Pender, John 78, 116
Peninsular and Oriental Steam Navigation Company (P&O) 54–5, 63, 240;
P&O steamer 54, 297
peons for delivery 56–8, 99, 120;
gift to 86–7*n*74;
see also runners; messenger pigeons
periodicals in Hindi 11;
see also journalism; vernacular newspapers
Peterson, Indira Viswanathan 118
Phoenix 268, 270;
Latest News section in 287
pigeon post 47
pigeon service, Orissa state police 48
pigeons 25, 46–8, 69;
in times of war 47;
see also carrier pigeons; Ladysmith pigeons; messenger pigeons;
Pike, Robert 24, 76
Pilkington, J. W. 130–3
Pioneer 156, 182, 206–7, 215, 221–2, 225, 227–8, 231–2, 244, 246, 252
Pitman, Charles Edward 246
plague 28, 242, 268, 304–7, 310, 312, 314
Ponsonby, Henry 223
Poona 28, 105, 185, 268, 285, 300, 304, 306–7, 310, 312–14;
assassination at 304–14, 327
Poona Observer 245
Post Office Act XVII of 1854 44, 59
postal communication 2, 44, 46, 51, 59, 61, 64, 74;
between Britain and India 51–64
postage, uniform rate of 49, 59;
see also subscription fee; tariff
Prasad, Amba 107, 124

Prasad, Babu Sheo 119
presidencies 44, 61, 169, 211, 233, 236, 241
Press Trust of India 20
press: commissioner 30, 100, 205, 223–5, 229–38;
 commissionership 204, 224–38, 253;
 freedom of 8, 13–14, 211, 216;
 history 8–9, 11–12, 14–15, 20;
 messages 74, 75, 179, 181–2, 228;
 regulations 155, 205, 212–16;
 telegrams 24, 30, 165, 168, 176, 179, 181, 189, 228, 235
print, explosion of 7, 19;
 printers 19, 152, 158, 161, 191, 208, 271, 314;
 printing 7, 10–11, 156–7, 162, 168, 215, 328
privatization 73, 80, 113
professionalization 10, 117, 149, 152, 156
progress 96, 121–8
proprietors 12, 63, 157–8, 160–1, 171, 191, 208, 236, 246, 314
public works 24
Public Works Department 45, 234
publishers 19, 169, 249, 253;
 see also printers; printing; newspapers; periodicals
Pulitzer, Joseph 33, 204
Pulvermacher, Isaac Louis 115
Punjab 13, 62, 107, 129, 156, 158, 184, 233

quadruplex telegraphy 97

radical journalism 152, 211;
 see also journalism; newspapers
Raghavan, G. N. S. 20–1
railways 6–9, 24, 26, 43, 45–6, 48–9, 61–2, 73, 79, 118–19, 123–7
Railways Conveyance of Mails Act 62
Ranchoddas, Rav Saheb Mohanlal 120
Rand, Walter C. 28, 304, 307, 309;
 in hospital 309;
 struggle of 307, 311–12
Rast Goftar 13, 161
Ratanbai 105, 186
Ray, Satyajit 122
Red Sea 26, 52–3, 97, 171
Red Sea and India Telegraph Company 76
Red Sea line 116
Reeves, E. A. 275
Reform Act (of 1832) 127
Reis and Rayyet 255*n*4
Reporter, Darashah Dorabji 161–2
Reuter telegrams 239, 241, 245–6, 251–2, 282, 293, 297, 299–300, 303, 313, 324
Reuter, Baron Julius 47, 239, 246
Reuter's Journal 251
Reuters 20, 30, 47, 181–2, 192, 205–7, 238–41, 243–8, 251–4, 289–91, 313–14, 326–8;
 archival holdings 251;
 in India 238–47;
 Indian Journal of 251;
 news service 244;
 office in Bombay 240;
 selling telegraphic news 50;
 Telegram Company of 327;
 telegrams 244, 246–7, 281–3, 293, 301;
 Telegraphic Office of 240
Reuters Archives (RA) 239
revolutions 5, 25, 167, 329–30;
 American and French 152
Riach, William 232
Riddell, H. B. 62
Rippon, Lord 229, 236

Robinson, D. G. 72–4, 180–1
Rochefort, Comte 151
Roy, K. C. 327
Roy, Madhub Chundra 119
Roy, Ram Mohan 211–12
rumours 3, 44, 108, 132, 223, 238, 291, 312
runners (*harkaras*) 25, 43–6, 48–9, 58, 60, 79;
from Ajmer to Ahmedabad 45;
between Calcutta and Madras 46;
Joshi on 46;
tiger attacks on 46
Russell, William Howard 55, 160, 290, 302, 304

Sahni, Ruchi Ram 176, 178–9
Samachar Chandrika 154
Sambad Kaumudi 211
Sandys, John Francis 110
Sanjibanee 158
Santi Prodaini 154
Sanyal, Ram Gopal 12
Sapru, S. 20, 295
Sathe, G. M. 185
Saugor (Sagar) Island 48, 69, 190
Saunders, J. O'B. 241, 243, 295
Saxony 289, 299
scandalous items 152, 208
Schudson, Michael 18
scientists 19, 110
Scotsman in East 316*n*28
seditious 13, 154–5, 207, 214, 253
Select Committee on East India Communications 61, 72, 240
semaphore telegraphy 48, 64–5, 68–9, 79, 280
Sen, Babu Narendra Nath 225
Sen, Brajendra Nath 161
sensationalism 161, 167, 290
Serampore Mission 11, 158, 183;
Baptist missionaries of 11, 120
Serfoji II 118
Seymour, Captain George 277
Shastree, Bap Deb 245
Shewshunker, Narayen 119
Ship Letter Act of 1814 51
Shivaprasad, Raja 118
Shree Venkateshwar Samachar 282
Shrihatta Prakash Press 156
Shrikrishnadas, Khemraj 282
shutter telegraphy 64, 68–70, 79, 110
Siemens & Halske 72
signallers 1, 68, 73–4, 99, 120, 129–31, 134, 147*n*148
Silberstein-Loeb, J. 255*n*4
Sinclair, Alexander 165
Singh, Dhyan 111
Singh, Jemadar Khooshyal 111
Singh, Prithvi Pal 156
Singh, Maharaja Ranjit 111
Sinha, Nitin 24
Sinnett, A. P. 225
siphon recorder 171, 199*n*94
Sir Charles Metcalfe's Act XI 208
Skalitz battle 289
Skrine, F. H. B. 12
Smith, Taylor, & Co. 183
Societa Anonima Italiana di Navigazione Adriatico Orientale 55
Society for Securing the Interests of Native Christians in India 107
Som Prakash 229
sorting clerks 56
Southampton 54, 56, 60, 62, 170
Spalding, A. J. 252
Speaker 319*n*88
speed 121–9: and Grand Trunk Road 61;
of information at 5, 18, 21;
mail horses 47;
and newspaper press 117;

of runners 45;
telegraph and 72, 77, 80, 97, 101;
of vessel 56
St. James Gazette 250
Stafford Advertiser 159
Stark, Ulrike 15, 188, 269, 327–8
Statesman (Calcutta) 12, 157, 185, 225–7, 231–2, 240, 253, 272, 327
steam navigation 20, 52;
steamers 4, 6, 8, 24, 26, 43, 51–2, 54–6, 79, 123, 190–1, 297;
from Alexandria to Southampton and Marseilles 56
Steel, Flora Annie 130
Steele, Thomas 124
stimulus–response model 18
Stockwell, G. 183
Stocqueler, J. H. 12, 52–3, 148, 270
Stokes, Whitley 204, 237, 249
Storey, Graham 20, 290
submarine cables 29, 76, 78, 97–8, 172
subscription fees 230, 245
subscription telegrams 242, 293, 295
Suez 29, 50, 52–4, 56, 63, 79, 172;
canal 63
Sulav Samachar 188, 229
Sumatra 282
superficiality 161, 167

tariff 75, 181, 279;
see also subscription fees
Taylor, James 183, 189
technologies 4–7, 15–18, 20–1, 23–5, 29–30, 43, 79–80, 98–101, 121–9, 135, 323–4;
of communication 3, 7, 15, 20, 25, 28–9, 124, 129, 149, 239, 325;
innovations in 7, 14, 17, 97;
and journalism 149;
and modernity 5, 29, 98–9, 104, 121–8;
and religion 123
telegrams 43, 69, 75, 100–2, 166–7, 174, 180–2, 228, 235, 244, 247, 252, 280–3;
price of 74;
see also subscription fees
telegraph 69, 99–104;
connecting India and Britain by 76–9;
and imperialism 23;
Indian and Indo-European 2;
and journalism 8, 23, 329, 2;
and language 17, 30–1, 56, 74–5, 104, 119, 176;
and literature 17, 29, 48, 100, 108;
mechanical 64;
memorializing the 129–35;
network 1–2, 47, 67, 73, 77, 97, 99, 130, 297, 326;
and religion 123;
wireless connection of 26;
and work 99, 120
Telegraph Department 26, 43, 65, 72–4, 120, 130, 132, 134, 173–5, 181, 234–5
telegraph lines 73, 77, 109, 122, 124, 162, 248;
via Ottoman Empire and Persia 26
telegraphic communication 66–9, 96–8, 101–5, 114–17, 171–6, 241–6, 282–3, 285–7, 292–3, 297–8, 300;
between Britain and India 77;
cost 6, 30, 74, 76, 102–3, 164, 166, 175–6, 206, 235;
and postal communication 2

telegraphic imaginary 120–1
telegraphic news 2, 64, 167, 172, 176, 278, 280, 282, 286–7, 292–3, 302;
compression of 298
Telegraphic Press Messages Bill 252
telegraphy 5–6, 15–21, 23–30, 64–6, 98–100, 108–10, 114–17, 119–21, 135, 162–6, 323–7;
history of 6, 16, 26, 98, 100, 114, 135, 149, 324, 326;
journalism 162–8;
popularizing of 109–17;
in nation-building 21;
role of 23
Templeton, A. N. 252
Thiaga Rajan, S. P. 9–10
Thomas, John 58
Thompson, John B. 23, 220
Tilak, Bal Gangadhar 13;
arrest of 28, 240, 304, 306, 313
Times of India 1–2, 12–13, 27–8, 115, 160–2, 185–6, 236–7, 240–3, 272–3, 291–9, 301–3;
Telegraphic Agency 30, 241, 290, 293
Times, The 1–2, 160, 162, 185–6, 221–2, 236–7, 239–43, 250, 272, 289–99, 301–3
Todd, Charles 130, 132
Tomlinson, John 126, 128
topical reporting 4, 11, 19–20, 160, 285; *see also* news reporting; journalism
science and technology, transfer of 71
transmission 16–7, 43, 46, 50, 61, 68, 75, 77–8, 97, 112–13, 168–71, 173–5, 324–5;
cost of 24;
of intelligence 8, 42, 47;
of messages 74
transportation revolution 18;
see also railways; steamers
Transvaal War 281
Trautenau, battle at 289, 299
tri-weekly 184, 269
Tuback, Manockji Pestonji 241, 243, 293, 295
Tully, John 137*n*14
Tyabji, Amiruddin 253

UNESCO-endorsed vision of communication 19
United Service Gazette 169, 286
United States (of America) 3, 7, 10, 15, 108, 123, 128, 151, 267, 269, 304, 326
Upper Assam Sarbajanik Sabha 107

van der Weyde, Peter Henri 48, 70–1
Vanity Fair 160
Venkatachalapathy, A. R. 11
vernacular languages 19, 29, 58, 120, 323, 327;
see also vernacular newspapers; vernacular press
vernacular newspapers 14, 28, 188, 206, 214, 229–30, 232–5, 237, 327–9;
in British India 26
vernacular press 13–14, 28, 107, 152, 154–5, 184, 186, 206–7, 214, 226, 228–30
Vernacular Press Act (1878) 13, 154, 206, 214–15, 223, 229–30, 232, 235–6, 253
Victorian journalism 153, 222;
see also journalism
Vienna 77, 115, 282, 301
voyage 51, 54, 63

Wacha, Dinshaw E. 104, 122, 187, 252, 275

Waghorn, Thomas Fletcher 52–4, 84*n*43;
and Company 240
Waghorn, T. Comyns 84*n*43
war 47, 160, 163–4, 167, 233, 245, 252, 267, 278, 287–93, 299–302;
correspondents 232, 288, 290;
reporting 288
Ward, Rev. William 158
Watson, A. H. 272
weekly 26–7, 59–60, 62, 169–70, 183–5, 189, 229, 234, 269–71, 281–2, 305–6;
see also periodicals
Wellesley, Marquis 209–10
Wells, H. L. 102
Wenzlhuemer, Roland 125, 325
Wheatstone, Charles 72;
automatic telegraph of 171, 199*n*93
Wheeler, S. 155
Whig model 8, 149
Wigram, W. 208, 212
William, Russell 303
Wilson, James 225
Winseck, Dwayne 24, 76
wireless telegraphy 10, 16, 26
Wolff 47, 238
Wollen, William B. 46
Wolseley, Roland E. 10
Wood, Charles 217
Wood, William Martin 160
Wright, Arnold 154
Württemberg 289

yellow journalism 10, 204;
see also journalism; newspapers; telegraphy
Yokohama 170, 295
Yokohama Mainichi Shimbun 244
Young, Keith Colonel 107

ABOUT THE AUTHOR

Amelia Bonea is a postdoctoral researcher at St Anne's College, University of Oxford. She is a historian of modern South Asia, with an interest in the history of technology and media. She has been educated at the universities of Tokyo and Heidelberg.